D1714671

THE POLITICAL VISION OF THE
DIVINE COMEDY

The Political Vision
of the
Divine Comedy

Joan M. Ferrante

PRINCETON UNIVERSITY PRESS

Library of Congress Cataloging in Publication Data will be
found on the last printed page of this book

ISBN 0-691-06603-5

Publication of this book has been aided by a grant from
the Paul Mellon Fund of Princeton University Press

This book has been composed in Sabon

Clothbound editions of Princeton University Press books
are printed on acid-free paper, and binding materials are
chosen for strength and durability

Printed in the United States of America by
Princeton University Press, Princeton, New Jersey

FOR MY PARENTS,
who taught me to love Dante
and to honor his long struggle

Contents

Acknowledgments

I WOULD like to thank my friends and colleagues, John W. Baldwin, Edward P. Mahoney, John H. Mundy, Edward M. Peters, and Robert Somerville, for reading parts of the manuscript and for making very helpful suggestions and criticisms at various stages of this work, and particularly Teodolinda Barolini, for commenting on the whole and for encouragement at every stage. Elizabeth A. R. Brown and Charles T. Davis generously supplied needed texts. The readers of the manuscript for Princeton offered extensive and valuable criticism for the final revision. The National Endowment for the Humanities provided the grant that helped me complete the research and write the first draft.

All citations of the *Comedy* in this study are from the Petrocchi text as presented by Charles S. Singleton, *The Divine Comedy* (Princeton: Princeton University Press, 1970–75); the translations are mine.

THE POLITICAL VISION OF THE
DIVINE COMEDY

Political Theory and
Controversy

THE *Divine Comedy* purports to be a description of the state of souls after death. So Dante describes it in his dedicatory letter to Can Grande. But this refers only to its literal sense; allegorically, the subject is man as he, by the exercise of his free will, merits reward or punishment. Dante's focus is on men's actions and their responsibility for them. Thus, though the setting of the poem is the three realms of the other-world, and though almost all the characters are dead, there is a persistent concern throughout the work with what is going on on earth, not because of the punishments that might result in the next life, but because of the disruption being caused in this one. The most violent attacks are directed against corruption in the church and the secular state, and they are voiced through the highest regions of heaven. Far more attention is given to public issues and their effects on society than to personal moral questions, the assumption being that personal morality is virtually impossible within a corrupt society. It is obvious from the poem that Dante, whose political career was cut off by false accusations and condemnation to death, who was forced into exile from his own city but not from the political situation which had troubled it, continues to be concerned with political issues throughout his life and throughout his works.

The political issues of primary concern to Dante fall into three large categories: the individual and society, city and empire, the church and the secular state. These were major topics for philosophical discussion and political controversy in his time, and they occupied him in one form or another in the *Convivio*, the *Monarchy*, the letters, and the *Comedy*. Like the *Monarchy*, the *Comedy* is a political tract, although it is also much more, and both occupy, or should, a position in the church-state polemic of the early fourteenth century. The purpose of this study is to analyze the political concepts expressed in the *Comedy* in relation to contemporary history and theory, and to define the political message(s) of the poem. This is offered as one perspective on an unusually complex and multifaceted work. It is not meant to deny the importance of other aspects—religious, aesthetic, philosophical, cultural, allegorical—but rather to emphasize one that was far more important to Dante than it has been to many modern critics.

Among those writers who do discuss the political side of the *Comedy*, there is some disagreement about its relation to Dante's other political works. Some critics see a change from the *Monarchy* toward a more religious orientation in the *Comedy*, though they do not deny the political side of the poem. A. P. d'Entrèves says that Dante deliberately subordinates politics to religion in the *Comedy*, that Rome's mission was to provide the seat for the church; but he also notes that the *Comedy* is as much a political as a religious poem, and that for Dante religion involved changing this world.[1] Jacques Goudet states uncompromisingly that the politics of the *Comedy* does not continue from the *Monarchy*, that Dante's reasons for being a monarchist are quite different, and that the *Comedy* has a fundamental religious orientation; but since the shift lies in the empire's taking on the reformation of

---

[1] A. P. d'Entrèves, *Dante as a Political Thinker* (Oxford: Clarendon, 1952), 62–66. Paolo Brezzi, in "Il Pensiero politico di Dante," *Dante*, ed. Umberto Parricchi (Rome: De Luca, 1965), 149–58, notes that Dante gives greater importance to the church and ecclesiastical problems in the *Comedy* than he had in the *Monarchy*, but also that he did not give up the empire as the guarantor of justice in the world, or the independence of the two powers and the parallelism of the two ends of man. A. Chiavacci-Leonardi believes that the earthly end is clearly subordinate to "the other" in the *Comedy*, but the theses of the *Comedy* are the same as those of the *Monarchy*, perhaps because in order to achieve the perfect earthly order, one has to base it on something absolute beyond the earth, "La *Monarchia* di Dante alla luce della *Commedia*," *Studi medievali* 18 (1977), 147–83, particularly 157–58, 164.

the church, in its assuming an active part in the economy of salvation, one could say that this mission gives the empire even greater scope than it had in the *Monarchy*.[2] Charles Davis does not take a position on the question in *Dante and the Idea of Rome*, though he notes that there is no contradiction between attitudes in the *Convivio* and *Monarchy* and those of the *Comedy*, even if there is a development, a difference in emphasis depending on a difference in subject. In a recent article, however, he argues for the essential connection between ecclesiastical poverty and the restoration of empire in the *Comedy*.[3]

Most critics who concern themselves with the subject emphasize the similarities in Dante's political views throughout his works. Francesco Mazzoni, in his introduction to an edition of the *Monarchy* and the political letters, proves the connections by juxtaposing specific passages in the *Convivio*, the letters, the *Monarchy*, and the *Comedy*.[4] Like Mazzoni, Felice Battaglia draws on all of Dante's political works to make his points, assuming a continuity of vision in them.[5] Arrigo Solmi says quite explicitly that there is nothing new in the *Comedy*, that Dante's political program, from his acts as a council member and his philosophical works, to his concep-

[2]Jacques Goudet, *Dante et la Politique* (Paris: Aubier Montaigne, 1969), 8–9, 147.

[3]Charles T. Davis, "Poverty and Eschatology in the Commedia," *Yearbook of Italian Studies* 4 (1980), 59–86. In *Dante and the Idea of Rome* (Oxford: Clarendon, 1957), Davis emphasizes the unity in Dante's ideas of Rome, the ancient city, the Christian empire, and the papal see. In "Dante's Vision of History," *Dante Studies* 93 (1975), 143–60, Davis traces Dante's belief in the providential pattern through history, and suggests that the *veltro* of the *Comedy* is to be a secular ruler, a precursor of Christ's second coming, as Augustus was of the first.

[4]Francesco Mazzoni, "Teoresi e prassi in Dante politico," in Dante Alighieri, *Monarchia, Epistole politiche*, ed. Francesco Mazzoni (Turin: ERI, 1966). Mazzoni dates the *Monarchy* 1314, after the deaths of Henry and Clement, which allows greater scope in interpreting the political prophecies of the *Comedy*; if the *Monarchy* was completed after Henry's death, Dante must still have believed in the possibility of, or at least need for, a secular leader.

[5]Felice Battaglia, *Impero, Chiesa, e Stati particolari nel pensiero di Dante* (Bologna: Zanichelli, 1944).

tion of the *Comedy* or the *Monarchy,* are one "compact structure."[6] Recently, George Holmes has written, "The main political conclusions of *Monarchia*—the necessity for a universal Roman Empire and a Church without money or jurisdiction—are entirely in agreement with the views expressed in the *Commedia.*"[7]

Etienne Gilson does not address the question directly, but he points out that even in the *Convivio,* Dante derives imperial authority immediately from God and secularizes the church's ideal of universal Christendom, though the state, however independent of the church, is never independent of God. Gilson also notes that the Christian God of Dante is interested at least as much in protecting the empire from the church as the church from the empire.[8] Similarly, Ernst Kantorowicz, as he demonstrates the working out in the Earthly Paradise of the goals posited in the last chapter of the *Monarchy,* and the man-centered concept of kingship throughout the *Comedy,* argues implicitly for the continuity of thought between the two works.[9] A number of other critics primarily concerned with the *Comedy* rather than with the strictly political works

[6]Arrigo Solmi, "Stato e Chiesa nel pensiero di Dante," *Archivio Storico Italiano* s. 6, 79 (1921), 59: "Sicchè il programma politico dell'Alighieri, dagli atti della sua vita civile come membro dei consigli e dell'amministrazione della sua patria, alla sua prima opera filosofica, alla concezione della Commedia o della Monarchia, si presenta come una compatta struttura."

[7]George Holmes, "Dante and the Popes," *The World of Dante,* ed. Cecil Grayson (Oxford: Clarendon, 1980). He goes on to say: "The Dominican defender of the papacy, Guido Vernani, who wrote a rebuttal of *Monarchia* about 1330, was entirely justified in saying that Dante undermined orthodox views not only by that book but also by the 'poetic figments and fantasies' and the 'sweet siren songs' of the *Commedia.*"

[8]Etienne Gilson, *Dante and Philosophy,* trans. David Moore (1949; reprint, New York: Harper and Row, 1963), 147, 166, 301, 307. Gilson does say that the essential postulate of Dante's thesis is simply "that natural reason is perfectly competent to confer on man earthly felicity in the sphere of action. This sphere of action is the sphere of politics, together with its *sine qua non,* the sphere of ethics. I cannot see that Dante ever said anything else: he hardly stopped repeating this between the beginning of the Banquet and the Divine Comedy" (304).

[9]Ernst H. Kantorowicz, *The King's Two Bodies* (Princeton: Princeton University, 1957), chapter 8.

emphasize Dante's concerns for this world in the poem: Erich Auerbach, Allan Gilbert, Dorothy Sayers, Marjorie Reeves, Karl Maurer, and most recently, E. L. Fortin.[10]

I hope to show in the course of this study that the political views of the *Comedy* are indeed consistent with those of the *Monarchy,* but that by expressing them in poetry rather than in discursive prose, Dante is able to put them far more forcefully. As Antonio de Angelis puts it, "the *Comedy* is to the *Monarchy* what the proof is to the doctoral thesis."[11] Before

[10]Erich Auerbach, *Dante, Poet of the Secular World,* trans. Ralph Manheim (1929; reprint, Chicago: University of Chicago, 1961; Allan Gilbert, *Dante and his Comedy* (New York: New York University, 1963). Dorothy Sayers, *Introductory Papers on Dante* (London: Methuen, 1954), describes Hell as Dante's picture of human society in a state of sin and corruption, Purgatory as the restoration of society that must come from within, and Paradise as the projection of the regenerate world (112 ff.). Marjorie Reeves, "Dante and the Prophetic View of History," *The World of Dante,* ed. Cecil Grayson (Oxford: Clarendon, 1980) focuses on the prophecies in the *Comedy,* which point to a secular savior: "I take the view that the *Commedia* is in many ways a this-worldly poem, still concerned with all that hinders the realization of the earthly beatitude, as well as with the soul's pilgrimage towards the heavenly beatitude" (51). Karl Maurer, "Dante als politischer Dichter," *Poetica* 7 (1975) 158–88, commenting on the *Comedy,* says there is no doubt that Dante looks for the victory of a strong German emperor or his vicar, the return of the pope to Rome, the separation of church and state, and the union of Italian cities under the empire (179). E. L. Fortin, *Dissidence et philosophie au moyen âge,* Cahiers d'études médiévales, no. 6 (Montreal: Bellarmin, 1981), suggests that the political message of the *Comedy* is paramount, that Dante exalts the empire and philosophy over the church and religion, but that the message is hidden and can only be reached through acrostics and complex allegorical interpretations.

[11]Antonio de Angelis, *Il concetto d'Imperium e la comunità soprannazionale in Dante* (Milan: Giuffrè, 1965), 183. Cf. U. Limentani, "Dante's Political Thought," *The Mind of Dante* (Cambridge: Cambridge University, 1965), where Limentani suggests the *Monarchy* deals scientifically with one aspect of mankind's pilgrimage on earth, the *Comedy* deals poetically with the whole (130). Limentani also says that Dante does not alter his views in the *Comedy,* that the *Monarchy* focuses on the regeneration of the empire, the *Comedy* on the regeneration of the empire and the church (129). Bruno Nardi, who thought the *Monarchy* was written before the *Inferno,* comments that the passion which pervaded the *Monarchy* erupts in an impetuous torrent of poetry in the *Comedy,* which transforms it into a lucid prophetic vision, "Il concetto dell' Impero nello svolgimento del pensiero dantesco," *Saggi di filosofia dantesca* (1930; 2nd rev. ed., Florence: La Nuova Italia, 1967), 274.

turning to the *Comedy*, however, I would like to trace briefly the major political issues of concern to Dante as they were treated by more or less contemporary writers whose ideas he most probably knew. Dante's views of government reflect both the influence of Aristotle's *Politics* on thirteenth-century philosophers and the contemporary political situation in northern Italy and western Europe. The practical reality Dante saw was the independent city-state, torn by factions within, pressed by papal and imperial claims from without, but nonetheless an economic and political force to be reckoned with. The theory he learned in his studies presented the state as a natural extension of the individual, a necessity not only for survival, but for peace and well-being. The basic political unit, in reality as well as in theory, was the city. The problem was to find a way to preserve the city as the essential unit and, at the same time, to ensure peace and prosperity to all citizens. This could be accomplished only by placing the smaller unit under the protective jurisdiction of a ruler who could mediate between warring parties and control them; for Dante that was the emperor, for papalists, the pope. Dante does not really discuss the problem of independent kingdoms, which had more practical power in his time than the empire; theoretically for him they are simply larger forms of the city-state, vulnerable to the same destructive forces and therefore in need of the same universal protector.

In the *Monarchy,* 1.5 and 6, Dante says that kingdoms and cities have the same ends, though the kingdom has a stronger bond of peace, and therefore the same need for a governing authority; but all cities and kingdoms must be subordinate to the rule of the single monarch, the emperor, in order for mankind as a whole to achieve its goal. In the *Comedy,* Dante does mention specific kings and kingdoms, but only to criticize particular abuses of power (see chapter one).[12] The papacy, of

---

[12]B. H. Sumner, "Dante and the *Regnum Italicum*," *Medium Aevum* 1 (1932), 2–23, notes that Dante rarely speaks about the *regnum,* never uses *regnum italicum* in his writings, and frequently attacks the *regnum* he knew best, the French.

course, claimed universal jurisdiction by virtue of the unity of Christendom, a claim that was opposed both by the empire and by the French monarchy, which also contested the supremacy of the empire in the secular sphere. Although Dante's sympathies are entirely with the empire—indeed, for him the French monarchy presents as serious a threat to peace as the church and is as fiercely condemned in the *Comedy*—the arguments put forth by the French apologists are probably more influential in his thinking than imperial propaganda, but he twists them to support the empire as the only secular authority with a claim to universal jurisdiction. The *Comedy* can in fact be seen as Dante's final word on the controversy between the papacy and the secular powers, where all the arguments and analogies of the historical conflict are translated into potent poetic images (see chapter two).

The positive attitude towards the secular state, prevalent among political theorists of Dante's period, is a significant shift from the earlier Augustinian view that secular authority was based on force and that government was a remedy for and necessitated by man's fallen state. Moerbecke's translation of Aristotle's *Politics* (c. 1259) made available to western Europe a very different position, much more congenial to the expanding states of the north Italian cities and western European kingdoms. Although, as Gaines Post has shown, there are indications that society and the state are natural institutions for twelfth-century writers, particularly John of Salisbury, and these views were available in Latin writers such as Cicero, in Chalcidius's version of the *Timaeus*, and in Roman law, it is nonetheless Aristotle's *Politics* which gives the solid theoretical support to secular government as a moral entity and an essential part of human life.[13] Aristotle emphasized the social-political nature of man: that he, alone among animals, has speech means he is supposed to communicate, to associate with his fellows; he is related to them as a part to the whole, and

[13]Gaines Post, *Studies in Medieval Legal Thought* (Princeton: Princeton University, 1964), particularly 291, 301, 496–519. For the use of the word "state" in the medieval context, see below, fn. 21.

the whole can offer him the best setting for a happy life. It can provide him with both necessities and knowledge, which will enable him to pursue virtue, the basis of happiness. In return, he owes the community his support, his obedience and virtuous action. In other words, it is natural to man as a human being, not as a sinful creature, to live in society with others, and it is advantageous to him to do so, not just physically but morally. The state is a community that exists for the good of its citizens, to maintain order and administer justice.

Thomas Aquinas, a central figure in Dante's Paradise, is probably the most important Christian disciple of Aristotle for Dante.[14] Thomas makes it clear that man is intended by his very nature to depend on his fellows: if he were meant to live alone, reason would suffice for his needs as instinct does for animals, but it does not. What nature gave other animals (covering, defense), man has to procure by his reason (clothing, weapons), which he cannot do entirely for himself; man therefore needs the help and knowledge of others, not only for his physical needs, but for stimulation to good and restraint from evil.[15] Man needs the help of other men in order to attain his

[14]Albertus Magnus, Thomas's teacher, whom Dante places next to Thomas in the circle of the sun, also commented on the *Politics,* and Siger, who appears on the other side of Thomas, was believed to have written on it as well, though no evidence of the work remains. See Martin Grabmann, "Die mittelalterlichen Kommentare zur Politik des Aristoteles," *Sitzungsberichte der Bayerischen Akademie der Wissenschaften,* Munich (1941[2]), 24. Jeremy Catto, "Ideas and Experience in the Political Thought of Aquinas," *Past and Present* 71 (1976), 3–21, suggests that Albert's teaching on friendship and on societies had political implications which Thomas drew out.

[15]These remarks are based on the *De regno* and the *Summa contra Gentiles,* henceforth cited as ScG; the *Summa Theologiae* will be cited as ST in the text. On man's need for the help of his fellows, see Thomas's commentary on the *Nicomachean Ethics* (*In decem libros Ethicorum Aristotelis ad Nicomachum expositio,* ed. Angelo Pirotta [Taurini: Marietti, 1934]); the needs that the individual cannot furnish for himself he must get as part of a group, the necessities of life from the domestic group, the necessities of living well from the civic group. I used the *Opera omnia iussu impensaque Leonis XIII* (Rome, 1882–1979) for the major Latin texts and consulted the following translations: for the *De Regno,* "On Kingship to the King of Cyprus," trans. Gerald B. Phelan, rev. Thomas Eschmann (1949; reprint, Toronto: Pontifical Institute, 1967); for

own end (ScG 3.117.4); only the most superhuman men can live a thoroughly ascetic life, for all others anything but the political life would be bad.[16] In other words, man would have led a social life even in a state of innocence (ST 1, q.96, a.4). Since man is·a part of the state, it is impossible for him to be good unless his will is proportionate to the common good (ST 1.2ae, q.92, a.1); all parts are ordered to the perfection of the whole, they exist for the sake of the whole (ScG 3.112.5). The end of the multitude gathered together is to live virtuously (De regno 3.106), forming a group in order to achieve the good life (the virtuous life), which they could not achieve alone.

The common good is judged by right reason to be better than that of the individual (ST 2.2ae, q.47, a.10).[17] Thomas considers even virtue and sin from a social perspective, that is, in relation to other men. The virtues do not pertain only to the good of the individual, because that would be contrary to charity, which seeks not her own; justice always involves others and all acts of virtue can pertain to justice insofar as justice directs man to the common good (ST 2.2ae, q.58, a.5). Even suicide has its public aspect: it injures the community since every part belongs to the whole (ST 2.2ae, q.63, a.5). Sin is judged more grievous as it affects more persons, and it is particularly serious to injure a person in authority because that injures the whole community (ST 2.2ae, q.65, a.4). A prince's actions are judged partly according to the numbers they affect: since virtue conduces to happiness, there is great virtue in

---

the ScG, On the Truth of the Catholic Faith, trans. Vernon J. Bourke (New York: Doubleday, 1956), 2 vols.; the ST, trans. the Fathers of the English Dominican Province (New York: Benziger, 1947), 3 vols.

[16]See Thomas's commentary on the Politics, cited by A. P. d'Entrèves, in the introduction to Aquinas, Selected Political Writings, trans. J. G. Dawson (Oxford: Blackwell, 1948), vii–viii.

[17]Although Thomas did not write a treatise on the common good, he was quite concerned with the concept, and mentioned it frequently in his works. Thomas Eschmann has collected the passages in which it appears in "A Thomistic Glossary on the Principle of the Preeminence of a Common Good," Medieval Studies 5 (1943), 123–65, where he also traces the concept through Roman writers, the Latin fathers, and canon law.

guiding others; the more people a prince rules, the greater his virtues (*De regno,* 1.9.68). Conversely, if a man who despoils a single man deserves death and damnation, how much worse a tyrant who robs all of goods and freedom and kills whom he will (*De regno,* 1.11.87). Because it can affect more men, a government is more perfect to the extent that it is more universal (ST 2.2ae, q.50, a.1), for it is better and more perfect to procure and preserve the good of a whole city than of one man. It is more divine, more like God, to preserve the good of whole nations and cities than of one man (commentary on *Ethics,* 1.2.30).

It is presumably because the rule of one, a king, is most like the rule of God that Thomas in the *De regno* prefers monarchy to Aristotle's city, though he speaks of the city as the perfect community.[18] The rule of one is, of course, "natural": the heart rules over members of the body, the reason over powers of the soul, and bees have one "king," just as there is one God (*De regno,* 1.2.19). The king is to his kingdom what God is to the world (1.9.72) and what the soul is to the body (2.1.95). Ultimately all kings are subject to the pope, as to Christ, because the ministry of God's kingdom is entrusted to priests (2.3.110), since it is only through divine power that man can attain to the possession of God. There is no question that Thomas means secular authority to be subordinate to spiritual (ST, 2.2ae, q.60, a.6); nonetheless the emphasis throughout Thom-

---

[18]The rule of one is also more likely to preserve peace, *De regno,* 1.2.17. For Thomas, the city is the perfect community; the ruler of the perfect community is the king (*De regno,* 1.1.14). Since the *De regno* was written for a prince, it emphasizes the argument for monarchy; Thomas himself came from southern Italy and lived in France, both monarchies. In the ST, 1.2ae, q.105, a.1, Thomas affirms the need for one to be at the head in a state, to ensure peace, but he also argues the need for others to have administrative powers, and for the ruler to be elected by and from all, combining elements of monarchy, aristocracy and democracy. Catto discusses the political involvements of Thomas's family and the influence of the Italian situation on his political thought; he also points out that Thomas's political views do not change in his later works, "Ideas and Experience," 20–21.

as's works seems to be on the secular state.[19] The state seems
to have a life of its own; it is an organism that lives indepen-
dently of individuals. Though men are mortal, government
should be perpetual (*De regno,* 2.4.120).[20]

The concept of the state as a necessity with a positive func-
tion for life on earth, contributing towards a better life phys-
ically and mentally, offering a greater opportunity for happi-
ness and peace than the individual could achieve on his own,
is a basic premise of political writers in this period no matter
where they stand on other issues. They also generally accept
the city as the basic unit of political life, because it is more or
less self-sufficient, but they see more perfection, more similar-
ity to the divine, and the greatest hope for peace in larger enti-
ties, in monarchies. What kind of monarchy, however, is very
much a matter of dispute. The same arguments for unity can
be used to support hereditary or elected temporal or spiritual
authority. The prime contenders in the thirteenth century are
the papacy, representing the spiritual unity of Christendom,
the Roman empire, with historic claims to universality in the
temporal sphere (both elective), and the French kingdom
(hereditary), offering the strongest argument for independent
temporal authority both in its practical power and in the intel-
lectual force of its apologists. Most of the works on these three
"monarchies" are written in terms of the controversy between

[19]Temporal power should be subject to the spiritual only to the extent
ordered by God, in those matters that affect the salvation of the soul. But in
those that concern civil welfare, the temporal should be obeyed, except where
both powers are found in one person, as in the pope, whose power is supreme
in both spheres, Commentary on the *Sentences* of Peter Lombard (*Commen-
tum in quatuor libros Sententiarum Magistri Petri Lombardi*), 2 q.3 a.4. Dante
did for the empire what Aquinas did for the smaller state: he gave it a positive
ethical goal set clearly in this world.

[20]On the community or corporation as more or less than a multitude of indi-
viduals, see Ewart Lewis, *Medieval Political Ideas* (New York: Knopf, 1954),
199–206; P. Michaud-Quantin, *Universitas, Expressions du Mouvement com-
munautaire dans le moyen-âge latin* (Paris: Vrin, 1970, and Otto Gierke, *Polit-
ical Theories of the Middle Age,* trans. Frederic W. Maitland (Cambridge:
Cambridge University, 1958).

13

the church and the secular state and will be discussed later in that light. But before coming to that, I would like to mention a few writers who influenced Dante, writers who had also directly experienced the Italian city-state, and whose views of the secular state in one way or another are comparable to his, whatever their position on the church-state issue.[21]

Giles of Rome, who is cited by Dante in the *Convivio* (4.24.9), wrote an important work on papal supremacy (*De ecclesiastica potestate,* 1301), but earlier he had composed what Lewis considers the most emphatic medieval defense of kingship, *De regimine principum,* c. 1285, for Philip IV of France.[22] Giles starts from the premise that human life is political life, "homo quia homo est naturaliter animal sociale, civile et politicum" ("man as man is naturally a social, civil, and political animal"), that of the three possibilities, to live the life of desire is to live as a beast, the life of contemplation to live as an angel, but to lead the civil (political) life is to live as a man (1.3). He describes human life in all its social aspects, the virtues of the individual man and king, the regime of the home and of the state, both the city and the kingdom. The king is a man and the minister of God (1.12); he must seek the common good, see that his people have what they need to achieve peace, virtue, and knowledge, remove any obstacles to such achievement, and direct them to that end (3.2.7–9). In other words, he has a guiding as well as an administrative function. Giles defines the city as *the* chief community (*principalissima com-*

[21]"Church-state," or "church and state," are modern terms, but used for convenience by many scholars writing about the medieval situation, e.g., Watt, Tierney, Ladner, Post, Ullmann, Battaglia, in works cited in this introduction. I have done the same. Post even argues that some medieval rulers practiced a "reason of state," 242–43, and that the thirteenth-century *regnum* was, in the legal and official views of its purpose, very similar to the modern state, *Studies in Medieval Legal Thought,* 250.

[22]Lewis, *Medieval Political Ideas,* 253. For the text of *De regimine principum,* I used the edition of Rome: Bladum, 1556. Although Giles points out that an elected monarchy is better in theory, he argues that a hereditary one works better in fact. Those who support the monarchy of the empire or the papacy, on the other hand, favor the concept of election.

munitas) in comparison to the home and village, but the kingdom is higher still (*principalior*): the community of the kingdom contains the community of the city and is much more perfect and more sufficient for life (3.1.1). The city, where different men can exercise their different arts, offers what is needed to live sufficiently and virtuously, but the kingdom can supply even more sufficiency (supplementing the deficiencies of one city from the assets of another), and more virtue (the prince has more power to restrain and enforce), as well as better defense (through the confederation of cities). Giles takes up the issue of the rule of many, the consensus that operates in Italian cities, versus the rule of one, and seems to be seeking a compromise between them, an eminently practical approach for the Italian situation. He points out that rule by one offers greater unity and peace, greater civil power; it is natural for one to organize the functions of all parts, and experience shows that other situations present a greater chance for war and poverty. At the same time, several eyes see better than one, several hands do more work; if each cares for his "own," the more "owns" involved, the closer to the common good; and finally, one man can be corrupted more easily than many. The ideal seems to be a monarchy in which the king surrounds himself with many wise men (3.2.2–4).

Ptolemy of Lucca also seems to hold both positions in that he is an ecclesiastical monarchist and a secular republican. Charles Davis calls him "the first self-conscious medieval republican."[23] He considers republican government more appropriate than royal government to man in a state of innocence, that is, more natural, and more suitable to virtuous, intelligent societies, like ancient Rome and contemporary Italian cities. He championed the heroes of the Roman republic,

[23]Charles Davis, "Ptolemy of Lucca and the Roman Republic," *Proceedings of the American Philosophical Society* 118 (1974), 49; cf. Charles Davis, "Roman Patriotism and Republican Propaganda: Ptolemy of Lucca and Pope Nicholas III," *Speculum* 50 (1975), 411: "the first Italian republican who could justify his position in a theoretically competent way." My remarks on Ptolemy are based on these two papers.

drawing much of his material from Augustine's *City of God*, but in Davis's words turning "Augustine's moral on its head."[24] In his continuation of Aquinas's *De regimine principum*, c. 1305, Ptolemy suggests that the Romans acted not out of self-love, lust for power and glory, but patriotism, moved by charity, a desire for the good of their people. (Dante will add divine providence as a cause of their action.) To both Dante and Ptolemy, the Romans are a chosen people, but for Dante it is the Roman empire that carries the providential destiny to save the world, while the papacy attempts to obstruct the divine plan. For Ptolemy, on the other hand, the papacy is the heir, not of the empire, but of the Roman republic. The church is the fifth kingdom prophesied in Daniel; the Roman republic was the fourth. Since the empire had usurped its power, Constantine was simply recognizing the legitimate authority when he left Rome to the papacy. The pope's dominion surpasses all others because it is both sacerdotal and royal. Davis's suggestion, which I find convincing, is that the only way Ptolemy could reconcile the papal position on the Donation of Constantine (stated by Innocent IV in *Eger cui lenia*) with his own glorification of classical Rome was to exalt the republic and demote the empire. Republican virtues (austerity, justice, self-sacrifice) do lend themselves to presentation as suitable foreshadowings of the apostolic life.

Remigio dei Girolami, a Florentine who, like Dante, was involved in the public life of the city, and whose family also suffered exile and confiscation of property for political reasons, similarly praised the virtues and patriotism of great Roman heroes.[25] But his concern was to contrast them with the self-

---

[24]"Ptolemy and the Roman Republic," 33. Remigio and Dante also twist Augustine and emphasize the patriotism of the Romans; it is not coincidental that both were Florentine, and that Florence self-consciously cast itself as the modern heir to Rome (see chapter one). Davis discusses the possible influence of Ptolemy on Dante, 35–38, and concludes that contact is probable although not proven.

[25]Remigio was a public preacher in Florence, the brother of "one of the most successful Priori," possibly a mediator in political crises, according to L.

interest and factionalism that was disrupting Florence. His political attention is focused on the commune, the city-state of Florence, and in this sense he is closer to Aristotle than the other theorists mentioned above, but he carries the concern for the common good, for the whole over the parts, to its logical extreme, probably, as Davis suggests, as a result of his experience of factionalism.[26] Dante may be doing something similar in the *Monarchy,* in the importance he gives to actualizing the potential of the human race as distinct from the individual. The city, according to Remigio, exists to create peace in which men may aid each other intellectually as well as physically; a political community must be based on the "union or conjunction of hearts, of wills willing the same thing"; one should love the city more than oneself, indeed next to God, because of the resemblance it bears to God.[27] It is because the part is more similar to the whole than to itself—in that a part as a part exists only potentially, whereas the whole exists in act—that the citizen should love the city more than himself.[28] The part cannot function except in relation to the whole as a severed hand is not really a hand any more than a sculpture or a painting of one, for it cannot bring food to the mouth. So, when a city is destroyed, the citizen is like stone or paint, because he lacks his virtue and operation; thus, if Florence were

Minio-Paluello, "Remigio Girolami's *De bono communi:* Florence at the Time of Dante's Banishment and the Philosopher's Answer to the Crisis," *Italian Studies* 11 (1956), 56.

[26]Charles Davis, "An Early Florentine Political Theorist: Fra Remigio de' Girolami," *Proceedings of the American Philosophical Society* 104 (1960), 671.

[27]See *De bono pacis,* text by Charles T. Davis in "Remigio de' Girolami and Dante: A Comparison of their Conceptions of Peace," *Studi danteschi* 36 (1959), 129; the union of hearts and wills is from *Speculum,* cited by Davis in "An Early Florentine Political Theorist," 668; the love of the city and its resemblance to God is in *De bono communi,* cited by Richard Egenter, "Gemeinnutz vor Eigennutz, Die soziale Leitidee im 'Tractatus de bono communi' des Fr. Remigius von Florenz," *Scholastik* 9 (1934), 88.

[28]"Ex natura civis praeamat civitatem sibi propter maiorem similitudinem, quam habet pars ad totum, quam habeat ad seipsam, tum quia pars ut pars est ens in potentia tantum, ut dictum est, totum autem ut totum est ens in actu" (102rb), Egenter, "Gemeinnutz vor Eigennutz," 87.

destroyed, a citizen could no longer be called a Florentine, but a "flerentine" (a weeper). If one is not a citizen, he is not a man, for a man is naturally a civic animal, according to "the Philosopher."[29] By turning Aristotle's statement around, Remigio makes a significant shift in emphasis.

Because the individual takes his identity from the city, he must be prepared to sacrifice himself for the good of the city; to achieve peace and concord among cities or communities, individual injuries may have to be disregarded, one must even run the risk of excommunication rather than obey the pope if his commands involve crimes against peace.[30] A citizen should, Remigio says, choose damnation for himself rather than for his city, if he can do so without offending God; of course, as Davis points out, it is inconceivable for the commune to be in hell or for the individual to take its place, just as it is for one to go to hell without offending God; so it seems unlikely that Remigio meant this passage to be taken literally.[31] In any case, Remigio makes it clear that the interest of the community cannot be in conflict with the individual's true interest, since the good of the part is always included in the good of the whole. Although his emphasis on the needs of the community over those of the individual may seem extreme, Remigio is essentially moderate in his thinking: he concentrates on the city, but he acknowledges the higher claims of larger entities, of the province, which contains many cities, the kingdom, which includes many provinces, and the universal church, which contains the world. He accepts the authority of the pope and the preeminence of the ecclesiastical over the temporal, the pope over the emperor, but he does not allow that jurisdiction to be

[29]"Ut qui erat civis Florentinus per destructionem Florentiae iam non sit Florentinus dicendus, sed potius flerentinus. Et si non est civis, non est homo, quia homo est naturaliter animal civile secundum Philosophum" (100ra), Egenter, "Gemeinnutz vor Eigennutz," 84.

[30]*De bono communi* (99vb), Egenter, "Gemeinnutz vor Eigennutz," 86; *De bono pacis,* Davis, "Remigio and Dante," 107–09.

[31]For text, see Egenter, "Gemeinnutz vor Eigennutz," 89 (104va); for comments, Davis, "An Early Florentine Political Theorist," 670. Egenter, like Kantorowicz, 480, takes Remigio literally.

"directe" and "principaliter" and he condemns the Donation of Constantine for poisoning the church with material wealth.[32]

The church's right to material possession and temporal power is at the core of the church-state conflicts. The Bible offers sufficient material on both sides: Christ tells the chief priests and scribes "Render therefore to Caesar the things that are Caesar's" (Luke 20:25); he called himself a king but insisted that his kingdom was not of this world (John 18:36); he gave Peter the keys of the kingdom of heaven and told him that whatever he bound on earth should be bound in heaven (Matt. 16:19). Peter preached: "Fear God. Honor the king" (1 Pet. 2:17), but "we ought to obey God rather than men" (Acts 5:29); and Paul: "there is no power but from God: and those that are, are ordained of God" (Rom. 13:1), that is, civil authority is divinely ordained. Christ continuously rejects worldly power and riches (John 6:15); he insists that he was sent not to judge but to save (John 3:17), not to be served but to serve (Matt. 20:28). Peter also makes clear he has no gold or silver (Acts 3:6), and the author of Second Timothy asserts that a soldier of Christ cannot get entangled with the affairs of this life (2.3–4). But later writers could and did interpret the more ambiguous messages of the keys and the two swords (Luke 22:38) as assertions of temporal as well as spiritual authority.[33]

[32]*De bono pacis,* Davis, "Remigio and Dante," 131, and *Contra falsos ecclesie professores,* Davis, "An Early Florentine Political Theorist," 673.

[33]On the church-state conflict in general, see John A. Watt, *The Theory of Papal Monarchy in the Thirteenth Century* (New York: Fordham, 1965); Geoffrey Barraclough, *The Medieval Papacy* (London: Thames and Hudson, 1968); Brian Tierney, *The Crisis of Church and State, 1050–1300* (Englewood Cliffs: Prentice-Hall, 1964); Ugo Mariani, *Chiesa e stato nei teologi Agostiniani del secolo 14* (Rome: Edizione di Storia e Letteratura, 1957); Walter Ullmann, *Medieval Papalism* (London: Methuen, 1949), and *A Short History of the Papacy in the Middle Ages* (London: Methuen, 1972). For the conflict as reflected in the canonists and theologians, see A. M. Stickler, "Concerning the Political Theories of the Medieval Canonists," *Traditio* 7 (1949–51), 450–63, and "Sacerdozio e Regno nelle nuove ricerche intorno ai secoli XII e XIII nei Decretisti e Decretalisti fino alle decretali di Gregorio IX," *Miscellanea Historiae Pontificie* 18 (1954), 1–26; Michele Maccarrone, "Potestas Directa e

That a thirteenth-century pope should claim powers in the temporal sphere is not surprising given the increasing tendency in the twelfth and thirteenth centuries to think of the church as a monarchy in its own right, over all churches, "Monarcha omnium ecclesiarum."[34] Watt calls the papacy the first monarchy to exploit the services of Roman law, whose techniques ensured the sovereignty of its central authority (*Theory of Papal Monarchy*, 79); Roman terminology was the most suitable, since Rome was the common fatherland, "communis patria omnium," for Christendom as it was for the empire (83). Innocent IV described the college of cardinals as the Senate of the church; Hostiensis, in the late thirteenth century, equated the *ecclesia* with *mundus*, making it coterminous with the entire world.[35] The idea of Christendom as a supranational society is not new in the thirteenth century, but it is more forcefully expressed. There were, of course, other aspects of the concept that did not serve the cause of the papacy and, in fact, strengthened its opponents: by the end of the thirteenth century, the concept of the church as the whole congregation of the faithful was used by the conciliarist movement, an attempt to locate authority in councils representing

---

Potestas Indirecta nei Teologi del XII e XIII Secolo," *MHP* 18 (1954), 27–47. Ullmann's views have been disputed by Stickler, G. B. Ladner ("The Concepts of *Ecclesia* and *Christianitas* and their Relation to the Idea of Papal *Plenitudo Potestatis* from Gregory VII to Boniface VIII," *MHP* 18 [1954], 49–77), and Tierney ("Some Recent Works on the Political Theories of the Medieval Canonists," *Traditio* 10 [1954], 594–625). Ullmann emphasizes the primacy of the spiritual in Christian society, others the dualist aspects, the tension between spiritual and temporal. James Muldoon, "Boniface VIII's Forty Years of Experience in the Law," *The Jurist* 31 (1971), 449–77, mentions an anonymous gloss on the two swords which cites eight passages from the *Decretum* proving that the pope possessed both swords, as well as five passages from the *Decretum* and one from the Bible proving that he did not, 466. See below, chapter two, for more on the swords and keys in the church-state debates and in the *Comedy*.

[34]Rufinus, cited by Watt, *Theory of Papal Monarchy*, 1.

[35]On Innocent IV, see Brian Tierney, *Foundations of the Conciliar Theory* (Cambridge: Cambridge University, 1955), 176; on Hostiensis, see Muldoon, "Boniface VIII's Forty Years," 475.

the whole church, rather than in the pope.[36] The heightened awareness of *communitas*, of *universitas*, also contributed to a sense of patriotism, hence of nationalism, in the secular states (Post, *Studies in Medieval Legal Thought*, 434).

Just how far the pope's jurisdiction extended, whether inside the church or into the temporal sphere, was an issue that was never really resolved. This is not the place to attempt a history of *plenitudo potestatis*,[37] but it is relevant to mention that the phrase was used in connection with both the pope's ordinary jurisdiction over the church and his extraordinary powers beyond standard procedures, which had implications for the temporal sphere (Watt, *Theory of Papal Monarchy*, 94–98). Ladner, however, points out that the term did not normally include temporal power except in the papal states, where the pope was the temporal ruler (57); he defines *plenitudo potestatis* as the full sovreignty of a ruler in his realm (66). Papal extremists claimed that the pope's fullness of power included judging *de feudo* and *temporalia,* as well as *spiritualia,* and assuming jurisdiction in cases of vacancies in secular positions; Innocent IV applied *plenitudo potestatis* to the political order, as a prerogative power throughout Christendom (Watt, *Theory of Papal Monarchy*, 98–102). Nonetheless, there is a significant difference between a pope's claim to jurisdiction *de jure* and his ability to exercise it *de facto,* which was never granted outside the papal states.[38] That is, whatever claims

[36]See Brian Tierney, *Conciliar Theory* and *Origins of Papal Infallibility, 1150–1350* (Leiden: Brill, 1972), 154 ff.

[37]On the development of the concept in the church up to the twelfth century, see Robert L. Benson, *"Plenitudo Potestatis:* Evolution of a Formula from Gregory IV to Gratian," *Studia Gratiana* 14 (1967), 193–218; for aspects of its history in the thirteenth century, see Watt, *Theory of Papal Monarchy*, pt. 2, and for limitations in its meaning, G. B. Ladner, "Concepts of *Ecclesia* and *Christianitas."* For the term as it was used in secular government, see Post, *Studies in Medieval Legal Thought*, 91 ff. For its use in papal claims to temporal power, see William D. McCready, "Papal *Plenitudo Potestatis* and the Source of Temporal Authority in Late Medieval Papal Hierocratic Theory," *Speculum* 48 (1973), 657–58, 669–70.

[38]Brian Tierney, "The Continuity of Papal Political Theory in the Thirteenth Century," *MS* 27 (1965), 239 and 245. He also suggests that if dualism means

were made in the name of papal power, the political reality affirmed the separation of powers.

There was, however, one tangible claim to temporal power, and that was the celebrated forgery, the Donation of Constantine, which purported to leave the governing of the city of Rome and the imperial provinces of Italy and the West to the pope, exalting the holy see above imperial authority and ascribing imperial honors, garments, and insignia to the pope because Peter was the vicar of the son of God on earth.[39] Before the emergence of this document, papal claims had been limited essentially to the superiority of the spiritual over the temporal sphere. The church accepted imperial authority in the latter, even over bishops, on the authority of Pope Gelasius, whose remarks would often be used by both sides, either to present the pope as supreme guiding authority with the emperor as the executive organ of the papacy, or to distinguish the two spheres of authority by which the world is ruled.[40] The Donation, on the other hand, makes a claim for papal authority in a temporal sphere, which canonists took as a recognition by the empire of powers Christ had already transferred to Peter, while civilists denied the right of the empire to transfer impe-

---

acknowledging that two orders of jurisdiction were needed for the governance of human affairs, one secular, one spiritual, all medieval popes were dualists, 234.

[39]The text of the document can be found in *Das Constitutum Constantini,* ed. Horst Fuhrmann (Hannover: Hahn, 1968); for a translation see S. Z. Ehler and J. B. Morrall, *Church and State through the Centuries* (New York: Biblo and Tannen, 1967), 16–22. (I cite their translations of short pieces for the convenience of the reader). For details about the Donation, see Fuhrmann's article on it in *Theologische Realenzyklopädie* 8.1/2 (1981), 196–202. The Donation was first invoked in the eleventh century. Papal claims to central Italy began much earlier, with the gifts of Pepin and Charlemagne (Daniel Waley, *The Papal State in the Thirteenth Century* [London: Macmillan, 1961], 1), as did the papal use of imperial insignia (Kantorowicz, 193, and Walter Ullmann, *The Growth of Papal Government in the Middle Ages* [London: Methuen, 1955], 310–11).

[40]See Ullmann, *Short History,* 32–33, and Tierney, *Crisis,* on the semantic problem of *auctoritas* and *potestas,* 10 ff., citing Gratian, that the world is ruled by two powers, secular *potestas* and ecclesiastical *auctoritas.*

rial power.[41] For Italians, it meant an excuse for the pope to interfere in local politics, and was therefore of particular importance to Dante, who denies its validity, though not its authenticity, in the *Monarchy* and condemns its effect, though not its intent, in the *Comedy*.

The moral danger of a pope becoming too involved in worldly affairs is most clearly stated by Saint Bernard in his advice to Pope Eugene III, *De consideratione,* a document which was widely cited through the later Middle Ages.[42] Bernard emphasizes papal responsibility rather than powers; his concern is to prevent his former student's becoming the tool of greedy and ambitious men, or becoming one of them. Wealth, Bernard reminds him, is to be used for good, not profit; Eugene's care should be for administering not possessing; his power is over sin, not property. (Sin, *ratione peccati,* was to be a major excuse of papalists for interference in temporal matters.) The words "all the earth shall be his" refer to Christ, not to the pope, who should leave possession and rule to God (3.1); by caring for riches, the pope becomes the successor of Constantine, rather than of Peter and thus denies the connection by which he claims the possession. Bernard exhorts the pope to attack with the word, not the sword, that is, not

[41]As Tierney ("Continuity," 240, fn. 29) points out, the legal validity of the document was open to question, making it necessary for papal publicists to find other bases for their political claims. A charter of Otto III denied the authenticity of the Donation in 1001. Stickler ("Sacerdozio," 16) points out that the Donation is not mentioned by Gratian, and not given much consideration by twelfth-century canonists, but was used more later, as scriptural arguments in favor of hierocracy proved less effective. The attention Dante gives it is a response to its political effects in northern Italy.

[42]Dante uses Bernard's letter in the third book of the *Monarchy,* chapters, 3, 8, 9, 15, and cites it directly in the letter to Can Grande, 10.28; for the text and translation of the letter, see *Epistolae, The Letters of Dante,* ed. Paget Toynbee (1920; 2d ed., Oxford: Clarendon, 1966), hereafter cited as Ep. See E. Jordan, "Dante et St. Bernard," *Bulletin du Jubilé* 4 (1921), 267–330. For the text of Bernard's letter, see *Sancti Bernardi opera,* ed. J. Leclercq and H. M. Rochais (Rome: Cistercian Editions, 1957–77), vol. 3. For a translation, see *Five Books on Consideration, Advice to a Pope,* trans. John D. Anderson and Elizabeth T. Kennan (Kalamazoo: Cistercian Publications, 1976).

to usurp the sword he was commanded to sheathe (4.7); both swords are in the hands of the church, the spiritual to be drawn by the priest, the material by the knight at the bidding of the priest and the command of the emperor. Bernard is referring to the passage in Luke 22:38: "But they said: Lord, behold, here are two swords. And he said to them: It is enough," which was interpreted by both sides to their advantage and frequently cited in the later controversy. On the one hand, the passage gives the pope the authority to tell temporal rulers how to act, on the other it states clearly that the pope is not to wield temporal power but must work through the accepted temporal authority.[43]

The early political conflicts between papal and secular authority arose from action by temporal rulers which affected the ecclesiastical sphere, particularly in lay investiture of bishops or taxation of clergy. Gregory VII, in the course of the dispute with Henry IV over the king's right to invest bishops, claimed that spiritual power is superior to temporal because the former derives from God, the latter originates in despicable human passions; therefore the church can judge, punish, and depose rulers if necessary, and he cites examples of kings who were excommunicated and deposed.[44] Christ, he says, despised secular kingship, preferring to come as a priest, an ingenious twist of the words "my kingdom is not of this world." The *Dictatus Papae,* which may be Gregory's and certainly comes out of the same conflict, is more extreme: only the Roman Pontiff may be called universal, may use imperial insignia; all princes are to kiss his feet; he may depose emperors but may himself be judged by no one, and he may absolve the subjects of unjust men from fealty. Gregory not only made claims, he took action, offering lands on the fringes of Europe as fiefs to rulers, encouraging rebels against rulers allied to his enemies;

[43] According to Mariani, the *forsitan,* "perhaps," Bernard used in the passage on the two swords was dropped by Boniface and Giles when they cited the passage, 150.

[44] See the letter of Pope Gregory VII to the Bishop of Metz, 1081, Ehler and Morrall, 29–39.

Henry accused him of sitting on the apostolic chair through the violence of an invader rather than the care of a shepherd, of usurping the kingdom and the priesthood and insisted that his own right to rule came from God not from the pope.[45] Henry used the two swords to support royal power and the dependence of the church on secular power: the sacerdotal sword should cause the king to be obeyed for God's sake, the royal sword should defeat the enemies of Christ and cause people to obey the priesthood.

Henry claimed the right to lay investiture because bishops were feudal lords and therefore had temporal responsibilities. Hadrian IV reversed the situation and claimed that the emperor was his vassal. Because Rome was the seat of both the church and the empire, at least in name, it was the object of claims on both sides: popes could scarcely deny Rome to the emperor, but they could claim that it lay in their power to bestow. Some rulers agreed to be vassals of the pope for their own purposes; Lothar III had accepted disputed territories in Italy from the pope as a fief in 1133. When Hadrian claimed that the government of Rome belonged to Saint Peter, Frederic Barbarossa insisted he held the crown by right of election by the princes, through God who subjected the world to *two* swords; if the imperial title conveyed no rights in Rome, he argued, it conveyed none anywhere.[46] Innocent III moved much further into feudal and secular matters.[47] He accepted

[45]For the *Dictatus,* see Ehler and Morrall, *Church and State,* 43–44; on Gregory, see Ullmann, *Short History,* 150; for the letter summoning the bishops to the Diet of Worms, 1076, see Ehler and Morrall, 45–47.

[46]On Lothar, see Tierney, *Crisis,* 99–100. A later mosaic showing the emperor kneeling at the pope's feet was taken by some to mean he had received the whole empire from the pope. On Frederick Barbarossa, see Tierney, ibid., 99, Ehler and Morrall, *Church and State,* 60–62.

[47]Although, according to Stickler, "Concerning the Political Theories," 455, he did not invent the concept of *translatio imperii,* as Ullmann claims, *Medieval Papalism,* 168. For a translation of Innocent's bulls, see Ehler and Morrall, *Church and State* 64–73. For a study of Innocent III, see H. Tillman, *Papst Innocenz III* (Bonn: Röhrscheid, 1954), particularly Exkurs 1, "Zum angeblichen Anspruch Innocenz' III auf die Fülle der weltlichen Gewalt"; also Michele Maccarrone, *Chiesa e stato nella dottrina di papa Innocenzo III*

the request of a league of Italian cities to protect them, using as his justification the analogy of the two luminaries, the sun and moon, the papacy and the empire set by God to preside over the days of souls and the nights of bodies; since both powers had their seat in Italy, the pope must be particularly watchful over it. In other words, he could participate directly in Italian politics (*Sicut universitatis conditor,* 1198). He also claimed the right to interfere in imperial elections, to examine candidates and to choose between two in a divided election on the basis of papal authority over the empire. Because the papacy had transferred the Roman empire from the Greeks to the Germans with the coronation of Charlemagne (by no means an undisputed reading of that event), the princes derived their right to elect the king, who would become emperor, from the pope (*Venerabilem fratrem,* 1202). Although Innocent insisted he would not interfere in feudal matters, he made an exception when sin was involved, a position which offered a good deal of latitude (*Novit ille,* 1204); in this connection he cited a rather suggestive passage from Jer. 1:10: "I have set thee this day over the nations and over kingdoms, to root up and to pull down. . . . " On the other hand, he also acknowledged, in letters to secular rulers, that the power of kings comes from God. Although it has been argued that Innocent interfered in the temporal sphere for spiritual motives, that his theory of church and state was a cautious dualism, the texts suggest a theocratic idea of papal world-monarchy, and that is how canonists who commented on them read them; it is true that Innocent III rejected any number of particular requests to exercise jurisdiction in temporal matters, but at the same time he frequently used the occasion to establish a general principle of papal jurisdiction.[48]

(Rome: Lateranum, 1940); and Brian Tierney, "'Tria Quippe Distinguit Iudicia . . . ' A Note on Innocent III's Decretal *Per venerabilem,*" *Speculum* 37 (1962), 48–59. Watt, *Theory of Papal Monarchy,* also discusses the political theories of Innocent III and Innocent IV.

[48]See Tierney, "Continuity," 230–31, and Watt, *Theory of Papal Monarchy* I, sec. 2. Cf. Tierney, *Crisis,* 128 and 130, and "Tria Quippe," 48: "He wanted

The more extreme claims and actions of later popes not surprisingly evoked counteractions from temporal rulers. When Frederick II proposed his own candidates for ecclesiastical benefits, Gregory IX was not content to remind him of the Donation of Constantine, or of the transfer of the empire to Charlemagne, but complained "you do not recognize your own creator." Frederick tried to move the cardinals against him, an overt attempt to weaken the pope's power within the church, and when Gregory died, Frederick had the cardinals locked up until they chose his successor. Frederick's interference with church procedures drove the curia to remove itself to Lyons in 1244, where it remained until his death in 1250. From that relatively safe distance, Innocent IV deposed Frederick in 1245 and absolved his subjects from their oaths to him in a bull which detailed Frederick's attacks on God and the church, his heresy, sacrilege, perjuries, destruction of physical property, taxation of clergy, and imposition of secular justice on the clergy. Frederick countered with threats to revoke the Donation of Constantine and to institute a radical reform of the church, returning it to the poverty of the early church by confiscation of its wealth.[49] Frederick was the last significant holder of the imperial title for some time. Between 1250 and 1355, only two others were serious contenders, Henry VII, who died a year after he was crowned, and Ludwig of Bavaria, who was elected king of the Germans in 1314, which should have made him emperor, but he was not crowned until 1328, and then not by the pope and only after he had captured Rome.[50] Several of Dante's letters and probably the *Monarchy*

---

there to be no doubt that the pope did have extensive powers in secular affairs even though he was not choosing to exercise them in this particular case." Apparently Innocent's view of what constituted "spiritual" was quite broad.

[49]For Gregory's letter to Frederick, see Ehler and Morrall, *Church and State,* 76–78. For the other details, see Tierney, *Crisis,* 141–43. Watt calls the deposition of the emperor "the most dramatic papal political act of the century," 5.

[50]The pope, John XXII, assumed full powers in 1317 on the basis of the imperial "vacancy" which he had helped to cause. Ludwig declared the election by the German princes sufficient to make him emperor in 1338, see Geof-

were written in support of Henry's position in Italy, but Henry died in 1313. Dante may well have had hopes for Ludwig; if so, they are expressed only obliquely in the *Comedy* (see chapter two).

During this period, the most powerful secular force in Europe was the French monarchy. Although Frederick's often violent opposition to the church had encouraged better relations between the papacy and the French king, the power, wealth, and ambition of the latter made such an alliance tenuous. The French king was in some ways more of a problem than the emperor—a pope could refuse to crown an emperor and thereby refuse to recognize his authority, but the "making" of a king was out of his hands. The church-state controversy reached a climax in the struggle between Philip IV and Boniface VIII, which produced some of the most extreme statements of papal authority and some of the strongest defenses of secular authority. Major works by Giles of Rome, John of Paris, and James of Viterbo were written as part of this polemic, along with striking pieces of political propaganda of unknown authorship.[51] Although Dante, like Marsilius of Padua, took up the controversy in terms of church and empire rather than church and national monarchy and considered the French royal line a dangerous threat to the empire and to peace, his political works are essentially a development of the same arguments and owe a good deal, positively or negatively, to them.

The papacy may have been at a low point in its actual power under Boniface VIII, but it was probably at the crest of its theoretical expression, after over a century of development by canonists. The popes during the previous century, if they were not themselves lawyers, were surrounded by lawyers who

---

frey Barraclough, *The Origins of Modern Germany* (Oxford: Blackwell, 1952; 1st pub. 1946), 309–12.

[51]See Jean Rivière, *Le problème de l'Eglise et de l'Etat au temps de Philippe le Bel* (Louvain: Spicilegium Sacrum Lovaniense, 1926), 253 ff., and 300 ff., and Lewis, *Medieval Political Ideas*, 486 ff. Dante's part in the controversy is discussed below in chapter two.

wrote, gathered, or commented on papal decrees and produced a theoretical assertion of papal authority that could not be equalled by anything in the secular sphere. It is only at the beginning of the fourteenth century that men of the calibre of John of Paris, Dante, and Marsilius, undertook the defense of the secular state against papal claims. Earlier expositors of the secular state, such as John of Salisbury and Thomas Aquinas, had not dealt directly with the conflict between the two authorities within a Christian state.[52] Secular rulers had accepted the notion of the preeminence of the spiritual sphere as long as it did not interfere with the operations of the temporal, but the language of the papalists reveals a sense of the pope as an imperial monarch well before James of Viterbo speaks of the papacy as a separate *regnum*. Popes had worn imperial insignia from the end of the eleventh century, the crown, the scarlet cloak and shoes, and the scepter; the Donation specifies the wearing of imperial insignia among the privileges Constantine bestowed on Sylvester.[53] The pope is described in imperial language as *dominus mundi, coelestis imperator* ("lord of the world," "heavenly emperor") by canonists; he, not the emperor, is the vicar of God on earth, and like God is not answerable to any but God.[54] The papacy saw itself as the head of an international society, composed of all

[52] For Thomas's comment on the relation of temporal and spiritual powers, see fn. 19. Thomas Gilby, *Principality and Polity, Aquinas and the Rise of State Theory in the West* (London: Longman, Green, 1958), says that Aquinas did not hold that all rights were communicated through the visible church; he was not a "papal caesarist," 329.

[53] See Ullmann, *Growth of Papal Government*, 311–19. "Solus uti possit imperialibus insigniis" ("He alone can use imperial insignia"), claims the *Dictatus pape*. The pope did not wear the imperial sword, but he did confer it on secular princes (Ullmann, *Short History*, 95). There was considerable argument over whether the pope delegated imperial power or merely sanctified it, Watt, *Theory of Papal Monarchy*, 234.

[54] On the *vicarius Christi*, see Watt, *Theory of Papal Monarchy*, 67–71. The pope had been described as the true emperor and the emperor as his vicar in the earlier *Summa Parisiensis*: "Ipse [papa] est verus imperator et imperator vicarius eius" (ed. T. P. McLaughlin [Toronto: Pontifical Institute, 1952], C.II, q.vi., p. 108).

Christian states. It is not surprising then that some canonists saw the pope as the lawful owner of the entire world and princes as holding their possessions unjustly unless subject to his spiritual authority; the pope could thus claim to confiscate property of delinquent sons of the church. From this perspective, the Donation of Constantine is not a gift, but merely a recognition of papal rights, already conferred by Christ on Peter.

The pope claimed, or papalists claimed for him, authority to confirm or depose emperors, to transfer the empire, even to "make" kings and emperors; the most moderate statement might be that the pope's blessing gives the temporal ruler the power to act. The ultimate issue behind these arguments is whether the temporal ruler derives his power directly from God or indirectly through the pope. Papalists claim the latter, royalists and imperialists, including Dante and Marsilius, take extreme positions on the other side.

Probably the most forceful statement of papal power was made in *Unam Sanctam* by Boniface in 1302. Since there had been no universally recognized emperor after the death of Frederick II in 1250, the pope was the only "visible" head of the Christian world, and the bull is his expression of that position. In it Boniface draws on all the biblical imagery used in the tradition in order to make the claim of domination over temporal powers: the mystical body of Christendom can have only one head or it would be a monster, and Christ gave that function to Peter; it is for the spiritual power to establish and judge earthly powers, while only God can judge the spiritual power.[55] Any one who resists this power resists the divine will,

[55]In a solemn discourse prepared to receive Albert of Austria, Boniface's candidate for emperor, Boniface went even further, using the sun-moon analogy: as the moon has no light except from the sun, so earthly power has only what it receives from the spiritual, see Rivière, *Le Problème*, 91. Muldoon says that the bull reflects Boniface's awareness of the tension in the canonist tradition between the concepts of a unified society and the duality of powers, "Boniface VIII's Forty Years," 477. For a discussion of the text in relation to Dante, see below, chapter two.

unless, like the Manichees, he pretends there were two beginnings for heaven and earth; in other words to dispute the supreme authority of the pope is to be a heretic. The individual claims are not new, but the combination and emphasis are.[56] This document is the climax of Boniface's battle with Philip, which grew out of Philip's imposition of taxes on the French clergy without seeking papal permission; Boniface answered with a bull forbidding clerics to pay (*Clericos laicos*, 1296) and this began a series of moves and countermoves, with Philip's becoming more aggressive and Boniface alternately attacking and withdrawing from earlier positions.[57] Finally, Boniface prepared a bull excommunicating Philip and putting his subjects under anathema unless they renounced their oaths to him. But before he could publish it, Philip had him captured.

The struggle between the head of the church and the most powerful secular ruler in Christendom spawned a number of theoretical documents, many of them dedicated to either Boniface or Philip. Of these, three are of particular interest for this study: Giles of Rome's *De ecclesiastica potestate,* James of Viterbo's *De regimine Christiano* (1302), both dedicated to Boniface, and John of Paris's *De potestate regia et papali* (1302–03), dedicated to Philip.[58] Both Giles and James wrote in support of the papal position and applied rational theories of society and of the state as a necessity for man to the church.[59]

[56]Both Stickler, "Concerning the Political Theories," 457, and Watt, *Theory of Papal Monarchy,* 60, following Rivière, note that Boniface drew on Hugh of St. Victor and Saint Bernard.

[57]For a history of the conflict, see Rivière *Le Problème,* and Georges Digard, *Phillippe le Bel et le Saint-Siège de 1285 à 1304* (Paris: Sirey, 1936) 2 vols.

[58]For the text of Giles, see the edition by Richard Scholz (Weimar: Böhlaus, 1929; reprint, Scientia Aalen, 1961); for James, see H. X. Arquillière, ed. (Paris: Beauchesne 1926); for John, Jean Leclercq, *Jean de Paris et l'écclésiologie du XIIIᵉ siècle* (Paris: Vrin, 1942), and recent translations by Arthur P. Monahan, *On Royal and Papal Power* (New York: Columbia University, 1974) Records of Civilization, 90, and John A. Watt, *On Royal and Papal Power* (Toronto: Pontifical Institute, 1971). Dante cites Giles and probably knew James, since, as Mariani points out, he answers many of his arguments, 172.

[59]See Georges de Lagarde, *La Naissance de l'esprit laique au déclin du moyen âge* (Paris: Droz, 1942), 170.

Giles turns from the defense of the monarchy, which he had undertaken some twenty years earlier, to a strong defense of theocracy, arguing for the supremacy of spiritual or sacerdotal power over temporal, and defending the concept of ecclesiastical property. It is the order of the universe, he points out, for the lower to be subject to the higher through an intermediary, so the state is to God through the church. Sacerdotal power precedes royal in four ways: tithes (all men are bound to pay tribute to God for their possessions, and tribute is a sign of service); benediction (the priest consecrates the king and the one who blesses is greater than the one blessed); institution of power (royal power having been instituted by priests at God's command in the Old Testament); and mode of government (every corporeal substance is governed through a spiritual). Temporal things are under the church's jurisdiction because the temporal substances were created for the service of the spiritual, as souls dominate bodies and bodies material goods, as superior animals rule inferior, and inferior animals inanimate objects. Giles dates the beginning of the priesthood with Abel's sacrifices to God, making it predate the state; both the worldly and the other-worldly authorities were entrusted to Moses and his successors, and both are concentrated in the pope, who uses the spiritual directly, and yields the temporal to sovereigns at his pleasure. All worldly possessions must be held through the church, which alone can restore man to grace through the sacraments; without that mediation, they would be held in sin. In order to forestall the argument that Christ opposed worldly possessions, Giles posits three phases in church history: in the early community, all possessions were held in common; later the clergy acquired a right to material goods without divine assistance; now, however, it has the right to possess by God's providence.

James of Viterbo, a student of Giles, is said to be the first person to treat the church consistently as a *regnum* (Lewis, *Medieval Political Ideas,* 181 ff.). Although he concedes that the state predates the church, he argues that the church is preeminent because more perfect; only within it can the natural community attain its highest destiny; so the church must control the state. The church itself is like a state, indeed everything that makes up the glory of a state is found in it, including wealth, age, justice, tranquillity, scope. It is universal and therefore can truly be called *respublica.* It has its own king, Christ, whose vicar is the pope. Like Giles, James sees the problem for his argument in Christ's flight from worldly honors and refusal to be king, but he pleads other times, other needs, and argues that the pope must exercise all the means God has put into his hands. For those who cannot accept a duality of power on earth with pope and emperor equal powers in their separate spheres (which projects the apex of the hierarchy, God, into the other world), but demand a head here, it must be the pope. Among antipapal writers, only Marsilius is prepared to shift the balance entirely in the other direction.

In contrast to Giles and James, John of Paris insists that the two spheres must be kept distinct; both powers are derived directly from God, both have functions in their own spheres. Kingship, though it precedes priesthood in time, is less perfect in its dignity; nonetheless, secular power may be greater in temporal matters. A pope may excommunicate a king if the king errs in spiritual matters, but he can do no more than warn a king who is at fault in temporal affairs, and that only at the request of the barons and peers of the realm, whose responsibility it is to deal with the king. Conversely, he argues with perfect equity, if the pope is guilty of an offense against civil law, the emperor can warn and then punish him, whereas, if he commits an offense against ecclesiastical law, it is up to the cardinals to depose him.[60] If he is intransigent, the secular authorities, at the request of the cardinals, can force the people to refuse to obey the pope. A pope can resign because his is a title of jurisdiction, therefore changeable, unlike that of priest; in other words, it is a function of the church, not a holy office in itself. John recognizes certain powers in the cardinals and in the whole community of the church, although he acknowl-

---

[60]*De potestate regia et papali,* chapter 13, Leclercq, *Jean de Paris,* 214.

edges that in spiritual affairs, since man has one end, there must be a unified church with one head.[61] He also argues the need for diversity in temporal power; different interests want different leaders. He is starting from the viewpoint of the Aristotelian self-sufficient community, but as applied to a national kingdom. Each community chooses the ruler appropriate to its situation. Dante will argue in the *Monarchy* that this diversity of interests is what requires one overall head, to settle disputes and insure peace, but John points out that empires have not kept the world at peace. John allows the church no right to possess property; the pope may act as steward of ecclesiastical goods which actually belong to the Christian community, but not as lord of them. Only in case of need can he compel the faithful to contribute. Since Christ exercised no jurisdiction over personal property, he did not pass it on to Peter and therefore the church does not have it; the power of the keys is purely spiritual, to forgive sins, to teach, not to command.[62] John goes systematically through the major arguments for papal supremacy, as Dante will, answering them with simple logic, for instance, transfer of empire did not occur because of emperors' sins; there have, after all, been heretical popes with no effect on the authority of their successors. Perhaps the most significant argument is the dismissal of the body-soul analogy: royal power is not corporeal; its purpose is the common good, which is to live according to virtue, and that pertains to souls.

Dante also argues for the monarch's importance in achieving the most ideal life on earth for mankind, but he adds a new twist, that mankind can only translate its full intellectual potential into action as one entity, not as an individual or a single community (*Monarchy*, 1.3).[63] Applying the philosoph-

[61]Tierney, *Conciliar Theory*, 177, says John's work "provides by far the most consistent and complete formulation of conciliar doctrine before the outbreak of the Great Schism."

[62]Cf. Pierre Dubois, who wrote *De recuperatione terrae sanctae*, c. 1305–07; he thought that the church should be purely spiritual, its possessions handed over to the French king to administer, but he stops short of making the church an organ of the state, see Rivière, *Le Problème*, 345.

[63]For the text, see Gustavo Vinay, ed., *Monarchia* (Florence: Sansoni, 1950), and the more recent edition by Mazzoni cited above; for a translation, see Don-

POLITICAL THEORY

ical principle that a whole has a different end from its separate
parts, Dante argues that the human race as a whole has a dif-
ferent goal from the individual, the family, the city, or the
kingdom. Since the specific capacity that distinguishes man as
a species is his possible intellect (*intellectus possibilis*), the spe-
cific capacity of mankind must be intellectual, and since the
potentiality of the whole cannot be realized by one man or by
a particular community of men, there must be a community of
the whole in order to realize it. But peace is essential for the
potential to be fulfilled, and that can only be accomplished by
a universal monarch. United under one ruler, mankind can be
most like God. The rule ordained by God to govern the world
is the Roman empire, whose legitimacy was proven by a series
of miracles in Roman history and by Christ's birth and death
under its jurisdiction (*Monarchy*, 2, cf. *Convivio*, 4.4–5). In the
third book of the *Monarchy*, Dante comes to the central issue
of secular authority: does it derive directly from God or from
his vicar the pope? He answers, point by point, the main papal-
ist arguments, denies the emperor's right to destroy the empire
thereby rendering the Donation invalid, and denies, by refer-
ence to Scripture, the pope's right to receive temporal power.
Although he leaves the pope supreme in the temporal sphere
and acknowledges the reverence the emperor owes the pope as
a firstborn son to his father, Dante makes it quite clear that the
emperor's authority derives directly from God and precedes
the church in time.[64] God ordained both the pope and the

---

ald Nicholl, *Monarchy* (London: Weidenfeld and Nicolson, 1954). In the *Con-
vivio*, Dante had spoken more traditionally of man as a social animal, of the
need for a monarch to keep peace in society and among political units, 4.4.
Although Dante mentions Averroes in connection with the passage cited, he
does not believe in a single universal intellect. He goes out of his way in Pur-
gatory 26 to explain how the mental powers of the soul retain their individu-
ality after death. For a philosophical discussion of Dante's position, see B.
Nardi, "Dante e la filosofia," *Nel Mondo di Dante* (Rome: Istituto Grafico
Tiberino, 1944).

[64]Dante may not have known Engelbert of Admont's *De Ortu et Fine
Romani Imperi*, written, perhaps like the *Monarchy*, to support Henry VII,
but their views are similar: Engelbert gives four reasons for the single rule of

35

emperor to guide man, but in different spheres and for different ends: the emperor's function is to lead mankind to happiness in this life, to a restoration of the earthly paradise through virtuous action, the pope's is to lead to eternal salvation and the enjoyment of the divine presence in the heavenly paradise (3.15–16).[65] Dante continues to argue the separation of the two spheres even more vigorously in the *Comedy*.

Marsilius carries Dante's argument to extremes in the *Defensor Pacis:*[66] the prince is the vicar of Christ, the representative of God on earth, charged with bringing about peace, which is essential to life and helpful to salvation. He is the supreme authority on earth, not only as the vicar of God, but as representative of the collective will of the people. The church is the whole body of the faithful; the function of its

---

the empire, the example of universal nature, the order of the political community, the unity of church and Christian commonwealth, and the righteousness and beauty of order of divine providence and grace. He recognizes the problems of the Roman empire through history, but insists that the union of Christian nations is essential for the safety and peace of the world and for the defense of the faith; those who weaken the empire hasten the coming of Anti-Christ (see Lewis, *Medieval Political Ideas,* 473–84). Dante may, however, have known an earlier imperialist writer, Jordan of Osnabrück who, in *De prerogativa Romani imperii,* presented the empire as the supreme universal political power and argued that Christ gave Rome the charge of bringing peace to the world for his birth, that he paid tribute to Caesar and died under imperial jurisdiction, arguments Dante uses in *Monarchy* 2. On Dante's possible knowledge of the work, see Chiavacci-Leonardi, "La *Monarchia* di Dante," 171–72.

[65]In the last chapter of the *Monarchy*, Dante says that temporal happiness is in some way, "quodam modo" subordinate to spiritual. Michele Maccarrone, "Il terzo libro della 'Monarchia'," *Studi danteschi* 33 (1955), 129, points out that *quodam modo* was applied in a similar context to the two powers by Uguccione in a *Quaestio,* to deny the subordination of the emperor to the pope, and employed similarly by Remigio along with other terms such as "indirecte," "mediate," and "aliqualiter."

[66]For the text, see C. W. Previté-Orton, ed. (Cambridge: University Press, 1928); for a translation, see Alan Gewirth (New York: Columbia, 1956; reprint, Medieval Academy of America, 1980). Relevant studies of his work have been done by Jeannine Quillet, *La Philosophie politique de Marsile de Padoue* (Paris: Vrin, 1970), and Nicolai Rubinstein, "Marsilius of Padua and Italian Political Thought of his Time," in *Europe in the Late Middle Ages,* ed. J. R. Hale, J. R. Highfield, and B. Smalley (Evanston: Northwestern University, 1965), 44–75.

priests is to teach men what is necessary for eternal salvation, with no coercive power in the world. Indeed, though the church can declare men heretics, only the state can take action against them, just as a doctor may diagnose leprosy, but only the state may quarantine the leper. Most of the problems in the contemporary world arise from the doctrine of papal plenitude of power, a power Marsilius denies, as he denies the essential primacy of the Roman bishop (saying the bishop of Rome has no more authority than any other, as Peter had no more than other disciples), not only in jurisdictional questions but even in questions of religion, which are properly the concern of a general council composed of all Christians, or the weightier part (2.20–22). In other words, he reduces the authority of the pope in all spheres, and relegates the church to being an organ of the state, though he never denies the higher purpose it serves in guiding towards salvation.

We do not know if Dante had any direct contact with Marsilius, but since they were both at Verona for some time during the second decade of the fourteenth century, both under the patronage of Can Grande della Scala, and were both staunch defenders of the Roman (German) empire, it seems highly likely that they knew of each other and of each other's ideas.[67] Although the *Defensor Pacis* appeared three years after Dante's death and cannot therefore have influenced him in its present form, Dante's treament of the church in the *Comedy* does have elements in common with Marsilius's views. It is, of course, perfectly possible that each came to his position independently as a result of his personal and political experiences, and his connection with the imperial cause, but it is not impossible that they may have encouraged each other to a much

[67]Felice Battaglia, *Marsilio da Padova e la filosofia politica del medio evo* (Florence: Le Monnier, 1928), notes the possibility of Marsilio's having met Dante while they were both at Verona; while it cannot be proved, he points out, there is no reason to reject the idea, 32. Another writer who supported the imperial cause, the jurist and poet, Cino da Pistoia, was a friend with whom Dante exchanged poems; for a discussion of his legal works, see Gennaro Maria Monti, *Cino da Pistoia Giurista* (Città di Castello: Il Solco, 1924).

stronger position than any previously taken. It is also not coincidental that Marsilius served Ludwig of Bavaria, who was elected emperor after the death of Henry VII, and had himself crowned in Rome "by the grace of God and the will of the Roman people," thereby realizing, however briefly, the dream of the *Monarchy*.[68] The connection between the event and Dante's work was felt strongly enough for the tract to be declared heretical and publicly burned by the papal legate, Bertrando del Poggetto; before Ludwig's march on Rome, not much attention had been paid to the work, although its heretical theses had been pointed out by Guido Vernani after Dante's death.[69] Boccaccio claims that Ludwig's followers picked up the *Monarchy* when they came to Italy and used it to support their cause.[70]

The *Monarchy* was written as a political tract to support the concept of the Roman empire and defend its authority from papal usurpation, a less direct message, perhaps, than the political letters, written to the princes and peoples of Italy, to the Florentines, and to Henry VII, but no less clear a message. If the *Comedy,* as most writers on Dante's political views agree, espouses the same basic ideas, does it also have a similar function? Was it meant to be, at least in part, political propaganda? By "political," I mean what Dante seems to have meant, having to do with the proper functioning of society, the forms of government, the aims of civilization, the subject matter of the

[68]See Robert Davidsohn, *Storia di Firenze,* (Florence: Sansoni, 1956–68), 8 vols. *Le ultime lotte contro l'Impero* (Italian trans. G. B. Klein, rev. Roberto Palmarocchi) 4.1125.

[69]For discussion and text, see Thomas Käppeli, "Der Dantegegner Guido Vernani OP von Rimini," *Quellen und Forschungen aus Italienischen Archiven und Bibliotheken* 28 (1937–38), 107–46. Guglielmo da Sarzano makes no direct reference to Dante, but does argue for the authority of the pope in a work also thought to be written in response to the *Monarchy*. See Ovidio Capitani, "Tractatus de potestate Summi Pontificis di Guglielmo da Sarzano," *Studi medievali* 12 (1971), 997–1094.

[70]See B. Nardi, "Fortuna della 'Monarchia" nei Secoli XIV e XV," *Nel Mondo di Dante* (Rome: Edizioni di Storia e Letteratura, 1944), 164.

Monarchy:[71] what a society should and should not be, how it functions in all its aspects, not simply the technical workings of government. The audience Dante envisaged for the poem is clearly an audience of important and intelligent people, those in a position and with the capacity to influence others, a point Dante makes firmly and frequently by discouraging those in little boats from trying to follow him and by having Cacciaguida tell Dante that his message, like the wind, will strike hardest on the highest peaks (*Comedy*, Pr. 17.133–34). That is why he, and through him his audience, has been shown only the famous, because their example will have a greater effect. One might add their example will be most forceful for those in similar positions, tempted by the same possibilities. This poem is not so much a manual to prepare the soul for heaven, a moral guide for a general audience, as it is a polemic preaching the need for improvements on earth in the running of religious and secular affairs, to those who can bring them about. The political message is not thrown in at discreet intervals, it is an integral part of the entire poem, and it involves every aspect of human life that has public implications, and all aspects do. For Dante, morality involves much more than personal salvation; every sin and every virtue, as it is presented in the *Comedy*, has social and therefore political overtones. Every action, every failure to act, has repercussions on others and, in the case of important secular and ecclesiastical officials, as so many of the figures in the *Comedy* are, often on whole cities or peoples.

The *Comedy* deals not only with the main issues of the *Monarchy* and the letters, but with all the political issues

[71]Cf. *Monarchy* 1.2: "Cum ergo materia presens politica sit, ymo fons atque principium rectarum politiarum, et omne politicum nostre potestati subiaceat, manifestum est quod materia presens ... ad operationem ordinatur.... quod est finis universalis civilitatis humani generis, erit hic principium per quod omnia que inferius probanda sunt erunt manifesta sufficienter...." "Since the present subject is political, indeed the origin and source of all proper polities, and everything political is within our power, it is clear that the present matter ... is directed towards action.... the goal of the universal civilization (society) of mankind will be the principle by which everything which is to be proved below will be sufficiently obvious...."

treated by the other political writers, as outlined above. Dante presents the empire as the bearer of a divine mission, to bring justice to earth, to establish the ideal society, and he makes it clear that only the Roman empire can fulfill such a destiny. The main obstacles to its efforts are the church, particularly the papacy, which usurps temporal power and wealth to which it has no right (although the neglect and corruption of the curia, of the monastic and mendicant orders, and of the clergy in general are not overlooked), the French monarchy (which seems to embody all the dangers laid to national states in the *Monarchy*), and Florence, the model of the powerful, rich, and corrupt city. Dante demonstrates the need for just and virtuous guides by showing the effect on the individual of a society that lacks them (in Hell) and one that has them in abundance (in Paradise). Instead of simply stating the abstract arguments of the political controversies, Dante presents them through striking images and the personal experiences of well-known individuals. He sets his arguments in the context of a divinely inspired journey to the other-world for two essential reasons: it enables him to use the authority of the great saints to support his position out of their own mouths, but more important, it provides him with the divine model, the organization of heaven and of the universe on which human society and government must be based. On the one hand, Peter, the first pope and the source of many papal claims, condemns the temporal ambitions of later popes. On the other, God, as "emperor," with his "court," his "barons," all dedicated to his service and sharing its rewards, gives us the model for society on earth. The political message of the poem is ultimately a religious one in that by striving for the ideal society as Dante (inspired by God) imagines it, mankind serves God most fully; at the same time, the religious structure reinforces the political message, the heavenly empire providing the strongest possible argument for its earthly counterpart.

In order to arrive at some idea of what Dante's audience might have gotten from the poem, I have consulted contemporary documents, chronicles, political and philosophical tracts, historical sources, and five of the earliest commentaries on the poem, by Dante's son, Pietro Alighieri (Pietro di Dante), Jacopo della Lana, the Ottimo, Guido da Pisa (for Hell), and Benvenuto da Imola, all from the fourteenth century.[72] Although I have also read and drawn on the work of modern scholars, historians, literary critics, and economists, I have concentrated on the earlier material because I was more concerned with the fourteenth-century northern Italian's view of figures like Boniface VIII or Frederick II, however prejudiced, than with historical details which might not have been known to Dante's audience. I wanted to determine what preconceptions Dante might have expected his audience to bring to his presentation, in order to understand the message he was offering them.

The dominant political-social realities of Dante's world, northern Italy in the late thirteenth and early fourteenth centuries, are the independent city-state, the claims of the empire, the church, and commerce. I have therefore considered Dante's treatment of each of these in the *Comedy* in a separate chapter, beginning with the city and its relation to the empire, the political entities which provide the structural models for Hell and Paradise: the contemporary earthly city, which stands for the self and against the common good, best exemplified by

[72]The commentaries appear in the following editions: *Petri Allegherii, super Dantis ipsius Genitoris Comoediam Commentarium* ed. Vincent Nannucci (Florence: Piatti, 1845); Pietro did other recensions of the commentary, of which only those on Hell have so far been published, by Roberto della Vedova and Maria Teresa Silvotti, eds., *Il "Commentarium" di Pietro Alighieri* (Florence: Olschki, 1978), hereafter referred to as V/S, but cited only when it offers a reading that differs from or adds significantly to the earlier version. *Comedia di Dante degli Allagherii col commento di Jacopo della Lana,* ed. Luciano Scarabelli, 3 vols. (Bologna: Tipografia Rebia, 1866). *L'Ottimo Commento della Divina Commedia, testo inedito d'un contemporaneo di Dante,* ed. Alessandro Torri, 3 vols. (Pisa: Capurro, 1827). Guido da Pisa, *Expositiones et Glose super Comediam Dantis,* ed. Vincenzo Cioffari (Albany: State University, 1974). *Benvenuti de Rambaldis de Imola, Comentum super Dantis Aldigherij Comoediam,* ed. Philip Lacaita, 5 vols. (Florence: Barbèra, 1887). References to these editions will be given throughout the text by page and, where relevant, volume number.

Florence, and the abstract ideal of the city, which stands for the world, united in peace and justice, Rome, the nominal center of the empire. The second chapter deals with the church and its conflict with secular powers and Dante's use and treatment of the traditional arguments of the controversy within the poem. Dante's position on the relation of individual states, cities, and kingdoms to the empire and on the distinct separation of functions of the spiritual and temporal powers is fundamental to an understanding of his political vision in the *Comedy,* as they are the basic issues of the *Monarchy.* Once they have been established, I can show how Dante sees the individual's relation to and responsibility for society through the three models presented in the three cantiche: the corrupt society based on greed and selfishness without order or justice (Hell), the transitional society of men working together to rid themselves of disruptive elements and to achieve a common goal (Purgatory), and the ideal society, based on love, wisdom, and justice, in which all share in the joy and harmony, presided over by the supreme Emperor, God (Paradise). The final chapter treats the basic elements of social exchange—commerce and language. Commerce is essential to the healthy life of a complex society, and a particularly important aspect of life in northern Italy, which Dante accepts as a necessity provided it serves the public interest. Money, as a basic tool of commercial intercourse, bears a close relation to language, the other basic instrument of exchange and communication. The abuse of either can be a serious obstacle to political and social stability, as the proper use can be a great benefit, points Dante makes forcefully by connecting the two kinds of exchange, both literally and figuratively. Dante's views on commerce and language underlie his whole political presentation in the *Comedy,* and are therefore essential to complete that picture. Since language is Dante's particular instrument of social action, as commerce is for so many of his fellow citizens, this seems a fitting place to end the study.

The issues raised in the *Comedy* are complex, the treatments infinitely varied, but the lessons are simple: greed and selfishness are destructive to the public good and to the individual soul, whereas love, concern for the needs of others, and a sense of social responsibility bring personal rewards and strengthen society. As Dante says at the end of the *Monarchy,* it is only by mutual effort, by all men working together in one society, that each man can realize his own highest potential, because it is only in that ideal society, which in the *Comedy* is portrayed in Paradise, that the proper atmosphere for such realization is achieved. In Hell, the souls, however gifted, are held back by their own sinful inclinations, but in Paradise, each soul attains the highest potential in him (or her) for wisdom and love, and thereby increases the light and joy, the wisdom and love, of all his fellows.

Given the temptations of life on earth, men cannot always be expected to lead the good life—even if it is in their own best interest—without guidance and direction. Those must be provided in spiritual things by a pure (uncorrupted by worldly wealth or power) church, and in all other things by a virtuous monarch, who has the power to establish and maintain peace and justice. Dante, a politician who was unable to continue to act directly or effectively in the political sphere, shifted his activity after his exile to the only other sphere in which he might have considerable public influence, writing, and he chose the mode in which he would have the greatest freedom and potentially the greatest force, poetry. Because neither the empire nor the church was functioning as the guide God intended it to be, the poet had to fill the vacancy. To emphasize that point, Dante has himself crowned emperor and pope over himself in the Earthly Paradise by Virgil, another poet, one who had had the ear of an emperor for his political message, the only figure able to bring Dante to the home divinely ordained for mankind, as Dante is the only one who can begin to lead his audience there.

ONE

City and Empire in the *Comedy*

THE POLITICAL VISION of the *Comedy* is firmly rooted in what are, for Dante, the essential political structures of city and empire.[1] He states his views quite clearly in the *Convivio,* 4.4, and in the *Monarchy,* 1.5: man needs the help of his fellows in order to achieve a happy life on earth, government is essential if men are to live together in society, cities are the smallest self-sufficient structures that meet man's needs, though kingdoms serve the same function and can also keep peace among cities, but only a world-monarchy, an empire, can control the greed and aggressions of individual cities and princes. The *Monarchy* devotes a book to each of three arguments: (1) the empire is essential to the well-being of the world; (2) the office was invested in the Roman people by right; and (3) the authority of the monarch is derived directly from God, not through a vicar, the pope, and his functions are separate and distinct. In the *Comedy,* Dante reiterates the human need for a structured society in Paradise: Charles Martel asks Dante if it would not be worse for man if he were not a citizen (8.115–16: "sarebbe il peggio/per l'omo in terra, se non fosse cive?"), and goes on, with a nod towards Aristotle, to explain why it would be, that different men have different functions, different talents, and therefore need each other.[2] Dante also reinforces the

[1] Parts of this chapter were published in "Florence and Rome, the Two Cities of Man in the *Divine Comedy,*" *Acta, Binghamton Conference on the Early Renaissance* 5 (1978), 1–19.

[2] Similarly, because of different local needs and customs, mankind needs different forms of government, different states, but since unity is the greatest need of all, they must all be under the jurisdiction of one sovereign ruler. On the relation of separate states to the empire in Dante's thought, see Felice Battaglia, *Impero, Chiesa e Stati particolari nel pensiero di Dante* (Bologna: Zanichelli, 1944). Pietro Alighieri, commenting on the sixth canto of Purgatory, lists as

other major arguments of the *Monarchy,* the proper relation of papacy and empire (which will be discussed in the next chapter), the divine destiny of Rome, and the need for empire. He deals with the question of empire as the ideal form of government by dramatizing through Hell the dangers of the lack of strong central authority and through Paradise the benefits of a well-functioning empire. He does so by presenting both as cities, the basic political unit, and the one most familiar to Dante's north Italian audience: Hell is the greedy, self-centered, self-enclosed city-state which serves its own needs at the expense of its neighbors, which ignores the common good, and which is ultimately self-destructive. It is best exemplified by Florence, while Paradise, the city of justice, wisdom, love, and harmony, in which the citizens work together for the benefit of all, is the one city which encompasses the world, its peoples and their needs, Rome. Dante underscores the divine destiny of Rome all through the *Comedy,* by choosing Virgil as his guide, by pairing Aeneas with Paul as the models for his journey, by using Rome and Israel as the chosen people whose virtues and vices provide the exempla in Purgatory, by having the Roman eagle represent divine justice in Jupiter, and by making Christ a "citizen" of the heavenly Rome (Pg. 32.101–02).[3]

---

the fifth "moral article" in the canto: "imperatorem non superessendo, abundare tyrannos," when an emperor does not prevail, tyrants abound. He goes on to explain that man is a social animal, that he proceeds from home to neighborhood to city to kingdom, and that, according to the philosopher, the empire and monarchy (single rule) are necessary not by force but by reason (Petri Allegherii, *super Dantis ipsius Genitoris Comoediam Commentarium,* ed. Vincent Nanucci [Florence: Piatti, 1845], (325, 331).

[3]"Cive di quella Roma onde Cristo è romano" ("citizen of that Rome of which Christ is a Roman"). The divinely ordained destiny of the Roman empire is argued in *Monarchy,* 2; cf. letters 5, 6, 7 *Epistolae, The Letters of Dante,* ed. Paget Toynbee (1920; 2d ed., Clarendon, 1966). On Dante's views of Rome, see Charles T. Davis, *Dante and the Idea of Rome* (Oxford: Clarendon, 1957) and "Rome and Babylon in Dante," *Rome in the Renaissance, the City and the Myth,* ed. P. A. Ramsey (Binghamton: CMERS, 1982), 19–40. For general background, Eugenio Dupré-Theseider, *L'Idea imperiale di Roma nella tradizione del medio evo* (Milan: Istituto per gli Studi di Politica Internazionale, 1942).

Between the corrupt city of Hell and the ideal city-empire of Paradise, there is Purgatory, which is neither city nor empire, but a loosely knit kingdom without a center, like Italy. Purgatory is a transitional state, in both senses of the word, a passage from the bad city to the good. Both Hell and Paradise are frequently described as cities, Hell as the grieving city, *città dolente* (Hell 3.1, 9.32, also as the city called Dite, 8.68; the city of fire, 10.22; the red city, 11.73), Paradise as the true city (Pg. 13.95, 16.96; as our city, Pr. 30.130; and as God's city, Hell 1.126 and 128). Purgatory is never called a city in the *Comedy;* instead it is a kingdom (Pg. 1.4, 23.133, 24.92; once a series of kingdoms, 1.82), but a kingdom not sufficient in itself, which looks continually upwards to the moment when it will be absorbed into the empire of Paradise. Paradise is also a kingdom (Pg. 22.78, 32.22, Pr. 3.83, 8.97, 10.72, 11.116, 19.103, 24.43, 31.117, 32.61; a holy kingdom, 1.10; blessed, 1.23; deiform, 2.20; true, 30.98; secure and joyful, 31.25, as well as a series of kingdoms, 5.93). In contrast to Purgatory, however, Paradise is a kingdom in more than name, because its king is always present, ruling directly, a point Virgil makes at the beginning of the poem:

> quello imperador che là sù regna
>
> . . . .
>
> in tutte parti impera e quivi regge;
> quivi è la sua città e l'alto seggio

> that emperor who reigns up there
>
> . . . .
>
> rules as emperor everywhere, and there as king;
> there is his city and his high seat.
>
> (Hell, 1.124, 127–28)

God reigns as emperor through all the universe (through subordinate powers, vicars), but in the city and kingdom of heaven, he rules directly. Hell is a city, Purgatory a kingdom; only Paradise is city, kingdom, and empire, the ideal model for government on earth, containing all the smaller units within the single, unified whole.[4]

In the sixth canto of each cantica, which always has an overtly political subject, Dante focuses on the political entity that serves as the model for that cantica: in Hell, it is Florence, in Purgatory, Italy, and in Paradise, the Roman empire. But the models function in very different ways. Paradise is based on an idealized Rome, a concept of empire based on Roman law, on Roman history, and on Roman literature, in other words an intellectual and cultural reality rather than a physical one, and an abstract ideal to be striven for. The Italy evoked in Purgatory is partly the physical entity, in that Purgatory is a mountain surrounded by sea; but it is primarily cultural. Italy's only political unity is linguistic, as Dante points out in *De vulgari eloquentia,* 1.18.19; for those educated people (*doctores illustres*) who wish to write in the vulgate, there is a language that is essentially the same throughout the peninsula. Unity through language is one of Dante's concerns in Purgatory. In Hell, however, Dante's model is neither cultural nor abstract; it is the physical and historic reality of contemporary Florence, not only the greed and ambition, the political faction and violence, but the walls and towers and caged animals. Florence, as I will show later in this chapter, is the quintessential "earthly" city.[5]

[4]Hell is called a *regno*, but only by its inhabitants, the devils (Hell 8.85, 8.90), who would glorify their realm, and once by Virgil (Pg. 7.22), perhaps for the same reason. Dante, when he sees Lucifer frozen in the ice, immobile and impotent, calls him "lo imperador del doloroso regno" (Hell 34.28), the "emperor of the sorrowful kingdom," but under the circumstances that can only be sarcasm.

[5]The analogy between Hell and Florence has been made by several critics. J. B. Fletcher, "The Crux of Dante's Comedy," in *Essays in Memory of Barrett Wendell* (Cambridge: Harvard, 1965), 90: Hell mirrors Florence as it is, Paradise what his hope would make it. Louis R. Rossi, "The Devouring Passion, Inferno VI," *Italica* 42 (1965), 30, writes that the infernal city of the living is Florence, Satan's plant. Giuseppe Toffanin, "Canto VIII," in *Lectura Dantis Scaligera, Inferno* (Florence: Le Monnier, 1967), 257, says, "La città di Dite simboleggia il mondo disertato dalla giustizia in quanto disertato dall'impero

Like Augustine in the *City of God,* Dante presents his audience with a choice between two cities, the city of God and good, Paradise, and the city of evil, Hell. The conflict between the two, in history as in the individual moral struggle, is between the principles of selfishness and self-indulgence, and devotion to divine law. But for Augustine, the heavenly city, Jerusalem, is embodied in the church; the earthy city, Babylon, in the pagan state.[6] Dante's two cities, instead, are models for man's political as well as spiritual life on earth, since for Dante morality and politics cannot be separated; as long as man is alive, he is a citizen as well as a Christian, and his activities must be judged in relation to society as well as to God. Because he is concerned with the contemporary situation in Italy, Dante shifts from the traditional types for heaven and hell— Jerusalem and Babylon—to the more immediate counterparts, Rome and Florence.[7] Rome, as the nominal center of empire and of church, has direct political significance for Dante's audience. Florence is the contemporary Hell not only because

---

... Firenze." "The city of Dis symbolizes the world abandoned by justice inasmuch as it is abandoned by the empire ... Florence.

[6]At least in theory; the concepts of the two cities were not necessarily embodied in actual organizations. Augustine was not unaware of immoral church officials or good, Christian, officials of state, but he did think that the church must imbue the state with her principles and remain above the state. Edward M. Peters notes that Dante opposes the city of God both to the injustice of human society on earth and specifically to Florence, "The Failure of Church and Empire, *Paradiso,* 30," *Medieval Studies* 34 (1972), 326–35, particularly 328–29. Commenting on canto 3 of Hell, Pietro Alighieri cites Augustine and asserts that a city is nothing but a multitude of men bound by some chain of association; so the state of the vicious may properly be called a city, 66. Benvenuto da Imola describes Hell as a city at some length in canto 34, alerting the reader to the order and disposition of the city he has just been through, see below, p. 195; he calls this the greatest city of all, "istam civitatem maximam omnium," which contains a great part of the citizens of all the cities of the world, 2.561–62. (Benvenuti de Rambaldis de Imola, *Comentum super Dantis Aldigherij Comoediam* ed. Philip Lacaita [Florence: Barbèra, 1887], 5 vols.).

[7]He probably makes the change in part because the New Jerusalem was associated with a purely spiritual state or with the triumph of a purified church. See Henri de Lubac, *Exégèse Médiévale* (Paris: Aubier, 1959–61), 4.vols., 1^2 645–50; $2^1$400, 466–67; $2^2$154, 349.

it is one of the largest, most powerful, and most corrupt cities in Italy, and the one Dante knew best and cared most about, but because it is also one of the major secular obstacles to empire in Italy, and the self-styled heir to classical Rome, though without divine sanction. If Rome, as the empire chosen by God for the birth of his son and the seat of his church and of world government (*Monarchy*, 2.11; *Comedy*, Hell 2.20–24), is Dante's model for the ideal society, then Florence, the Italian city most responsible for impeding Rome's function, is the obvious model for the corrupt society. The opposition is determined by Florence, not by Dante.

Dante makes similar analogies in his letters: of his fellow Florentines he asks, "Why, like the men of Babylon, do you attempt new kingdoms, deserting the pious empire, so that the government of Florence is different from that of Rome?"[8] Dante is not the first to make the analogy with contemporary cities. Jacques de Vitry, in a sermon to citizens and burghers (*sermo ad cives et burgenses*) calls the city of the devil the image of the communes (*communitates*), formed to exert force over their neighbors, to destroy their liberty, to ruin the nobles in the country around them and usurp jurisdiction over their men, to usurp ecclesiastical rights, favor theft and usury, even practice usury, extort money from strangers, and encourage feuds and wars.[9] And Henry VII, in a sentence proclaimed against the Florentines, calls them "proud sons and heirs of

---

[8]"Quid . . . tamquam alteri Babylonii, pium deserentes imperium nova regna tentatis, ut alia sit Florentina civilitas, alia sit Romana?" (Ep. 6.2.49–52). Cf. Ep. 7.8, having lamented Florence's rebellion against Rome, Dante comments: "But just as we, remembering the very holy Jerusalem, lament as exiles in Babylon" (144–46). In Ep. 8.1–2, he compares the widowed Rome to Jerusalem. Jeremy Catto, "Florence, Tuscany, and the World of Dante," in *The World of Dante*, ed. Cecil Grayson (Oxford: Clarendon, 1980), 15, comments that this letter "treats *Romana civilitas* as a moral state." On the more conventional identifications of Babylon with Rome (the empire or the corrupt church), and the importance of apocalyptic imagery in political prophecy, see Marjorie Reeves, *The Influence of Prophecy in the Later Middle Ages* (Oxford: Clarendon, 1969).

[9]Cited by A. Lecoy de la Marche, *La Chaire française au moyen âge*, (1868; 2d rev. ed., Paris: Renouard, 1886), 406–07. I am indebted to Robert Somerville for this reference.

Lucifer," "superbi Luciferi filii et heredes," making the implicit connection between Florence and hell.[10]

The political reality of Italy in Dante's time was a mass of self-seeking smaller states: the cities of northern Italy, the kingdoms of southern Italy and France (as little interested in the common good as the cities), and the papal states of central Italy. All had constantly shifting alliances, of which the only unifying force appeared to be the papacy, which secular rulers acknowledged as their spiritual leader, though they followed the pope's leadership only when it served their purposes. Since Dante would not accept any role for the papacy in secular affairs, he had to look to the empire as the one organ that could transcend and unite the other secular powers. The empire was still a factor in Italian politics, not only with the descent into Italy of Henry VII, 1310–13, but again shortly after Dante's death with that of Ludwig of Bavaria, who reached Rome in 1328. It is no wonder then that Dante should have continued to look to the empire as the one hope for Italy, or that he should have found its highest sanction in the model he provides of the imperial Rome in heaven.

The Rome of Dante's Paradise (and I begin with the heavenly rather than the earthly city, because that is the positive model against which the other must finally be seen) is not the contemporary city Dante knew. Although some of the ancient buildings still stood, reminding visitors like Villani of its former glory—and the Jubilee of 1300 brought many such visitors—the city was in decline; it had receded from its outer walls to the small space between the Capitoline, the Quirinale, and the Tiber, leaving the rest meadows and farmlands.[11]

[10]Cited by Michele Maccarrone, "Il terzo libro della 'Monarchia'," *Studi danteschi* 33 (1955), 5–142, 120.

[11]Villani's visit in 1300 is cited and discussed by Nicolai Rubinstein, "The Beginnings of Political Thought in Florence," *Journal of the Warburg and Courtauld Institutes* 5 (1942), 214. On the decline of the city of Rome, see Arsenio Frugoni, "Dante e la Roma del suo tempo," in *Dante e Roma*, Atti del Convegno di Studi (Florence: Le Monnier, 1965), 86–87. For a study of various aspects of Rome in this period, see Robert Brentano, *Rome Before Avignon: A Social History of Thirteenth Century Rome* (New York: Basic, 1974). Alfred

Nonetheless, it was still thought of as the center of the civilized world; Brunetto Latini, speaking of Cicero, comments "where he says . . . 'our commune' I read Rome, since Tully was a citizen of Rome . . . Rome *is* the head of the world and the commune of everyone."[12] Its citizens identified themselves with the ancient city: from the mid-twelfth century, the Roman Senate defined the "commune" as the *senatus populusque Romanus,* reviving the ancient abbreviation SPQR, and looked to the restoration of the empire ("restauratio imperii Romani"); they addressed emperors as "lord of the city and the world" ("urbis et orbis dominus"), described Rome as the *caput mundi,* and occasionally asserted the city's right to confirm the emperor;[13] and they glorified the city's past in books about its buildings ("Mirabilia urbis Rome") and its ceremonies ("Libellus de cerimoniis aule imperatoris").[14] This self-conscious revival of Roman language and traditions may have

Basserman suggested that Dante modeled Hell on the Colosseum, *Dantes Spuren in Italien* (Munich: Oldenbourg, 1899), 10, but I think it more likely that the *Malebolge,* with the series of concentric arched moats, rather than the whole of Hell, may owe something to the Colosseum.

[12]Commenting on the *Rettorica,* cited by Charles T. Davis, "Brunetto Latini and Dante," *Studi medievali* S.3, 8 (1967), 427–28. Battaglia, *Impero,* 107, notes that Dante makes the empire Roman because Rome stands for universality; its values are neither German nor Italian, but universal.

[13]Robert L. Benson, "Political *Renovatio:* Two Models from Roman Antiquity," in *Renaissance and Renewal in the Twelfth Century,* ed. Robert L. Benson and Giles Constable (Cambridge: Harvard University, 1982), 342–43. The medieval tradition that the emperor did not have real authority within the city of Rome, which was under the temporal control of the pope because of the Donation of Constantine, is not accepted by Dante, who questions the validity of the document. In the *Monarchy,* he states flatly that the emperor did not have the right to give away the prerogatives of empire, any more than the church had the right to receive them, 3.10; in the *Comedy,* Paradise 6.1–2, the emperor Justinian says that Constantine carried the eagle, the imperial standard, against the course of the heavens, that is, in opposition to God's will, and the eagle (20.55–60) says that Constantine, who made the laws and empire Greek to yield to the pope, now knows that the evil he caused with good intentions does not harm him, though it may destroy the world.

[14]The texts can be found in *Codice Topografico della Città di Roma,* ed. R. Valentini and G. Zucchetti (Rome: Istituto Storico Italiano, 1946), vol. 8.

been more rhetoric than political reality, but it is a rhetoric some, including Dante, would have made true. And it was reinforced by the reality of Roman law, which increasingly from the twelfth century on was a factor in contemporary society. Roman law, codified under the emperor Justinian, was in a sense proof that only Rome could properly govern the world. All of this was reinforced by the history of Rome, which Dante draws on so heavily in the second book of the *Monarchy* and in the *Comedy,* by the examples of the Roman leaders, by the teachings of Cicero, Seneca, and Livy, and by the poetry of Virgil, Lucan, and Statius. And this was coupled with the role of the Christian empire in protecting the church, with God's choice of the empire as the government under which his son could be born and legally executed (*Monarchy,* 2.11 and 12), and of the city as the seat of his church. For these reasons, Rome was the inevitable and only possible model for Dante's Paradise.

The Roman empire is the political entity that dominates Paradise from canto 6, where Justinian traces its history from Aeneas to Dante's time, to canto 30, where Dante sees the seat in the rose reserved for Henry VII, the emperor who might have saved Italy and Europe if individual cities and kingdoms and the church had not interfered. The importance of the empire in Dante's scheme is suggested much earlier in the *Comedy:* at the very beginning of Hell, the first character to speak to Dante is Virgil, the poet of empire, who identifies himself in terms of the emperors under whom he was born and lived (1.70–71: "I was born under Julius . . . and I lived at Rome under the good Augustus"), and whose last words in the canto are of the "emperor" of heaven and the "city" he rules. In Hell 34, the two assassins of the emperor are placed in Satan's mouths on either side of Judas, the enemies of the empire punished on the same level as the enemy of God. In Purgatory 30, Beatrice is heralded by three phrases which connect her first with the church as Christ's spouse, then with Christ himself, and finally with the emperor; Dante's personal savior is made to represent God, the church in the body of the faithful, and the empire.[15]

In Paradise, Justinian shows the will of God working through the empire not only in his actions, the reform of the laws and the establishment of order, but in those of the pagan emperors to whom God gave the task of carrying out his justice, first by crucifying Christ to save mankind, and then by taking revenge for Christ's death in the destruction of Jerusalem. It is ironic, of course, that pagan Rome under the emperors served God in the salvation of mankind, while Christian Rome, under the popes, does the devil's work. Peter, speaking of his successor, says he has "made a sewer of my cemetery, from which the perverse one who fell from up here takes pleasure down there" (27.25–27: "fatt'ha del cimitero mio cloaca . . . onde 'l perverso/che cadde di qua sù, là giù si placa"). In the heaven of justice, Jupiter, it is once again emperors who represent God's will. They appear in and speak through the eagle, the imperial sign, which is placed above the martyrs in the sign of the cross because the justice embodied in the empire is the cause which the sacrifice of Christ and the crusaders serve. The rulers serve that cause at times without fully understanding it: "Ora conosce," the eagle keeps repeating, "*Now* he understands why. . . ." The church, which claims to know and tries to impose its will rather than God's, may itself run counter to God's intentions, withholding the bread that God does not deny anyone (18.129). But God will accept even those who lived outside the church: at the Last Judgment, the eagle tells us, many who did not know Christ in his historic form

---

[15]The phrases are: "Veni, sponsa, de Libano" ("Come, my bride, from Lebanon"), drawn from the Song of Songs 4:8, which was taken to represent the marriage of Christ to man or to Christianity in the church) "Benedic*tus* qui venis" ("Blessed are you [masc.] who come") based on Matt. 21:9, which greets Christ's entry into Jerusalem as king; and "Manibus, oh, date lilia plenis" ("Give lilies, oh, with full hands") from the *Aeneid,* 6.883, a prophecy of the early death of Marcellus, who should have been a great emperor. On Rome's role in the redemptive process, see Giuseppe Mazzotta, *Dante, Poet of the Desert* (Princeton: Princeton University, 1979), chapter 1.

will be closer to God than those who now cry "Christ, Christ" (19.106).

Among the leaders who form the eye of the eagle, the highest position in the figure, there are two who did not know Christ while they lived: the pagans Trajan and Ripheus;[16] and two who could only have known the Christ to come, David and Hezekiah. Only two, Constantine and William II, a twelfth-century king of Sicily, actually lived their lives as Christians. They are all here because they served God's justice most completely as kings, and they appear in the eagle, the symbol of the Roman empire, "the sign that made the Romans revered through the world" (19.101–02: "il segno/che fé i Romani al mondo reverendi"), not because they were Roman emperors—only Trajan and Constantine actually were—but because it is the Roman empire that carries the burden of imposing God's justice on earth. Anyone who serves that justice serves the empire. Divine justice is one, no matter what earthly form it takes, a point Dante emphasizes by having the souls in the eagle speak with one voice, saying "I" and "mine" for "we" and "our" (19.11–12). It is the only symbol in Paradise from which the individual souls never emerge singly, a powerful exhibition of the unity and harmony Dante attributes to the supreme monarchy.

Nestled within the figure of the eagle, which represents God's justice as administered by the Roman empire, some of the souls form lilies, symbols of France, of Florence, and of the Guelphs, who should have been united under the protective guidance of the empire. Only the empire can make the individual cities and kingdoms serve God's purpose, and that is why the political figures in Paradise are predominantly emper-

[16]There is a legend of Trajan's being brought back from the dead to be reborn and die a Christian, but nothing of the kind about Ripheus. Although Ripheus is not a prince in the *Aeneid*, Dante makes it clear that he thinks of Ripheus as a leader by including him in the eye of the eagle and placing him in the sphere of Jupiter, which is identified as the realm of world leaders, those who oversee justice on earth (see Pr. 18.93, 18.116, 19.101–02, 19.112 ff., 20.8, 20.36).

ors: Justinian, in Mercury, Charlemagne, in Mars, where the future imperial vicar, Can Grande, is praised, Trajan and Constantine in Jupiter, the mother of the last effective Roman emperor, Frederick II, in the Moon, and the empty seat for Henry VII in the rose. There are a few good kings in Paradise, but very few: William II of Sicily, in Jupiter; Godfrey, who fought God's war and became king of Jerusalem, in Mars; Solomon, who asked only for wisdom to be a sufficient king (13.95–96: "fu re, che chiese senno/acciò che re sufficiente fosse"), who, in other words, accepted the limitations of kingship; and the thirteenth-century Charles Martel, whom Dante apparently met in Florence, who might have united a good part of Europe had he lived, as the heir to Naples, Provence, and Hungary and son-in-law of the emperor Rudolph I. But these kings are few and far between in human history as in Paradise. Most of those who govern the separate states of the world fail to serve justice, and Dante, through the eagle, indicts a long line of contemporary rulers for their failures, contrasting the abuses of the Christian kings with the just pagans in the eagle's eye, and with unidentified just pagans still alive (19.112: "What will the Persians say to your kings . . . ?"). The list (19.115 ff.), given by country rather than individual names, covers most of Europe from north (Scotland, England and Norway) to south (Sicily and Serbia, as far as the Middle East), and from east (Bohemia and Hungary) to west (Spain and Portugal), emphasizing the need for a central authority to unite the disparate parts. (The list also recalls the kings in the valley of negligent princes in Purgatory 7, many of them fathers of these, whose own defects perhaps contributed to the greater failures of their sons.) This wide sweep over Europe, extending our perspective to include most of Dante's world, is echoed in other parts of Paradise that are not overtly political: the list of territories held by Charles Martel (8.49 ff.); Folco's description of his home in terms of the Mediterranean basin, lands united by ancient Rome (9.82 ff.); the wise men in the circles of the Sun, which include Italians, Frenchmen, Greeks, Jews, Flemish, Spaniards, an Englishman, a Scot, and a Swabian, who together form the symbol of wisdom; and in the lives of Saints Dominic and Francis, the former born in the western limits of Europe, who carried his message eastward across the continent, the latter born in Italy, who carried the Word to the Sultan in Egypt. These geographic leaps are meant to show the oneness of the Christian world and faith, which, when properly observed, represents a unity only the empire can achieve. Conversely, Dante's journey from hell (or earth) to heaven is described metaphorically by Beatrice as from Egypt to Jerusalem (25.55–56), the shortest geographical distance to describe the longest spiritual voyage. Dante, from his new perspective, can look down on Europe and see the whole of it as a threshing floor (22.151 and 27.86).

Dante builds slowly through the *Comedy* to this perspective, from which he and his audience can see the inhabited world as a whole. Moving out from the focus on Florence in most of Hell, adding other cities of north Italy in the *Malebolge,* he begins to speak more of regions in Purgatory, and even of kingdoms. Purgatory itself is simply a realm of transition between the opposing models of Hell and Paradise, in every way an intermediate stage. Though not itself a city, its inhabitants are all citizens of the "true" city (Pg. 13.94–95: "ciascuna è cittadina/d'una vera città"), waiting until they are ready to enter there. If Purgatory is reminiscent of one contemporary reality more than another, it is of Italy, though without the symbolic force of Rome in Paradise, or the graphic power of Florence in Hell. Like Italy, which is the object of Dante's attack in canto 6, Purgatory is a mountain that rises out of the sea, all its sections separate but connected by a single road, as Italy's separate states are connected by a common language.[17]

[17]Cf. Charles T. Davis, *Dante and the Idea of Rome* (Oxford: Clarendon, 1957), 187: "Italy to him [Dante] was certainly a geographical and cultural unity, but not a self-sufficient political one, for it was the center of the greatest polity, the Empire, and separateness would have cost it glory rather than added it." Peter Damian's description of his hermitage, which begins "between the two shores of Italy rise cliffs" (Pr. 21.106), is somewhat reminiscent of Purgatory. On Dante's sense of Italy as a geographic and linguistic unity, see Battaglia, *Impero,* 88–89.

Like Italy, it is a kingdom with laws, but no ruler to enforce them, although the results are quite different because the inhabitants of Purgatory accept the rule of the universal emperor. Italy, on the other hand, which was meant to be the "garden of the empire" (6.105), its king the emperor of Christendom, is now filled with tyrants and rebels (6.124–25), torn by wars and factional strife because it has no leader. Its center, Rome, is now a widow mourning the absence of her emperor (6.112–14). Italy is a ship without a pilot, a horse without a rider in the saddle (6.77, 88–92). The horse and rider imagery also suggests that Italy is a macrocosm in relation to the individual soul: in *Convivio*, 4.9.10, Dante speaks of the emperor as the "rider of the human will," "cavalcatore de la umana volontade"; in Purgatory 6, Italy is the horse that goes astray because the church has kept Caesar out of the saddle, and the souls on each ledge are restrained and encouraged by the reins and whips or spurs of the examples of vice and virtue.[18] The souls in Purgatory are pilgrims working their way from the evil to the "true city" where they can once again be citizens, as Beatrice tells Dante:

> Qui sarai tu poco tempo silvano;
> e sarai meco sanza fine cive
> di quella Roma onde Cristo è romano.

> Here you will be for a short time a rustic;
> and [then] you will be with me an eternal citizen
> of that Rome of which Christ is a Roman.

(Pg. 32.100–02)

To prepare themselves for that city, the souls not only purge themselves of their vicious impulses, they also outgrow their political narrowness. They begin to think in larger terms, identifying themselves with and by their regions rather than their cities, so that they can eventually think of themselves as Italians—Sapia tells Dante that they all lived as pilgrims in Italy

---

[18]Dante also compares himself to Italy, Pg. 30.85–99, the ice in his heart like the snow that freezes Italy's back.

(13.96), an unusual instance of a soul speaking for all Italians in common—and finally as members of the empire which includes all mankind.

The steps Dante climbs out of the first ledge of Purgatory remind him of the steps leading to San Miniato outside Florence, as though he too were moving away from his city towards the rest of Italy. Like Dante, the poets in Purgatory, who should guide men towards the right life, provide a model for this broadening of perspective. Virgil, who wrote of the origins of the empire, spans the peninsula in his life: born at Mantova, he lived in Rome, he tells us at the beginning of Hell, and adds in Purgatory 3 that he died at Brindisi and was buried in Naples. Statius says he was from Toulouse,[19] but lived in Rome and sang of Thebes. Sordello, an Italian-born poet who lived in France and wrote in Provençal, attacked most of the rulers of Europe in his poetry, as Dante does in his. The last two poets Dante meets in Purgatory, the Italian Guido Guinizelli and the Provençal Arnaut Daniel, are not political poets, but their words provide the most effective example of international harmony: each speaks in his own language, united by Dante's rhyme scheme and meter. It is an instance, one of many in the *Comedy,* of the poet's accomplishing in his work what politicians and statesmen fail to do in theirs. Poets bring generations and even nations together through their use of language. Throughout Purgatory, communication, and therefore harmony, is facilitated by an apparent unification of language: Latin, Italian, Provençal, French are treated as one tongue, just as the people whose cultures are based on those languages should be one under the empire. The Latin poet, Virgil, is called "gloria di Latin ... per cui/mostrò ciò che potea la lingua *nostra*" (7.16–17: "the glory of the Latins ... through whom *our* language showed what it could do") by Sordello, an Italian who wrote in Provençal. The Italian Guido

[19]Ettore Paratore, in his article on Statius in the *Enciclopedia Dantesca* (Rome: Istituto delle Enciclopedie Italiane, 1970–78), 5.419, notes that Statius identifies Naples as his birthplace in the *Silvae,* but that Dante probably knew only the *Thebaid* and the *Achilleid.*

Guinizelli calls the Provençal poet Arnaut Daniel "miglior fabbro del parlar materno" (26.117: "a better craftsman of the maternal tongue").

Unfortunately, those who are most responsible for bringing the world together and leading it in the right direction—its secular princes—have not done their part. It is not only Italy that lacks proper guidance; the rest of Europe is also suffering from the defects of its leaders. Dante criticizes the rulers of Europe at length in two regions of Purgatory, among the negligent in canto 7, and among the greedy in canto 20. Negligence and greed are traits for which he condemned the German emperor Albert I and his father, Rudolph I, in canto 6. In the valley of negligent princes at the foot of Purgatory, Dante sees kings from Bohemia, France, Navarre, Aragon, Naples, and England, along with a German emperor, sitting in a flower-filled valley which is a reflection of the Earthly Paradise. The duty of these rulers while they were alive was to work towards the establishment of an earthly paradise in the world, as Dante pointed out in the *Monarchy,* but they failed out of negligence. The irony, as Dante would have expected his audience to recognize, is that despite the fact that many of them are related by marriage, a recognized means of uniting or at least allying nations, they were frequently at war with each other, sometimes fomenting war between brothers. Part of their present suffering is the knowledge that most of them have spawned sons whose sins are far worse.[20]

[20]Philip III of France was married to the daughter of Henry I of Navarre, Pedro III of Aragon was the son-in-law of Manfred (who appears in an earlier group of negligents), Charles I of Naples (Anjou) and Henry III of England were married to sisters, and Ottokar's son eventually married Rudolph I's daughter after his defeat. James II of Sicily (Anjou) fought his brother Frederick II, ceding Sicily to his father-in-law, Charles II of Naples. Charles is mentioned only by epithet, *maschio naso,* and *nasuto,* whereas his nephew, Philip III, is a *nasetto,* the family decline echoed in the size of the nose. The kings of Bohemia, France, Naples, and Sicily all have worse issue; only Henry III of England is said to have better. Dante does not mention Charles of Anjou's grandson here, but he does meet him in Paradise 8, and receives a lesson from him on the importance of civil community in human life.

On the ledge of avarice, in canto 20, Hugh Capet carries the theme of degeneration within the family to its furthest extreme, tracing his line from himself, "the root of the bad plant," from which good fruit is seldom plucked (20.43–45), through a series of kings whose greed and ambition caused them to take by force and fraud, to conspire with popes and local political factions (Charles of Valois was involved in the exile of the Whites from Florence, which drove Dante out of the city), to sell their own children, to attack the pope and seize the possessions of a religious order. The last kings he mentions are Charles II of Naples and Philip IV of France, who were so severely criticized in canto 7. It is no coincidence that the kingdoms of France and Naples were the two that most consistently and effectively fought the true heirs, as Dante saw it, to the empire. The failures and abuses of these kings, even those whose defects were not serious enough to condemn them to Hell, is a strong reminder of the limitations of national monarchy and the need for a strong emperor to control them. That message is reinforced at the end of Purgatory when Dante sees the procession of the books of the Bible and the pantomime of the history of church and empire, which makes clear the role God intended for both in providential history and shows once again how the French monarchy, in the person of the giant, attempts to interfere with God's plan by removing the church from the tree in which the imperial eagle lives and taking it forcibly to France.

The problem of greed and selfishness, which prevents kingdoms from working towards peace in the world and the common good of mankind, is the same problem that faces the city-states; Purgatory simply expands the scope of the problem as it was outlined in Hell, but it is in Hell that we are really shown the dangers of an independent political entity. Here Dante focuses much more directly on his model city, Florence, and the analogy between the city and the individual sinner is not made just by allusion to an image like the riderless horse, but by a series of identifications of Florence with particular sins. Because it serves both as a macrocosm of individual moral

sins. Because it serves both as a macrocosm of individual moral corruption and as the symbol of secular resistance to the empire in Italy (the self-styled anti-Rome), it is the most suitable model for Hell. There are also personal reasons for Dante to model Hell on Florence: what better way to avenge himself on the city that exiled him than to cast it as Hell, a city no rational being would want to enter, and then force his way back into it with the aid of divine intervention only to show it up for what it is? In this sense, writing the *Comedy* is a way of returning to Florence and rejecting it, turning the tables on it. But this is not Dante's main reason for writing the *Comedy*. What he wants to do is cure the corruption in Florence and Italy, and he focuses on Florence not only because he knows it best, but because it, in fact, offers his audience the most striking example of corruption in Italy. It represents most completely the rich and powerful political unit, which lives for itself alone and exploits rather than supports its fellows.

While Dante was writing, Florence was one of the four largest cities in Italy, indeed in Europe (only Paris rivaled the major Italian cities in size), with a population of about ninety thousand, trade relations all over the known world, predominance in banking, which enabled it to finance the politics and wars of kings as far away as the British Isles, and a policy of expansion into the neighboring territory by attack and by colonization. Between 1299 and 1360, Florence planned six new towns.[21] In its ambitions, Florence consciously modeled itself on ancient Rome. Historical writings from the early thirteenth century emphasize the Roman origins of the city, which were in the main legendary. The *Chronica de origine civitatis* says it was first called "parva Roma," little Rome, when it was founded under Julius Caesar, and its original buildings were

[21]On the population, see J. K. Hyde, *Society and Politics in Medieval Italy* (New York: St. Martin's, 1973), 153: on finance, see references in chapter six, below, and also John Larner, *Culture and Society in Italy, 1290–1420* (New York: Scribner's 1971), 25–26; on the new towns, see David Friedman, "Le terre nuove fiorentine," *Archeologia Medievale* 1 (1974), 235. I am indebted to Paula Spilner of Columbia for much of the information about the contemporary city.

copies of Roman models; after its (also legendary) destruction by Totila, it was rebuilt by Rome, again in conscious imitation of the mother city.[22] The Florentine chronicler Villani reports that he was impressed when he saw the great and ancient buildings of Rome, but when he considered that Florence, "daughter and creation of Rome, was rising and achieving great things, whereas Rome was declining," he decided to collect the deeds and origins of Florence and record them. In other words, he sees Florence as the successor to Rome. The same sentiment is echoed more arrogantly in an inscription on the facade of the Palazzo del Popolo, built in the mid-thirteenth century: "Florence is full of all wealth; she defeats her enemies in war and civil strife; she enjoys the favour of fortune and has a powerful population . . . she possesses the sea and the land and the whole earth; under her leadership the whole of Tuscany is happy. Like Rome she is always triumphant."[23] A similar inscription on the reconstructed Badia of San Simone proclaimed that Florence was at the head of all other Latin cities, therefore of the world.

Other cities were rich and powerful and growing during this period, but none to the extent of Florence. Florence was building and rebuilding at a rapid rate. It had what Guido Pampaloni calls a vast urban program at the end of the thirteenth and in the early fourteenth century: three of the four bridges over the Arno were built in thirty-two years, churches were expanded "for the honor and beauty of the city," new roads were opened up and old ones widened.[24] Dante himself was the head of a committee to widen the Via Santi Proculi, although he had reservations about the extent of destruction and

[22]For a discussion of such legends, see Rubinstein, "Beginnings," 201 ff. Dante calls Florence "la bellissima e famosissima figlia di Roma" ("the most beautiful and famous daughter of Rome") in the Convivio, 1.3.4, ed. G. Busnelli and G. Vandelli (Florence: Le Monnier, 1954), 2 vols.

[23]Cited by Rubinstein, "Beginnings," 213, with the original text.

[24]Guido Pampaloni, Firenze al tempo di Dante (Rome: Archivi di Stato, 1973), particularly xxiv ff. On the bridges, see Robert Davidsohn, Storia di Firenze, I primordi della civiltà fiorentina: il mondo della chiesa, spiritualità ed arte, vita publica e privata (Italian trans. Eugenio Dupré-Theseider), 7.531.

rebuilding.[25] And Florence was expanding its territory, building a third set of walls around itself, the most famous new walls in contemporary Italy (Hyde, *Society and Politics,* 153). To live within the walls of a city meant that one enjoyed the freedom and protection of a citizen; it was a privilege people in the outlying areas sought. But Dante saw the increasing population as a threat to the purity of Florence, as he makes clear in Paradise 15 and 16, where Cacciaguida describes the city of his time, the early twelfth century, as the ideal: simple, morally upright, and one-fifth its size in 1300. For Dante, all men could ideally be Romans, but only a small number should be Florentines.

The original Roman walls around the inner city of Florence, where Dante's family lived, were gone by his time, although people were still aware of them and perhaps confused them with Byzantine ruins; the second circuit of walls was built after 1172, three times the original size, and a third, enclosing roughly eight times the area, was begun in 1284.[26] It was not completed until 1333, but was effective enough to withstand the attack of Henry VII two decades earlier (Davidsohn, *Storia di Firenze,* 7.478–79). This is the unforgivable sin for Dante, that Florence in its arrogance should not only rival Rome, but should oppose the divinely ordained destiny of the empire, the only hope, as he saw it, for all of Italy. Florence was, in fact, at the center of Guelph resistance to the emperor, bringing major cities, including Bologna, Lucca, and Siena, together in a Guelph league in 1310, which was to field a cavalry force of 4,000. Florence also treated Henry as a foreign intruder,

---

[25]Pampaloni gives the document that names Dante for the project (April 28, 1301), no. 70, *Firenze,* 125. Dante's views on rebuilding are apparent in his letter to the Florentines, 6.4.75–76: "Videbitis aedificia vestra non necessitati prudenter instructa, sed delitiis inconsulte mutata . . . ruere" ("You will see your buildings, raised not prudently out of need, but thoughtlessly altered for your pleasure . . . fall").

[26]See Pampaloni, *Firenze,* vi, and Davidsohn, *Storia di Firenze,* 7.479. On the Byzantine walls, see Charles T. Davis, "Il Buon Tempo Antico," in *Florentine Studies,* ed. Nicolai Rubinstein (Evanston: Northwestern University, 1968), 56, fn. 3.

addressing him in letters as "King of Germany" in 1311 and solemnly banning him; it appealed to the king of Naples, Robert of Anjou, for support against Henry, as well as to the pope and the king of France, making it clear that it was concerned not so much with the foreign element as with the imposition of authority.[27]

Dante keeps coming back to the problem in letter 6 cited above and in Purgatory, 6.127 ff., where Florence's willingness to shoulder the burdens of the world is an implicit reference to the rivalry with Rome:

> Fiorenza mia . . .
> Molti han giustizia in cuore . . .
> . . . .
> ma il popol tuo l'ha in sommo de la bocca.
> Molti rifiutan lo comune incarco;
> ma il popol tuo solicito risponde
> sanza chiamare, e grida: "I' mi sobbarco."

> My Florence . . .
> many have justice in their hearts . . .
> . . . .
> but your people have it on the tip of their tongues.
> Many refuse the common burden;
> but your people answers solicitously
> without being called, and shouts: "I will take it on."

and again in Paradise 15, where the reference is explicit: "Non era vinto ancora Montemalo/dal vostro Uccellatoio" (15.109–10: "Montemalo was not yet conquered by your Uccellatoio"), naming hills outside the two cities. In a letter to Henry VII, Dante tells him not to waste his time attacking other Italian cities, but to go straight to the root of all the trouble: "Florence is the name of this terrible bane. She is the viper that turns against the viscera of her own mother . . . when she sharpens

---

[27]See William Bowsky, "Florence and Henry of Luxemburg, King of the Romans: The Rebirth of Guelfism," *Speculum* 33 (1958), 177–203, particularly 184, 195, 199, 201.

the horns of rebellion against Rome, which made her in her own image and after her own likeness." [28] As long as Florence is permitted to go her own way, there is no hope for the empire, for the world, or for Italy.

Such are Dante's reasons for using Florence as the model for Hell. His methods are twofold: Florence is present both in echoes of the physical city and as the prime sinner in many of the circles, either in itself or through its famous sons. Technically, Dante uses the physical city because he presents Hell in graphic, physical terms, with emphasis on sense perception (sounds and smells, as well as sights) and weight. One is very aware of the encumbrance and pain of the physical body of individual souls and the physical setting that contributes to the pain, in contrast to Paradise—the realm of spirit and mind—which is dominated by light and motion rather than weight and physical detail. That is why the Rome on which Paradise is modeled must be an abstract ideal, while the Florence of Hell is a concrete, physical reality. Didactically, Dante uses the city his audience knew or knew about, because that drives home the principal message that they are living in the Hell they create for themselves, which not only hurts them but seriously endangers the common good. The political corruption cannot be dissociated from the moral, since the bad state corrupts its citizens, as bad citizens corrupt the state.

Some of the characteristics medieval Florence shares with Hell would be true of other medieval cities, such as the narrow, curving streets filled with the traffic of vendors, muggers, the crippled and mutilated, the stench of human excrement. But the larger the city, the worse the problem. Other cities also had ruins, but Florence's were mainly the results of civil strife: towers torn down by the *popolo* because they represented the power of the aristocracy, houses destroyed by rival factions. Still, there are more telling signs of Florence in Hell: the series of walls around the city, outer walls in canto 3, seven moats

[28]"Florentia . . . dira haec pernicies nuncupatur. Haec est vipera versa in viscera genitricis. . . . dum contra Romam cornua rebellionis exacuit, quem ad imaginem suam atque similitudinem fecit illam, "Ep. 7.7.111–12, 119–22.

and gates around the castle in Limbo, walls around the inner city of Dis, the ten moats of the *Malebolge,* and finally what appear to be towers surrounding the lake at the center. These last turn out to be chained giants, a reference, perhaps, to the towers of the aristocracy which were limited in their height by the *popolo,* a symbol of the restrictions on their powers.[29] In any case, Dante seems to be saying that only Hell has more walls around it than Florence, and Hell is what Florence is really striving to be.

Two of the three animals which prevent Dante from climbing the mountain at the beginning of the *Comedy,* forcing him down through Hell, had their real counterparts in Florence: the lion, a symbol of the city, was sculpted on the northern gates (on one side a lion protecting a bull, on the other a lion tearing a bull apart, as a not-very-subtle warning to Florence's neighbors), but it was also to be seen live inside the city. Cages containing up to two dozen lions were kept near the Battistero from the mid-thirteenth century as the "pride of the citizenry and symbol of communal power"; in a separate cage there was a leopard. All the animals were maintained at the expense of the commune.[30] The statue of a wolf, the third animal of Hell 1 and the emblem of classical Rome, was located near the Lateran, where it served as a symbol of papal power.[31] The Flor-

[29]See Ferdinand Schevill, *History of Florence* (1936; reprint, New York: Ungar, 1961), 155, and Edward M. Peters, "Pars, Parte: Dante and an Urban Contribution to Political Thought," in *The Medieval City,* ed. H. A. Miskimin, David Herlihy and A. L. Udovitch (New Haven: Yale, 1977), 117.

[30]See Davidsohn, *Storia di Firenze,* 7.513. Giovanni Villani, *Istorie Fiorentine* (Milan: Società Tipografica dei Classici Italiani, 1802), tells of lions given to the city: one, c. 1273, escaped from his pen in the Piazza San Giovanni and captured but did not harm a little boy, 6.70; another was given to the city by Boniface VIII, c. 1302, but was killed by a donkey, which was taken as a sign of changes to come, 8.62.

[31]See Adalbert Erler, "Lupa, Lex and Reiterstandbild im Mittelalterlichen Rom," *Sitzungsberichte der Wissenschaftlichen Gesellschaft an der J. W. Goethe-Universität* Frankfurt/Main 10[4] (1972), 125–26; and Franco Lanza, "Roma e l'emblema della lupa," *Dante e Roma,* Atti del convegno di studi (Florence: Le Monnier, 1965), 255–61. Dante, of course, connects the wolf with greed in Purgatory, 20.10, but he also calls the Florentines wolves indi-

entine lions and leopard were famous sights which people paid a fee to see, so it seems likely that Dante's audience would have made the connection. None of this, incidentally, is meant to deny the allegorical significance of the animals; I am simply suggesting that they might also have had an immediate contemporary relevance for Dante's audience, inviting the identification with Florence.

Dante gives us several hints within the *Comedy* that he equates Florence with Hell: at the top of Paradise (31.37–39) the pilgrim says he has come from the human to the divine, from time to the eternal, and from Florence to the just and sane people; in Paradise 9 (127 ff.), he calls Florence the "devil's plant," which scatters its seed—the florin—everywhere, corrupting all it touches, turning shepherds (the church) into wolves (of greed), and leading the sheep astray. The inscription on the gates of Hell describes it as a "città dolente," which might remind those familiar with the *Vita Nuova* of the passage in which Dante calls Florence a "città dolente" after the death of Beatrice (chapter 40, sonnet, line 6). That lower Hell is also called the "città di Dite," "city of wealth," also suggests Florence, which was the richest, or financially the most important, city in north Italy (see chapter six). But Florence's presence is most clearly felt in the separate circles where it is either the object of discussion or the place of origin of the principal sinner, or both, and often it emerges as the strongest example of the sin. Among the gluttons, in Hell 6, Dante meets the Florentine Ciacco, who describes the city as if *it* were the glutton, not for food, but for money and power, "your city, so full of envy that it already overflows its sack" (6.49–50: "la tua città, ch'è piena/d'invidia sì che già trabocca il sacco"). The rhyming of *sacco* with Ciacco joins the city with the glutton; Florence feeds itself on power and wealth beyond what it can

rectly (Pg. 14.50), and says the florin turned the church (the shepherd) into a wolf (Pr. 9.132). The wolf was also the symbol of Siena, according to Dino Compagni, *Cronica,* ed. Gino Luzzatto (Turin: Einaudi, 1968), 2.28, who cites a prophecy, "La lupa puttaneggia," "the wolf whores", that is, Siena toys with the Florentine political refugees, the Ghibellines and the Whites.

contain, and becomes so diseased that even its best people are tainted.[32]

Dante asks Ciacco two significant questions about Florence: first, what will happen to the citizens of the divided city, a question that implies the basic problem. If the city is the smallest political unit, how can one be a citizen of a divided city? To divide it is to destroy it, and Ciacco's answer is indeed a prophecy of feud and bloodshed. Hell, too, is a divided city, each section separate unto itself, filled with inhabitants hostile or, at best, indifferent, to each other. Dante's second question is about five Florentines he had respected, men who strove to do good, but who are now, Ciacco tells him, among the blackest souls in Hell. Thus, from very early on we know that Hell is peopled by the famous citizens of Florence, that the city is so corrupt even its great men are damned. Guido da Pisa, commenting on canto 26, which begins with the sarcastic eulogy of Florence's prestige through all the world and Hell, notes how many Florentines there are in Hell and lists them in some detail, beginning with Ciacco and ending with five among the traitors in the last circle.[33]

The kind of violence and hatred that is destroying Florence is demonstrated in Dante's next two encounters with Florentines in Hell, canto 8 with Filippo Argenti and canto 10 with Farinata. Filippo, who attacks Dante and tries to pull him out of his boat, is described as "il fiorentino spirito bizzarro" (8.62), "the irascible (or strange) Florentine spirit," an ambiguous phrase which might mean either that the spirit is *from* Florence or *of* Florence, that is, the spirit that dominates Florence. Inside the city of Dis, the first soul Dante meets is the heretic Farinata, the Florentine patriot and Ghibelline. He is the first person to name the city in the poem, Dante's acknowledgment of the fact that he was the only one who spoke in its defense when it was almost destroyed after Montaperti, though he had

---

[32]Cf. Pg. 20.75, Charles of Valois, by deceit, bursts Florence's belly ("a Fiorenza fa scoppiar la pancia"), which also evokes the image of a glutton.

[33]Guido da Pisa's *Expositiones et Glose super Comediam Dantis*, ed. Vincenzo Cioffari (Albany: State University, 1974), 514–15.

not hesitated to fight against it.[34] His conversation with Dante reflects the Florentine feud in miniature: because Dante's ancestors were Farinata's enemies, he forces Dante into an extreme Guelph position, although Dante, as a White Guelph, is closer to Farinata's Ghibelline views than to those of the Black Guelphs with whom he is here classed. The common bond between the two, love for their city, gives way to factionalism and drives them to attack each other. In the wood of the suicides, Dante intensifies our sense of the self-destructiveness of the city by his encounter with another Florentine, who identifies himself only by city, not by name. He tells Dante in the last line of the canto (13.151) that he made himself a gallows of his own home. Since the next canto begins with Dante gathering the scattered leaves of the suicide's tree out of love for his birthplace (14.1: "carità del natio loco"), and the canto break between the two lines calls particular attention to them, one assumes that Florence itself is the suicide, bent on self-destruction by its own greed and violence.[35] In Purgatory, Florence is described as a dismal wood that does not reforest itself (14.64–66: "trista selva ... che ... non si rinselva"), which recalls the wood of suicides. Dino Compagni lends support to this view of Florence when he comments that the Blacks would rather see the city destroyed than lose control of it: "I Neri di Firenze, volendo più tosto la città guasta che perdere la signoria" (2.28). In one sense, what Dante does in the Comedy is to gather the fragmented parts of his city, out of love and the desire to restore it.

[34]It is interesting that Farinata, who saved Florence, is in Hell, while Provenzan Salvani, who wanted to destroy it, is in Purgatory (canto 11). Might Dante have thought that the destruction of the corrupt city would have served a higher purpose? Dante does imply that the defeat at Montaperti destroyed Florence's pride and wrath (Pg. 11.112–14).

[35]Davidsohn, Storia di Firenze, 7.727, says that suicide was a common occurrence in Florence, and not treated as severely there as elsewhere. He suggests that the anonymous suicide in Hell represents the type of the Florentine suicide. Leo Spitzer, "Speech and Language in Inferno XIII," Italica 19 (1942), identifies the anonymous suicide with Florence.

The city is not named directly by the suicide, but is identified by its two patrons, Mars and John the Baptist: "Io fui de la città che nel Batista/mutò il primo padrone" (Hell 13.143–44: "I was from the city which exchanged its first patron for the Baptist"). Both patrons continue to dominate it, Mars through the constant violence, John the Baptist, unfortunately, only through the coin that bears his picture. Indeed, Benvenuto says that when Florence gave up Mars, representing fortitude and power in arms, for the Baptist, meaning the florin, it gave itself over to greed (1.462); he cautions that unless virtue and prudence protect the city from the wrath of God, its own ills will subvert it (1.463). Benvenuto also relates the story of Attila talking his way into Florence with the promise that he would destroy her enemy, Pistoia, but instead destroying Florence; here the city's desire to hurt its enemies is suicidal (1.463–64). The implication is that the Florentines cannot give up Mars completely—the statue of Mars remains in the city—so they are destined to go on fighting, but since they fight only for selfish reasons, they must destroy themselves. The life-denying aspect of suicide is echoed in the next "Florentine sin," sodomy. Not only are all the main figures in this section Florentines (Brunetto Latini and the three civic leaders in canto 16, not to mention the bishop Andrea dei Mozzi), but they speak of the city as "our depraved land" (Hell 16.9: "nostra terra prava"). And Brunetto tells Dante that Florence, that ungrateful people, will make him an enemy because of his good deeds, perversely denying itself its good fruit, like the sinners of this circle, and rendering itself sterile. Ironically, Dante is the "plant" that rises from the dung, in whom the holy seed of the Romans lives again (15.74–75); in other words, what is good in Florence is the Roman heritage, which Dante carries. Brunetto himself may have betrayed the Roman heritage by drafting a letter which Florence sent to Rudolph of Hapsburg asserting its traditional independence.[36]

---

[36]See Richard Kay, *Dante's Swift and Strong* (Lawrence: Regents Press of Kansas, 1978), 21. The other Florentines in the circle recognize Dante from his dress; since, as Villani points out (*Istorie Fiorentine,* 12.4), the Florentines dressed in the most noble costume of any Italians, like the togas of the ancient

The other sins of lower Hell specifically connected with Florence are, in one way or another, commercial sins, reminding us of Florence's major sphere of activity and the source of its political power in the world. First there is usury, the sin on which most of Florence's prosperity is based, the making money from money, however cleverly it might be concealed by a variety of financial arrangements (see chapter six). Dante does not recognize these men by their faces but by the family crests on the pouches that hang from their necks; although those signs would no doubt have sufficed to identify them to Dante's audience, he rubs it in by having a Padovan identify them all as Florentines. Theft, the deceptive taking of another's goods, boasts five Florentines, who evoke one of Dante's most ringing invectives, "Godi, Fiorenza, poi che se' si grande ..." (26.1–3), "Rejoice, Florence, that you are so great you beat your wings over land and sea, and your name resounds throughout Hell" as it does like that of no other city; these lines may echo the inscription on the Palazzo del Popolo cited earlier. Theft elicits one of Dante's most horrifying punishments, the metamorphoses and fusion of the souls and serpents. Like them, Florence continually "renews" itself: "poi Fiorenza rinova gente e modi" (24.144: "then Florence renews its people and customs"), echoed later in Purgatory, "Quante volte ... hai tu [Fiorenza mia] mutato e rinovate membre!" (Pg. 6.145–47: "how many times ... [my Florence] have you changed and renewed your members!"). Florence is a thief on a much grander scale. Florentines figure among the falsifiers as well: Gianni Schicchi, who takes on another's identity to forge a will, and master Adam, who counterfeits Florence's coin, the florin, the most important monetary unit of Europe, both deceiving for gain, doing on a smaller scale what Florence does in national and international politics.[37]

Romans, Dante may intend a contrast between his dignified Roman appearance and their grotesque nudity.

[37] In the other *bolge* of the eighth circle, where the various categories of fraud are placed, Florence shares the honors with a number of other Italian cities, but is rarely left out of the discussion. In the circle of simony, the holes of the sinners are compared to the baptismal fonts in Florence; in hypocrisy,

Lower Hell moves out from the focus on Florence towards other cities of northern Italy that share the same destructive characteristics.[38] Different cities dominate separate sections, all hostile to their neighbors and to one another, suggesting the anarchy of Italy, but Florence is not spared. In the *Malebolge,* the circle of fraud, almost each section has its city: Bologna for pimps, Lucca for flatterers, Rome, by implication, for simoniacs, Mantova for false prophets, Lucca and the island of Sardegna for barrators, Bologna and Florence for hypocrites, Pistoia and Florence for thieves, the Romagna for false counsellors, the Puglia for fomentors of discord, Siena and Florence for falsifiers. In the seventh circle, Siena and Padua are also singled out for wastrels, and Padua and Florence for usury; in the ninth, Pisa and Genoa produce traitors. Padua, founded by Antenor, is also connected with treachery: one Paduan defoliates the Florentine suicide, another identifies the Florentine usurers. By combining Florence with other Italian cities, or different cities with each other as evildoers in the lower sections of Hell, Dante seems to be reflecting the historical fact of Florence's involvement in the politics and wars of most Tuscan, and many other Italian, cities, and the shifting alliances of all those cities as they moved back and forth between Guelph and Ghibelline, White and Black, and even "Green" factions.[39] And Dante frequently alludes to Monta-

Dante meets the two Bolognese friars who were sent to Florence to preserve peace between the factions but instead favored the Guelphs; among the disseminators of scandal and schism is the man who instigated the murder that was said to have begun the Guelph-Ghibelline feud.

[38]Nicolai Rubinstein, "Some Ideas on Municipal Progress and Decline in the Italy of the Communes," in *Fritz Saxl, A Volume of Memorial Essays from his Friends in England,* ed. D. J. Gordon (London: Thomas Nelson, 1957), 165–83, points out that various thirteenth-century chronicles of north Italian cities, like Genoa and Padua, explain the city's crises in terms of its vices, and that various writers treat the growth and decline of cities as a natural phenomenon, among them, Jacopo de Voragine on Genoa, Villani on Florence, and Dante in Paradise 16.

[39]See Villani, *Istorie Fiorentine,* 8.107, for reference to the "parte Verde," and Peters, "Pars, Parte," on various aspects of party in contemporary Florence.

perti, Florence's terrible defeat in 1260, as a constant reminder and threat of overweening pride humbled. In the ninth circle, among the traitors, Dante, as an instrument of divine justice, allows himself to take some revenge for the defeat at Montaperti against a traitor to Florence (32.76 ff.).

Florence not only dominates Hell, it continues in Purgatory and Paradise to be a symbol of the worst kind of corruption and a major obstacle to achieving the ideal society. Although in Purgatory Dante shifts his focus to include the much larger areas of the church and the major states of Europe, he does not give up his attacks on Florence (see 6.127–51, 14.49–51, 23.94 ff., 24.79 ff.). In Paradise, too, though he concentrates on the two institutions provided for mankind's guidance on earth, the church and the empire, attacking corrupt churchmen and offering the empire as the solution for the world's ills, Dante frequently alludes to the corruption of his native city. The first Florentine he sees in Paradise is Piccarda, who failed to keep her vow to God, reminding the audience of the many failures of the city to keep its word; Piccarda was forced to break her vow by her violent brother, Corso Donati, who committed similar outrages against the city. Cacciaguida, Dante's ancestor, is a positive example of a Florentine; he served the city's first patron, Mars, in the proper way, by fighting for God's cause on the second crusade, as well as its second patron, John the Baptist, by becoming a martyr in that cause. But he too lashes out against the corruption of the modern city, providing another, more subtle, contrast between Florence and Rome. He appears in a scene which evokes the meeting of Anchises and Aeneas in *Aeneid* 6, but the prophecy he gives his descendant is not one of future glory. Florence's glory, unlike Rome's, was its past, when it was small and virtuous; its future holds only evil for itself and suffering for its best citizens. The tradition Dante must serve and reestablish is Rome's, the return of the Roman empire to world dominance. Thus, at the center of Paradise, as he does at the end (canto 31), Dante brings together the corruption of Florence and the divine destiny of Rome.

Dante's movement through the corrupt city (Hell/Florence), standing for all that is selfish and destructive in human life, takes him further and further from civilization. As he descends through the city of Hell, Dante moves away from the earthlike castle and meadows of Limbo to the tombs inside the city of Dis, then to a river of blood, a wild forest, a desert, and finally a series of moats encircling not a castle but a lake of ice, with its lord frozen at the center. The movement in the good city, Paradise (the ideal Rome) is just the opposite: from the outer spheres where souls are still seen as individuals, to the higher realms where they submerge themselves in symbolic figures, putting their love, wisdom, self-sacrifice, and justice to the service of the common good, and finally to the rose, which contains all the souls, each retaining his or her individual features, but as a petal helping to form the flower—the perfect unity of the divine city. In such a city, citizens are bound by love and loyalty and a mutual desire for peace and good; this city can be the core of a strong state. Even Florence, in her early, simpler days, was that kind of city (so Cacciaguida claims, perhaps stretching the truth), before she tried to rival Rome. Any city may model itself on the ideal city, as the early Florence did, but none may challenge Rome as the center of imperial authority. However corrupt the earthly Rome becomes—the "cemetery of Peter's army" (Pr. 9.140–41) and the market "where Christ is daily bought and sold" (17.51)—it remains the ideal for Dante.

The final mention of the two cities fixes the contrast once for all; as Dante looks at the city of God in the rose, the heavenly Rome, he thinks of the barbarians seeing the earthly Rome for the first time. If they were amazed at that sight, he says, imagine his "stupor" as he came from the human to the divine, from time to the eternal, and from Florence to the just and sane people:

> Se i barbari . . .
> . . . .
> veggendo Roma e l'ardüa sua opra,

> stupefaciensi, quando Laterano
> a le cose mortali andò di sopra;
> ïo, che al divino da l'umano,
> a l'etterno dal tempo era venuto,
> e di Fiorenza in popol giusto e sano,
> di che stupor dovea esser compiuto!
>
> (Pr. 31.31–40)

This is the journey Dante wants his audience to make, from Florence, the city of evil, to the eternal Rome, the city of good, the seat of church and empire. Like Rome, Paradise is at once the circumference of the universe and its center, the city where the emperor, God, rules directly, as Virgil described it in the first canto of the Comedy: "In tutte parti impera e quivi regge;/quivi è la sua città e l'alto seggio" (1.127–28). Paradise as both the center—outside of time and space, where the blessed dwell eternally with God—and the whole of the physical universe, is the Rome of which Christ is a Roman. The souls in the rose (*nostra città,* 30.130) are eternal citizens of that Rome. Rome is the only earthly city that can reflect the heavenly model because it is both *urbs* and *orbis,* both city and world.[40] To be at once the smallest and the largest political unit is a paradox which should exist only in heaven and yet it was achieved by Rome on earth.

[40]See Ovid, *Fasti,* 2.684: "Romanae spatium est urbis et orbis idem." Cf. Antonio Russi, "Canto xxxii," *Lectura Dantis Scaligera, Paradiso,* 1,175–176: "non abbiamo qui l'immagine di una Gerusalemme celeste; ma piuttosto di una Roma celeste . . . in armonia non solo con la teoria politica di Dante, esposta nel *De Monarchia,* per cui alla Roma imperiale come 'città terrena' corrisponde la Rome celeste come 'città di Dio'; ma si accorda anche con altri luoghi della *Commedia.* . . ." "we do not have the image of a celestial Jerusalem here, but rather of a celestial Rome . . . in harmony not only with Dante's political theory, expounded in the *Monarchy,* by which the heavenly Rome as 'city of God' corresponds to imperial Rome as 'earthly city;' but it also accords with other passages in the *Comedy.* . . ."

TWO

Church and State in the *Comedy*

THE PROPER FUNCTIONING of the empire on earth depends not only on its relations with individual cities and kingdoms, but also on its relations with the papacy. The jurisdictional dispute between secular and ecclesiastical authority, the third and certainly the most controversial question Dante takes up in the *Monarchy,* also permeates the *Comedy.* He deals with it directly in Marco Lombardo's discourse on the two suns (Pg. 16) and in the various attacks on the Donation of Constantine, and indirectly in his own frequent and clear denial of any but a spiritual and didactic function to the church and in his unrelenting criticism of the greed, corruption, and abuse of their position by individual popes and churchmen. In the *Monarchy,* Dante deals with the questions theoretically; in the *Comedy,* he confronts them more practically. The emperor is the only figure who can keep peace on earth because only he is not vulnerable to greed (*Monarchy,* 1.11); greed for money and power is the dominant characteristic of the churchmen in the *Comedy.* Christ told his disciples his kingdom was not of this world, that they were not to possess gold and silver (cited in *Monarchy,* 3.10.14), but churchmen in the *Comedy* pursue little else. The nature of the church is its form, and its form is the life of Christ, sacrifice, teaching, good example (*Monarchy,* 3.15), a life which in the *Comedy* is eschewed by all but the early popes and martyrs and a handful of later reforming saints, all men who avoided worldly power and possession. The *Monarchy* ends with the statement of man's two goals, befitting his two natures: the earthly paradise, to which he is led by the emperor through reason, philosophy, and morality, and the heavenly paradise, to which he is guided by the church through faith and spiritual teaching. In the *Comedy,* Dante is led to the Earthly Paradise by Virgil, the poet of empire, who glorifies the empire's meaning and history, and to heaven by Beatrice, the figure of theology, the faith on which the church is based. Both Dante's guides are surrogates for the malfunctioning organs of empire and church which they represent, and which Dante comes to represent when he is crowned in the Earthly Paradise.

The major moral obstacle to achieving the perfect state is greed for wealth and power; the major political obstacle is the papacy. The church interfered in local and international politics and asserted its right to do so on the basis of Scripture and canon law. Papal jursidiction in temporal affairs was opposed by both monarchists and imperialists, but the former dominated the debates in the thirteenth century. The most interesting material and the largest volume in the church–state controversy during this period was produced by the struggle between Pope Boniface VIII and the French king Philip IV. Giles of Rome wrote on both sides of the issue in different periods; John of Paris, James of Viterbo, a series of clever but anonymous pamphleteers, and a virtual army of skilled and learned canonists took part in it (see introduction). The basic arguments for and against papal supremacy are similar; monarchists differ from imperialists mainly in their assertion of the independence or autonomy of individual states. When Dante draws on the monarchist arguments, he turns them to the support of the empire; in the *Comedy,* he condemns the French royal house almost as severely as he does the papacy because it offers the most powerful secular opposition to the empire outside Italy.

Boniface, who brought the conflict to a head, is an important figure in Dante's Hell, although he does not appear as a character in it. Dante had personal as well as philosophical reasons to condemn him, which he does by assigning him a place in Hell, although he is not yet dead in 1300 when the journey is supposed to be taking place. Boniface's role in Italian, particularly Florentine, politics and in Dante's own exile, along with his extreme position on papal supremacy, would be enough to explain Dante's animosity towards him.[1] But Boniface inspired the same kind of fierce hostility in much larger circles during his lifetime and for many years after his death, well into the period when Dante was writing the *Comedy* and long after the French king had effectively gained control of the papacy by the election of French popes and the transfer of the curia to Avignon. It is not surprising that Boniface is a powerful presence in the poem and seems to personify the corruption of the papacy for Dante even though he died years before Dante wrote most of it.

A brief survey of Boniface's actions and the stories that circulated about him should explain Dante's presentation of him. The troubles between Philip and Boniface began with jurisdictional clashes of various kinds: Philip imposed taxes on the clergy without first getting papal permission, and the pope, in response, forbad payment (*Clericos laicos,* 1296); the king then stopped all passage of money out of the country, a blow to papal finances.[2] Boniface created a new bishopric separating Palmiers from Toulouse, and the bishop he appointed to it proclaimed that he was subject only to the pope, in temporal as well as spiritual matters, not in any way to the king, whom he went out of his way to insult; eventually the king had him arrested (Dupuy, *Histoire du Differend,* 197–98, Digard, *Philippe le Bel* vol. 2, 51 ff.). Boniface produced a series of bulls,

[1]On Boniface and Florence, see Guido Levi, "Bonifazio VIII e le sue relazioni col Comune di Firenze," *Archivio della Società Romana di Storia Patria 5* (1882), 365–474; George Holmes, "Dante and the Popes," in *The World of Dante,* ed. Cecil Grayson (Oxford: Clarendon, 1980), 18–43; and T. S. R. Boase, *Boniface VIII* (London: Constable, 1933). Levi points out that Boniface worked for the triumph of the Guelph party in Italy and that his actions were not always taken to advance pontifical politics but often out of personal antipathy and preference.

[2]For detailed accounts of the conflict see Pierre Dupuy, *Histoire du Differend d'entre le pape Boniface VIII et Philippes le bel Roy de France* (Paris: Cramoisy, 1655; reprint, Tucson: Audax, 1963); also Jean Rivière, *Le problème de l'Eglise et de l'Etat au temps de Philippe le Bel* (Louvain: Spicilegium Sacrum Lovaniense, 1926) and Georges Digard, *Philippe le Bel et le Saint-Siège de 1285 à 1304* (Paris: Sirey, 1936), 2 vols.

some asserting his claims, some retracting them, and the situation was complicated by false bulls and letters circulated in his name, which made more extreme claims and elicited strong responses from the king's party.[3] It did not help that the king's party included disaffected Italian cardinals of the Colonna family, old enemies of Boniface whom he had removed from their posts. Perhaps the best known of Boniface's authentic statements is the bull *Unam Sanctam,* 1302, claiming a divine hierarchy in which spiritual power excels any earthly power in dignity and nobility and establishing the earthly power; the spiritual power can judge the earthly, whereas only God can

[3]Perhaps the most striking forgery is the brief letter cited by Dupuy, *Histoire du Differend,* 44: "Bonifacius Episcopus servus servorum Dei, Philippo Francorum Regi. Deum time, et mandata eius observa. Scire te volumus, quod in spiritualibus et temporalibus nobis subes. Beneficiorum et praebendarum ad te collatio nulla spectat: et si aliquorum vacantium custodiam habeas, fructus eorum successoribus reserves: et si quae contulisti, collationem huiusmodi irritam decernimus; et quantum de facto processerit, revocamus. Aliud autem credentes, haereticos reputamus." Dat. Laterani Non. Decembr. Pontificatus nostri anno 7. "Boniface, Bishop, servant of the servants of God, to Philip, King of the French. Fear God, and observe his commands. We want you to know that in spiritual and temporal matters you are subject to us. The collection of benefices and prebends is not your affair: and if you have the care of other vacancies, you must reserve their fruits for their successors: and if you have collected any, we declare that collection invalid, and whatever proceded from that, we revoke. Those who believe anything else, we consider heretics." The Lateran, the ninth of December, in the seventh year of our Pontificate. The answer was even stronger: "Philippus Dei gratia Francorum Rex, Bonifacio se gerenti pro summo Pontifice, salutem modicam, seu nullam. Sciat tua maxima fatuitas in temporalibus nos alicui non subesse. Ecclesiarum ac praebendarum vacantium collationem ad nos iure regio pertinere, fructus earum nostros facere: collationes a nobis factas, et faciendas fore validas in praeteritum et futurum, et earum possessores contra omnes viriliter nos tueri: secus autem credentes, fatuos et dementes reputamus." Datum Parisius, etc. "Philip, by the grace of God, King of the French, sending Boniface, for his high Pontificate, little or no greeting [as though God had designated Philip, but not Boniface]. May your great foolishness know that in temporal affairs we are subject to no one, that the collection of vacant churches and prebends is ours by royal right, to make their fruits ours; the collections made by us and to be made are valid in the past and future, and we will protect their possessors firmly against all: those believing otherwise, we consider foolish and demented." Paris, etc.

judge the spiritual. Anyone who does not accept the pope's position is a heretic, and it is essential to the salvation of any human creature to be subject to the Roman Pontiff.[4]

Boniface tried to excommunicate Philip at different times. On one occasion, 1301, when no one would publish the decree, the pope complained to a French official: "Nos habemus utramque potestatem" ("We have both powers," spiritual and temporal); the Frenchman replied "Utique Domine, sed vestra est verbalis, nostra autem realis" ("That may well be, my Lord, but yours is verbal, ours is real," Dupuy, *Histoire du Differend,* 193, Rivière, *Le Problème,* 121). Boniface tried again, in 1303, to excommunicate Philip and place his subjects under anathema unless they renounced their oaths to the king; but before he could publish the bull, Philip had him captured in a rather blatant display of real power. Boniface's position as pope was complicated by the fact that questions had been raised about his legitimacy because he had ascended while the previous pope, Celestine V, was alive. If the pope was the bridegroom of the church, there could be no other husband while he lived, divorce being frowned upon even in regard to an institution. The objection, as stated in the records of the hearings held on Boniface after his death, was:

... sicut vir non debet adulterare uxorem suam, ita nec Episcopus Ecclesiam suam, id est, ut illam dimittat ad quam consecratus est; et sicut uxori non licet dimittere virum suum, ita ut alteri se vivente eo, matrimonio societ, aut eum adulteret, licet fornicator sit vir eius; ... absit enim quod Romano Pontifice vivente alter possit eligi: Iam enim Ecclesia non esset una unius, sed una plurium; ... non esset formosa et electa, sed deformis et mon-

---

[4]The text can be found in *Corpus iuris canonici* (Extravagantes Communes, 1.8) ed. E. Friedberg, vol. 2, 1,245; the translation in S. Z. Ehler and J. B. Morrall, *Church and State through the Centuries* (New York: Biblo and Tannen, 1967), 90–92. For a study of the background of the bull, see James Muldoon, "Boniface VIII's Forty Years of Experience in the Law," *The Jurist* 31 (1971), 449–77.

struosa, dum in uno corpore Ecclesiae duo capita forent, quod esset omnino monstruosum, ridiculosum et absurdum.

... just as a man should not defile his wife, so the bishop should not defile his church, that is, put away her to whom he was consecrated; and as it is not permitted to a wife to put away her husband, so that she might join in matrimony with another while he is still living, even if her husband is a fornicator, ... it is not fitting that while the Roman pontiff is alive, another be chosen: for then the church would not be one of one but one of many; ... it would not be beautiful and elect, but deformed and monstrous, while there were two heads in the one body of the church, which would be in every way monstrous, ridiculous and absurd. (Dupuy, *Histoire du Differend*, 449)

There are a number of interesting points in this passage besides the marriage imagery: (1) the husband as fornicator, compare the Ottimo's commentary on Purgatory 32, calling Boniface the lover (*drudo*) of the curia, not her legitimate spouse 2.576–77;[5] (2) the two-headed monster, an image the church often used to support its own claims to supreme power in Christendom, which Dante turns around in the *Comedy* (see below); and (3) the separation of a bishop from his diocese, a touchy point, since Boniface was himself criticized for abusing the practice.[6] It did not help matters that Boniface was popularly believed to have tricked Celestine into renouncing the papacy and retiring to a monastery. A contemporary Italian chronicle claims that Boniface had a tube inserted in the wall of the former pope's bedroom, which he spoke through for three nights, pretending to be the angel of God and telling Celestine to

---

[5]*L'Ottimo Commento della Divina Commedia, testo inedito d'un contemporaneo di Dante*, ed. Alessandro Torri, 3 vols. (Pisa: Capurro, 1827).

[6]Innocent III had made the action legal, but it was not altogether accepted. Richard Kay, *Dante's Swift and Strong*, (Lawrence: Regents Press of Kansas, 1978) 114–17, says that Boniface transferred more bishops than any pope before him.

renounce his position.[7] When he did, Boniface had him imprisoned in a monastery in case he should change his mind—or get a different message—until he died. Thus, Boniface's papacy was tainted from the beginning. When Boniface died, chronicles report, he fulfilled the prophecy that he came to power like a fox, he would rule like a lion, but die like a dog.[8]

While he reigned, Boniface was accused of almost every imaginable vice; the attacks range from plays on his name to criminal allegations. Guillaume de Nogaret, one of Philip's advisers who was to play an important role throughout the conflict, publicly called Boniface a master of lies even in his name: "faciens se, cum sit omnifarie maleficus, Bonifacium nominari et sic nomen falsum sibi assumpsit," "though a malefactor in every way, he took on a false name and had himself called Boniface."[9] An official act, made in the presence of king and court by several nobles, accused Boniface of various heresies and blasphemies, of fornication, simony, idolatry, demon-worship, war-mongering, sodomy, assassination, violation of the confessional, political intrigue, embezzlement of crusade funds, and of saying he would rather be a dog or an

---

[7]*Cronica Fiorentina* for the year 1294, cited by Singleton in his commentary on Hell, 50.

[8]"Ascendisti ut vulpes, regnabis ut leo, morieris ut canis," according to Thomas of Walsingham's *History,* cited by Dupuy, *Histoire du Differend,* 196; the same thought is expressed in the past tense as a comment in French chronicles also cited by Dupuy, ibid., 199–201, the latter in French. Dino Compagni, *Cronica,* ed. Gino Luzzato (Turin: Einaudi, 1968), 2.35, reports Boniface's death more soberly, but nonetheless damningly: "Many rejoiced over his death, because he ruled cruelly, and fomented wars, undoing many people and amassing a good deal of treasure: and the Whites and Ghibellines were particularly happy because he was their heartfelt enemy; but the Blacks were very sad."

[9]Dupuy, *Histoire du Differend,* 56. Cf. Dante's play on Boniface's name in Hell 19, rhyming Bonifazio with *sazio* both sounds echoing the hissing of flames, as though the name suited the chosen destiny in Hell, and emphasizing the fact that Boniface never was "sated." Guillaume de Nogaret also called Boniface a thief, "fur et latro," which may be a play on papalist comments on kings of the Gentiles who possessed by invasion and usurpation, that they were "fures et latrones" (cf. Giles of Rome, *De ecclesiastica potestate,* ed. Richard Scholz [Weimar: Böhlaus, 1929; reprint, Scientia Aalen, 1961], 1.5)

ass than a Frenchman. The point of the last accusation was to show that he did not believe the French had souls, though it sounds more like the outburst of a strong temper. The same accusations were made for years after his death. Philip threatened to have him tried for heresy as a means both of controlling subsequent popes and of blackmailing them to dissolve the Templars, and Philip compelled the church to hear witnesses and take depositions against Boniface for eight years after his death. It is a curious irony, and one that must have appealed to Dante, that Boniface is a presence throughout the *Comedy,* although he cannot actually appear in it because, according to the fiction, he is still alive, just as he was a constant presence in the hearings against him, though he could not appear at them because he was already dead.

Boniface was posthumously accused of the same variety of sins: of fornication and sodomy with specific partners (Dupuy, *Histoire du Differend,* 527, 539–41), of political intrigues, particularly against the Ghibellines. When told that the church in which a group of Ghibellines was taking refuge had not been destroyed because it contained the bones of saints who would be angry when the resurrection came, the pope said: "You're trying to do penance before you sin—destroy the church and don't worry about them, they'll no more rise from the dead than my horse that died yesterday" (Dupuy, 543). This story must remind readers of the *Comedy* of Hell 27: after Boniface tricks Guido into sinning by promising absolution, a devil comes for Guido's soul and points out that one cannot be absolved who does not repent, and one cannot repent and will at the same time (27.118–19). The situation is reversed here, but the words are similar and both incidents reveal the abuse of religious belief to lead others into sin for political advantage. The most persistent accusations against Boniface are those of blasphemy and heretical beliefs: that he denied the resurrection; that he disparaged the Eucharist as "no more Christ's body than I am," "it's only dough" ("immo pasta est"), and Christ's mother, "no more a virgin than my mother was" (Dupuy, 538).

Whether there is any truth to these charges, they indicate the scope and persistence of the tradition of Boniface as an archvillain. The same view is to be found in early commentaries on the *Comedy:* Pietro, Dante's son, calls Boniface "princeps clericorum hypocritarum," "the prince of hypocritical clerics" (240); Guido describes him as "perversa conscientia depravatus et arroganti superbia elevatus," "depraved by a perverted conscience and exalted by arrogant pride" (559). The Ottimo misses no opportunity to pass on rumors about him: on Hell 3, he remarks that Boniface deceived Celestine with tricks; on canto 19, that he got his position by simony, that he sold church positions or bestowed them on unworthy relatives, and that he corrupted cardinals with money, gifts, or promises; on 27, speaking of the war between Boniface and the Colonnesi, the Ottimo tells a gratuitous story about Boniface's nephew, sick for love of a woman. Boniface invited the woman to a banquet, had her seated before a door so that during the dinner she could be pulled into another room, where his nephew was waiting to rape her (1.468). On Purgatory 16, discussing the separation of powers, the Ottimo says that Boniface crowned himself and girded on the sword, and made himself emperor, "e fecesi egli stesso imperador" (2.291); on canto 20, he mentions that Boniface excommunicated Philip over the see of Palmiers; on 32, in connection with the corrupt curia, he notes that Dante had had experience of it in the time of Boniface when he went there as ambassador for his commune, and that he calls Boniface the lover, not the legitimate husband, of the church (2.577). On Paradise 9, he explains that the prophecy that Rome will soon "be freed of the adultery" refers to Boniface, who came to the pontificate by simony and deception; on 17, he describes Boniface's intrigues with Corso Donati, and finally, on canto 27, we are told that Peter's indignation at his place being usurped refers again to Boniface, elected by simony and deception. It is clear from the Ottimo's frequent remarks, as well as from the French records, that Dante's view of Boniface as *the* corrupt pope is a popular contemporary view.

The papacy, even after Boniface, was at a low point while Dante was writing the *Comedy*. Popes had allowed themselves to be removed, with the curia, from the traditional seat of the church at Rome to Avignon, where the French monarchy could exert a powerful influence. Clement V undermined the empire by withdrawing his support from Henry VII and refusing to crown him at St. Peter's, at Philip's insistence; he further undermined it after Henry's death by claiming that the emperor swore fealty to the papacy (*Romani Principes*) and that the pope could assume power in the empire when it was vacant (*Pastoralis cura*). But he also contributed to the decline of the papacy by giving in on the Templars and exempting the French monarchy from *Unam Sanctam* (in *Meruit*).[10] Popes had made extravagant claims and practiced continual intrigues. They were perceived by their enemies as greedy, petty men, leading the church in the wrong direction and giving a bad example to the Christians they were supposed to guide, and that is how Dante portrays them in the *Comedy*, where their corruption is condemned from the beginning of Hell to the summit of Paradise. A pope is included among the first souls Dante sees in Hell, because he rejected the task God set for him, but probably also because his abdication left the way open for Boniface.[11] In the circle of gluttony, a reference

[10]Henry had also turned *Unam Sanctam* to his own purposes, changing the end to claim that "every human spirit must be subject to the Roman prince." See William M. Bowsky, *Henry VII in Italy* (Lincon: University of Nebraska, 1960), 181.

[11]Four of the five early commentators identify the "one who out of cowardice made the great refusal," "colui che fece per viltade il gran rifiuto," Hell 3.60, as Pope Celestine V. Properly so, Pietro Alighieri says, because Celestine forgot Gregory and Sylvester, who had been able to be holy and spiritual even in the papacy (69). Guido da Pisa says Celestine renounced the papacy because he did not know how to pilot the ship of the church (59). Jacopo della Lana reports the story of the deception to explain how Celestine could be persuaded to leave thinking it was God's will, when he was having such difficulty dealing with the corruption he found (*Comedia di Dante degli Allagherii col commento di Jacopo della Lana*, ed. Luciano Scarabelli, 3 vols. [Bologna: Tipografia Rebia, 1866], 131–32. The Ottimo implies that Celestine's renunciation left the way open for Boniface, noting the report that his successor, Boniface,

is made to the political intrigues of the pope (Boniface) in Florence, when he pretended to favor peace but really encouraged one party against the other. In greed, all the condemned souls Dante notices are clerics, among them popes and cardinals, their greed set in direct opposition to God's will as manifest by Fortune, who disposes wealth and power according to a divine plan. The canto begins with the guardian monster shouting "Pape Satan, pape Satan," probably suggesting "Pope Satan."[12] Among the heretics, there is a cardinal and a pope, Anastasius, who either was led into heresy by his deacon, or led him; the Italian is purposely ambiguous: "lo qual trasse Fotin de la via dritta") Hell 11.9: "whom Photinus drew away from the right road" or "who drew Photinus from the right way") and either meaning is shocking, since it is the pope's responsibility to protect the faithful from heresy. In any case, the pope presents a striking contrast to Virgil, who delivers a lecture on the categories of sin to Dante later in the same canto. The poet, as so often in the *Comedy*, provides the guidance the church fails to give.

Among the sodomites (homosexuals) in Hell, there are several clerics and a bishop who was "transferred" by the pope (Boniface):

... dal servo dei servi
fù trasmutato d'Arno in Bacchiglione
dove lasciò li mal protesi nervi

... by the servant of servants

---

tricked him with the consent of the cardinals, because he was more fit for the solitary life than the papacy, from which the church and the world are in great danger (30). Only Benvenuto da Imola rejects the identification, although he admits that most people accept it and think of the reunuciation as cowardice, but he considers it an act of magnanimity; like the Ottimo, he lays great stress on the corruption of the churchmen around Celestine (117–18).

[12]Guido da Pisa suggests that since Pluto "in suo episcupatu" cannot stop Dante, he turns to a higher authority, as our bishops turn to the pope, 137. Marsilius, in a different context, identifies his pope with Satan, *Defensor Pacis* (2.26.19). On a possible connection of "Pape" with Boniface's coins, see below, chapter six, fn. 37.

he was transferred from Arno to Bacchiglione
where he left his badly stretched nerves.

(15.112–14)

The word *trasmutato* combined with *mal protesi nervi* suggests that the pope seduced him; Boniface was often accused of the sin (cf. Jacopo, 1.286). The circle of simony, graft within the church, is, of course, dominated by popes, who commit adultery with the "bride of Christ," who prostitute her for their own greed; Boniface is awaited in this section. The hypocrites are clothed in heavy lead cloaks in the style of the monks of Cluny, a *faticoso manto* meant to remind us of the papacy, since *manto* is associated with the papacy through the *Comedy*.[13] Finally, the fraudulent counsellor, Guido da Montefeltro, tells Dante that it was a pope who tricked him into committing his sin one last time and, worse yet, into thinking he had been absolved of the sin before he committed it, so that he died technically unrepentant. Thus the pope, Boniface again, not only leads him into sin, but directly into damnation. Boniface, and with him the papacy, emerges from the *Inferno* as a malevolent spirit, inducing others into all kinds of sins and creating disorder all around.

Even in Purgatory we are reminded of Boniface, though less critically: in connection with the indulgences offered to souls

[13]See Hell 2.27; *papale ammanto* is a figurative reference to Peter's position; he did not want to assume a royal mantle as later popes would. In Hell, 19.69, the simoniac, Nicholas, tells Dante he was "clothed in the great mantle"; in Purgatory, 19.104–05, Hadrian learns how the mantle weighs on one who would keep it out of the mud (perhaps an echo of Marco Lombardo's remark about the church of Rome falling in the mud and soiling itself and its burden because it combines the two governments in itself, Pg. 16.129); in *Paradise,* 21, 133–34, modern pastors, who cover their palfreys with their cloaks are contrasted to Peter and Paul. Historically, when the elected pope accepted the office a scarlet cloak was thrown over him by the archdeacon of the Roman church (Walter Ullman, *A Short History of the Papacy in the Middle Ages* [London: Methuen, 1972], 230). The symbolism of the mantle no doubt underlies a remark reported to the French assembly by Guillaume de Plaisians after a public attack on Boniface, purportedly by King Philip, that he would have preferred to cover his "father" (Boniface) with his own cloak to save the honor of the church (Dupuy, *Histoire du Differend,* 107, Rivière, *Le Problème,* 113).

during the Jubilee he proclaimed (Pg. 2.98–99) and in the midst of a catalogue of the sins of the French king, who "captured Christ in his vicar" (20.86–90).[14] It is, of course, ironic that the only way Boniface imitated Christ was in suffering an attack he had brought on himself. It is also worth noting that the only one in the *Comedy* to call the pope the vicar of Christ is an ancestor of the French king, the other serious obstacle to the empire. But near the end of Paradise, Dante brings us back to the infernal view of Boniface and sets him forever in his place: Beatrice, pointing out the seat reserved for the emperor Henry in the heavenly rose, tells Dante that Henry will be opposed by a pope (Clement V) who will be thrust into the circle of simony, pushing "quel d'Alagna" (Boniface) further down into the hole (30.148); since this is the last line of the canto, it is particularly emphatic.[15]

[14]When Boniface was captured by Philip's men and there seemed no way to escape, the pope, feeling himself betrayed like Christ, according to Giovanni Villani *Istorie Fiorentine* [Milan: Società Tipografica, 1802], 8.63, determined at least to die like a pope: wrapping himself in the mantle of Saint Peter, with the crown of Constantine on his head, and the keys and cross in his hand, he sat on the papal throne. It is perhaps not surprising that the Italian Villani grants him some dignity at the end, while the French reports emphasize his rage, claiming that he died of a "flux de ventre," "une frenesie" (Dupuy, *Histoire du Differend*, 191, 199).

[15]Though Boniface is the focus of attention, there are various other churchmen in Hell who took part in political intrigues: Nicholas against Charles of Anjou, which culminated in the Sicilian Vespers, alluded to in 19.98–99; Frate Gomita, a Sardinian friar who sold public offices and took bribes, 22.81 ff.; two Frati Gaudenti among the hypocrites, who served together as *podestà* in Florence ostensibly to keep the peace, but in fact to allow the pope to maneuver in favor of the Guelphs and expel the Ghibellines, 23.103 ff. Like Guido da Montefeltro, these friars allow themselves to be used by a pope, and Dante holds them reponsible for their actions. In the lowest circle of Hell, Dante sees Tesauro dei Beccheria (32.119–23), an abbot and papal legate, executed by Florence in 1258 on a charge of conspiring with the Ghibellines, and Archbishop Ruggieri, canto 33, leader of the Pisan Ghibellines, who intrigued with secular leaders encouraging them against each other then turning the people against all of them in order to gain full control, even betraying the members of his own party. Ruggieri is the nephew of Cardinal Ottaviano, the heretic who boasted of losing his soul for his party, canto 10; Ruggieri's father, on the other

Along with the condemnation of individuals, there are possible allegorical allusions to the church in Hell: one is the Veglio di Creta, the statue drawn from Daniel, which the Ottimo glosses as representing the ages of the world, with the leg of clay representing the current age of the church all intent on worldly delights, and the foot of clay the seventh age, those completely given over to greed; he also mentions the great worldly possessions of the church beginning with the gift of Constantine, which he considers the source of temporal cupidity in the church (1.275–76).[16] Pier della Vigna may also stand for the corrupt papacy, but this will be discussed later in this chapter; Ulysses as pilot taking his boat on a disastrous journey has been connected with the corrupt church.[17] Since the church in Purgatory is represented by angels, the devils in Hell may well represent corrupt churchmen; in canto 18 they direct the traffic of Hell, as the church did Rome's during the Jubilee, and in canto 34, the last view of Lucifer's legs, upside down, recalls the popes' feet in the circle of simony. That the living body of a friar, Frate Alberigo, is inhabited by a demon because his soul is already in Hell, reinforces this interpretation. If these analogies are correct, the devils, the "black angels" (23.131), in the circle of barratry represent the clergy who manipulate politicians and throw them into the pitch; indeed, the scene between Dante and Virgil and the devil Malacoda reminds Benvenuto of his own experience at the papal court of Urban at Avignon (2.118).

---

hand, the layman Ubaldino della Pila, is in Purgatory, canto 24. Also in the bottom of Hell is Frate Alberigo, another of the Frati Gaudenti, who had two of his relatives killed in revenge for an unsuccessful attempt to wrest political power from him (33.118 ff.). Even in Paradise, there is a striking allusion to a Guelph bishop of Feltro who betrayed, out of party loyalty, the Ghibellines who had taken refuge with him, and thus caused their deaths (Pr. 9.52–60). In each case, the churchman's involvement in secular politics is so strong that he chooses to damn himself for political necessity.

[16]Cf. Jacopo, 1.272–73. Marsilius interprets the statue in Daniel's dream as the pope and the papal curia (*Defensor Pacis*, 2.24.17).

[17]See J. A. Scott, "Imagery in *Paradiso XXVII*," *Italian Studies* 25 (1970), 27–28. Ulysses will also be discussed in chapters three and six.

In Purgatory, Dante allows the church a positive function through the recognition of the sacraments and religious ritual, but he carefully divests it of human features which might suggest actual churchmen. The whole rock of Purgatory may well represent the church, which Christ founded on "the rock," Peter (Matt. 16:18).[18] Dante is baptized before he begins to climb it, and makes two confessions as he passes through it; the whole realm is filled with hymns, with biblical examples, didactic sculpture, even sermons, and it ends with the procession of the books of the Bible and the drama of church history. The permanent residents of Purgatory, however, are not churchmen but angels; they carry the symbols associated with the papacy, Peter's keys and the swords, but they are pure spirit. There can be no question of their being lured into the temporal realm. Pietro Alighieri clearly identifies the angel at the gate of Purgatory as a "figure" of a priest (361), as does Benvenuto (3.263), and Statius, within the poem, calls him "il vicario di Pietro" (Pg. 21.5); Jacopo della Lana says the keys represent the power to loose and bind, which is held by ministers of the church in the world. Apart from the angels, there is only Cato at the bottom and Matelda at the top, a pagan hero (who committed suicide) and a woman, neither one a traditional churchman, though Matelda served the church's cause. To some extent, the papacy is vindicated in Purgatory by Dante's acknowledgment of its power to grant indulgences and to excommunicate, but the latter is qualified by the fact that the effect of excommunication can be modified by the prayers of individuals; that is, the love of laymen outweighs the anger of popes in God's justice. It does not increase our sense of papal dignity to learn from one of the souls (Manfred) that a pope had his body disinterred and left to the mercy of the elements because he had died excommunicate; we are reminded of this gratuitous violence to a lifeless body when

[18]In Hell, the rock of the *Malebolge* is partially inhabited by popes who perverted the church on earth by abusing its functions and are now upside down in baptismal fonts, representing the sacraments they misused. See J. A. Scott, "The Rock of Peter and *Inferno* XIX," *Romance Philology* 23 (1970), 464.

another soul (Bonconte da Montefeltro) tells how his unburied body was attacked by a frustrated devil who was denied possession of the soul. It would be hard to avoid the analogy between the frustrated churchman and the frustrated devil. If the angels represent what the church should be, devils in Hell represent what it has become; like Lucifer, they start higher and therefore fall lower than other creatures.

We are also told several times in Purgatory of popes interfering in political affairs: in canto 6, it is because of them that there is no emperor to enforce the laws; in 16, by taking on temporal authority, "confounding two governments in itself," the church soils itself and its burden and deprives the world of the two organs ordained by God to guide it, the empire, which cannot function, and the church, which malfunctions. "Now I understand," Dante says, all innocence, "why the sons of Levi [the priesthood] were excluded from inheritance" (Pg. 16.131–32). The one pope Dante meets in Purgatory, Hadrian V, in canto 19, is an example of greed corrected, but only when he achieves the height of earthly wealth, the papacy, and learns how little it means.[19] Then he turns to spiritual matters, an ironic instance of the papacy teaching virtue to the pope. In any case, he was pope for only thirty-eight days, enough to save himself, but not to do much for others. Mention is made of one very early pope, Gregory I, whose prayers helped to save the soul of the emperor Trajan, a rare example of the proper relation of church and state (cf. Sylvester, who cured and converted Constantine, and Agapetus, who saved Justinian from heresy), but the featured story of conversion in Purgatory is that of Statius, who was rescued from sin and pagan beliefs by the words of the pagan poet Virgil (see chapter four).

At the end of Purgatory, in the Earthly Paradise, Dante presents a brief reenactment of the major stages in the history of the church (represented by the chariot), particularly in its relations with secular government. Although the focus in the

---

[19]Martin IV is pointed out among the gluttons, but does not come forward or speak.

91

drama is on the church's struggle to survive various attacks from religious and secular forces, the message is that the church is corrupted by secular power and wealth, and must be saved ultimately by the empire. The chariot which represents the church is described as more splendid than any which pleased Scipio or Augustus at Rome (29.115–16), or than the sun's, which was destroyed to save the earth (29.117–18). This moves Benvenuto to remark that Dante exalts the chariot by naming two glorious leaders, one who wondrously rescued the public state from danger, the other who felicitously ordered it (4.197–98). The sun's chariot refers to Phaethon's disastrous journey, with the implicit suggestion that the church could be destroyed if its lack of control threatened the safety of the world. In Dante's letter to the cardinals, he berates them, reminding them of God's wrath:

> Vos equidem, ecclesiae militantis veluti primi praepositi pili, per manifestam orbitam Crucifixi currum Sponsae regere negligentes, non aliter quam falsus auriga Phaëton exorbitastis . . .

> But you, who are like the commanders of the first rank of the church militant, neglecting to guide the chariot of the Spouse of the Crucified along the open track, have gone astray no differently than the false charioteer Phaethon . . .

> (Ep. 8.4)

When the chariot is fixed to the tree of divine justice, in which the eagle of empire lives, the tree is renewed, because the church gives new life to divine justice, whose living exponent is the Roman empire. However, when Christ first established the church, the empire was pagan, so the eagle attacks the chariot; later, when the empire becomes Christian, the eagle bestows its feathers on the chariot (the Donation of Constantine), and later still, the chariot is covered with more feathers (new gifts of temporal possession and power from major secular leaders) and becomes a monster with seven heads and ten horns, like the beast of the Apocalypse. The church that was meant to be the spiritual vessel for God's grace is given life artificially and becomes a dangerous beast. The heads and horns represent the distortion of the Ten Commandments and the seven gifts of the Holy Spirit (or the seven virtues), the bases for moral life on earth.[20] Once the chariot has become a monster, a whore takes her place on it (the papal curia, which prostitutes the gifts of the church) and dallies with a giant (the king of France, Philip IV), who abuses her when she looks at Dante (the good Christian or the Italian people), and drags her off along with the monster (the removal of the papal court to Avignon). The church that first appeared drawn by Christ and bearing theology (the griffin and Beatrice) has become a monster carrying the corrupt curia and dominated by the king of France.

There is general agreement among the early commentators on most of the imagery in this drama, with minor exceptions: Jacopo identifies the whore with the pope and the giant with the kings of France who raped and adulterated the church and whored with popes (2.388); the Ottimo interprets the giant as Boniface, who was the illicit lover, not the legal husband, of the church (2.577);[21] to Jacopo, Dante represents the Christian people (loc. cit.), to Benvenuto, the Italian people (4.265). Pietro interprets the dragon that rends the chariot, usually identified as a schism, as Anti-Christ, who inflames the cupidity of the pastors of the church for temporal things (528); the Ottimo identifies it with the beast of the Apocalypse (2.574), while Jacopo and Benvenuto connect it with Mohammed. But the major lesson of the drama, the danger to the church when it takes on temporal power or possession or gives itself over to secular domination by the wrong leader, is the same for all of

[20]In Paradise 12.106–08, the two wheels of the church's chariot are identified with Francis and Dominic, suggesting that the contemporary church must be based on the reform orders rather than on the ecclesiastical hierarchy.

[21]Richard Kay, "Dante's Razor and Gratian's D.xv," Dante Studies 99 (1979), 65–96, also suggests that the giant is the pope, but that the whore is the heresy of plenitudo potestatis.

them: when the church works with the empire, it serves the divine purpose; when it invades the temporal sphere, it becomes its victim and loses the ability to perform its divine function.

The attacks on the church for failing to do what it should and for getting into areas it has no business in, continue through Paradise, for the most part put in the mouths of saints whose purity and, presumably, judgment are beyond question.[22] Bonaventure and Thomas Aquinas, Peter Damian and Benedict, all decry the corruption of the modern church in contrast to the poverty and self-sacrifice of the early saints, and all make it clear that the church should not be concerned with worldly goods. Though their attacks are most often directed at their own orders, they also implicate the papacy, either directly or indirectly, as the rotten head from which corruption flows through the body.[23] Bonaventure describes the papacy as the seat that once was kinder to the poor, but is now degenerate, not in itself but in those who hold the office; he tells us that Dominic sought not the church's wealth, which belongs to the poor, or position, but permission to fight heresy, and that he himself also put temporal cares below spiritual, even when he held high office (Pr. 12.128–29). He and Thomas

[22]Dante and Beatrice lack the historical authority of the saints, but they are presented in the *Comedy* as the chosen messengers of God and Mary, so their attacks on corrupt churchmen also have divine sanction. Beatrice, in the highest realms of heaven, complains about the abuse of Scripture by those who preach to show off and to enrich themselves (Pr. 29) and about the pope's betrayal of an emperor (Pr 30). Dante's blast, evoked by the sight of the eagle, symbol of divine justice, attacks the buying and selling in the temple (Pr. 18.121 ff.) and the self-serving use of excommunications; he ends with the fiercely sarcastic reply of the pope, who makes flippant references to John the Baptist, Peter, and Paul, affirming his devotion to John (whose image is on the florin).

[23]There is a good reason for Dante's connecting the pope and the mendicant friars, who depended directly on the pope and therefore usually defended his supreme authority, as Brian Tierney points out (*Origins of Papal infallibility, 1150–1350* [Leiden: Brill, 1972] 58–59, 83. Bonaventure supports the idea of Christ's authority residing entirely in the pope rather than in the successors of the other apostles, the bishops, which makes his attack on the papacy in Dante's poem particularly effective.

both lament the corruption of their respective orders, which had been instituted to reform the church, and Thomas indirectly identifies the church with Poverty, by speaking of Poverty as Christ's widow (11.64 ff.) just after Dante has spoken of the church as Christ's bride (10.140) and shortly before Bonaventure does (12.43). Benedict also speaks of the decline of his rule in his order and the misuse of church funds that properly belong to the poor; Peter Damian contrasts current luxury (modern pastors whose mantles are so large they cover themselves and their elegant horses, "two beasts under one hide") with apostolic poverty (Peter and Paul, thin, barefoot, taking food where it was offered, 21.127–34).

But the most striking attack on the church is made by Peter, the first pope, who rages against those who have exploited his face on the "lying privileges" they sell (27.53), and "usurped" his place, now vacant in the eyes of God (27.23–24). According to the fiction of the poem, this vacancy must refer to Boniface, who either had no right to be pope, or who has lost that right by abusing the position, or both. However, to a contemporary audience, it would also suggest the more recent popes, Clement V and John XXII, who failed to support properly elected emperors and claimed authority over the "vacant" empire. Dante turns the tables on them by having Peter declare the papacy vacant.[24] It is left to Peter, the pope on whom so many of the later papal claims to temporal authority were based, to make the strongest anticlerical attack of all. He himself denounces the claims that were made in his name. His speech in Paradise 27 can be read as an answer to Boniface's *Unam Sanctam:* both use the imagery of the Song of Songs to describe the church, Boniface calling it "my dove," Peter, "the bride of Christ," but Boniface emphasizes the mystical body whose head is Christ, Peter that it was born of the blood of the early martyrs. Boniface stresses the unity of the church, Peter

---

[24]The papacy was actually vacant from 1314–1316, which may be a subtext to this passage. Peter, drawing on his knowledge of the future, makes reference to both Clement V and John XXII, and decries the corruption of current popes who use the church to amass wealth and fight other Christians.

points out that the papacy is dividing Christians. Boniface cites the two swords and "feed my sheep"; Peter rages because popes are making war on other Christians and the shepherds have become rapacious wolves. Boniface claims jurisdiction over the temporal sphere, Peter cries that Christ's gifts were not made to acquire gold. Boniface cites Peter as the foundation of the church's power, through the keys to loose and bind, Peter says the keys are being used against Christians. And finally, Boniface claims that there is no salvation without subjection to the Roman Pontiff; Peter, the first Pontiff, ends with a promise of divine aid, of Providence working through secular Rome:

> Ma l'alta provedenza, che con Scipio
> difese a Roma la gloria del mondo,
> socorrà tosto. . . .

> But the high Providence, which with Scipio
> defended the glory of the world at Rome,
> will soon give aid. . . .
>
> (Pr. 27.61–63)

The language of Boniface's bull and of Peter's speech is drawn from traditional papalist material; it has its sources in Bernard of Clairvaux's *De consideratione,* his advice to Pope Eugene III, which emphasizes papal responsibility rather than rights, in Giles of Rome's *De ecclesiastica potestate,* dedicated to Boniface and supporting his position, in John of Paris's attack on the papal position, *De potestate regia et papali,* and echoes in Dante's *Monarchy* and political letters. The same images and arguments recur through the *Comedy* as well.[25]

[25]See the introduction for a general discussion of the controversy. I will also cite the *Quaestio de utraque potestate,* ed. Melchior Goldast, in *Monarchiae Sancti Romani Imperii* (Frankfurt: Biermann, 1614), 2.96–107. Rivière *Le Problème,* and Ugo Mariani *Chiesa e stato nei teologi Agostiniani del secolo 14 (Rome: Edizioni di Storia e Letteratura, 1957)* discuss the major works in the controversy. Some of the imagery used in the debates and by Dante in the *Comedy,* e.g., wolves in shepherd's clothing, is also found in anticlerical satire, from which resonances it derives even greater force.

I would now like to look at some of the major arguments and images from this tradition and show how Dante uses them in the *Comedy*. Papal claims to power in the temporal sphere were based not only on the interpretation of biblical passages, but also on the supposedly historical document the Donation of Constantine, which purported to give the pope political authority over the city of Rome and the provinces and cities of Italy and the western regions. That it was an eighth- or ninth-century forgery was not known at the time, so the main arguments against it questioned its legal validity, denying that the emperor had a right to diminish the empire and bind later emperors (John 21, *Monarchy*, 3.10), or tried to limit its scope to Italy or to the city of Rome ("in urbe non tamen in orbe," *Quaestio*, 106).[26] In the *Comedy*, there is a series of attacks on the Donation. In Hell, Dante seems to blame it for the corruption of the later church: "Ah, Constantine, how much evil was born not of your conversion but of that dowry which the first rich father took from you" (Hell 19.115–17); calling it a "dowry" suggests that the pope, unlike Christ, has to be paid to marry the church. The other reference to Constantine in Hell does not mention the Donation, but it would be difficult to miss the connection: when Guido da Montefeltro explains how the pope persuaded him to sin, he says that as Constantine asked Pope Sylvester to cure him of leprosy, so the pope asked Guido to cure him of his fever. The cure effected by Sylvester led to Constantine's conversion and thus to the Donation. In Guido's case, the roles are reversed: the pope, playing the emperor's role, is the afflicted one, with a fever for power or revenge, and he goes to the former political figure, now a monk, for a cure, a plan to undo his enemy. The modern pope

[26]Charles T. Davis, *Dante and the Idea of Rome* (Oxford: Clarendon, 1957), points out the similarity between Dante's views on the Donation and those of Remigio dei Girolami in *Contra falsos ecclesiae professores*, 84–85. Remigio reported that at the time of the Donation, a voice from heaven was heard saying: "today poison was poured into the church of God;" cf. the voice heard in Pg. 32.129.

is in a sense carrying on the tradition Sylvester began, of operating in the temporal sphere.

In the Earthly Paradise, at the top of Purgatory, the Donation is symbolized by the feathers which the eagle (the Roman empire) drops on the chariot (the church), turning it into a monster while a voice laments from heaven. In Paradise, the emperor Justinian begins a history of the empire and its place in God's plan with an allusion to Constantine's mistake: "Poscia che Costantin l'aquila volse/contr' al corso del ciel," "after Constantine turned the eagle against the course of heaven."[27] Justinian himself is an example of the proper relation between pope and emperor, in that a pope, Agapetus, led him back to the true faith and prepared him to undertake the task God intended for him—to reform the laws. Constantine himself appears in the eye of the eagle, aware now of the mistake he made and of the disaster it has brought on the world, although it is not held against him:

> ora conosce come il mal dedutto
> dal suo bene operar non li è nocivo,
> avvegna che sia il mondo indi distrutto
> (Pr. 20.58–60)

These words are spoken by the eagle, which is divine justice working through the empire. Thus heaven condemns the act because it runs counter to providential order.

The church also claimed supremacy in the temporal sphere on the basis of precedence in time: priests, they said, had preceded and even instituted kings, therefore kings were subject to them. The priesthood began with Abel and continued

[27]Constantine moved the empire from Rome to Constantinople. It was moved back to the West, that is, a western claim to the empire was made under Charlemagne; the papacy claimed that it had "translated" the empire as a proof of its authority over it. John of Paris, *De potestate regia et papali*, 15.9, and Dante, *Monarchy*, 3.11, point out that the church called on Charlemagne to defend it, and in so doing *recognized* the transfer of the empire, which had been *accomplished* by the emperor. Dante also points out that one might as well say that the authority of the church depended on the emperor from the day Otto deposed Benedict and put Leo back on the throne.

through the patriarchs to Samuel who "made" the first king of the Jews (Giles, *De ecclesiastica potestate,* 1.6, 3.1). John of Paris argues on the other side that there was no *true* priesthood before Christ, but there were true kings (*De potestate regia et papali,* 4), that it is kings who prefigure Christ in the Old Testament (18.26), and their power came directly from God (10); even prelates derive their powers not through the pope but from God, since Christ, not Peter, sent the apostles out (loc. cit.). In the *Monarchy,* Dante points out that seniority does not determine authority—there are, after all, young bishops with old archdeacons (3.5)—a point that should be considered in connection with the last passage in the *Monarchy,* where Dante grants that Caesar owes Peter the reverence of a firstborn son to his father (3.16). That does not mean he accepts papal supremacy, as is sometimes claimed, but simply the dignity accorded seniority. Dante calls Samuel, the supposed kingmaker, a messenger, not the vicar of God, one who has no discretion to act on his own, but is merely a tool, a "hammer" (3.6). In the *Comedy,* Dante emphasizes Jewish kings rather than priests or patriarchs:[28] Solomon, Joshua, David, and Hezekiah, are prominently placed, but the only priest who appears is Nathan, who rebuked David but could not be said to have "made" him and who supported Solomon's accession; that is, a moral guide and support to kings, not an authority over them. Nathan appears in the same circle with Solomon, who is singled out among all the saints there for great praise, and David is seen in a higher sphere of heaven with Hezekiah. By placing the two Jewish kings, David and Hezekiah, in the eye of the eagle, "the sign that made the Romans revered through the world," along with the pre-Roman pagan Ripheus, Dante

---

[28]We are told that Christ led Abel, Noah, Moses, and Abraham out of Hell (Hell, 4.56–58), but Melchisedech is only mentioned as a name synonymous with the priesthood (Pr. 8.125). Neither John of Paris, nor Dante (in the *Monarchy*) mentions Melchisedech, probably for the same reasons that Giles makes much of him, because he was both king and priest, that is, he wielded both swords, as Giles points out (*De ecclesiastica potestate,* 1.5,6,7 and 3.1).

makes it clear that the "Roman" empire in the providential plan is as old as divine justice on earth.

Precedence in time is related to the issue of hierarchy and the supremacy of the spiritual power. The biblical passage usually cited in support of the latter involves the "two swords" (Luke 22:38): when Christ tells the apostles to buy swords, Peter shows him the two he has and Christ says "It is enough." This passage is often connected with John 18:11: after Peter has cut off Malchus's ear with his sword, Christ tells him to put it back into its scabbard. Bernard, in *De consideratione*, tells Pope Eugene to attack with the word, not the sword, and not to usurp the sword he was commanded to sheathe; that is, not to use temporal means or interfere in temporal affairs. Although he says both swords belong to the pope (or else Christ would have said "That's too much" instead of "That's enough"), he cautions that only one is to be used *by* him, the other *for* him, at the request of the pope but at the command of the emperor (4.7), an important distinction.[29]

Bernard's emphasis is on discouraging the use of the swords; papalists were later to seize and build on the statement that both swords belonged to the church. Boniface cites it in *Unam Sanctam,* but adds that since everything in the universe is ordered hierarchically, one sword must be higher than the other. Giles comments that as body is subject to spirit, so is temporal sword to spiritual (*De ecclesiastica potestate,* 1.7); if earthly powers are subject to ecclesiastical, the temporal things they govern must also be; and with the spiritual sword the pope can cut off the right ear of the sinner, with which he would hear the word of God; that is, excommunicate him (2.5). John of Paris points out that doctors of the church do not interpret the swords as temporal and spiritual power, but as

[29]Bernard also uses the word "forsitan," "perhaps," which Boniface and Giles drop when they cite the passage (Mariani, *Chiesa e stato,* 150). For a thorough study of the early history of the two swords, see Gerard E. Caspary, *Politics and Exegesis: Origen and the Two Swords* (Berkeley: University of California, 1979). For further references, see Muldoon, "Boniface VIII's Forty Years," 451 and fn. 10.

the Old and New Testaments or the word and persecution (*De potestate regia et papali,* 18.30); even if they are taken to represent the two powers, Peter is told to sheathe the spiritual one so as not to abuse it, and he never touches the other. The *Quaestio* notes that God ordained two swords for two distinct and different jurisdictions; the material sword is for princes and this was used only once by Peter, when he cut off Malchus's ear, but he was told to sheathe it (99). Dante, like John, denies the interpretation of the two regimes in the *Monarchy;* for him, the two swords signify words and deeds to carry out what Christ said he had come to do by the sword. When he told his disciples to buy swords, he intended one each, so when he said "that's enough," he meant if they could not have twelve, two would do (3.9). In the *Comedy,* the angels who perform church functions carry a sword, but only one, and it is the spiritual one; the angel who sits at the gate of Purgatory etches the seven P's on Dante's forehead with that sword. The two in the valley of negligent princes carry one sword each, which has been glossed as representing the two equal powers.[30] The temporal sword by itself is mentioned in a passage on the division of powers and the need for a strong secular leader: when the pastoral staff is joined with the sword, both go astray (Pg. 16.109–11).

Boniface applies the meaning of the two swords to another image, the two great lights (*luminaria,* the sun and the moon), in a discourse welcoming Albert of Austria, whom he was then supporting for emperor: as the moon has no light except from the sun, so earthly power has only what it gets from the spiritual.[31] This is a more powerful image, because the hierarchical

[30]Antonio de Angelis, *Il concetto d'Imperium e la comunità soprannazionale in Dante* (Milan: Giuffrè, 1965), 187. The sword carried by the Apostle Paul in the procession of the books of the Bible signifies the word of God, a spiritual sword, like Beatrice's words, which strike Dante like a sword (Pg. 31. 2–3 and 30.57).

[31]Boniface's *Allegacio* was delivered before imperial legates and a multitude of *curiali,* according to Michele Maccarrone, "Il terzo libro della *Monarchia,*" *Studi danteschi* 33 (1955), 33, and was a well-known document in Dante's time. Innocent III (and others before him, see Muldoon, "Boniface VIII's Forty

relationship is built into it, and it aroused strong reactions: John of Paris again turns to a doctor of the church for a different interpretation, this time to Isidore, who equated the sun with the kingdom, the moon with the priesthood (the synagogue) in his gloss on Genesis (*De potestate regia et papali,* 14.4). Cino da Pistoia reverses the analogy in his *Lectura in codicem,* making the empire the sun and the papacy the moon.[32] But even if one accepted the papal analogy, John points out, the moon has a virtue of its own by which it can cause wet and cold, the opposite of the sun, so although a prince may take instruction from the pope and church on the faith, he has his own power direct from God (cf. *Quaestio,* 96). Dante, almost impatiently, notes the problems of interpreting Scripture, and warns that it is a crime to pervert the intentions of the Holy Spirit. The sun and the moon were created before man, he points out; if man had not fallen, he would not have needed the church and state, so God cannot have intended that meaning by them—he would be a stupid doctor indeed who prepared a plaster for an abscess on a person not yet born (*Monarchy,* 3.4). Nonetheless, like John, he assumes that some will refuse to reject the analogy; to them he says that the moon has its own powers and operation. In his political letters, Dante goes out of his way to address and describe the emperor as a sun of peace ("Titan pacificus"), as the bridegroom of Italy, a Moses who will deliver his people from Egypt, in other words, a Christ figure (Ep. 5.1–2).

At the center of Purgatory, Dante has one of the souls discourse on the "two suns" that were ordained by God to guide man along the two roads of life, but one, the church, has put out the other, the empire (16.106–09). The two suns is a startling image and states most forcefully, particularly in the

---

Years," 475) had used the image of the two luminaries: as God made the sun to dominate the day, and the moon the night, so he made the greater rule, the church, to preside over the days of souls, and the lesser, the monarchy, to preside over the nights of bodies, *Sicut universitatis conditor,* 1198.

[32]Codex 1.3, cited by Gennaro Maria Monti, *Cino da Pistoia Giurista* (Città di Castello: Il Solco, 1924), 200.

mouth of a blessed soul from the perspective of the other world, that the two should be equal powers on earth. However, it violates the natural order, so when Dante rises through the planets in Paradise he is limited to one sun which is necessarily higher than the moon, but he does the unexpected with the souls he finds there. The Moon contains not secular rulers, but religious women (nuns) who failed in their vows; in the Sun Dante finds great teachers, mostly religious men, but among them one acknowledged to have achieved the height of wisdom for his calling, Solomon, a king. He had, we are told, the greatest wisdom of all (10.109–14) because, as it turns out, he asked only for sufficient wisdom to be king (13.95–96), as if to be a good king were the highest role a man could play. Thomas Aquinas, who makes the remark, eventually explains that he was speaking of Solomon as without equal among kings (13.106–08), but that explanation comes a full three cantos after the initial praise, allowing us, all through the sphere of the wise, to think of Solomon as the wisest among them. This is Dante's way of emphasizing the importance of a king's judgment, and the distinction between the king's function to judge and rule, and the priest's to guide and teach.[33] And beyond the Sun, higher still, are more kings: among the crusaders in Mars, and as the sole representatives of divine justice in Jupiter, where they appear in the sign of the Roman empire. Only the monastic figures who rejected the world and the early apostles who lived without wealth or power are higher.

One of the most contested areas of jurisdiction between church and state is the judicial; the king as guardian of the law has fundamental rights in temporal cases, but the church made claims on the basis of sin (*ratione peccati*), a fairly loose and comprehensive category, to judge a wide variety of cases. The claim was based on the passage in Matt. 16:18–19 where Christ says to Peter: "Thou art Peter and upon this rock I will build my church . . . And I will give to thee the keys of the kingdom

[33]Cf. *Monarchy* 1.13. The universal monarch is in the best possible condition for governing because he surpasses all others in the power of his judgment and justice.

of heaven. And whatsoever thou shalt bind up on earth, it shall be bound also in heaven; and whatsoever thou shalt loose on earth, it shall be loosed also in heaven." Giles takes this passage to mean that Christ gave Peter, hence the pope, jurisdiction over soul, body, and possessions (*De ecclesiastica potestate,* 2.4); since the rules of property are based on the communion of men in society, the church, through excommunication, has power over possessions as well as over souls. Because of original sin, none can be the just lord of possessions except through the church, which absolves from original sin and therefore has *ius utile* over all temporal things; the church can deprive Caesar for *culpa* or *causa,* while earthly power can operate only over laymen (3.11).

Bernard had tried to keep property distinct from sin in his advice to the pope: your power is over sin *not* property, he said (*De consideratione,* 1.7), not because the pope did not have the right to judge in all matters, but because temporal matters were beneath his concern and involving himself in them might lead to corruption; the pope was entrusted with the stewardship not possession, of the world (3.1). John of Paris picks up that point (*De potestate regia et papali,* 6) and adds that even ecclesiastical property is given to the community, not to the pope, and that lay property is under the jurisdiction of lay princes. Christ, as man, did not possess the temporal kingdom, therefore he did not pass it on to Peter (8–10). The keys represent only the spiritual power to forgive sins, the authority to teach, not the power to command (13), and only in spiritual matters; it would be stupid to deduce from the biblical text any power to absolve from the bond of debts (14.2). A pope may judge an emperor guilty of heresy, and excommunicate his subjects until they depose him, but only they can depose him, while an emperor may force the deposition of a criminal pope (13), unless his offense is spiritual and then the cardinals must act.

In the *Monarchy,* Dante takes a moderate but firm position on the powers conferred by the keys: they are those which pertain to the pope's office as custodian of the heavenly kingdom, nothing more; they do not empower him to dissolve marriages or absolve the impenitent, or to bind and loose decrees of the empire (3.8). In the *Comedy,* the popes' misuse of their powers is severely criticized: excommunication as a political weapon is attacked by Saint Peter in heaven and undercut by Manfred in Purgatory. Manfred, an heir to Frederick's empire, was the object of every kind of papal weapon: Alexander IV and Urban IV excommunicated him several times, Urban preached a crusade against him, and Clement IV had his body disinterred. Manfred was also a terrible sinner by his own admission ("orribil furon li peccati miei," Pg. 3.121) and yet he is saved. Excommunication, he explains to Dante, can keep someone waiting longer to get into Purgatory, but it cannot keep him out of heaven as long as "his hope remains green" (3.135: "mentre che la speranza ha fior del verde"), a play on the river Verde, with which it rhymes, where the pope had his body thrown; his hope counteracts the pope's vindictiveness. In other words, those keys cannot be used to close heaven against souls. Peter had told the angel in Purgatory, to whom he entrusted them, to err in opening rather than in shutting, if people were sincerely repentent (Pg. 9.127–29).[34] It is not that Dante does not respect the power of the keys when properly used, but that modern popes use them for their own sordid purposes; they put them on the banners they carry when they fight other Christians (Pr. 27.49–51), they sell the gifts of the sacraments for gold and silver, flouting Christ's purpose, as Dante emphasizes with a sarcastic question to the simoniac Pope Nicholas III: how much did Christ want from Saint Peter

[34]The keys can also be used to modify vows (Pr. 5.55–57), depending on the sincerity of the vower's intention, which means they should always aid the soul who wants to be saved. When the angel in Purgatory opens the gate for Dante, the sound reminds him of the forced opening of the temple of Saturn, which contained the Roman treasury, a suggestion both that he fears he may be unworthy and that the real treasure of the church is to be found with these keys. It also suggests yet another connection between the empire and God's realm.

when he gave him the keys? (Hell 19.90–92). At the end of a fierce sermon delivered to the feet of this upside-down pope,[35] Dante says that if it had not been for his own reverence for the keys, he would have used even stronger words, though it is hard to imagine what they might have been. There is some irony in Dante's calling them the keys that you held "in the happy life;" what Nicholas held were the keys to *the* happy life, but since he failed to use them properly, for himself or for others, life on earth now seems "happy" in comparison to hell; there is further irony in that Christ told Peter when he gave him the keys that the gates of hell would not prevail against his church (Matt. 16:18).

The worst abuse of the keys in the *Comedy* is, of course, Boniface's boast of their power in order to entice Guido da Montefeltro back into the sin he was atoning for; Boniface told him that he had the two keys so that he could shut or open heaven, and he would absolve Guido of the sin before he committed it. The claim is totally unjustified since the keys do not work unless a sinner is truly repentant, and he cannot repent an act before he commits it. Boniface, in this case, perverts both his priestly functions in one act, by leading a soul into sin and exploiting the sacraments for political ends. He also makes a cynical remark at the expense of his predecessor who "did not hold the keys dear," that is, gave up his position; Bon-

[35]The position of the simoniac popes is significant not just because it turns them upside down, as they perverted their roles in dispensing the sacraments, but also because it exposes only their feet. Dante may well be playing on the custom of kissing the pope's feet as a symbol of his supremacy; the pope as universal bishop alone could demand that princes kiss his feet as part of the coronation ritual (Ullmann, *Short History,* 152). A famous Lateran mosaic depicted Emperor Lothar kneeling at the pope's feet (Tierney, *Crisis,* 99). Cardinals also kissed the feet of the elected pope. Giles, in the dedication of *De ecclesiastica potestate* to Boniface, offers himself as a humble creature in all submission to kiss the blessed feet, "cum omni subieccione seipsum ad pedum oscula beatorum," and later says that all should do so, 1.2. Dante also plays on the imperial footwear, the *zanca,* worn by popes. See Ernest N. Kaulbach, "*Inferno* XIX, 45: The 'Zanca' of Temporal Power," *Dante Studies* 86 (1968), 127–36, and Scott, "*Inferno* XIX," who notes that *zanca* is also used of Lucifer in 34.79, another pope-devil connection, 463–64, fn. 5.

iface seems to imply that Celestine did not understand the real value of the keys—what could be gained from them. There is one other reference to the keys which Dante does not connect directly with the church, but which is filled with suggestive allusions: in Hell 13, among the suicides, he meets Pier della Vigna, whose name means "Peter of the Vineyard," a perversion of Saint Peter who, as Dante says in heaven, died for the vineyard that contemporary popes are laying waste (Pr. 18.131–32). Dante may well have known that members of Frederick's court called it the "ecclesia imperialis," of which Pier della Vigna was the Saint Peter, the rock upon which the imperial church was founded, sometimes in contrast to the "false vicar of Christ," the pope.[36] Pier della Vigna was the secretary of the emperor Frederick, whose name in Italian, Federico, can mean "rich in faith"; Dante has already seen Frederick in the circle of the heretics, so he too is a perversion of his name.[37] Pier boasts to Dante, not unlike the way Boniface boasts to Guido, that he held both keys to Frederick's heart and turned them, locking and unlocking to keep everyone else from his secrets (Hell 13.58–60). He claims to have kept "faith" with his "glorious" (a loaded word) office, but he abused his powers since an emperor's heart cannot belong to one individual. Allegorically, then, we may have a pope (Pier/ Peter) abusing the gifts of his office to serve a false faith (Federico/Frederick), and, on another level, the church using its powers (the keys) to interfere with the proper functioning of

[36]Pier also punned on the other part of his name, Vigna. For a discussion of the language of the imperial court, see William A. Stephany, "Pier della Vigna's Self-Fulfilling Prophecies: the "Eulogy" of Frederick II and *Inferno* 13," *Traditio* 38 (1982), 193–212. From Dante's references to Caesar and Augustus, Hell 13.65 and 68, we know he was aware of Frederick's affectations of ancient Roman usage.

[37]It is Saint Peter who questions Dante on *his* faith in Paradise. And it is certainly not coincidental that Frederick's mother, Constance, whom Dante sees in Paradise, lacked "constancy" in her vows; she is called the mother of the third "wind of Swabia," suggesting a parody of the Holy Spirit and the Trinity, which makes little sense in the context of Paradise 3, but much more in the light of Hell 10 and 13.

the empire; by so doing, by usurping control over the political sphere and interfering between the emperor and his people, the pope is committing spiritual suicide.[38]

Basic to all papal claims of universal jurisdiction is the notion of Christendom as one entity, a mystical body of which Christ, or his vicar on earth, is the head, a ship of which he is the pilot, a bride of whom he is the groom, a family of which he is the father, and a flock of which he is the shepherd. The imagery comes from the long tradition of biblical exegesis, but it runs through the papalist documents as well, and most of it is in *Unam Sanctam.* Dante uses all of it, twisting it to his own purposes in the *Comedy,* as in the political letters, which are undisguised political propaganda. Boniface describes the church as a single body with one head—Christ or his vicar, Peter and Peter's successors—and warns that a body cannot have two heads or it becomes a monster. Even antipapalists accept the image of the body and the one head, but they insist on that head being Christ (John of Paris, *De potestate regia et papali,* 29, Quaestio, 103).[39] Bernard had used the image of the monster in a very different way, which Boniface does not take up; Bernard had said that Christ organized the church the way God wanted it, and any attempt on the pope's part to rearrange its members would be to create a monster (*De consideratione,* 3.17). Dante, however, presents the church not as a body, but

[38]The Ottimo mentions that Pier wrote a letter at the pope's instance revealing the emperor's secrets to the Church of Rome; in other words, that he conspired with the pope against the empire, a notion not found in the *Comedy,* so it is either based on a contemporary rumor or perhaps on the power of suggestion in the name. It is interesting that Jacopo connects Cecina and Corneto, mentioned at the beginning of the canto (Hell, 13.9), with the patrimony of Saint Peter, 1.252. For further discussion of the political implications of Pier's service to Frederick II, see chapter three.

[39]See Ernst H. Kantorowicz, *The King's Two Bodies* (Princeton: Princeton University, 1957), 196, on the use of the mystical body in a sociological sense, which he says is relatively new with Boniface. For Thomas Aquinas, the head of the *corpus Ecclesiae mysticum* was Christ (ST, 3, q.8, and Kantorowicz, op. cit., 203). John of Salisbury, in his comparison of the state to a body, makes the prince the head, churchmen the soul, *Policraticus,* 5.2.

as a chariot, an inanimate object which cannot move on its own; when the chariot takes on the eagle's feathers (imperial possessions), it begins to act like a body, but a monstrous one, sprouting heads and horns. Dante turns the church into the monster it has created.

The chariot is in itself a complex symbol, involving other aspects of the same themes; it may have been suggested by the wagons, which represented individual Italian cities at parlays and in triumphal processions,[40] but it is also an *arca*, which suggests both the ark of Noah and the ark of the covenant, which King David steadied on its journey (Pg. 10.56). *Arca* can also mean "coffer" (used figuratively in Pr. 23.131 ff.), implying that the church is the repository of treasure that was meant to be spiritual but is material to the popes in Hell and to Hadrian before his conversion (Pg. 19).[41] As the ark of Noah, it is also a boat, a traditional figure for the church, which must be properly guided if it is to save those it carries. When Beatrice appears on the chariot, she is like an admiral on a boat (Pg. 30.58–60) and when the eagle attacks it, it reels like a ship; when the eagle covers it with its feathers, a voice calls out from heaven "O navicella mia, come mal sei carca," "O my little boat, how badly loaded you are" (32.129).[42] Thomas calls the church the "barca di Pietro" (Pr. 11.119–20), which must be piloted by Francis and Dominic to save it from the corruption

[40]See Daniel Waley, *The Italian City-Republics* (New York: McGraw-Hill, 1969), 139 ff. The wagons are mentioned frequently by Villani *Istorie Fiorentine*, see particularly 6.20, 43, 76. They were usually drawn by oxen. Cf. Dante's letter to the cardinals in which he says he is concerned with the oxen who draw the ark, not the ark itself, Ep. 8.5.

[41]The play on *arca* as "ark" and "coffer" echoes a medieval Latin poem that makes a series of similar puns, all suggesting the corruption of the church: "Nummus est pro numine/et pro Marco marca,/et est minus celebris/ara quam sit arca." ("Money stands for the divinity/and the mark for Mark,/and less celebrated/is the altar than the ark.") (Utar contra vitia).

[42]The voice may be either God's or Peter's: the Ottimo gives God, saying that the church is the boat of God under Peter's guidance, 2.573–74; but since the boat which represents the church is also called Peter's boat, "barca di Pietro" (Pr. 11.119–20), the voice might be Peter's.

or neglect of the popes. It is possible that Ulysses' ship is also to be connected with the church, being led beyond its proper limits; Ulysses, like Adam, errs in "trapassar del segno," taking his followers beyond the bounds set by Hercules (Hell 26.107–09), leading them into damnation with false promises, as Boniface does. One of the promises made to Dante of divine intervention to set the church right is described in terms which recall Ulysses' end: "le poppe volgerà u' son le prore" (Pr. 27.146: "he will turn the sterns to where the prows are," recalling Hell 26.137–42, "un turbo . . . fé . . . levar la poppa in suso/ e la prora ire in giù," "a storm . . . made . . . the stern rise up and the prow go down").

One of the most popular figures for the church is the bride of Christ, from the Song of Songs, which is put to various uses in the political debate. Giles claims marital rights: since a clergyman is the husband of his church, he has a right to her possessions; that is, although the church's goods may belong to all the faithful, the priest, bishop, or pope, as her husband, has domination over them (2.1). Dante, as one would expect, emphasizes the marital abuses: the popes lead the church into adultery for gold and silver (Hell 19.3–4); they win it by deception and then outrage it (19.56–7); they pimp for it, turning it into a whore for kings (19.106–11, cf. Pg. 32.149 ff.). But, he reassures us, the whore will be killed by the eagle's heir (Pg. 33.37–45) and Rome will soon be freed of this adultery (Pr. 9.142). The bride of Christ, who paid for her love with blood (the sacrifice of Christ and the early martyrs, Pr. 27.40 ff.), will be restored. When Dante speaks of the bride of Christ in the *Comedy,* he usually means the whole assembly of the faithful, laity and clergy; the church bureaucracy by itself is a whore.[43]

[43]The rose, the assembly of all the faithful in heaven, is described as the "holy army which Christ married with his blood" (Pr. 31.1–3). Rahab, the good whore, is also a figure for the church, because she helped Joshua, a Christ figure, to take the Holy Land, in contrast to modern popes who forget the crusades and the mission to spread the faith (see Pr. 9.124–26, 15.142–44). Bernard, *De consideratione,* had also reminded the pope of his responsibility to convert unbelievers, 3.3.

The epithets most frequently used of the pope in papalist writings are "father" and "shepherd." When he speaks as a figure of authority to be revered, particularly addressing wayward princes, it is as a father: "Ausculta, fili carissimi, praecepta patris" (Boniface to Philip: "Listen, dear sons, to your father's precepts"). Giles says that all should call him most holy father ("omnes debent eum appellare sanctissimum patrem" 1.2).[44] Dante, in the *Monarchy,* acknowledges the pope's paternal position—the emperor owes him the reverence of a firstborn son to his father—but only after he has effectively denied him all authority outside the spiritual sphere. In the *Comedy,* however, the pope is called "father" only sarcastically, as when Dante calls the recipient of Constantine's gift "the first rich father" (Hell 19.117), and when Guido accepts Boniface's deceptive offer of absolution (Hell 27.108). Otherwise he reserves the title for those who actually guided him, the poets Virgil and Guido Guinizelli, and the saints Francis, Benedict, Peter, and Bernard.[45] God is the *pio padre* who should be the model for popes, but is not; they withhold the bread which the "pious father" denies no one (Pr. 18.128–29). Aeneas is a father to Rome (Hell 2.20–21), while the clergy is stepmother to the emperor (Pr. 16.58–59).

When he claims universal jurisdiction, the pope speaks as shepherd, based on John 2:16–17, "Feed my sheep." Boniface points out that Christ does not say "these" or "those" sheep ("has vel illas") but "mine," *meas,* by which he means *all* sheep, universally (cf. Giles, *De ecclesiastica potestate,* 2.4). Bernard had noted the shepherd's responsibility for his flock (*De consideratione,* 1.5); he should expel evil beasts so the flocks can pasture in safety (2.13); clergy of the past cared only for the sheep (4.3), now instead they adorn themselves in gold and colors; they pasture demons more than sheep (4.5) and dwell with wolves (4.6). Dante makes wide use of these images of wolves and sheep in the *Comedy,* and he uses the word

[44]See Maccarrone, "Il terzo libro," 130 ff., on father–son imagery.
[45]I am not including biological ancestors, like Adam and Cacciaguida, who are naturally spoken of as "father."

"shepherd" again and again to underline all kinds of priestly abuses.[46] The wolf throughout the *Comedy* stands for greed, which will eventually be driven back to Hell by the *veltro*, a secular leader (Hell 1.101). The pope as "sommo pastore" should be protecting the sheep from that wolf, but instead he becomes a wolf, transformed by greed, and leads all the sheep and lambs astray (Pr.9.130–32). The church is filled with wolves in shepherd's clothing (Pr. 27.55–56), Peter comments with disgust. Nicholas III openly admits that his only care was for his own family (Hell 19.70–71); in his desire to enrich "the little bears," the *orsati*, he completely ignored the sheep. Peter Damian contrasts the poverty of the apostles with the *moderni pastori*, so heavy they have to be propped on their mounts; a mounted shepherd is in itself a strange picture and a fat one, ludicrous. Hadrian's greed is stemmed only when he becomes the *roman pastore* and has as much wealth as he desires (Pg. 19.103 ff.), that is, "Roman shepherd" is the equivalent of enormous wealth.

The *Comedy* is filled with examples of popes who guide their flocks in the wrong directions; it may be true that we are "men, not mad sheep" (Pr. 5.80), and should not allow ourselves to be led astray, but the bad example that is set where a good is expected can be very powerful: "color che sono in terra/tutti svïati dietro al malo essemplo" (Pr. 18.125–26: "those on earth are all gone astray after the bad example"). After all, God gave us, along with the Old and New Testaments, "il pastor de la Chiesa" to guide us (Pr. 5.76–77), but instead of guiding, he prostitutes the church. It is you pastors the Evangelist was thinking of when he saw the whore forni-

---

[46]To distinguish the good shepherd, Francis, Dante uses the Greek word "archimandrita," "abbot," which probably involves a pun on "mandra," "flock" (Pr. 11.99, cf. Pg. 3.86). Uguccione, *Magnae Derivationes*, defines it as "head of the fold," cited by Singleton, Commentary on Paradise, 203. One wonders if the importance of the wool trade to Tuscany, and the fact that monasteries in England raised sheep and sold the wool to Italian merchants, did not add some piquancy to all the talk of shepherds' corruption for Dante and his audience.

cating with kings, Dante rages at the simoniac popes (Hell, 19.106–08). These "shepherds" feed their flocks either selectively (like the bishop in Pg. 24.30, "who fed many with his staff," presumably his courtiers), or with the wrong food (wind, the nonsense preached by vain and ignorant preachers, Pr. 29.106–07); they indulge themselves, neglect their duty (Pr. 15.142–44, possibly Hell 20.67–69), or commit crimes, actively harming their flocks (like the *empio pastor*, the "impious shepherd," who betrays the Ghibellines who had taken refuge with him, Pr. 9.53). There is only one instance in the *Comedy* of the pope as shepherd leading a soul back to the faith, and that is a very early one: Justinian tells how Agapetus, the *sommo pastore*, led him out of heresy to the faith by his words (Pr. 6.17–18). Dante describes himself as the victim of wolves who make war on the sheepfold where he slept as a lamb, Florence (Pr. 25.4–6), but he also sees himself as a goat, watched over by the good shepherds, Virgil and Statius (Pg. 27.76–87). In this rather tender simile, the shepherds are poets, not priests, who wake through the night to guard their charge. (In Purgatory, 20.139–41, Dante compares himself and Virgil to the shepherds who first heard the angel sing *Gloria* to announce the birth of Christ.) Dante, of course, takes on the function popes have abandoned of guide to Christendom when he becomes God's messenger in the poem.

The pope can no longer function as shepherd because he has joined the sword with the pastoral crook (Pg. 16.109–11). He attempts to rule the secular as well as the religious sphere without either the authority or the qualifications: "il pastor che procede/rugumar può ma non ha l'unghie fesse" (Pg. 16.98–99: "the shepherd who leads may chew the cud but does not have cleft hooves"), that is, he can mediate but not distinguish, so he leaves the world without its proper ruler, the king, who *can* discern at least the tower of the true city and can enforce the laws (16.94–96). The trouble began when Constantine moved the empire east to "yield to the shepherd" (Pr. 20.57), a particularly foolish move, since it was clear that God meant the empire to be Roman, and it is ludicrous to think of a shepherd replacing an emperor; the phrase may have been suggested by Clement's bull, *Pastoralis cura,* in which the "shepherd's care" is to oversee the vacant empire. Constantine's gift imposed a secular function on the pope which God had not intended, thereby distorting the one he had, the spiritual guidance of the shepherd. The force of the word shepherd, constantly repeated by Dante to point up the failures and abuses of episcopal responsibility, lies in the image it evokes of a being endowed with greater sense to watch over the weak and helpless, to defend them from their enemies, to see that they are fed and do not get lost. The shepherd is a figure with enormous responsibility but no tangible power or wealth; he is a wanderer in this world.

It is no accident that the shepherd is the only active image Dante uses for the pope, whereas the emperor is the husband of Rome (Pg. 6.112–14, but Rome is a widow), the horseman who should be in the saddle to keep mankind on the right road. The empire is itself an eagle, a living force, while the church is a chariot which must be driven to function properly. The only church symbol equivalent to the eagle as a living force is the bride of Christ, and in Dante's poem the bride usually represents the whole assembly of believers, while the curia by itself is a whore, prostituting God's gift of love. By turning their backs on the lessons of the gospels and the example of the early popes, recent popes have turned God's instrument for man's salvation, the church, into a monster and surrendered it to powers like the French king who use it for their own selfish ends. The only hope is the promise of a savior, the eagle's heir, who will kill the whore and the giant; that is, a new emperor who will destroy both the clerical and the secular enemies of mankind (Pg. 33.34–45), who will return the church to its proper function of spiritual guidance and remove it from the temptations of wealth and power which have corrupted it and endangered all mankind. We are assured that the church will not be allowed to continue on its corrupt course: in Purgatory, 33.34–36, Beatrice says that the vessel broken by the dragon (the chariot representing the church) "was and is not." The

114

church, in other words, has been fundamentally changed, but the guilty party will soon feel God's revenge. In the heaven of Saturn, the souls of the contemplatives cry out a promise of God's imminent vengeance for ecclesiastical corruption that will come before Dante dies (Pr. 21.140–22.18).

The two major prophecies in the *Comedy*, the *veltro* in the first canto of Hell and the DXV in the last of Purgatory, are both ambiguous, presumably because Dante has to allow for variations in detail. But it is clear from both that Dante believes there will be a change for the better, that a reformer will come to set Europe straight, although he cannot be sure exactly when it will occur. There is a third prophecy which Dante must have considered equally important, simpler than the other two because it offers no enigmatic hints, but perhaps more reassuring because of its source and certainty. This is Peter's promise at the end of his condemnation of ecclesiastical corruption, that God, the High Providence that with Scipio defended the glory of the world at Rome, will soon send aid (Pr. 27.61–63).[47] What Virgil told Dante in Hell and Beatrice told him in Purgatory is repeated by the first pope in heaven, that God, working through the Roman empire, will put an end to the corruption which destroys the Christian world. Dante may not know who the *veltro* or the DXV is, but he must be a secular ruler, since Dante has proved in the *Monarchy* that only a universal monarch can bring peace and justice and in the *Comedy* that secular power in the church is by definition corrupt.

There has been a great deal of speculation about the nature and identity of the *veltro* and the eagle's heir, but the identity can never be definitively established; we can only make intelligent guesses on the basis of the material Dante gives us.[48] We

[47]Scipio's name also appeared in connection with the chariot of the church, Pg. 29.116, which had once been more splendid than the Roman leader's, but had turned into a monster since it was covered with secular power and wealth.

[48]For a comprehensive survey, see the *Enciclopedia Dantesca* (Rome: Istituto, 1970–78) entries under *veltro* and *cinquecento dieci e cinque;* recent discussions that offer much information and very sensible readings are Charles T.

know the *veltro* is an enemy of the wolf, and the wolf throughout the *Comedy* is greed, frequently identified with the church, particularly in Paradise where the shepherds become wolves (9.132, 27.55). The wolf *s'ammoglia*, "marries" many animals (Hell 1.100), the promiscuity within marriage suggesting the sexual abuses of Christ's bride by the popes, but the *veltro* will drive the wolf back to Hell.[49] The *veltro* might be a religious reformer (Dominic, for example, is associated with a dog, but he is long since gone and his effects no longer widely felt, Pr. 11.124 ff.), but he must also be the salvation of *that* Italy ("*quella* umile Italia") for which Cammilla, Euryalus, Turnus, and Nisus died, heroes of the struggle to found Rome, ancestors of the great pagan Roman tradition, who must be associated in any medieval reader's mind with the empire, if only from their presence in the *Aeneid*. The Ottimo makes that association clear, saying the *veltro* will be a universal lord, following Virgil in the sixth book of the *Aeneid,* where he tells us that Rome will rule without end (1.11). Davis ("Dante's

Davis, "Dante's Vision of History," *Dante Studies* 93 (1975), and Robert Hollander, *Allegory in Dante's "Commedia"* (Princeton: Princeton University, 1969), particularly 181–91. Both Davis and Hollander associate the *veltro* with the DXV and suggest that Dante is prophesying a temporal leader, another Augustus, who may be sent to prepare the way for the second coming, but will not himself be a religious leader. Davis, 152: "It is natural to suppose that the heir of the Eagle and of Scipio will be Roman": in "Poverty and Eschatology in the Commedia," *Yearbook of Italian Studies* 4 (1980), 59–86, Davis points out that the Hohenstaufen themselves used the imagery of the eagle's heir, that Frederick's son, Conrad, was called "son of the Eagle, heir of the Emperor," 71. Cf. Floro di Zenzo, *Il Sistema morale e politico nella Divina Commedia* (Florence: Kursaal, 1965), 7: the *veltro* is a Roman emperor, corresponding exactly to the sovereign described in the *Monarchy*. The *veltro* prophecy was still alive and being applied by Italians to the emperor in 1355, see later in this chapter and fn. 68. For striking examples of the importance of prophecy in the political life of this period, see Villani, *Istorie Fiorentine,* particularly 6.81, 7.31, 9.3, 9.46.

[49]Cf. Benvenuto, 4.273: "that wise, just greyhound . . . will kill the whore, that is, the great whore, that is, the prelacy of the pastors of the church, whose wife is the wolf, for avarice flourishes in them." Davis, "Dante's Vision," 149, cites Dante's letter to the Italian cardinals, in which he says each of the clergy "has taken avarice to wife," Ep. 8.7.

Vision," 145), pursuing the same tack, suggests that Dante puts the prophecy in Virgil's mouth because it was the *Aeneid* which convinced him that "God had willed Rome's conquests and universal power ... and had revealed this fact to Aeneas and to Virgil." Pietro Alighieri describes the *veltro* as an emperor who will reign like Augustus, over the whole world. He also identifies him with the Last World Emperor, and with the ideal man of Alanus de Insulis (45–46), another ambiguous figure with overtones of Christ, but an ideal human figure rather than a second coming; in later recensions, however, Pietro identifies the *veltro* explicitly with the DXV, as an emperor and leader who will control avarice, bring peace, and despoil prelates of their wealth.[50] Benvenuto says the *veltro* can be both Christ *and* a future prince who will repair the Roman empire (1.55–60).

If we are meant to connect the *veltro* with the DXV prophesied at the end of Purgatory, as seems most likely, the Roman identity becomes even stronger.[51] The DXV will be God's messenger, the heir of the eagle:

> Non sarà tutto tempo sanza reda
> l'aguglia che lasciò le penne al carro
> . . . .
> ch'io veggio certamente . . .
> . . . un cinquecento diece e cinque,
> messo di Dio. . . .
>
> The eagle which left its feathers in the cart
> will not always be without an heir
> . . . .

[50]For Pietro's later views, see Charles T. Davis' article on the *veltro*, *Enciclopedia Dantesca*, 5.909. On Dante and the Last World Emperor, see Marjorie Reeves, "Dante and the Prophetic View of History," *The World of Dante*, ed. Cecil Grayson (Oxford: Clarendon, 1980), 57, and Davis, "Dante's Vision," 155.

[51]Benvenuto on the DXV, "messenger of God," says "hic est ille veltrus," "this is the greyhound," 4.273. Hollander, *Allegory in Dante's "Commedia,"* 184, notes the numerical symmetry of the two prophecies, Virgil's coming 101 lines after the beginning of Hell, Beatrice's 102 lines before the end of Purgatory.

for I see with certainty . . .
. . . a five hundred, ten, and five,
messenger of God. . . .

(Pg. 33.37–44)

Here the eagle is carefully identified with Constantine's donation; elsewhere, most notably in the sphere of justice in Paradise, the eagle is "the sign that made the Romans revered through the world" (Pr. 19.101–02); the eagle is also the bird of God ("uccel di Giove," Pg. 32.112, and "uccel di Dio," Pr. 6.4), the instrument of God. The Ottimo takes God's justice and the eagle's heir to mean that the empire will be restored and the judgment of God will take revenge on those who deceived it (2.583–84). Benvenuto calls the eagle's heir a "successor emperor" and points out that there was none at the time of Boniface (4.272). The Ottimo interprets the numbers of the eagle's heir, 500, 10, and 5, in their Roman equivalents, D, X, V, as an anagram for DUX, a leader sent by God who will bring the world back to God (2.584–85); he may come at the end of the world, but he will be a "most just and holy prince," who will reform the state of the church. One who will kill the whore and the giant (Pg. 33.44–45) is one who can not only thoroughly change the structure of the church, since the whore is the corrupt curia and is to be killed not cleansed, but one who can also destroy the powerful French king.[52] The only figure who would have the power and authority to destroy the bureaucracy of the church and the most powerful political figure in Europe would be a universal[ly accepted] emperor. It is tempting to connect the killing of the whore with Marsilius's reduction of the church to an organ of the state; although Dante never says so directly, it is possible, given his negative views on the secular powers and structure of the church, that,

[52]It seems unlikely that Dante means Boniface in the figure of the giant, as the Ottimo suggests in his comments on Purgatory 32 (2.576–77), since Boniface was already dead when Dante wrote the poem and he had certainly not been killed by a great reformer, nor had the curia been cleansed. The Ottimo, incidentally, does not repeat that identification when he discusses this passage.

like Marsilius, he may have foreseen a time when the empire would control the bureaucarcy of the church and restrict it to its spiritual function.

Although it is futile to try and determine a distinct historical identity for the *veltro* or the eagle's heir, one can and perhaps should consider the hints Dante gives us. The *veltro* is a dog, an animal with little positive value in the *Comedy*, except in the name of Dante's future patron, Can Grande, who is alluded to with considerable enthusiasm in Paradise because of his great deeds and his magnificence (17.76 ff.). Can Grande's family, the Scaligeri, have as their emblem "in su la scala ... il santo uccello" (17.72: "the holy bird on the ladder"), in other words, they are identified with the eagle. Can Grande will also be an imperial vicar under both Henry VII and eventually Ludwig of Bavaria and will win important victories in their service, though those for Ludwig come after Dante's death. Dante alludes to Henry and Pope Clement's betrayal of him in the midst of the passage about Can Grande (Pr. 17.82). Certainly Can Grande is a likely candidate for the *veltro*, at least as one who might rescue Italy from the wolf.[53] He does not, however, have the political scope within Europe to be the eagle's heir who will kill the whore and the giant. If that figure is to be a contemporary, the only possible candidate is Ludwig, since Henry died before Dante had written a good part of the poem and he clearly had not solved Europe's problems. Davidsohn identifies Ludwig with the DXV on the basis of the sum of the three numbers, 515, which he adds to 800, the year Charlemagne brought the empire back to the West, giving him 1315, a significant date for Ludwig.[54]

[53]J. B. Fletcher, "The Crux of Dante's Comedy," in *Essays in Memory of Barrett Wendell* (Cambridge Mass.: Harvard University, 1965), identifies Can Grande with the *veltro*, 74–84; Hollander, *Allegory in Dante's "Commedia,"* 187–88, suggests both Can Grande and Christ; Erich Auerbach, *Dante, Poet of the Secular World* trans. Ralph Manheim (1929; reprint, Chicago: University of Chicago, 1961), 129, Can Grande and the Great Kahn, or the Phoenix. For others who posit Can Grande, see Davis, veltro, *Enciclopedia Dantesca*, 5. 908–912.

[54]Ludwig had his German coronation and his victory at Morgarten in 1315,

It is not necessary to be quite so specific, particularly since no great changes of the kind Dante envisioned were apparent after 1315, but there are other connections to be made with the numbers. The eagle, when it appears in canto 18 of Paradise, rises out of the letter *M*, the end of the message spelled by the soul of the just kings, "Diligite Justitiam qui judicatis terram" (18.91–93). Well before we are given the whole message, however, we are told only the first three letters, *D, I,* and *L,* five hundred, one, and fifty (18.78). Since Dante also makes much of the fact that the message contains five words and five times seven letters, one must assume that five is somehow significant here, as it was in the enigmatic prophecy of Purgatory 33. As it happens, the first three letters of Ludwig's name in Latin, Ludovicus, are all fives, *L, V, D* (and the name also contains one, *I,* and one hundred, *C*). The coincidence of fives and ones may have suggested to Dante that Ludwig was to be the figure to oppose the beast of the Apocalypse, the 666.[55] Since

R. Davidsohn, "Il cinquecento dieci e cinque del Purgatorio," *Bullettino della Società Dantesca Italiana* 9 (1902), 129–31. Hollander makes a rather attractive point about the numbers: in Isidore's *Etymologiae,* Julius Caesar, the first emperor, is said to have been five years old in the 5155th year from the creation, in other words, he was born in the year 5150. Thus 515 would be the number of the first emperor, and fittingly of his (final?) successor. Kay, "Dante's Razor," suggests that DXV refers to Distinction 15 in Gratian and makes an interesting case based on Dante's frequent opposition to the authority of the decretals. There may well be some truth to this argument, but it cannot be the sole explanation, since the DXV must also be a human leader, if he is heir to the eagle. Robert Kaske, "Dante's DXV and Veltro," *Traditio* 17 (1961), 185–254, makes a strong case for Christ on the basis of the manuscript monogram of *Vere dignum:* more recently, in "Dante's Purgatorio XXXII and XXXIII: A Survey of Christian History," *University of Toronto Quarterly* 43 (1974), 193–214, he adds to his arguments for the second coming as the solution of Dante's prophecy.

[55]C. H. Grandgent, ed., *La Divina Commedia di Dante Alighieri* (Boston: Heath, 1933), 635–37, refers to commentators on Revelation who spelled out the number of the beast, 666, in Roman numerals, DCLXVI, an anagram for DIC LUX, Lucifer, who claims to be the light. Those six letters also suggest an anagram for Ludwig's name, Ludovicus, which often appears as LVDOVIC'. Cacciaguida dates his own birth, the beginning of Dante's family, from the Annunciation by the numbers 500, 50, 30 (D, L, XXX), combining the

Dante died long before Ludwig, it is at least possible that, as long as he was writing the *Comedy*, he cherished hopes of the great reformation to come from Ludwig, working with Can Grande.[56] Certainly Dante would have been taken with the fact that Ludwig's mother was a Matelda (daughter of emperor Rudolph I and namesake of the great Tuscan countess),[57] and that his wife was a Beatrice, both names connected with women who figure in Dante's personal salvation and who guide him to the Earthly Paradise, which the emperor is meant to restore for mankind. It is another interesting coincidence, though Dante would not have known it, that his *Monarchy* was burned as a result of Ludwig's march on Rome.

In this chapter, I have concentrated primarily on the church's abuse of its powers and functions, because that is what Dante emphasizes. What the church should be and do must be deduced mainly from what Dante tells us it should not be: it should not concern itself with wealth, except to distribute needed goods to the poor, and it should never interfere in political affairs—local or international.[58] It should spread

---

imperial number 5, with the divine number 3, and implicitly connecting Dante with the leader to come, of whom he is the herald (as John the Baptist was to Christ). Five is associated with good rulers in Paradise: Solomon is the fifth light of his circle (Pr. 10.109 and 13.48) and there are five lights in the eagle's brow (20.69).

[56]Francesco Mazzoni's view, that the last chapter of the *Monarchy* reflects the recent problems over the election of Ludwig of Bavaria, with the injunction that imperial electors should think of themselves as instruments of divine providence ("Teoresi e prassi in Dante politico," in Dante Alighieri, *Monarchia, Epistole politiche* [Turin: ERI, 1966], lxiv), lends some weight to this hypothesis, since it means that even in the *Monarchy*, Dante is looking to someone beyond Henry, and Ludwig is the most likely candidate on the scene.

[57]A description of Ludwig's mother as regent, ruling wisely and governing virilely after the death of her husband, echoes what was said of the earlier Countess Matelda (see below, chapter four: "Domina Mechthildis ... post mortem mariti sui—Dominium terrae sapienter regnans et viriliter gubernans," *Monumenta Dissensia*, cited by Joseph Schlett, *Biographie von Kaiser Ludwig dem Baier* (Sulzbach: Seidel, 1822), 12.

[58]On Dante and evangelical poverty, see Antoon Ariaens, "Dante e la Chiesa," in *Miscellanea Dantesca* (Utrecht: Spectrum 1965), 89–102; Raoul Manselli, "Dante e l'Ecclesia Spiritualis," *Dante e Roma*, Atti del Convegno di

God's message among non-Christians and guide Christians away from heresy or error. Its prime function for Dante seems to be to teach, by example or word. Apart from the earliest popes, who lived in poverty and died martyrs, the only churchmen who are praised in the Comedy or who can be looked to as good examples are the monks and friars, Benedict, Peter Damian, Francis, and Dominic, who renounced worldly things, although they continued to work in the world, and the great teachers, the scholars and theologians who appear in the circles of the Sun. Among the latter there is one pope, John XXI, but he is cited as a writer, Pietro Ispano, who still shines on earth in his twelve books. Dante does not even mention that he was pope, and he only served for eight months in any case, so what effect he had was as a scholar.[59]

Dante has presumably been influenced by the scholars and saints he names, and some of them lecture to him in heaven, but he does not choose any of them to guide him on his journey to God; his guides are a pagan poet, Virgil, and a woman, Beatrice (just as the two permanent human inhabitants of Purgatory are a pagan and a woman). It is Virgil, the poet of Empire, who leads Dante to the earthly paradise and crowns him emperor and pope over himself, and Beatrice, the woman and Christ figure, who leads him to heaven. In fact, Virgil and, to a lesser extent, other poets in the Comedy fulfill the functions of teacher and guide, which the church and the empire leave vacant. Dante, of course, takes on that role through his poem for his audience. Only for the last moment of the jour-

---

Studi (Florence: Le Monnier, 1965), 115–35; Holmes, "Dante and the Popes"; Scott, "Inferno XIX"; Davis, "Poverty and Eschatology," and Dante and the Idea of Rome (214–27) for connections with Ubertino da Casale. In "Imagery in Paradiso XXVII," Scott calls the canto "an absolute condemnation of papal policy, which is based on greed and opposition to the emperor, Christ's temporal vicar on earth," 29.

[59]We know that Gregory the Great is also in Paradise, not because Dante sees him, but because he tells us that Gregory was wrong about the order of angels and smiled at his mistake when he opened his eyes in the Primo Mobile (Pr. 28.133–35). Even on angelic hierarchy, Dante will not allow a pope to be right.

ney, the vision of God, does he choose a saint, Bernard, to guide him. Bernard is a mystic, devoted to Mary, and thus a suitable choice for the vision that Dante receives through her, but he is also a reformer and a political moderate (and something of a poet). It is no accident that the other churchmen with important roles in heaven, Thomas Aquinas, Peter Damian, Bonaventure, are also political moderates, men who recognize the need for a secular state and the practical separation of spheres (see chapter five).

The separation is essential to Dante's view of church-state relations; it is because the church interfered with the empire that Dante attacks it so fiercely, but that does not mean that he is blind to the faults of emperors. In fact, he condemns the man he considered the last functioning emperor in Italy, Frederick II, to Hell for heresy. This is a puzzling fact in some ways because Frederick was a significant force against the political ambitions of the papacy in Italy; he emphasized the Roman heritage of his title, he developed an efficient state, and he was a scholar and writer, all of which Dante admired.[60] That he was also accused of unorthodox beliefs is not enough to explain Dante's condemnation of him—Dante was ready enough to put others accused of heresy in Paradise. Perhaps what troubled Dante is that Frederick treated heresy as a crime against the state, as treason, and assumed all responsibility for it. This view is supported by a comment Benvenuto makes about the emperor, that he tyrannically usurped all spiritual matters, "omnia spiritualia tyrannice usurpavit" (3.443).[61] Fred-

[60]See Ernst Kantorowicz, *Frederick the Second* trans. E. O. Lorimer (1931; reprint, New York: Ungar, 1957) for a comprehensive study of the emperor. In the *Convivio,* Dante calls Frederick the last emperor of the Romans ("ultimo imperadore de li Romani"), 4.3.6.

[61]The passage is worth citing since it deals with the problem of the two powers: "'one has put the other out,' that is, the pope the emperor, and the emperor the pope, as was evident in Frederick II who tyrannically usurped all spiritual things, and Gregory IX, who occupied Frederick's kingdom when he was absent.... It can also be understood especially of Boniface, who girded on his own sword, as was shown above in chapter 6. Therefore he says: 'and he joined the sword,' that is, temporal power, 'with the staff,' that is, with

erick did what Dante objected to most strenuously in the popes, he claimed jurisdiction in the other sphere. He also kept Saracens and Jews as alien groups under his special protection and discouraged efforts to convert them (Kantorowicz, *Frederick the Second* 130–31), instead of extending Christendom, as Dante's ideal monarch would have done. One might expect Dante to condemn Constantine as well, since his ill-conceived gift to the church caused so much of the trouble, but he is in heaven, where he learns what a mistake he made. That act, he now knows, has just about destroyed the world, but his motives were pure (Pr. 20.58–60).

Apart from Frederick and Constantine, and the ineffective emperor Rudolph from Dante's period who is saved, though he did not attempt to restore order to Italy (Pg. 6.103–05,7.94–96), the emperors Dante sees—and they are many—are presented as model figures, while he sees only one model pope, and he was the first.[62] The emperors David and Trajan provide, along with the Virgin, the examples of humility sculpted by

spiritual power, which is represented by the pastoral staff. The poet sees this same thing a little later in Clement V against Henry VI [sic], when the authority of the Gospel testifies that two swords are employed by the Christian empire." Walter Ullmann, *Medieval Papalism* (London: Methuen, 1949), 185, notes that Frederick went further than Innocent in condemning even the suspicion of heresy and in punishing the failure of secular authorities to execute ecclesiastical sentences on heretics. Dante may also have been influenced in his judgment of Frederick by the fact that Frederick allowed his court to be described as an imperial church, "ecclesia imperialis," and himself as a kind of messiah (see Stephany, "Pier della Vigna's Prophecies"). Jacopo (1.219 ff.) tells some interesting anecdotes about Frederick's relations with the church: trying to curb the "mal reggimento" of the "mali pastori," the emperor asked the church to grant him more than one wife and when the cardinals answered with scriptural arguments against it, he pointed out how many wives (churches) they had; on another occasion, the pope, plotting against Frederick, wrote to the Sultan to take advantage of the rebellion of Sicily and Puglia which the pope had fomented, but the Sultan instead told the emperor.

[62]Hadrian, is presented as a figure of greed corrected, Martin as gluttony being purged, Peter of Spain as a scholar, none as a model pope. Gregory is mentioned in both Purgatory and Paradise, but not seen, whereas Trajan, in connection with whom Gregory is mentioned in Pg. 10.75–76, is seen both as a sculpted figure and as a soul in the eye of the eagle (Pr. 20).

God on the first ledge of Purgatory; Justinian is inspired by God to reform the laws of the Roman empire (Pr. 6.11); Solomon is presented as the supreme figure of wisdom (Pr. 10). Of the six souls who represent divine justice in the eye of the Roman eagle, all are secular leaders, two are emperors, three kings, and four lived their lives as non-Christians: David and Hezekiah were Jews, Ripheus and Trajan pagans; only Constantine and William of Sicily were Christians. Trajan, of course, was supposed to have been brought back to life through the prayers of Pope Gregory so he could be baptized and die the second time as a Christian, but he lived and ruled as a pagan. Ripheus was baptized, we are told, by the theological virtues, as if even baptism were available outside the church. In fact, Dante suggests that the church is not essential to salvation, in contradiction to Boniface's claim; not only will those who believed in Christ-to-come be saved, an accepted view, but some who do not now know Christ directly will be closer to him than many who cry "Christ, Christ" (Pr. 19.106 ff.); the Ethiop will condemn such Christians at the Last Judgment.[63]

It is the empire, when the church does not intefere with it, that does God's will on earth; the emperor is the guide who can discern "the tower of the true city" (Pg. 16.96), the horseman who can control human nature with the bridle of law.[64]

[63]This passage may owe something to Christ's words in Matt. 7:21–23: "Non omni qui dicit mihi: Domine, Domine, intrabit in regnum caelorum...." "Not everyone that sayeth to me, Lord, Lord, shall enter into the kingdom of heaven...." On Ripheus's status in the *Comedy*, see above, chapter one, fn. 16.

[64]Pg. 16.94–97; cf. *Convivio*, 4.9.10: "One can almost say of the emperor, wishing to describe his office with an image, that he is the rider of the human will. It is quite clear that that horse goes through the fields without its rider, and especially in poor Italy, which remains without any means for its governing"; in the *Monarchy*, Dante says that human cupidity must be controlled, that men would wander like horses if they were not held back "in camo et freno," "by bit and bridle," 3.16. One wonders if Dante has other passages from the controversy in mind, e.g. Giles, *De ecclesiastica potestate*, 2.6: there are four kinds of power, the lower always serving the higher; the art of making a bridle is not so high as that of using it; the horse is matter on which the

It is the empire that provided the peace into which Christ could be born, the legal setting in which he could be condemned, and the force to avenge that death (Hell 2, Pg. 21, Pr. 6). Henry VII, the divinely ordained emperor who will attempt, but fail, to save Europe, has a place waiting for him in God's rose, while the pope who opposed him, Clement, claiming power God did *not* grant him, is expected in Hell. Those who betrayed the empire, in the person of Julius Caesar, the first emperor, are at the very bottom of Hell, literally in the mouths of Lucifer on either side of Judas, who betrayed Christ; their evil is on a level with the betrayer of Christ and the leader of the rebellion against God. With the three mouths occupied, there is no room for the betrayer of a pope, not because there were none, but because the pope is not on the same level of importance. Only the emperor is God's vicar on earth; the pope is Christ's as priest, but not as ruler.[65]

Such are the main views of church and state that can be extrapolated directly from the *Comedy.* They are quite consistent with Dante's positions in the *Monarchy,* which was written as an overt polemic for the empire: the need for a single monarch to rule the world, the providential choice of the Roman empire as that monarchy, and the separation of church and state, with the secular power dominant in the temporal sphere. Dante's ideal is a world in which the emperor dispenses divine justice and the church dispenses knowledge and the sacraments. This is both a reactionary position, in that it is a return to the apostolic church and the ancient notion of empire, and a radical one, in that it proposes the reduction of power in national monarchies (the only ones with strong gov-

---

knight acts, matter disposed for his action by a bridle; earthly power is to prepare matter so that the ecclesiastical is not impeded in dealing with spiritual things. John of Paris (*De potestate regia et papali,* 19.32), in a discussion of control over the end and the means by which the end is attained, points out that to say man is master of all horses, and therefore of all bridles, does not follow.

[65]See Rivière, *Le Problème,* appendix 6, "Vicarius Dei," 435 ff., and Kantorowicz, *The King's Two Bodies.*

ernments at the time), and a reduction if not abolition of the oldest functioning bureaucracy in the Christian world—the church. In order to convey this message, Dante turns away from the normal form of political debate, the ordered series of logical arguments, and takes up a potentially far more powerful weapon, the poetic vision. He casts the most important images and arguments from the controversy in poetic form where they take on new life: the chariot that becomes a monster before our eyes is far more effective than the statement that a figurative body with two heads would be a monster. And he places them in a setting that gives them the sanction of divine revelation: it is not just Dante who condemns the modern papacy, it is Saint Peter himself, on whom many of its claims were based; it is not Dante who defends the destiny of the Roman empire, it is God who sends the message of divine justice through the Roman eagle.

That Dante's message was not well-received by the church is made clear by the various attacks on it; though they do not always spell out the objections, the attacks do bear witness to the power of the poetry. The Dominican, Guido Vernani, at the beginning of his refutation of the *Monarchy,* takes a lengthy shot at the author's poetry, calling it a poisonous vessel of the father of lies, covered with false and fallacious beauty, by which the author, with poetic phantasms and figments, and the eloquence of his words, his siren songs, fraudulently leads not only the sick and ignorant, but even the learned (studious), to destroy the truth which might save them.[66] The reading or study of "poetic books composed in the vulgate by the one called Dante" was prohibited at the Dominican chapter at

---

[66]See Nevio Matteini, *Il più antico oppositore politico di Dante: Guido Vernani da Rimini, Testo critico del "De reprobatione Monarchiae"* (Padua CEDAM, 1958), 93: Habet enim mendax et perniciosi pater mendacii sua vasa que, in exterioribus honestatis et veritatis figuris fallacibus et fucatis coloribus adornata, venenum continent ... Inter alia vero talia sua vasa quidam fuit multa fantastice poetizans et sophista verbosus, verbis exterioribus in eloquentia multis gratus, qui suis poeticis fantasmatibus et figmentis ... non solum egros animos, sed etiam studiosos dulcibus sirenarum cantibus conducit fraudulenter ad interitum salutifere veritatis.

Santa Maria Novella in Florence in 1335, although it apparently continued to be popular among the *frati;* twenty years later, Jacopo Passavanti, in *Specchio della vera penitenza,* advises against reading worldly poets like Juvenal, Ovid, and Terence, for whom one scribe substituted Dante.[67] In the same period, Dante's poem was used in a political cause: another emperor came from Germany to be crowned in Rome in 1355, Charles of Bohemia, and much was made of Dante's prophecy of the *veltro* in connection with him, though he did not fulfill Ghibelline hopes.[68] A fourteenth-century inquisitor, Nicholas Eymerich, calls the doctrine of Christ's poverty the root of the troubles of his time (Matteini, *Guido Vernani,* 79), a doctrine Dante certainly advocates and which was condemned as heresy by John XXII in 1323, only two years after Dante's death. Cavallari cites a number of contemporary poems, by Dante's son, Pietro, and others, attempting to defend the orthodoxy of his beliefs (44 ff.) and one legend that the Friars Minor, angered by his attack in Paradise 12, tried to have him condemned as a heretic, which he forestalled by setting in terzine the Credo, the Ave Maria, the Pater Noster, the Sacraments and the Commandments (46). Questions had certainly been raised about Dante's orthodoxy. However, it is the political implications of his attacks on the church that seem to be the major irritant. Several passages from the *Comedy* were condemned by the Spanish Inquisition: Hell, 11.8–9, on the heresy of Pope Anastasius; Hell, 19.106–17, on the identification of the whore of the Apocalypse with the corrupt church and the Donation of Constantine; and Paradise, 9.136–42, another attack on the pope and the ecclesiastical hierarchy (Matteini, 48). Although

[67]See Michele Maccarrone, "Dante e i teologi del XIV-XV secolo," *Studi romani* 5 (1957), 20–28, on Guido; on Jacopo, Elisabetta Cavallari, *La fortuna di Dante nel trecento* (Florence: Perrella, 1921), 44.

[68]See Cavallari, *La fortuna di Dante,* 48, who cites the sonnet by Menghino Mezzani attacking the emperor they all thought would be "quel veltro a dar salute a Italia umile/che terra o poltro non dovea cibarlo," "that greyhound to bring salvation to humble Italy, whom earth or dust would not feed," words drawn from the *Comedy,* Hell 1.101–06.

the antipapal views expressed in the *Comedy* troubled many, they also gave the work a special appeal to conciliarists, who had the poem translated into Latin and commented by Giovanni da Serravalle at the Council of Constance (1414).[69]

It was, of course, the *Monarchy* (which was on the papal index from 1554 to 1881) that elicited the strongest and most direct attacks. This was due as much to the part it played in contemporary politics as to its arguments. It apparently influenced the supporters of Ludwig of Bavaria, after whose successful descent into Italy the attacks on the work began in earnest.[70] According to Boccaccio, the *Monarchy* was condemned by Cardinal Beltrando del Poggetto, papal legate of John XXII, because Ludwig had come to Rome against the pope's will and had himself crowned by his own pope using Dante's book in defense of his own authority; Beltrando then had the book condemned and burned for its heretical content ("sì come cose eretiche contenente") and would have done the same to Dante's bones if he had not been stopped.[71] Little attention seems to have been paid the work before the break between Ludwig and Pope John XXII, but afterwards the attacks are frequent: two Franciscans, Guglielmo da Sarzano and Francesco di Meyronnes, writing between 1324 and 1328, do not name Dante but do attack the argument that imperial authority derives directly from God (Maccarrone, "Dante e i teologi,"

[69]Carlo Dionisotti, "Dante nel Quattrocento," *Atti del Congresso Internazionale di Studi Danteschi* (Florence: Sansoni, 1965), 1.335.

[70]For Dante's influence on imperial propaganda, see Richard Scholz, *Unbekannte Kirchenpolitische Streitschriften aus der Zeit Ludwigs des Bayern* (Rome: Loescher, 1911), 254–56. Antonino, bishop of Florence, said Dante's error was spread by William of Ockham, see Cavallari, *La fortuna di Dante,* 42–43.

[71]In the *Vita di Dante,* chapter 26, ed. Bruno Cagli (Rome: Avanzini e Torraca, 1965), 103–04. The same story is told by the jurist Bartolo del Sassoferrato, see Maccarrone, "Dante e i teologi," 20, Matteini, *Guido Verrani,* 32, and Bruno Nardi "La fortuna della *Monarchia,*" *Nel mondo di Dante* (Rome: Istituto grafico Tiberino, 1944), 164, where Nardi notes that Bartolo cites arguments from the *Monarchy* against the bull *Pastoralis cura.* The use of the *Monarchy* by jurists commenting on the Justinian Code is also attested by Cavallari, *La fortuna di Dante,* 67.

23). Several of the errors imputed to Ludwig and his followers by John XXII are Dante's, and various people write about them without naming him but clearly having him in mind.[72] Probably the best known, certainly the most thorough, attack is the direct one by Guido Vernani, *De reprobatione Monarchie composite a Dante,* which rebuts Dante's arguments with little sympathy for the author, usually called "ille homo" (Matteini, *Guido Vernani,* 42). Guido wrote in direct response to Ludwig's conflict with the pope; indeed, it was Guido who announced the excommunication of Ludwig to the city of Rimini and explained the document to the clergy and the people (Matteini, 15). Many years later, in 1400, Guglielmo da Cremona wrote a *Tractatus de iure Monarchie,* turning Dante's thesis upside down to support universal monarchy but under the pope. Discussing the statement that Pilate justly executed Christ, Guglielmo calls its author "that nefarious man," "iste nefarius homo," and suggests that the book, with its author, be publicly consigned to the flames: "unde opus quod super hoc iste edidit, dico libera voce, cum suo autore publice ignibus esse tradendum."[73]

There is no question that Dante takes an extreme stand against secular power and wealth in the church, but Dante had seen what a worldly papacy could do in Italy, where it exercised some temporal power. He knew that by striving for more, well beyond its proper sphere, it had reduced itself to a virtual prisoner and tool of one ruler, thereby disrupting a delicate balance in the secular sphere and destroying its own ability to influence to good. The only way to return the church to the role God ordained for it was to remove it entirely from temporal affairs. To strip it of all temporal wealth and power

[72]See Aldo Vallone, "Il pensiero politico di Dante dinanzi ad A. Trionfi e a G. Vernani da Rimini," *Atti del Convegno Internazionale di Studi Danteschi* (Ravenna: Longo, 1971), 173–201, particularly 191 and 194. Vallone, 187, cites one of the texts given by R. Scholz (*Unbekannte Streitschriften,* 2.113–14), which attacks the idea of God's two vicars, pope and emperor, as heretical, saying "this heretical error seduced many."

[73]Nardi, "La Fortuna," 174–91, particularly 182.

was to restore its spiritual power. In the *Comedy,* even more forcefully than in the *Monarchy,* Dante argues for the empire as the ultimate world government, and for the church as the ultimate spiritual force, but to be such a force, the church must destroy the monster it has become and return to the purity of its origins.

THREE

The Corrupt Society:
Hell

THE PROPER RELATION of individual states (cities or kingdoms) to the empire and the separate and distinct functions of ecclesiastical and secular authority discussed in chapters one and two provide the political framework for the *Comedy.* Within that framework, each cantica presents a different but related model for human society. Paradise is the ideal society in all its essential elements working harmoniously; Purgatory is a society in transition, moving from self-centeredness to concern for and commitment to others, but not yet organized within an effective structure. Hell reveals what society is when all its members act for themselves and against the common good. The souls here are condemned not just for their selfish motivations but also for the effects of their actions on others.[1] Dante's point is that as civic beings, we are responsible not only for our actions, but also for their results. The people he presents were all men and women of prestige and/or power, people in a position to influence others either directly or by example, and in one way or another they all failed. The suffering, the violence, the anarchy of Hell are a result of their failure to act up to their responsibilities or their outright abuse of those responsibilities. Selfishness, greed for money, power, or

[1] W. H. V. Reade, *The Moral System of Dante's Inferno* (1909; reprint, New York: Kennikat, 1969), is so intent on distinguishing God's justice from man's and on showing Aquinas's influence on Dante that he neglects the importance of the effects of human action, which Dante weighs along with the motivation. Allan H. Gilbert, *Dante's Conception of Justice* (1925; reprint, New York: AMS Press, 1965), gives a much better sense of the relation between earthly and divine justice in the *Comedy.*

pleasure, is the basis of the injustice that reigns in Hell, as charity is the basis of the justice that operates in heaven.

Bonaventure and Aquinas name four objects of love or sin: God, ourselves, our neighbors, and our bodies; Dante adds a fifth, our community. It is not that the theologians are not concerned with the effects of our actions on others, but that they are not primarily concerned with the public aspect of those actions, with their consequences for society as an entity.[2] Dante, in contrast, shows how all sins contribute to social disorder, not only the overtly disruptive sins of violence, fraud, and treachery but even those that seem most personal. Lust, gluttony, greed have sociopolitical overtones; even heresy and suicide are presented within a political context. Barratry (graft within the government) is placed in a lower section than simony (graft in the church) because corruption within the state has a greater effect on society; both are treated as aspects of fraud, that is, as social rather than religious sins. Flattery and hypocrisy are lower than robbery and murder (except for murder committed by treachery), not because in themselves Dante considers them more serious sins, but because their effects on society are more insidious and ultimately more damaging. Dante reverses Aquinas's consideration of theft and rob-

[2]For the four objects, see Bonaventure, *Speculum animae*, 3 (*Opera omnia,* vol. 7); Aquinas, ST, 2.2ae, q.25, and 1.2ae q.73, a.9. I do not mean to imply that either of them is not concerned with man's actions in relation to society; on the contrary, Bonaventure says that for a harmonious political life, man must be rightly ordered to society as well as to God and his fellows (*Collationes in Hexaemeron 5*); see also Matthew M. de Benedictis, *The Social Thought of St. Bonaventure* (1946; reprint, Westport: Greenwood, 1972), 28. Aquinas considers a sin against a public person more serious than one against a private person because of the numbers affected, but taken as individuals, not as an entity. Aquinas also recognizes the three orders the individual must respect of reason, of human, and divine law and is concerned with the state as an organ of justice on earth. But he separates political issues from questions of sin, whereas Dante intentionally confuses them, or sets the treatment of sin and virtue in a political context. Brunetto Latini comes closer to Dante in the *Trésor,* Bk. 2, in which he discusses vices and virtues in terms of Aristotle's *Ethics,* and the governing of cities, and notes that pride, envy, etc., lead to enmity and fighting, which disrupt law and destroy cities (2.131.8).

bery: for Aquinas, theft, which is secret, is not as bad as rob-
bery, which is open and violent and does more physical harm
to its victim (ST, 2.2ae, q.66). The secrecy is what makes theft
worse for Dante, since it opens the way to various kinds of
injustice, like the incrimination of the innocent, and threatens
economic stability in a much graver way. For Aquinas, blas-
phemy is also worse than murder or theft because it is a direct
attack on God (ST, 1.2ae, q.73, a.3), but Dante places blas-
phemy in the seventh circle, theft far below it in the seventh
section of the eighth circle.[3]

The most serious sins for Dante are those that deny the trust
on which social and political relations are based—fraud and
treachery. Although treachery is the worst of all because of the
special relation between "perpetrator" and victim, fraud is the
one that occupies Dante's attention. He devotes thirteen cantos
(from 18 to 30) to it, more than a third of Hell, and he subdi-
vides it into ten different sections. It is not unusual to subdivide
sins; the capital vices are normally discussed in terms of the
sins they spawn.[4] But Dante differs in two ways from others
who make the distinctions: (1) he presents the first five sins
without any real subdivisions, (2) he moves into three sins
which would normally be offshoots of others, violence, fraud,
and treachery, and subdivides them, violence into three sec-
tions (the second with two parts, the third with three), fraud
into ten (the tenth with four parts), and treachery into four. By
introducing all these complexities, he is clearly calling atten-
tion to these sins, forcing us to shift the emphasis from the
traditional moral view of greed and pride as the worst of evils
to the more sociopolitical distinctions of violence, fraud, and
treachery. The cantica seems to draw more from legal codes

[3]The social implications explain all the differences between Dante and Aqui-
nas, which G. Busnelli lists, *L'Etica Nicomachea e l'ordinamento morale
dell'Inferno di Dante* (Bologna: Zanichelli, 1907), 153: for Aquinas, neutrality,
heresy, blasphemy, suicide are worse; for Dante, theft, lying, hypocrisy, bad
counsel.

[4]Bonaventure, Aquinas, Vincent of Beauvais, Brunetto Latini all deal with
sin this way.

than manuals on vice; several of the punishments, particularly in the eighth circle, are based on contemporary penal codes. The very concept of Dante's Hell peopled with sinners well known to Dante's audience may itself be a reflection of the contemporary practice of painting the portraits of certain criminals on the walls of public buildings.[5]

Dante emphasizes the political message of Hell in other ways as well. One is the identification of specific places with sins. I suggested above in chapter one that Florence is presented as the central sinner throughout the cantica, but that in the lower parts of Hell other cities or regions of Italy share the stage; two classical cities, Thebes and Troy, also echo through Hell as emblems of self-destructiveness and pride. Rivers are often used to identify cities and regions, suggesting the spread of corruption from one place to another,[6] and Dante uses dialect words particularly in the *Malebolge* to suggest the atmosphere of different regions. A more subtle way, perhaps, of underlining the interdependence of men in society is Dante's placing members of the same family in different parts of Hell (and in other cantiche for contrast). In a malfunctioning society, sinners seem to lead even their relatives into sin: the Navarrese barrator Dante sees in canto 22 is the son of a wastrel, the implication being that wasting oneself or one's goods leads naturally to abusing the government, which is an extension of the self. Michel Zanche, another barrator, was killed by his son-in-law, who appears among the traitors to guests in the ninth circle, as though the deception of one's fellow citizens by the subversion of government led to the betrayal of still closer bonds. The bishop, Ruggieri, among the traitors, is a nephew of Cardinal Ottaviano, who is mentioned with the her-

[5]See R. Davidsohn, *Storia di Firenze, I primordi della civiltà fiorentina: impulsi interni, influssi esterni e cultura politica* (Italian trans. Eugenio Dupré-Theseider), 5.598.

[6]See Hell 15.113, 20.73 ff., 21.49, 23.95, 27.30,49,52, 30.65, 32.26,27,56, 33.83; cf. Pg. 14.24, 92, 16.115. The Arno is the river most frequently cited, but it is by no means the only one.

etics, implying that the lack of faith in eternity facilitates the betrayal of faith to other men.[7]

In every way, Dante tries to show that we are responsible not only for our own actions, but for the effects they have on others; we are responsible not only for our own salvation, but for the good of our fellows. Dante moves in Hell from vices which seem to be personal and simple (although complications are revealed in them) to more and more overtly social faults. The victims become more numerous, from single individuals to large groups and even whole nations; the simple impulse to sin is replaced by the more complex manipulation of that impulse in others. We see the corrupt society built up from its basic element—the self-indulgent individual—and when we reach the center, we discover that the lowest sinner is not so different from the souls in the upper circles: Ugolino's story echoes Francesca's in many ways because the love that is dominated by lust can be as destructive to its object as hatred. For Dante, individual morality cannot be dissociated from social responsibility because the individual is a citizen, and to be a good individual, he must be a good citizen. Thus, to retrace the moral journey of the pilgrim through Hell, Purgatory, and Paradise, is to follow the journey of the citizen from a corrupt society, through the transition from selfishness to social responsibility, to his goal in the ideal society. The moral level of Dante's allegory is also the political level because it is impossible to be a moral human being without being a good citizen, and it is difficult to be either a good citizen or a moral person in a bad society. In Hell, Dante leads his pilgrim-persona step by step through a knowledge of what constitutes a corrupt society and a corrupt person and shows how even a basically good individual can be affected by the evil around

[7]Dante also uses families for contrast: Frederick II is in Hell, his son, Manfredi, in Purgatory, his mother, Costanza, in Paradise; Forese Donati is in Purgatory, his sister, Piccarda, in Paradise, his brother, Corso, destined for Hell; Guido da Montefeltro is in Hell, his son, Bonconte, in Purgatory; Ubaldino is in Purgatory, his son, Ruggieri, in Hell; Ezzelino da Romano is in Hell, his sister, Cunizza, in Paradise.

him. By analyzing the structure of Hell, investigating each region in the order in which the pilgrim goes through it, since each sin has political implications, we can see how Dante reveals the hidden corruption that undermines society and how he unmasks the respected public figures. By the end, Dante's audience should understand what constitutes evil in a society as well as in an individual and be able to see the part we play in the evil around us.

The first point Dante makes in Hell is his own social responsibility. The pilgrim begins outside society in the woods,[8] alone, severed from all human connections, as Dante found himself in exile, banned under pain of death, cut off from his family, his city, and any public function. The inner man on his own is threatened by vice (the three animals), particularly greed (the wolf)[9] as the outer man is endangered by the enmity of Florence and the papacy (see chapter one). Aid comes in the form of a man who has all the public connections and purpose Dante lacks. Virgil is a poet, a Roman who served the highest form of political society, the empire, with his poetry. He must prepare Dante to become like him, a Roman and a poet of the empire. He is the first character in the *Comedy* to speak and he identifies himself by region, city, period, government, and role, bringing the poem abruptly from the moral allegorical into the real historical sphere. He was a Lombard, from Man-

---

[8]The wood is this life, both as Augustine describes it, an immense forest of traps and dangers (*Confessions* 10.35), and as the romance hero encounters it when he goes off into the wilderness to seek adventures, trials which test and perfect him so that he can return to society and serve it properly.

[9]The wolf is connected with greed throughout the *Comedy*, particularly clerical greed, see Hell 7.8, Pg. 20.10, Pr. 9.132, 27.55. Benvenuto da Imola, discussing the prophecy of the *veltro*, notes that if the author intends it to be a Roman prince, the avarice he will oppose is that of prelates and pastors of the church, in whom avarice has its source, continually increasing, 1.57. I prefer to follow the early commentators who gloss the three animals as lust, pride, and avarice, as befits the moral allegory of the inner man in the first canto (see Pietro, 32 ff., Guido, 9, the Ottimo, 1.6, Benvenuto, 1.38–40; Jacopo gives vainglory for the *lonza*, but agrees on the other two, 1.109). At the same time, the animals suggest Florence and Rome, as mentioned in chapter one, and therefore also have a political meaning for the public man.

tova, born under the emperor who formed and spread the empire, Julius Caesar;[10] he lived under Augustus, who established the peace in which Christ was to be born, and he sang of the "just" Aeneas, who brought the seeds of that empire to Italy. Virgil connects himself with the origin and high moments of the empire, and provides all the social identifications Dante so far lacks: nationality, citizenship, public function as poet. Virgil also prophesies the figure who will kill the wolf and send it back to Hell, the restoration of empire and reform of church (as Dante eventually learns, see chapter two), in which Dante's poem is to play an important role. Virgil will show Dante the way through Hell and Purgatory, but not to Paradise, not to the ideal society, because he was a rebel to God's law. The language of the outlawed rebel associates Virgil with Dante, who is historically in that position when he writes the poem, although he was not when the poem is supposed to take place. But Dante is in rebellion only against an unjust government of man, Virgil against the law of God: "quello imperador che là sù regna/perch'io fui ribellante a la sua legge,/non vuol che in sua città per me si vegna" (1.124–26: "that emperor who reigns there will not allow any to enter his city through me, because I was a rebel to his law"). Virgil recognizes the authority of God and the rule of law with a metaphor drawn from the highest secular authority; this statement establishes from the very beginning of Hell that however attractive a soul in Hell may be, he or she is in rebellion against God's law. Virgil began his speech with the Roman empire on earth; he ends it with the empire in heaven, making a connection between the two which Dante will carry through the poem, reinforced by the souls in Paradise. The last to make the

[10]Benvenuto comments that Virgil was really born under consuls, not under Julius Caesar, and claims Dante intentionally has him change that fact because Virgil admires Caesar and prefers to derive his origin from his reign, 1.45–46. For a detailed study of Dante's treatment of Virgil and his poetry in the *Comedy*, see Robert Hollander, *Il Virgilio Dantesco: Tragedia nella "Commedia"* (Florence: Olschki, 1983), and Teodolinda Barolini, *Dante's Poets: Textuality and Truth in the "Comedy"* (Princeton: Princeton University, forthcoming).

poem, reinforced by the souls in Paradise. The last to make the connection is Bernard, who points out at the end of the journey the main figures of "this most just and pious empire" (Pr. 32.117: "questo imperio giustissimo e pio"), recalling in his adjectives the hero of Virgil's poem.

It is because Virgil is a poet and Dante is a poet that heaven sent Virgil to guide Dante; his "parola ornata" will move Dante as Dante's must move his audience. What Dante does not recognize when he hesitates ("I am not Aeneas, I am not Paul," Hell 2.32), is that as the poet of the Christian empire, he has the same mission as Aeneas and Paul, as the state and the church. The allusions to their journeys establish certain important points. Aeneas is described in the first canto as the son of Anchises who came from Troy (1.74); in the second, he is the father of Silvio, Aeneas's son by Lavinia, the first Trojan born in Italy of an Italian race. God, the "enemy of all evil" (2.16)—God is always the enemy in Hell, as the emperor is in corrupt societies on earth—grants Aeneas the journey to the otherworld because of the "high effect" that is to proceed from him. He was chosen by heaven to be the father of Rome and of its empire (2.20–21), which was established as the seat of the papacy, "the holy place where the successor of the greatest Peter sits" (2.22–24). The empire had to prepare the way for the church. Long after Aeneas, Paul, also chosen by heaven, the "vas d'elezione," made his journey to the otherworld, but his mission was spiritual. What Aeneas learned in Hell was the cause of his victory and also of the papal mantle (2.26–27); what Paul learned in heaven supported the faith that leads to salvation (2.29–30). The temporal institution of the church depends not on Paul but on Aeneas's heirs, which is why Dante takes fifteen lines to describe the reasons for Aeneas's journey and only three for Paul's. It is perhaps a coincidence, but the sort that would have assured Dante of the correctness of his position, that there is an Aeneas in the same chapter of the Acts of the Apostles in which Paul's conversion is described and in which Paul is called the "vas electionis" (Acts 9:15). This Aeneas is a man who has lain in bed with palsy for eight years,

but Peter cures him saying, "Aeneas, the lord Jesus Christ heal-
eth thee; arise, and make thy bed" (9:34). Can Dante have failed
to understand this as meaning that the Christian faith restored
the empire? Dante's mission, like Paul's, will be to spread the
truth, to reform and restore both empire and church.

The first lesson Dante learns towards this mission after he
enters Hell is the importance of making a commitment, the
first step in social action; the neutrals, men and angels who
never took sides, never made a public commitment.[11] Their
failure is *viltade* (3.60), a baseness of spirit like Dante's hesi-
tation (2.45), which is not humility, but a denial of God's gifts,
a lack of courage to accept one's responsibilities. The neutrals
lived for themselves alone, refusing to choose either good or
evil and are therefore scorned by both heaven and hell, by
mercy and justice (3.50) because they have done nothing to
merit either. Cut off from all recognized human and divine
laws, they are men without a country; the world has forgotten
them (3.49), heaven and hell will not receive them. It is worse
in Dante's view to take no part at all in civic life than to take
the wrong part. Among them, Dante recognizes "the one who
made the great refusal" (3.59–60: "colui/che fece per viltade il
gran rifiuto"). Most early commentators take this to be Celes-
tine V, whose abdication left the papacy to Boniface VIII, one
of the major villains of the *Comedy*.[12] It is quite possible that

[11]The neutral angels are an apocryphal concept, but effective in making
Dante's point. For a discussion of the issue, see John Freccero, "Dante's *Per Se*
Angels: The Middle Ground in Nature and in Grace," *Studi danteschi* 39
(1962), 5–38.

[12]See the Ottimo, 1.30, Guido, 59, Jacopo, 1.131, and Pietro, 69. Pietro does
not accept the notion that Celestine had to retire from the world to lead a holy
life ("he could be as holy and spiritual in the papacy as in a hermitage") and
says that he acted "pusillanimously" in renouncing the papacy. In a later recen-
sion, he expresses some doubts about Celestine and suggests that the figure
might be Diocletian or Develicianus, who renounced the empire (V/S 80, 81).
Benvenuto, who denies the identification, admits that Celestine's renunciation
was generally attributed to "great baseness," but insists that Dante could not
have meant Celestine because he was "magnanimus" before, during, and after
the papacy, though he notes that Celestine was unable to keep the incorrigible

Dante does not name the figure because for him all those who refuse to act when called upon deny their own identities; the point is not just what you fail to do, but what you open the way to by your denial of responsibility.

There is one group of souls in Hell who chose good action, the inhabitants of Limbo, but they too failed in one crucial respect. They did not acknowledge the existence of God and therefore their action was not directed to his purpose. The moral life alone is not sufficient, it must serve the creation of the perfect society according to the divine plan. In every other respect, the three groups of virtuous pagans Dante sees together constitute an almost ideal society: the poets, who taught others the highest values and who accept Dante as one of them; the great spirits, who sacrificed themselves for country or principle; and the philosophers, who sought the truth. The last include moral and theological writers, scientists, and commentators; together they represent all aspects of human knowledge, but that is not sufficient to save them or to enable them to succeed. In the sun, Dante will see, side by side, philosophers who took opposing views now completing the figure of perfection, the circle, because they were all motivated by faith. The society of Limbo is peaceful, the only harmonious community in Hell, but it lacks joy because it lacks the deepest motivation for the good society, the salvation of its citizens. Of the four roles Dante recognizes in civil life (see Pr. 8.124–26), craftsmen (and intellectuals), lawgivers (and statesmen), warriors, and priests, Limbo lacks the priests.

Beyond Limbo, Dante sees souls who felt no responsibility outside themselves; the next three sections of Hell are devoted to different kinds of selfish action: lust, gluttony, greed. But Dante makes it clear that the self is not the only victim. The circle of lust is filled with figures of great social responsibility, queens and princes, who chose indulgence of their passions over duty to their peoples. The queens are given a lot of atten-

cardinals from their simony and other cupidity, 1.117–18. Busnelli, *L'Etica*, 21, comments that the problem with the renunciation is the evil that came with Boniface's election.

tion by the early commentators, particularly Benvenuto da Imola, who details their great deeds as rulers as well as their vices (1.194 ff.). Semiramis twists the laws in order to cover her own guilt: "libito fé licito in sua legge" (5.56: "she made her libido licit in her law"), as if by changing a word she could obliterate morality, an attitude that is particularly disturbing in a guardian of the law. The next three queens were not only self-indulgent but also obstacles in one way or another to the Roman empire: Dido, who killed herself for love, leaving her land and people unprotected, also held Aeneas back temporarily from founding his dynasty in Italy; Cleopatra, also a suicide, had affairs with Caesar and Marc Antony which complicated the course of empire in her time; and Helen's affair with Paris caused the destruction of Troy, the old Rome. The only men named are Achilles, Paris, and Tristan, all princes: Achilles died ignominiously fighting over love, Paris and Tristan both stole the wives of kings, one of his host, the other of his uncle, and their affairs led to serious trouble for their countries. The violence such love engenders, spreading the effects of self-indulgence well beyond the immediate actors, is part of the responsibility they must now bear for their sin, which in life interfered with their fulfilling their assigned obligations as leaders of their people.[13]

The next stage of self-indulgence is to satisfy the body without even the excuse of a nobler impulse, simply to feed it as an animal does. Gluttony is so completely centered on the physical senses that it becomes virtually impossible for the gluttonous individual to give of himself, even with words, to others. This self-indulgence leads to a self-absorption that necessarily interferes with social exchange. The gluttons lose the power to act or to communicate with others. Dante finds it very dif-

[13]Dante also condemns himself to some extent in this section through identification with Francesca and her exploitation of noble-sounding lyric conventions; he too engaged in the selfish and self-deceptive aspects of the love tradition about which he began to have doubts as early as the *Vita Nuova*. By the *Comedy*, he has come to see his role in that tradition as antisocial rather than ennobling.

ficult to get anything out of them; he has to keep coaxing "tell me, tell me": "Ma dimmi chi tu sei," 6.46, "ma dimmi, se tu sai," 6.60, "e dimmi la cagione," 6.62, "dimmi ove sono," 6.82, "ancor vo' che mi'nsegni/e che di più parlar mi facci dono" (6.77–78: "I still want you to instruct me and make me a gift of more speech"). But always the soul stops before Dante is satisfied: "e più non fé parola," 6.57, "qui puose fine," 6.76; and finally the soul declares "più non ti dico e più non ti rispondo" (6.90: "I tell you no more and I answer you no more"), and falls back with the others.

For a city as for a man, overfeeding is self-destructive; more wealth and power than it can handle will first disrupt its natural processes and then destroy it. Florence, which is the subject of Dante's conversation with the glutton, and the way the soul first identifies himself, suffers from political gluttony, which is both greed and envy: "la tua città, ch'è piena/d'invidia sì che già trabocca il sacco" (6.49–50: "your city, which is so full of envy that its sack overflows"), an image echoed in Purgatory, 20.73–75, where Florence's paunch, presumably overstuffed, is burst by the lance of Charles.[14] Even its best men are flawed: all the Florentines Dante asks about, "who were so worthy," are lower down in Hell, and only two just men are left in the city, an allusion to Gen. 18:23 ff. where Abraham attempts to save Sodom on the basis of the just men in it and cannot find even ten.[15] As in Ezek. 14:14, the sins of the world

[14]Louis R. Rossi, "The Devouring Passion, *Inferno* VI," *Italica* 42 (1965), 24, making a connection with Paradise, 27.106–10, comments that the breakdown of the moral organism is an effect of the dissolution of the social order, and the fault lies with the leaders. He also notes that there are covert allusions to Corso Donati and Charles of Valois in Hell 6, and that Corso comes up again on the ledge of gluttony in Purgatory 24, where the destruction of his body and the ruin of his city are discussed, 26–28.

[15]Benvenuto says the two just men are Guido Cavalcanti and Dante (1.236), although Dante gives no hint of this; in Purgatory, 16.121, Dante suggests there are only three just men left in the whole region of Lombardy. Early commentators try to place all the other men Dante asks Ciacco about: the Ottimo has Tegghiaio, Jacopo, and Arrigo in canto 16, Mosca in 29 (1.100); Benvenuto puts Theghiaius and Jacobus among sins against nature, Musca and Arrigus

are such that even the best men, Noah, Daniel, and Job, could only save themselves. The implication is that a modicum of virtue can stem the corruption of society, but the corruption of Florence is so great that its good men cannot save it.

Greed and gluttony are aspects of the same impulse, the amassing of more material than can be used. Like food, material wealth was intended by God to serve men's needs, but misuse of wealth is potentially harmful to one's fellows. What the miser hoards cannot serve others' needs. Fortune, which Dante the pilgrim sees as a monster holding the goods of the world in its "claws" (7.69), is in fact a minister of God, ordained to supervise the transmission of worldly goods and power from one people to another as well as from one family to another (7.73 ff.). In other words, the distribution of worldly goods and power seems random to man because he cannot understand it and wrongly blames fortune (7.91–93), but it follows a divine plan, whereas the action of misers and prodigals on earth and in Hell, in their continuous semicircles, seems ordered, but is really futile or worse, because it runs counter to providence.[16] Thus greed, on the personal or public level, is a serious social sin for Dante because it interferes with the proper functioning of government and of providence. It is not accidental that the group Dante concentrates on in this section is identified by their tonsures; they are all churchmen, whose function was to give, not to possess, and to teach others the vanity of earthly goods.[17] They substituted the things of this earth for heaven in

among sins against others, while Farinata sinned against the faith (1.238). Farinata, Tegghiaio, and Jacopo all question Dante about life in Florence when he meets them. Unfortunately, no one identifies Arrigo, though Pietro calls him Arrigus de Arrigucijs (V/S, 129); the point may be that everyone knows some Arrigo who belongs in Hell.

[16]Boethius, in the *Consolation of Philosophy*, defends Fortune's acts as beneficial to those she abandons, but he does not see her as a positive force; Dante himself presents different views of fortune: as random chance, *Convivio*, 4.11, as the fate of an individual, Pr. 8.139, and as providence, Pr. 27.145 and *Monarchy*, 2.9. For connections between fortune and history in Dante, see Giuseppe Mazzotta, *Dante, Poet of the Desert* (Princeton: Princeton University, 1979), Appendix.

[17]The tonsure on their heads and the broken circle they form in their move-

their own desires, a particularly serious sin in a cleric, who is supposed to reject temporal goods, but a common one, as Benvenuto notes (1.255–56) and as Dante stresses throughout the *Comedy*.

Dante follows a logical progression in sinful impulses from the indulgence of natural physical desires for sex and food to the indulgence of desires for less natural, but still necessary, goods like wealth, which is essential to social existence. The more the sins are centered on the self, the more hostile they render the individual to others. The glutton is only noncommunicative, the miser is aggressive. The rage that begins to surface in the circle of greed in the accusing shouts of the souls, but without a specific object, erupts in the next three circles against very specific objects, other people, the self, and God. It bursts out like the stream that has boiled underground but pours forth into the Styx (7.100–08). As we learn later, all the rivers of Hell are connected, just as tendencies to sin are connected, so the Styx must flow underground from the Acheron; in other words, wrath is latent in all the sins of self-indulgence, but after greed it comes to the surface and finds its object in another being. In the upper circles, the sins and sinners are wrapped up in themselves; from wrath down, there is much more interaction between the souls and between them and Dante. Filippo Argenti, who was a political enemy of Dante's, a Black and a member of the family which received Dante's confiscated goods after his exile, attacks Dante as he approaches the city, eliciting a fierce reaction from the pilgrim with Virgil's approval.[18] What Dante exhibits, in contrast to

---

ment may both be reflections of the wheel of Fortune, whose turning they have obstructed and which operates as an instrument of providence. Dante lures the reader into making the same mistake they did with the line "mal dare e mal tener lo mondo pulcro" (7.58), which seems to mean "the bad giving and holding of the beautiful world" until the first three words of the next line, "ha tolto lor," corrects that impression; "the beautiful world" becomes the object of *tolto* rather than of *dar* and *tener,* that is, their bad giving and holding robbed them of the beautiful world, which we now understand to be heaven, not this earth.

[18]Landino, cited by Natalino Sapegno, in his notes to his edition, *La Divina*

the soul's unprovoked hostility, is righteous indignation, a mean between the extremes of wrath and sloth, both of which are socially harmful: wrath strikes out wildly in any direction, sloth rejects action and turns inward, while proper anger, when guided by reason (Virgil), upholds the cause of good against its enemies.[19] Filippo's wrath is a threat to his society; Dante's is essential to its proper functioning. Dante consciously aligns himself with divine justice and against the attacking soul, making it clear, as he has not before, that he is an alien in Hell.

This change in Dante's attitude heralds a change in the entire presentation. The scene is dramatic, with a much larger cast of active characters than has been seen heretofore, and the atmosphere is much more overtly civic. Beginning with the exchange of signals between towers, which suggests a hostile setting, the approach of an alien, perhaps an enemy, as Benvenuto notes (1.275–76), we are aware of entering a more structured, more complicated organization than Dante has encountered before, indeed a city. In the earlier circles, there were guards who objected ineffectually to his presence. Now there is sophisticated communication among beings he cannot see. He is about to enter the inner city of Hell, the city of Dis, "wealth," in which greed dominates, with its *gravi cittadin*— the serious citizens of Hell—its "army" of devils, and its mosques, a city of infidels whose citizens work to deceive and exploit each other. Dante and Virgil enter this city as hostile aliens, although Virgil is himself an inhabitant of Hell, a fellow countryman from a different region, so to speak; for

Commedia (Milan: Ricciardi, 1957), 98. Fiorenzo Forti, in his article on Filippo in the *Enciclopedia Dantesca,* 2.873–74, reports that Filippo's brother, claiming offenses by Dante, received Dante's confiscated goods as a concession from the commune, and henceforth, according to Benvenuto, opposed Dante's return to Florence. Forti also notes that the *Chiose Selmi* related a quarrel between Filippo and Dante in which Filippo slapped the poet.

[19]Cf. Aquinas on kinds of anger, deserving of praise if in accord with right reason, whereas unreasonable patience can be the hotbed of many vices (ST, 2.2ae, q.158, a.1).

Dante, the experience is one he lived in his own life, an alien everywhere but in Florence, where he was an unwanted outlaw. If the devils who guard the city gates represent corrupt churchmen, as suggested in chapter two, it is clear why Dante sees them as dangerous enemies; in any case, fallen angels are rebels who try to close the city to representatives of the true emperor, God, just as Florence, with the church's support, closed its gates to Henry and to Dante. Dante perhaps will be the divine messenger who with a seemingly small weapon, his poem, like the angel's wand, will open them again. The action of the fallen angels is, of course futile; they cannot shut this gate against the divine will. Their whole rebellion won them only the loss of heaven, not even the control of their own domain, which, like the Italian cities that defy the emperor, is filled with chaos and self-destructive violence. The angel who brings divine help asks the devils why they bother to resist a will that cannot be thwarted, an action which can only increase their pains, 9.94–96. That is an important question for Dante and the reader to ponder before entering the lower circles where the sins are a conscious and continuous affirmation of evil and rejection of God, but it is also a reminder to Florence that, however successful it may be at thwarting the emperor temporarily, the divine will must ultimately prevail on earth as in Hell.[20]

The city of Dis is the core of the corrupt society. Inside it, Dante concentrates on four large categories of sin, those which are the most socially destructive: (1) heresy, the limited or distorted truth, which prevents acceptance of the larger truth and kills the soul, is the equivalent of factionalism in politics, the narrow view that destroys the body politic; (2) violence, the flouting of the most basic natural laws which rule men in their relations with others, with themselves, and with God; (3) fraud, the willful deception of others in order to exploit them; and

[20]Robert Hollander pointed out to me that the source of the storm simile which heralds the angel's appearance in canto 9 is the storm simile in *Aeneid* 2.416 ff., which precedes the destruction of another proud city, Troy.

CORRUPT SOCIETY

(4) betrayal, the willful and harmful deception of those to whom one owes a special kind of loyalty.

Heresy was intimately associated with politics for Dante's audience: Frederick II had condemned and executed heretics as traitors to the state; an inquisitor in Florence condemned Farinata and his wife as heretics posthumously in 1283 because of the fierce hatred inspired by Farinata's part in the defeat at Montaperti; and Pope John XXII instigated trials for heresy against his political enemies, like Matteo and Galeazzo Visconti, Can Grande, and Federico da Montefeltro.[21] In Hell, Dante uses the charge of heresy not as a political weapon, but as a symbol of political factionalism. The souls he concentrates on are Epicureans, a sect which indulges the body and denies the immortality of the soul;[22] politically, these souls deny the larger reality of empire or even city in order to indulge the smallest segment, their party. Each heretical sect has its own quarter in Dante's Hell, emphasizing the narrowness and factionalism, the refusal to see beyond one's own obsession, whether in religion or in politics, and the heretics are condemned not just in themselves, but in their followers, for whom they are responsible. They are buried along with those they misled, a point that is carefully made twice (9.128 and 10.14) and emphasized by the word which first identifies them, *eresïarche* (9.127), meaning leaders of sects or groups of heretics.

[21]See N. Ottokar, "La condanna postuma di Farinata degli Uberti," *Archivio storico italiano* 77 (1919), 155–63, on Farinata. For the other trials, see Nicolai Rubinstein, "Studies on the Political History of the Age of Dante," *Atti del Congresso internazionale di studi danteschi* (Florence: Sansoni, 1965), 1.227, and Friedrich Bock, "I processi di Giovanni XXII contro i Ghibellini delle Marche," *Bullettino dell'Istituto Storico Italiano per il Medio Evo* 57 (1941), 19–68. According to Davidsohn, *Storia di Firenze,* 5.609, the remains of heretics were exhumed and their tombs defaced, which may also be behind Dante's presentation of them in open tombs.

[22]See Joseph A. Mazzeo, "Dante and Epicurus," *Comparative Literature* 10 (1958), 106–20, for contemporary views of the Epicureans. According to Aquinas (ST, 2.2ae, q.11), a heretic is one who picks and chooses what he wishes to believe.

There is a suggestion that Dante is himself vulnerable to this kind of factionalism, both in the fear he feels when Farinata addresses him and in the accusation implicit in Farinata's words, "La tua loquela ... ," (10.25), which echo the words spoken to Peter before he denies his connection with Christ (Matt. 26:73). Dante will, in fact, be led to deny his true loyalties to the imperial side in response to Farinata's attack. Farinata feels a deep loyalty to Florence, "quella nobil patrïa," so strong still that it elicits a rare (for Hell) statement of regret: "to which I was perhaps too hostile" (10.27: "a la qual forse fui troppo molesto"), a reference to his part in the battle at Montaperti, where the exiled Florentine Ghibellines fought with Siena against Florence. That love for Florence was strong enough while he was alive to make him oppose alone the destruction of Florence, (10.91–93: "fu'io solo ... colui che la difesi a viso aperto"), but it is not strong enough to overcome his loyalty to party, and it leads him into an exchange with Dante, his countryman, that is painful to both of them. Benvenuto comments that the Florentines are worse partisans than any other people in Italy (1.346: "Florentini sunt magis partifices quam alius populus Italiae"). Ironically, Farinata's attack on Dante's family forces Dante to identify with the Guelphs as a party, which in Farinata's time was the church party, although Dante is in fact a White Guelph and therefore, like Farinata, of the imperial party. As in most factional disputes, they hurt each other to no purpose: Dante tells Farinata that the Ghibellines never returned to Florence, and Farinata counters with a prophecy of Dante's exile. And both of them, in their zeal to attack each other, ignore the feeling of their fellow Florentine. Farinata's neighbor in the next tomb, Cavalcanti, is closely connected with him not only by the sin they share and their native city, but also by the marriage of their children, a union arranged to end enmity between the two factions; yet each is so wrapped up in his own obsession that he is completely impervious to the other's. And Dante, the third Florentine, bound to both, to Farinata by love of Florence and the imperial cause, to Cavalcanti as the father of Dante's close friend and fellow poet, Guido,[23] is so preoccupied with his own concerns that he manages to wound both of them, one with political taunts, the other with a comment about his son.[24] He strikes them in two loyalties, to party and to family, which can most obstruct the higher loyalty to country. Cavalcanti, a member of an important commercial family, may also represent the class that put its financial interest ahead of the needs of the city or the country, another aspect of factionalism quite prevalent in Dante's world (see below, chapter six).

Dante suggests the responsibility of church and empire to save mankind from the effects of factionalism by mentioning only two others among the more than a thousand souls who lie with Farinata and Cavalcanti: the emperor Frederick II, and "the Cardinal." Both were eminent leaders, men with great social responsibility to others and spiritual responsibility to God, whose vicars they were, but both denied the existence of God or eternity and pursued their personal ambitions to the detriment of their larger obligations. The cardinal, Ottaviano, is reputed to have said, "My soul, if it exists, I have lost for the Ghilbellines"; the emperor is supposed to have made a similar remark: "If I had one foot in Paradise, I would withdraw it to take revenge on Viterbo."[25] Frederick also engaged in discussions on points of faith and in experiments to test the life of the soul after death, and he persecuted heretics as threats to

[23]Cavalcanti's son, Guido, was apparently also involved in factional struggles; Dino Compagni describes a feud in which both he and Corso Donati were involved *Cronica,* ed. Gino Luzzato (Turin: Einaudi, 1968), 1.21.

[24]Dante's error was in assuming that Farinata and Cavalcanti were aware of the present, a natural mistake since they know the future. The irony is that the present, which was all they cared for or believed in, is the one thing now denied them; at the end of time, when there is no future and all is present in eternity—the one present they did not acknowledge—their knowledge will be altogether dead, "tutta morta." Their perception of time is yet another indication of the limitations of factionalism; concentrating on the immediate, the local, they fail to comprehend the larger context.

[25]The cardinal's remark is cited by both the Ottimo (1.192: "se anima è, io l'ho perduta per li Ghibellini") and Guido (200); the emperor's is cited by Ernst Kantorowicz, *Frederick the Second* trans. E. O. Lorimer (1931; reprint, New York: Ungar, 1957), 352.

imperial power, so there is a certain poetic justice to his loca-
tion in Hell.[26] The only other heretic Dante mentions is a pope
whose tomb' he sees in a different section of heresy. The pope
is Anastasius, who was thought not to have believed in the
divine nature of Christ; in fact, medieval tradition confused the
pope with an emperor of the same name who was actually
the heretic, but it is important for Dante's view to balance the
emperor Frederick with a pope.[27] It is bad enough for the
emperor, God's regent, to reject God, but it is shocking when
the highest placed guardian of the faith falls into heresy
instead of guarding others from it.

Dante focuses our attention on the special nature of the
other sins inside Dis by breaking his narrative pattern before
he leaves the circle of heresy and devoting the better part of a
canto (11) to a discussion of the sins of the last three circles of
Hell. Pietro comments that this canto is in some ways like a
gloss of the whole cantica: "hoc capitulum . . . quodammodo
est glosa totius hujus libri Inferni" (136). This is an unusual
pause in the poem, the only purely didactic, nondramatic canto
in Hell. It is made partly because the lower sins are compli-
cated by subdivisions, and Dante the pilgrim, like the reader,
must be prepared in order to understand them properly; but
also because Dante the author is about to make a break with
traditional presentations of sin, and he is calling attention to
that. The sins he presented outside the walls of Dis are among

[26] Guido repeats the story of Frederick asking how the soul of a man who
was enclosed in a vat to die could escape (200). Dante's positive and negative
views of Frederick were discussed in chapter two. Giovanni Villani, *Istorie
Fiorentine* (Milan: Società Tipografica dei Classici Italiani, 1802), also praises
Frederick for his wisdom and valor, but calls him an enemy of the church,
who led an "epicurean" life with no thought to the next life (6.1), and describes
his part in Florence's factional squabbles (6.33).

[27] The early commentators accept the identification of the pope as the here-
tic. Bruno Nardi, *Nuova Lectura Dantis: Il canto XI dell'Inferno* (1951;
reprint, Rome: Signorelli, 1955), discusses the historical confusion. He shows
that Dante followed Gratian's *Decretum*, making Pope Anastasius an adherent
of the Acacian heresy, presumably because he had favorably received the dea-
con of the eastern church, who did follow the heresy.

the standard capital vices: lust, gluttony, greed, wrath, which in Dante's Hell also have political overtones. Heresy, which is inside, is treated more as a political than as a theological problem. The remaining sins are presented, with some reference to Aristotelian categories, essentially as sins against society, sins against others within a social context: violence, fraud, treachery. Pietro remarks, apropos of violence, that if man were a solitary animal, the double order of reason and divine law would suffice, but since he is a political and social animal, as Aristotle says in the *Politics*, there must be a third order by which men are ordered to other men, hence violence is divided into three sections (140).

The Aristotelian distinction serves mainly to divide the lower sins of malice from those of incontinence, which are outside the city of Dis. Whether the third disposition, "mad bestiality," is meant to be equated with a specific circle, violence or treachery, has been much argued. Aristotle opposed it to superhuman virtue, which is found only in heroic and divine natures, and says it is rarely found among men. Aquinas, in his commentary on the *Ethics*, makes the same point (7.1.1,296–1,303); he notes that men can be bestial in three ways, like barbarians who operate without rational laws, like those who lack certain human faculties, or with great increase in malice, which is rare. Bestial malice, he says, is worse than human malice or incontinence if men become like animals; men can progress beyond the limits of human life in taking on the desires of beasts. Modern commentators take one of two positions on bestiality in the *Comedy*: they either equate it with one section or they see it as part of other sins.[28] Dante's earliest commen-

---

[28]Reade, *The Moral System*, devotes an entire chapter to explaining why Dante drags it in at all and argues for the seventh circle as the section of bestial malice on the basis of sodomy and cruelty, suggesting that if fraud is peculiarly human, force must be bestial. Alfred Triolo places bestiality in the ninth circle, as excessive malice, "Matta Bestialità in Dante's *Inferno:* Theory and Image," *Traditio* 24 (1968), 247-92; he makes an interesting point about the guardians of Hell, that they become less bestial and more human as the sinners themselves become more bestial. Busnelli points out cautiously that any excess of

tators made no attempt to fix bestiality in one circle: Pietro points out how rare it is and specifically says that Dante does not distinguish a place for it, unless it is the Minotaur (138); he and Benvenuto both define it as something that goes beyond human limits (Pietro, 139, Benvenuto, 1.374). Benvenuto also notes how rare it is among men; he connects it with madmen who cut open the wombs of pregnant women to eat the embryos and barbarians who eat human flesh and live without rule in the open (cf. the Ottimo, 1.207). In short, they equate bestiality with the absence of civilization; since it is men's nature to form a political society, if they do not do so, they are no more than animals. Inasmuch as they indulge their lower impulses without the control of reason, they are bestial and antisocial. But the only "pure" bestiality in Hell is to be seen in the superhuman inhabitants, Satan and the giants, who began as more than human and have been reduced to something far lower.

What is most significant in canto 11 is the discussion of the three lower sins and their various subdivisions, which emphasize the social nature of the sins, particularly in their focus on the victim. In violence and treachery, the divisions are made according to the nature of the victim or his relation to the sinner; in fraud, the sinner manipulates his victim to involve him in the sin which in turn has other, often numerous, victims. Malice, the willful harm to others either by force or fraud (11.22–24), is the essence of all these sins. But fraud, for Dante, is worse than force because it is an evil peculiar to man (11.25: "frode è de l'uom proprio male"); animals cannot conceive it, since they communicate by instinctive action; angels cannot practice it, since they communicate by direct intuition. Only men can deceive each other. Fraud is the quintessential social sin because it plays on the natural bond of love that should

---

vice, even lust and gluttony, had its bestial aspect for Aristotle; similarly, Dante shows bestial lust in the Minotaur, a combination of fraud and violence in the man/beast, Gerione, and bestiality in the thief, Vanni Fucci, *L'Etica*, 71–72, 107, 150.

unite all men with their fellows. It can be practiced indiscriminately on any available victim or, and far worse, on those to whom one is bound by special trust, and then it is treachery, the worst sin of all. But in either case, the effects of the act have wide-reaching repercussions. The three sins discussed in this canto, which fill the lowest circles of Hell and command fully two thirds of the cantica, are the sins most harmful to society and, Dante declares by his placement of them, most displeasing to God, because they disrupt the order he instituted for man's life on earth.

All three sins involve a perversion of the reasoning process, a conscious decision to harm others in order to satisfy personal desires. This is why in order to move through the lower circles Dante must give himself consciously into the power of the monster who symbolizes it: in violence, he rides through the river of blood on the Centaur's back;[29] in fraud, he flies on Gerione's back; in treachery, he is lifted and lowered by the giant Antaeus. Violence is a combination of "blind greed" and "mad wrath" (12.49), wrath towards people, greed towards their possessions. The circle of violence is divided into three sections according to the object of the violent act—others, the self, or God. It is further divided within those sections into the person of the victim or his goods, the objects respectively of wrath and greed. Possessions, as we know from Virgil's lesson about Fortune, play their part in the divine order as well as in the political structure, where due sense of ownership is essential to social stability. Therefore, violence against others includes tyranny, which involves both persons and goods, murder and assault or robbery, extortion, and plunder; violence against the self is suicide or wasting of goods; violence against God is either direct in blasphemy, or indirect against his creation through sodomy or usury, one a perversion of the sexual act, which impedes the providential course of procreation, the

---

[29]The Ottimo (1.223) and Jacopo (1.243) identify the centaurs with the soldiers of tyrants; here, however, it is the centaurs who control the tyrants.

other the abuse of the proper function of money, which inter-feres with the providential distribution of wealth.[30]

Those who commit violence against others are grouped according to the nature and scope of their actions and stand more or less submerged in blood. The most deeply submerged, the guiltiest, are the tyrants, whose violence was felt by whole peoples. They perverted the governor's function as God's vicar, the one destined to maintain order in society, and created chaos instead. As the Ottimo comments, tyrants ruin the polit-ical regime by putting their own interests before the public good (1.213; cf. Jacopo, 1.234: "the tyrant's intent is com-pletely and solely on his own good, which by its perversity is bad for all others"). Among the tyrants are several who were known as the scourges of their people or their time, a reminder to Dante's audience that their own sins bring on their suffer-ing: Attila, "che fu flagello in terra" (12.134); Ezzelino da Romano, son-in-law of Frederick II and a cruel tyrant, accord-ing to Villani, who destroyed towns, blinded citizens, confis-cated their possessions, killed and tortured, in short was "a great scourge of his time . . . to punish the sin of their ingra-titude" (6.73: "fue uno grande flagello al suo tempo nella Marca Trivigiana e in Lombardia per punire il peccato della loro ingratitudine").[31] Ezzelino's own sister, Cunizza, calls him a "firebrand who made a great assault on the countryside" (Pr. 9.29–30: "facella/che fece a la contrada un grande assalto"). The next group, in blood up to their throats, are the murder-

[30]Dorothy Sayers, *Introductory Papers on Dante,* (London: Methuen, 1954) 141–42, cites an early commentator, Gelli, who suggested that the sodomite makes sterile what should be fertile, the usurer makes breed what was meant to be sterile. For more on usury and related sins, see below, chapter six.

[31]Also among the tyrants is Opizzo da Este, who was believed to have been murdered by his son and successor; Dante speaks of the latter as his "stepson" (12.111–12) either to emphasize the unnaturalness of the act, or as a gratuitous insult. According to Alfonso Lazzari, in "Il marchese Obizzo II d'Este signore di Ferrara nel poema di Dante e nella storia," *Giornale dantesco* 39 (1936), 127–50, Obizzo was supposed to be the man to whom Venedico Caccianemico pandered his sister (canto 18), as sordid in his private as in his public life.

ers, of whom only one is pointed out, whose deed, though committed for personal reasons, had international repercussions because it involved figures at the highest level of government: Guy of Montfort murdered his cousin, Prince Henry of Cornwall, in a church at Viterbo in 1271. The murder was committed to avenge his father, Simon, in the presence of his king, Charles of Sicily, whose vicar he was, thereby showing in the one act contempt for his earthly lord as well as for God. The result of this murder was that Henry's brother, Edward, later king of England, was never a friend to King Charles or his people, according to Villani (*Istorie Fiorentine, 7.39*). The other souls in this section are despoilers and plunderers; one, Rinier da Corneto, was reputed to have held all the Maremma in fear, acting like a tyrant without a political office.[32] The implication, particularly since this is a circle and Dante has been moving round it back towards the tyrants, is that tyrants and plunderers are much the same. Frederick II, considered by many to be a tyrant, cannot appear in this circle since he was placed among the heretics, but he is very much present through the various people who are connected with him, Ezzelino, Rinier, and in the next section, Pier della Vigna.

The second section of violence contains suicides, a sin that would appear to be the most personal of all, and indeed Dante classes it under violence against the self, although Aristotle considered it a crime against the city. Nonetheless, by his choice of suicides, Pier della Vigna and the anonymous Florentine, Dante makes political statements about both the empire and Florence. Pier, the central figure in the section, is a public man in two ways, a high and influential official at the imperial court of Frederick II, whose functions were diplomatic and legal, and a poet and rhetorician, whose epistolary collections were used as models.[33] Although Pier presents him-

---

[32]According to the Anonimo Fiorentino, as cited by Singleton in his commentary on Hell, 203. The Ottimo says Rinier robbed prelates of the church at the command of Frederick II, as a result of which he and his descendants were perpetually deprived of all rights in Florence (1.235).

[33]See William A. Stephany, "Pier della Vigna's Self-Fulfilling Prophecies,"

self as an innocent victim, he reveals that he in fact abused his office; so, whether or not he was guilty of the crime he was accused of, he is not undeserving of his fate.[34] Pier may blame others for turning the emperor against him, but he cannot altogether excuse his own actions, and he is completely responsible for his death by his own admission. He had, he boasts to Dante, held the keys of Frederick's heart, from which he excluded almost everyone else, although an emperor should be open to all his people; naturally this aroused the envy of others and they turned against him, eventually turning the emperor against him as well.[35] Like Farinata, who clings to his loyalty to Florence remembering how he had saved it but forgetting his contribution to her troubles, Pier insists on his loyalty to the emperor ("già mai non ruppi fede/al mio segnor," 13.74–75), but fails to see how much harm he did the state by his distorted view of service. What Pier did was turn a public office into a private domain, and the result was that he became the private victim of the public reaction. But he also abused his office by fostering the emperor's pride and arrogance through his extravagant eulogies, which drew on biblical as well as pagan imperial sources, whereas a courtier and advisor, not to

---

Traditio 38 (1982), 193–212, and A. Huillard-Brèholles, *Vie et Correspondence de Pierre de la Vigne* (Paris: H. Plon, 1895).

[34]Pier's responsibility for his fate may explain why Virgil says his own description of Polydorus is not sufficient for Dante; the soul who speaks from the tree in the *Aeneid* is not a suicide, but an innocent victim of treachery and murder, what Pier pretends to be. Cf. Kurt Ringger, "Pier della Vigna o la poesia del segno," *Medioevo Romanzo* 5 (1978), 87, who connects the soul's plant name with his fate. Benvenuto, who praises both Pier and Frederick, the first for his great knowledge of secular and canon law and the art of writing, the other for his magnificence and building, seems to hold the emperor indirectly responsible for Pier's suicide and that of his own son, Henry (1.444).

[35]Ironically, a rumor claimed that Pier wrote a letter at the pope's instigation in opposition to one of Frederick's and that he revealed all Frederick's secrets to the pope, according to the Ottimo (1.246), and Jacopo (1.255), which Jacopo offers as the cause of his disgrace. Stephany, "Pier della Vigna's Prophecies," points out that the courtiers who turned against him out of envy and brought about his disgrace were probably the "fruits of his vineyard," products of his curricular reforms at the University of Naples.

say a poet, is supposed to curb the evil tendencies in the ruler and guide him away from them. He became the victim of the tendencies he had failed to correct.[36] At the same time, though heavy responsibility rests with Pier, the story also reflects badly on the emperor, who first gave excessive power to him and then exacted excessive punishment from him, both serious failings in a ruler. The possibility that the name "Peter of the Vineyard" and the imagery of the keys are meant to suggest that Peter is also an allegory for the pope, using the keys to impede the proper functioning of empire, was discussed in chapter two. What is here imputed to Pier as a public official can also be imputed to the church in its relations with the empire.

The other suicide Dante sees, identified only as a Florentine and seeming to stand for the city in its self-destructiveness (see chapter one), also presents himself as a victim. When the hunted wastrel, fleeing from dogs (*veltri*, like the instrument of divine justice promised in canto 1), takes shelter beneath the suicide bush, the bush is caught in the dogs' attack. "What did I ever do to you?" he asks (literally, "what responsibility do I have for your evil life?" 13.135), as if he could dissociate himself completely from the guilt and suffering of his fellows. That is, the city that destroys itself, its people and its goods, by its greed, ambition, and violence, attempts to stand aloof from the guilt and suffering of its people and its fellows who look to it for protection. Through both suicides, Pier della Vigna and the anonymous Florentine, Dante raises questions about man's responsibility for his fellows: Pier, as a courtier or as a symbol of the church, takes on more imperial responsibility than he

---

[36]There is a simple justice to Pier's suicide; unable to endure the public scorn of his disgrace, he took his own life, robbing himself, by the same blow, of salvation. When Pier says "ingiusto fece me contra me giusto" (13.72: "he made me unjust against my just self"), he means that by executing himself he was unjustly punishing himself because he was innocent, but since his final act was a sin against the highest justice, it made him "unjust," guilty, so that his final act, ironically, vindicates the world's view of him. Though a public servant, Pier shows himself to be as self-centered in his death as he was in his life, and self-destructive in both.

should and therefore fails to fulfill his proper function as a public servant and interferes with the emperor's doing so; the Florentine refuses to take any responsibility for another, revealing a total rejection of social identity, as an individual with his city, as a city with its nation under the empire.

The self-destructiveness of the city is reflected in the allusion Dante makes to Attila, the Scourge of God, burning it down centuries before (13.149). Benvenuto's comment on this passage adds a significant detail about the event: that Attila was taken into Florence because he promised to destroy Florence's enemy, Pistoia, but once inside destroyed Florence instead (1.463–64). Thus Florence was destroyed by her vindictive pride. Villani, in *Istorie Fiorentine,* takes a similar position, that the city continues to make the same mistakes and God continues to send warnings that go unheeded. He describes fires and other disasters in Florence which he attributes to divine judgment for the city's sins: in 1177, a great fire was sent to punish the city's pride over the recent defeats of its enemies (5.7); in 1260, the city was defeated and nearly destroyed despite its strength as divine punishment for its sins (6.80).

The remaining sinners in the seventh circle commit their violence against God, but they too are carefully set within a social context: blasphemers are represented by a king, sodomites by teachers and statesmen, usurers by members of important families and commercial operations. Blasphemers abuse the gift of speech, the expression of the highest human faculty, reason, and the basic instrument of social communication, by using it to attack or defy God. By challenging the highest authority directly, they become the ultimate human anarchists, the equivalent of the rebel angels. When a king, Capaneus, challenges the only authority above him, he undermines the basis of his own. Capaneus compares himself to the giants who rebelled against the gods (and were defeated), but the reader is reminded of the futile defiance of the fallen angels outside the walls of Dis; they all began as creatures of greater strength than Capaneus, but were defeated by the divine power they

challenged. Dante condemns any disruption of the providen-
tially ordered chain of authority, even from a king, but he also
reminds us that arrogance in a ruler has repercussions on his
subjects: the story of Capaneus recalls the devastating war
against Thebes, and allusions to the armies that suffered in the
burning deserts of India and Libya remind us of Alexander's
insatiable lust for conquest (14.31 ff.). The figure who brings
together everything Dante is saying about blasphemy and defi-
ance of the providential order is the statue described at the end
of the canto, the "Veglio di Creta," which represents the moral
history of mankind. The statue suggests classical and biblical
traditions, the four ages of man (as in Ovid, *Metamorphoses*,
1.89 ff.) with the implication of continuing moral degeneration
and corruption, and the four kingdoms of Nebuchadnezzar's
dream (Dan. 2:31–44), which represent the transfer of power
from one nation to another through human history. The statue
faces west, following the movement of empire, with its face
mirrored in Rome (14.105), which in God's plan is the climax
of human destiny.[37] It stands on two feet, the empire and the
church (cf. Benvenuto, 1.491), both intended by divine plan to
have their seat in Rome (cf. Hell 2.20–24), but though one foot
is iron, the other is only clay and the statue is now leaning too
heavily on the more vulnerable one; the implication is that the
church now has more power in the world than the empire, but
cannot sustain it.[38] The statue is cracked in all its members,
except the gold head, and tears flow from the cracks forming
the rivers of Hell, the suffering of mankind; that is, man's
defects create his hell. Whether it is national or individual,
moral corruption is harmful to all: the polis is contaminated

[37]See Mazzotta, *Dante, Poet of the Desert,* chapter 1, for an interesting dis-
cussion of this passage and the suggestion that Rome here is an anti-Eden.

[38]Benvenuto, for whom the statue represents the ages of the world, identifies
the church with the terra-cotta foot because it was originally simple and hum-
ble like earth but, after the Donation of Constantine, became richer, stronger,
and more beautiful and flourishes while the empire declines (1.491). See chapter
two, fn. 16, for other early interpretations of the Veglio.

by the acts of a single person, individuals are touched by the acts of the polis. All men suffer potentially for any man's sins.[39]

The section on sodomy (by which Dante means homosexuality), which follows the description of the statue, offers a striking illustration of the contamination of public life by the private sins of public figures. That Dante is concerned primarily with civic life in this section is clear not only from the focus on Florence and its vices in his conversations with the souls, but even more from the fact that he groups the souls in this section by their public functions, their professions, and that every major sphere of civic life is represented: politics, law, the church, letters, and commerce. These are all men professionally committed to maintaining order in their own spheres. Richard Kay has amassed a stunning amount of evidence to show that all the men named in canto 15 were guilty of professional perversion.[40] It is Dante's technique to begin with the

[39]Dante does not depart from the historical-political significance of the statue, as Busnelli suggests, L'Etica, 163, but joins it with the moral; see Busnelli for a discussion of medieval moral interpretations, 176–80.

[40]See his *Dante's Swift and Strong* (Lawrence: Regents Press of Kansas, 1978), from which the information in the rest of this paragraph is drawn. The book is extremely useful despite Kay's denial that homosexuality is the sin punished in this section. Even if sodomy was a social as well as sexual perversion in the Bible, for Dante the one does not preclude the other. Dante suggests homosexual overtones in Brunetto's greeting, giving Dante the eye, pulling at his hem, following his skirts, and it is clear from the earliest commentators that sodomy meant homosexuality for Dante's audience: Pietro is particularly specific, calling it coitus with males, "coitum cum masculis" (178); Jacopo and the Ottimo discuss various kinds of sexual aberration, of which this, being against nature, is the worst. None of them objects to the claim that the men named in this section were homosexual. Jacopo even notes that Boniface, who transferred the bishop, Andrea dei Mozzi, "fu simile sodomita" (1.286). A Pézard, *Dante sous la pluie de feu* (Paris: Vrin, 1950), had, of course, also raised the question and supplied an interesting substitute, the perversion of language, which is effective for Brunetto, Priscian, and Andrea, but not for the others. Like Kay's work, it adds to our understanding of the section, even if one cannot accept the premise that these sinners were not homosexual. Dante may well have perceived a certain ambivalence in Brunetto's loyalties to Florence, since Brunetto chose to write the *Trésor* in French, which he called "la

sin named and move into larger implications, such as the "professional perversion" Kay so amply illustrates. The same perverted thinking that allows the indulgence of one's sexual appetites permits the abuse of one's professional position. Priscian wrote a textbook for his fellow grammarians in which he glorified his own craft, whereas Donatus, whom Dante puts in Paradise, wrote a simple textbook for the use of students.[41] Francesco d'Accorso, the son of the man who did the *Glossa Ordinaria* to the *Corpus iuris civilis,* used his father's work and name, taking credit for the work as if it were his own, and also supported the king of England and the pope against the empire; since Roman law is the empire's responsibility, he, by his allegiance to its enemies, abused and misrepresented the law he taught. Bishop Andrea dei Mozzi came from a great banking family that had gone from Ghibelline to Guelph and financed the papacy against the emperor Frederick. Andrea himself tried to tax the clergy to pay for his own promotion,

parleure la plus délitable et plus commune a toutes gens," 1.1.1. On the larger question of homosexuality in the Middle Ages, see John Boswell, *Christianity, Social Tolerance, and Homosexuality* (Chicago: University of Chicago, 1980).

[41]The connection between rules of sexual behavior and rules that establish order in language is found in Alanus de Insulis, *De planctu Naturae,* who uses grammatical terms to discuss sexual perversion; laws of grammar were made to control the natural corruption of speech so men could communicate; sexual mores are established so that men can preserve the forms of family on which larger units of society are based. For Dante, the family is the first stage of human society (*Monarchy,* 1.5, and *Convivio,* 4.4.2); homosexuality, if indulged to the exclusion of other sexual activities, impedes procreation and eliminates families. Dante emphasizes this aspect of the sin by his use of the words *famiglia,* 15.22, *figliuol,* 15.31 and 37, and *imagine paterna,* 15.83. He describes the group of souls as a *famiglia;* Brunetto calls Dante his "son," not unusual usage among poets in the *Comedy,* but double-edged in this context. Dante is also the son of Florence, which will reject him; perverse, like so many of her distinguished men, she chooses to be sterile in respect of her good sons. She is too corrupt, Brunetto implies, to bear good fruit, 15.65–66. As Amilcare Iannucci puts it, "The homosexual steps outside of the natural order of birth, procreation, death, and seeks his own image. In so doing he refuses to accept his own mortality." He thinks he can live through his writings, but not even Brunetto's major work was to be of importance for any length of time ("Brunetto Latini: 'come l'uom s'etterna'," *NEMLA Italian Studies* 1 (1977), 17–28.

used excommunication as a personal weapon, and preached poorly besides; he was transferred by Boniface to oblige Andrea's family when the feud between him and his bishop got out of hand.[42] Brunetto taught civic humanism and public service through rhetoric, but upheld the independence of Florence from the empire; he was assumed to have drafted the letter Florence sent in 1281 to Rudolph of Hapsburg asserting her traditional independence; thus he must be associated with the Florence he condemns (15.73–78), because he too was disloyal to its "pure" Roman heritage. And finally, the three Guelph leaders in the next canto opposed the cause of empire, glorying in the power they had as partisans, which they would not have had as nobles within an imperial city.

Brunetto is the dominant figure in this section because he was a particularly respected personage and because, like Pier della Vigna (and Dante), he was not only a public official, but also a master of rhetoric, hence he had a two-fold responsibility to guide others. Brunetto indeed preached the highest principles of public life, that it was the responsibility of the virtuous orator to teach and civilize his fellows, that virtuous deeds, not noble birth, honor a man, that the more exalted the sinner, the more sordid his vice.[43] But as Pier della Vigna did with the emperor, Brunetto supported his city in its mistakes and aggressions instead of correcting it: despite his attachment to the Roman heritage, "the holy seed of those Romans" (15.76–77: "la sementa santa di quei Roman"), he furthered the cause of the Guelph anti-imperial Republic, he was the official notary for the government of Charles of Anjou, and the chosen public orator to urge war against Arezzo. Villani calls him a

---

[42]The possibility of a pun in the words Dante uses to describe that transfer, implying other relations between the bishop and Boniface, was discussed in chapter two.

[43]In the *Trésor*, discussed by Charles T. Davis, "Brunetto Latini and Dante," *Studi medievali* s. 3, 8 (1967), 421–50. Davis gives details of Brunetto's life and work and points out interesting connections between Brunetto and Pier della Vigna. See also H. Wieruszowski, "Brunetto Latini," *Dizionario biografico degli Italiani* (Rome, 1970), 3–10.

great philosopher and supreme teacher of rhetoric, praises his books, and notes that he began the refinement of Florence, guided it to speak well and to judge and rule the republic according to the science of politics, but he also calls him a "mondano uomo," a worldly man, in contrast to his virtues (*Istorie Fiorentine*, 8.10). Even in Hell, Brunetto seems more concerned with the circulation of his book and with Dante's literary career than with either's salvation.[44] Benvenuto makes an interesting judgment on Brunetto's vanity; he says that he was a man of great intelligence and eloquence, but that he had a high opinion of himself, and when he made a small error in his writing, instead of correcting it, as he might easily have done, he preferred to accuse and blame others lest he appear ignorant, for which Benvenuto claims he was exiled from Florence and condemned to burn. He avoided that fate in his life, the commentator notes, but not in his afterlife (1.502–03).

If there is something superficial about Dante's conversations with Brunetto, it is even more evident in his exchange with the three Florentines. Naked themselves, they recognize Dante as a Florentine not by his words but by his dress,[45] and what con-

[44]His prophecies of Dante's glorious future and the benevolence of heaven refer to Dante's fame on earth; Dante's remark, "you taught me how man makes himself eternal" (15.85), does not refer to his soul, in the sense that Statius will attribute his own salvation to Virgil, but to his writing. That is the eternity Brunetto wanted and got for himself: "Sieti raccomandato il mio Tesoro,/nel qual io vivo ancora, e più non cheggio" (15.119–20: "Let me commend to you my *Treasure*, in which I yet live, and I ask no more"). It is an ironic twist of fate that Dante is more effective in keeping Brunetto eternal by mentioning the book in his own poem.

[45]A lot of attention is paid to dress in this section of Hell: Brunetto grabs Dante's hem (15.24), follows "at his skirts" (15.40), the Florentines recognize his dress (16.8), and at the end, Dante takes off his *corda* and Virgil uses it to summon the monster of fraud. Villani says the Florentine dress was the most noble and honorable of all Italian garb because it was like the ancient Romans' (*Istorie Fiorentine*, 12.4). Dante's dress clearly contrasts with the nakedness of the sinners, the corruption that lurks beneath the noble dress they wore in life. The *corda* which summons fraud (16.106 ff.) must be connected with false appearance or posture; Pietro connects it with Dante's deceptions of women (180), Jacopo with attempts to acquire temporal goods (1.294).

cerns them in Florence is the state of *cortesia* and *valor* (16.67), good manners and worth or prestige. If *valor* is meant to have a moral overtone here, it is ironic that those who should have led by good example are concerned with such behavior now. They show good manners in their speech to Dante, wishing him long life and fame afterwards, like Brunetto, but their naked bodies, moving nervously like wrestlers in a circle, undercut the dignity their names would otherwise evoke, as did Brunetto's sudden sprint like a winning racer at the end of the previous canto. Dante unmasked Brunetto slowly in his conversation before he destroyed Brunetto's dignity with the image of the naked racer, but he makes us aware of the sordidness of the other three from the beginning by his description of their grotesque movements while they speak so graciously; the contortions of the bodies betray the lack of control which the voices conceal. In all, Dante presents in these two cantos a chilling picture of the hypocrisy and self-indulgence of Florentine public life. If men such as these are given to such behavior, it is no surprise that the city is troubled. The violent impulse that lies so close to the highly cultivated surface in these men is echoed in the natural allusion with which Dante ends the section, the river that roars down the Alps with strength for a thousand waterfalls, an image of nature uncontrolled, potentially dangerous, in sharp contrast to the dikes mentioned at the beginning (15.4 ff.), which represent man's attempts to control the harmful forces of nature within civilized life.

All the souls Dante groups among the violent against God abuse divine gifts, which were ordained for the good of men in society. Blasphemers abuse the gift of language, using it to attack the creator rather than to praise him and communicate with men; sodomites abuse sex, using it to indulge sterile desires instead of continuing the human race; the last group, usurers, abuse the gift of art, which follows nature, as Virgil explained in canto 11 (lines 97 ff.). Because the usurer does not labor as Genesis bids, he scorns both nature and art, a greater crime against the providential order than the miser's, who only attempts to interfere with Fortune (cf. canto 7). Thomas Aquinas points out that usury is especially contrary to nature because, according to nature, money should increase only from natural things, not from money; he describes the making of money from money as a kind of birth, "quidam partus," to emphasize the distortion of the natural function.[46] Following Aristotle, Thomas also associates usurers with tyrants, among those who make sordid gain at public cost (commentary on *Ethics*, 4.1). Dante gives little space to the usurers themselves, but he does take time to describe the emblems on the pouches which hang from their necks, the signs of their families and the only distinguishing feature of these souls. The sin committed to aggrandize the family (the major banking and trading operations were family companies) against the laws of God and man is now the cause of public disgrace to the family.[47] The importance of usury in Dante's world and the overlapping of usury and fraud, which Dante suggests by having the pilgrim see the usurers in the shadow of the monster of fraud, is discussed below in chapter six.

Gerione, the symbol of fraud, is the most striking of Dante's monsters, as fraud is the most important of his sins. Gerione is a hybrid, but stranger than those in the seventh circle (the centaurs and harpies) because it combines several types of being, as fraud is made up of many kinds of action. Fraud depends on trust, hence it has the face of a just man; it abuses positions of power to prey on others (the hairy arms and paws suggest a lion); it offers attractive but deceptive schemes (the body of a varicolored serpent), and it destroys without warning (the poisonous tail of a scorpion).[48] One must not only consciously give

[46]In his commentary on the *Politics*, cited by Singleton in his commentary on Hell, 182.

[47]The Ottimo (1.319) comments that one of the Gianfigliazzi is put here to represent all of them.

[48]The early commentators note the different aspects of fraud in the different parts of the monster. The Ottimo explains that it has the face of a just man because the beginning of fraud has a just and benign appearance, with the hairy parts of a beast of prey and the chest of a serpent because of varied and venomous wills, decorated with deceptive goods and pleasures, and the tail of a

oneself over to it (as Dante and Virgil ride on its back), but also actively seek it with the mind (they summon it with the *corda*); and its flight carries them deep into Hell because this sin is far more evil than the last. Fraud is the most social and the most socially destructive sin of all in that it involves deceiving others, manipulating them or exploiting their tendency to sin to one's own advantage and profit and frequently to the harm of many innocent victims. Fraud expands the scope of evil by increasing the number of actors and victims; it is a sin committed more against society than against the individual. Dante sets it in a series of moats surrounding not a castle, the center of a society, but a lake of ice, the denial of life, because fraud destroys the trust on which human life—society—must be built.[49] The antisociety of the eighth circle, the *Malebolge* ("sacks of evil" or "evil sacks"), is based not on trust but on deception, not on the common good but on the exploitation of the many for the profit of the few, not on justice but on the abuse of the innocent, not on guidance to the good life but on encouragement to evil.

Dante emphasizes the importance of fraud by dividing the eighth circle into ten sections and devoting thirteen cantos to it, more than a third of the entire cantica of Hell.[50] He arranges the ten sections so that they seem to be distortions or intensi-

---

scorpion because fraud hurts with its end, its goal, (1.314–15). The Ottimo also emphasizes the harm to others from fraud (1.309 and 313). Pietro connects Gerione with a king of Spain who had three kingdoms and with three kinds of fraud, in word (the face), deed (the scorpion), and in the thing itself, which includes merchandise (the serpent) (181–82). He notes that fraud travels far by letters and embassies. A modern commentator, Giuseppe Garrani, *Il pensiero di Dante in tema di economia monetaria e creditizia* (Palermo: Cassa di Risparmio, 1965), suggests that the monster represents fraudulent contracts. The commercial aspects of fraud will be discussed below in chapter six.

[49]The moats are spanned by a bridge, which suggests that fraud is the link from violence to treachery, a worse form of fraud practiced by denying all natural and assumed bonds; from fraud, one falls into the bottom of the abyss, where there is not even the semblance of a society, simply living death.

[50]For a discussion of the ten divisions in relation to the structure of Hell, see my *"Malebolge* as the Key to the Structure of Dante's *Inferno," Romance Philology* 22 (1967), 456–66.

fications of the larger categories of Hell's nine circles or the manipulation of the impulse to those sins in others, the organizing of sin for profit:

FRAUD, EIGHTH CIRCLE	CIRCLES OF HELL
sec. 1 panderers, seducers	2 lust
2 flatterers	3 gluttony
3 simoniacs	4 avarice
4 false prophets	prodigality
5 barrators	5 wrath
6 hypocrites	6 heresy
7 thieves	7 violence
8 counsellors of fraud	8 fraud
9 disseminators of scandal, schism	9 treachery, betrayal
10 falsifiers (of elements, persons, coins, words)	Satan

Seducers and panderers turn the lust of others to their gain; flatterers indulge the gluttonous appetite of others for praise; simoniacs feed their own greed for money on others' greed for position; false prophets squander their gifts of divining to feed others' reckless desire to know the future. Barrators attack the structure of the state, ultimately a self-destructive act, since the state is an extension of the self, just as the wrathful vent their passions on themselves when there is no other object to hand. Hypocrites deceive others with a false appearance of piety, while heretics, who search for truth, accept false beliefs; thieves take by stealth, the violent by force, both interfering with the providential order; counsellors of fraud advise others to use fraud; disseminators of scandal and schism advise others to treachery, the one case in which the act itself is worse than the inducement to it. The last section has no counterpart among the sins: if the falsifiers, who abuse all the essentials of human existence, making both civilized life and salvation impossible, have any counterpart, it can only be Satan, the perverse reflection of the creator of those elements. The souls in the eighth circle prostitute every aspect of human life, the body (sec. 1), the mind (2), God's gifts of the sacraments (3), of prophecy (4), of government (5); they practice willful deception in politics (secs. 6, 8, 9), commerce (7, 10), and religion (9).

Despite the attempts of the souls to order their "society" by the principles of greed and self-aggrandizement, a certain justice does prevail; the deceiver is deceived, the con man conned. The most striking example of this occurs outside of Hell, but is described by a soul, Guido da Montefeltro, who was seduced into devising yet another deception by Pope Boniface VIII. The great counsellor of fraud is tricked by the master deceiver. Like the clever inventor of the brass bull, mentioned in the same canto (27.7 ff.), who was his machine's first victim, Guido becomes the victim of his own cleverness; as the inventor did not consider that the cruelty of the tyrant for whom he made the bull might be turned on him, so Guido does not think that a pope who can deceive others on his advice could as easily deceive him. It is fitting, since the fraudulent incite others to sin, that in Hell they should become the objects of evil action, the perpetrators, so to speak, becoming the victims: the panderers and seducers, who incited others to sexual acts, are goaded to movement by the whips of devils;[51] flatterers squat in the excrement that they metaphorically showered on others; simoniacs are buried in baptismal fonts, a symbol of the source of eternal life which they stifled; the false prophets who twisted divine truth are twisted in their bodies; devils abuse the barrators as they abused the government; hypocrites literally bear the weight of their own hypocrisy; thieves cannot control possession even of their own bodies; counsellors of fraud who inflamed others with their tongues become tongues of flame; disseminators of schism who severed the members of church and state are continually severed in their bodily members; and

---

[51]The horned devils suggest cuckolds who are among the victims of this sin, and the whipping, artificial stimulation to sex; what they did to others is now being done to them.

falsifiers who corrupted the elements of human life are corrupted, diseased, in their bodies and minds.

The punishments of the souls also recall actual contemporary punishments in several instances, which reminds us once again that Hell is really an earthly city or state. Certain types of criminals were walked around the city before they were executed and whipped as they went, as the panderers and seducers are (Davidsohn, *Storia di Firenze* 5.611); some lost limbs for encouraging seditions (Davidsohn, 5.612), like the mutilated sinners in the ninth section. The upside-down burial of the simoniac popes recollects the punishment of assassins, buried alive upside down, as Dante himself notes (19.49–51); the hoods the hypocrites wear are lead, like the coverings Frederick II had placed on traitors before they were burnt, again noted by Dante (23.65–66). Other details reinforce the sense of the contemporary city. The second section provides the sight and odor of excrement, the first is densely populated, with groups of sinners moving quickly in opposite directions, their movement carefully ordered, as the Romans ordered their traffic during the Jubilee (18.28 ff.).[52]

The crowds in the first section of the *Malebolge* also suggest the vast extent of the sin, both of those who commit it and those who suffer from it. The number of people involved in these sins as victims and as participants is a significant factor in the social impact of fraud. Jason seduced and abandoned a

[52]The crowds in Rome had come on pilgrimage to receive the indulgences promised by the pope, complete pardon for all sins, remission of guilt and punishment, provided the sins were or *would be* confessed. This procedure reverses the normal order of awareness of sin, confession, absolution, and satisfaction. It is not too great a leap from the reversed order to the absolution of a sin before it is committed, which the same pope, Boniface VIII, fraudulently offered Guido da Montefeltro (canto 27). One wonders if Dante is not suggesting that the church has not only been ordering the traffic of sinners, but even defrauding them with false promises of salvation by undermining the importance of confession. Dante himself as pilgrim makes two confessions in Purgatory and acknowledges the power of papal indulgences indirectly through Casella's story (Pg. 2), but one assumes that Casella was sincerely repentant.

number of women, each of whom had already betrayed others, which suggests an endless cycle of deception and revenge and numerous, sometimes innocent, victims.[53] Victims are more and more obvious in the lower part of the circle: whole nations, like the Jews, because of Caiaphas's hypocrisy (sec. 6), Troy, because of the deceptions of Ulysses (8) and Sinon (10), and Islam, because of the schism of Mohammed (9). Cities suffer from the activities of hypocrites (6) and counterfeiters (10), the inhabitants of a castle from political deception (8), and individuals from false accusations (7 and 10). Even Dante is briefly caught up in the atmosphere of this circle and becomes its victim: Virgil, thinking that Dante is trying to gauge the distance, or perhaps attempting to direct Dante's attention to facts and away from temptation, gives him details and tries to hurry him away from the ninth section. Dante's answer is unusually aggressive: "If you'd known why I was looking, you might have let me stay," 29.13–15. Whether or not Virgil read Dante's thoughts, as he usually can, he has seen the person Dante was looking for, a cousin whose violent death is still unavenged.[54] Virgil did not point him out, because, as reason, he must guard Dante from the consequences of personal feuds. Dante missed his cousin because he was so intent on another sinner, the political poet Bertran de Born; thus the bad example of one political poet, Bertran, and the wisdom of another,

[53]Dante names Isifile (Hypsipyle) and Medea. Isifile had deceived all her countrywomen (18.92–93), the women of Lemnos, who had killed their husbands because they had been unfaithful, making the deceivers the victims on a national scale; Isifile deceived them to save her father, but was herself deceived by Jason. Medea killed her brother and deceived her father in order to run off with Jason and later killed Jason's new bride and her own children in order to avenge herself on him.

[54]Both the Ottimo (1.497) and Jacopo (1.455) relate that Geri del Bello, Dante's cousin, was a falsifier of money as well as a sower of discord, in order to explain why he is mentioned in canto 29, devoted to the falsifiers, although he is in the ninth section of disseminators of scandal. Benvenuto discusses Florence's particular problem with the thirst for revenge, both public and private, and commends the wise man, Virgil, for dissuading Dante from getting involved (2.391).

Virgil, prevent Dante from abusing his own gifts, from getting involved in a feud that would have had serious political consequences. His concern with the public, perhaps theoretical, aspect of the problem, represented by the two poets, protects him from the private aspect, which could have had public repercussions. Nonetheless, if only for a moment, the cousin has had the effect he had in life, of dividing those who should be united. Again in the tenth section, Dante is so fascinated by the exchange between two falsifiers, Virgil has to rouse him quite sharply. This time, Dante has no excuse, only shame, but that satisfies Virgil, so they leave the circle in harmony, reason in the good man having overcome the threat of fraud, which is to draw others into sin. "The same tongue first bit me," Dante comments, "and then gave me medicine" (31.1 and 3). This is the proper function of language and of poetry, to show what is wrong and guide to what is right, and it contrasts sharply with the fraud of the whole eighth circle.

There are many innocent victims of fraud because it is practiced by people who have official positions or functions, which they abuse to the harm of those who must depend on them. Many of the categories of fraud involve advisors, a role Dante was particularly concerned with since he cast himself in it: the flatterers in section two are courtiers, companions, advisors, who should use their access to lords and leaders to persuade them to right action, to correct and stem their sinful desires, but who instead pander to their vanity.[55] The false prophets in section four, instead of using their knowledge of the future to correct and guide, as the prophets of the Old Testament attempted to do, sell it to those who would use it for political

[55]Symbolically, Dante suggests that flatterers are whores in the person of Taide, a figure from a Terence play cited by Cicero; the words Dante quotes were actually spoken by the whore's lover to a parasite. Dante's change makes the indictment of flattery even stronger; the flattering parasite is a whore because he prostitutes language. They are set in dung because praise that is not only excessive but potentially harmful is mental excrement, the waste product of the human mind; Benvenuto comments that they are in human excrement which smells worse than other animals' because flattery is peculiarly human (2.25).

advantage. Counsellors of fraud (sec. 8) and disseminators of scandal (9) pervert their advisory functions altogether by guiding to sinful action, which is harmful not only to the souls of those who listen to them, but also to those against whom they act. Many of these advisors are themselves public officials, as are most of the souls Dante points out in the other sections: Venedico Caccianemico (sec. 1) was a podestà of various cities, as well as a pimp for his sister; church officials as high as popes practice simony (3); barratry (5) and hypocrisy (6) are the vices of political officers; religious and political leaders engage in fraudulent counsel and in scandal and schism (8, 9).

Because fraud is the core of the corrupt society in Dante's scheme, it is appropriate to look at relevant details of various sections, following Dante's order. He gives short shrift to the first two—pimps and flatterers—using them primarily to set the atmosphere for the circle, the prostitution of body and mind, the sordid traffic in what is essentially filth. The third section, however, is one of major importance, because it involves the church at the highest level, not only trafficking in the sacraments, but also interfering in secular affairs. Prostitution and adultery figure largely in the imagery of this section (canto 19), because the church used the language of marriage widely in its political propaganda as well as in religious texts (see chapter two). Dante speaks of simoniacs committing adultery for gold and silver (19.4), of Boniface taking the lady church by fraud and then raping her (19.56–57); the popes fulfill the prophecy of the whore who fornicates with kings in the Apocalypse (19:106–08). The whore in the Bible stood for secular Rome, but then the church became secular Rome with the Donation of Constantine, taking on its corruption with the possession (19.115 ff.). The church now trades in the "things of God" which were meant to be the "brides of goodness" (19.2–3); those "things" are the sacraments and spiritual gifts, which the church should administer freely to all.[56]

[56]Several of them are alluded to in the canto in a distorted way emphasizing the church's perversion of its functions: baptism by the fontlike holes in which the popes are buried; confession when Dante talks to the pope "like the brother

The simoniac popes are in their own holes, as the heretics are in their own tombs, a connection that Benvenuto points out (2.48); they too have rejected the faith, but with more far-reaching effects. They are buried upside down as they subverted their sacramental functions, the only sinners Dante sees in this position; Jacopo notes that they are upside down because they were concerned with things of the earth rather than of heaven (1.312). The position is not only a striking indictment of their abuses, but also serves to connect them with Satan, whom Dante sees upside down as he leaves Hell, suggesting that in perverting the functions God gave them and in usurping others not meant for them, they do the devil's work rather than God's.[57] Not only have they taken to themselves what properly belongs to all men, and Nicholas admits to Dante that he used the church to benefit his family, they also claim and use powers that God gave to the empire. They usurp or interfere with secular authority: Dante alludes to Nicholas's intrigues against Charles of Sicily (19.98–99), which, as early commentators make clear, were believed to have led to the carnage of the Sicilian Vespers;[58] he compares Clement's relations with the French king to the story of Jason in 4 Maccabees (19.85–87); he may be reminding the Florentines, in his remarks about the broken font, of the oath they took to stand

---

who confesses the perfidious assassin" (19.49–50), suggesting a comparison between the assassin who murders for money and the pope who contributes to the death of souls for money; the laying on of hands is the sacrament bought and sold by simoniacs; and the gift of tongues, which came to the apostles with the pentecostal flames, is parodied in the flames which dance on the feet of the sinners.

[57]Susan Noakes, "Dino Compagni and the Vow in San Giovanni: *Inferno* XIX, 16–21," *Dante Studies* 86 (1968), 46, suggests that the importance of simony for Dante lies in the harm it works on man and the earthly community, not principally in the insult it offers to God. Hence, presumably, Dante classes it as a category of fraud rather than of violence.

[58]Cf. Pietro, "the said pope caused the rebellion of Sicily and Apulia, or consented to it" (200), and the Ottimo, who claims that the pope was bribed to consent to the rebellion and wrote letters to the conspirators, although he did not use the papal seal (1.350).

together for the city, which was undermined by the treachery of the Blacks with the collusion of Pope Boniface VIII, as Noakes suggests; and his use of the curious word *zanca* to describe the papal leg (19.45) is probably, as Kaulbach argues, a reference to the slippers worn by the prefect of the city of Rome in papal rituals, symbolizing a temporal power once vested in the Roman consul, but taken over by the papacy. All we see of the popes in this section are their legs, which have taken the place of the head by usurping imperial power.

False prophets also abuse a divine gift that was intended to help mankind, of foretelling the future, which they put to the selfish purposes of political leaders or to their own profit. All the commentators make a distinction between knowing the future through divine revelation, which may come either directly in a vision or dream or through natural science, both of which are proper, and knowing it through demons, who use it to destroy souls.[59] Prophets, like Dante and Virgil, chosen to transmit the divine message, serve God and man, but they were also believed by some to be sorcerers. At the heresy trial of Matteo Visconti, a witness reported that Dante had been summoned by Matteo to practice magic against the pope.[60] Therefore, Dante takes pains to establish exact details in this canto in order to dissociate himself from the souls he sees, and he has Virgil correct the story he told in the *Aeneid* about the founding of Mantova and reprimand Dante sharply for show-

[59]See Pietro, 202–03; Guido, 379, the Ottimo, 1.357–58; Jacopo, 1.337. Demons, being angels, albeit fallen, have a higher intellect than men and can know things not accessible to men. See Aquinas on divination (ST 2.2ae, q.95). For a full discussion of many of the vexed problems of canto 20, see Robert Hollander, "The Tragedy of Divination in *Inferno* xx," in his *Studies in Dante* (Ravenna: Longo, 1980; Hollander shows how Dante rewrites his classical sources, particularly Virgil, to defend him from the charge of false prophecy.

[60]See Rubinstein, "Studies," 227. Paget Toynbee, *Dante Alighieri, His Life and Works* (1900; rev. 1910; reprint New York: Harper, 1965), 101–02, and Elisabetta Cavallari (La fortuna di Dante nel trecento [Florence: Perella, 1921], 40), tell the story apropos of Galeazzo Visconti. On Virgil as seer, see Domenico Comparetti, *Vergil in the Middle Ages* (1908; reprint from 2d ed., Hamden: Archon, 1966), pt. 2.

ing sympathy to the sinners. Prophets played an important role in political policy-making in Dante's time. Rulers depended on their forecasts to make key decisions. Villani reports several of the scholar Michel Scot's prophecies coming true much later, in 1328 when Can Grande took control of Padua (*Istorie Fiorentine*, 10.103), and in 1329, when he took Trevigi (10.139).[61] However, Villani also warns that not all astrologers or their prophecies can be trusted, although the point of his story seems to be rather that men may be misled by prophecies they do not fully understand. He reports a prophecy that Henry of Luxembourg would advance to the end of the world ("capo di mondo"), which was taken to mean that nothing could stop him; events seemed to belie the apparent meaning until a local abbot told them of a street named Capo di Mondo and they realized how badly they had misinterpreted the prophecy (9.46). The problem with prophecy may lie as much in the lords who rely on it as in the prophets; among those Dante mentions, Michel Scot served as court astrologer to Frederick II, and Guido Bonatti was astrologer to both Guido da Montefeltro and Ezzelino da Romano. Benvenuto notes that Guido consulted Bonatti in all his actions (2.89). It is surely no accident that Dante condemns these lords as well, Frederick for heresy, Guido for counseling fraud, Ezzelino for tyranny. By serving them, the prophets used their arts in the service of evil.

Barrators commit a much more direct political crime: they subvert government from within. According to Aquinas, the purpose of government is to imitate God in his goodness and in moving others to be good, but barrators not only fail to

[61] It is interesting that in the prophecies, Michel Scot refers to the "dog" (*catulus*) of Verona long before the birth of Can Grande, whose name means "big dog"; it gives an added significance to Dante's prophecy of the *veltro* if the audience had some knowledge of "dog" prophecies in the past. Dante, of course, died before the ones Villani mentions came true. Michel Scot also predicted his own death by a falling stone and always wore a helmet except at the consecration of the host, where a stone eventually fell on him. Benvenuto says he took off the helmet for public show, not out of love for Christ (2.89); Jacopo tells an amusing story about him, that he entertained by bringing in all his dishes by magic from the royal houses of Europe (1.351).

move others towards good, they actively subvert government for private profit.[62] They destroy the honor of their cities for money, Jacopo says (1.354). Dante gives much attention to this sin, two full cantos, a treatment he accords only two other sins in the *Malebolge,* because he is particularly concerned with the proper function of government, and because he himself was accused of the crime. The simile of shipbuilding and repairing in Venice, which begins canto 21, suggests what government is meant to be, everyone engaged in a different activity with a distinct purpose that serves the whole operation in order to keep the ship of state functioning.[63] What barratry makes of government, however, is a farce. The puns implicit in the word *barrateria* point up both the serious and the game aspect of the evil. Nine lines after the first mention of barratry in the poem, *baratro* occurs (11.69), meaning "the abyss," as if the subversion of government were itself the equivalent of hell, which it helps to produce on earth; *baratta* occurs in the cantos of barratry (21.63) as "scuffle," "contest"; in other words, a competitive game. In life, barratry is a game that you lose when you win, since to turn government, which is an extension of the self, to selfish purposes subverts its real purpose and therefore harms the self. In Hell, it is a game that has been lost before it is begun: the souls cannot get away from the devils and the devils cannot get away from them; they are unable to

[62]For Dante, Christ's death gave special meaning to human government in that redemption prepared the way for man to reestablish the earthly paradise; he implies this connection by the painstaking accuracy of his reference to the harrowing of hell (1266 years and one day less than five hours before, 21.112–14), which broke the bridge from this section to the next.

[63]This contrasts with the description of tourneys and skirmishes at the beginning of canto 22, reminiscent of Bertran de Born's *Be'm platz lo gais temps de Pascor,* which exalts the pleasure of fighting for its own sake, with no sense of a serious purpose. The furious action and noise of such events is compared to the devils' activity and the music of their leader, who made a trumpet of his ass (21.139). Since man is distinguished from animals by his political nature, abuse of the structure instituted to govern him in society is a denial of his humanity, so the sinners in this section are portrayed as little more than animals, dolphins, frogs, a mouse among cats, a duck, while the devils are like dogs, cats, and a falcon.

leave the section even to move into the next (see 23.55–57). Still they play: the souls trick the devils, the devils try to trick them, and everyone ends up in the pitch. If the devils miss a crack at the souls, they attack each other and have to be dragged out by their fellows' hooks. There is little difference in this section between the sinners and the devils; both play the same game to the same futile ends. The devil caught on his own hook is simply an extension of the barrator's plight and a direct result of their abuses; barratry sets up an endless cycle of corruption which extends upwards and downwards in the echelons of government. As Benvenuto points out, barratry is practiced at all levels of courts, from the greatest minister to the least mercenary (2.97); the greater barrators flay the lesser, the lesser sew strife among themselves (2.153); no lord can avoid their hidden plots, even good lords are vulnerable (2.136–37); and barratry is so contagious that if a saint entered a court and became involved in its functions, he would become a barrator.

Barratry afflicts religious as well as lay courts; indeed Benvenuto tells a story of his own experience at the papal court at Avignon, where the pope's treasurers expected him to offer a bribe even though his cause was just (2.118). Benvenuto claims that the best examples of barratry are to be found in the pope's court (2.97). He identifies Dante's devils as important officials, great masters of barratry or their ministers, presumably either lay or clerical (2.101), and offers a lengthy analysis of their names, showing how they illustrate different aspects of barratry (2.120–21).[64] I suggested in chapter two that the devils might represent corrupt churchmen trying to manipulate the politics of secular as well as of religious government; in any case, whether priests or laymen, Dante's message is that barrators will eventually be caught and hooked on their own intrigues. His devils are, incidentally, black (21.29 and 23.131), as the souls must also be since they are submerged in pitch, which may well suggest the Black Guelphs, the church party

[64]Attempts have been made to read the names of contemporary officials into the devils' names, see Edward Moore, *Studies in Dante,* 2d Series (Oxford 1899), 233.

and Dante's enemies. It was the Black Guelphs, supported by the church, who falsely accused and sentenced Dante, effectively exiling him from the city.[65]

Dante exonerates himself from the charges of false prophecy and barratry by his treatment of the sins; but this is not the case in hypocrisy. He seems to admit some slight guilt here by the precipitousness of his fall into the sixth ditch and the difficulty of his climb out of it. One can only assume that he adopted some self-righteous posture when he went into exile, perhaps during his brief and unhappy political association with other exiled Whites, to which Cacciaguida refers (Pr. 17.61–65). Hypocrisy is commonly associated with false piety, but it can also have far-reaching political effects, and that is the aspect Dante concentrates on. Among the souls he presents, Caiaphas is one whose hypocrisy brings suffering on an entire nation. Ironically, he advised the Pharisees to make one man suffer rather than the whole people (Hell 23.116–17), and that was the "seed of evil for the Jewish people" (23.123: "fu per li Giudei mala sementa"). He now lies crucified on the ground where all the hypocrites must pass over him, that is, he bears the full weight of the world's hypocrisy, as Christ in his crucifixion bore the full weight of the world's sin. The two Frati Gaudenti Dante speaks to in this canto were sent to Florence to keep the peace; of opposing parties, they were elected to serve together as one *podestà* for the city but actually worked as one for the pope, and instead of reconciling the two sides, they favored the Guelphs at great cost to the Ghibellines. The signs of the destruction wreaked on Ghibelline property could still be seen by Dante's audience (23.108). Benvenuto notes in his commentary that Frati Gaudenti sinned in both

[65]In this connection, it is interesting that Dante is threatened by devils twice in Hell, first at the gates of Dis, between the fifth and sixth circles, in an attempt to keep him out of the city, and again between the fifth and sixth sections of the *Malebolge*, to catch and punish him for a crime he did not commit. Both Benvenuto (2.113) and Villani (*Istorie Fiorentine*, 9.134) insist on Dante's innocence of barratry, Villani saying that he was banished for belonging to the White party, and for no other crime.

hypocrisy and barratry, since they were corrupted by the Guelphs, and that Dante quite properly places these hypocrites next to the barrators (2.178). Villani says they worked together under cover of false hypocrisy ("sotto coverta di falsa ipocrisia") more for their own gain than for the common good (*Istorie Fiorentine*, 7.13). Guido comments that they did the devil's work in the guise of holiness, "sub specie sanctitatis opus diabolicum perpetrarunt" (445). Religious orders are particularly susceptible to this sin because of their ascetic dress and customs, which is why all the hypocrites except Caiaphas wear robes cut in the Cluny fashion, with an abundance of material. Since these robes, however, are gilded lead, they pay for that extravagance with added pain. Dante emphasizes the weight of the cloaks by comparison with the lead coverings in which Frederick II burned traitors, a reference that underscores the political aspect of the sin.

Theft is also a special category for the poet, who devotes two cantos to it, but not because he was directly connected with the sin. Theft shakes the stability of a society by defying and complicating recognized rights of possession;[66] Guido comments that thieves introduce moral poison into society, that stealing what belongs to another corrupts and dissolves human fellowship (451). Because thieves refuse to recognize ownership in others, they lose all claim to it themselves, even to the possession of their own identities. Their punishment is to lose their bodies at random; they never know when they will be attacked, and, worse still, they cannot tell whether the

---

[66]Cf. Aquinas; property is necessary for three reasons: man makes more of an effort for his own things; there is more order in human affairs if each has charge of particular things; the state is more peaceful if each man is content with his own (ST, 2.2ae, q.66, a.2). But Aquinas considers robbery by force worse than theft by deceit because he is concerned with personal morality and effects on the individual, whereas Dante is concerned with the public. Jacopo points out that there are two kinds of possession: God's, who created all, and man's, who has the use of things; but clear title to possessions is important among men because without it there would be nothing but confusion and war (1.387–88). On the possibility that theft may also represent different kinds of financial crimes, see chapter six below.

snakes that threaten them are really their friends suffering similar metamorphoses. They suffer the effects of a society in which trust among men has been destroyed. The metamorphoses here are not really changes so much as a revelation of the truth within, which is that the thief reduces himself to the lowest form of animal life.[67]

Through the first thief, Vanni Fucci, Dante reveals several facets of the sin: that it is sacrilege (he steals sacred objects and defies God in a gesture which Dante connects with Capaneo's blasphemy, 25.14–15, as theft itself defies the divine order in the disposition of goods); that it harms the innocent victim (Vanni mentions that another was accused of the crime, and, according to Benvenuto, he was subsequently hanged for it, 2.217 ff.); that it can be committed by cities as well as by individuals. Like Farinata, a Ghibelline who prophesied trouble to the Guelph Dante, Vanni, the Black Guelph, prophesies trouble for the White Dante; but as he describes the events—the exile of Blacks from Pistoia and of Whites from Florence—the cities seem to undergo metamorphoses like the souls, so we come to see them as thieves: "Pistoia first strips herself of Blacks, then Florence renews her people" (24.143–44; cf. 25.10 ff.: "Ah, Pistoia, why do you not turn yourself to ashes?"). In Purgatory, 6.145–47, Dante comments on the frequency with which Florence changes and renews its laws, money, customs, and members, which Benvenuto echoes in his commentary on theft, saying the thief forecast the *mutationem* of his city (2.189). Since cities confiscated the personal property of their political exiles, it is not difficult to picture them as thieves.

One of the thieves named in this section, Agnolo, is identified as a Brunelleschi by the early commentators; his family had been Ghibelline, but turned Guelph, and Agnolo himself began as a White and became a Black, a stunning example of

---

[67]For political overtones in the classical allusions in this episode, e.g., the destruction of cities and political exiles from tyranny, see my article on canto 24, in the forthcoming *California Lectura Dantis,* ed. Allen Mandelbaum, where I also discuss the possibility that Dante presents himself as a thief insofar as he steals from the classical poets, but for a socially beneficial purpose.

political metamorphosis for personal advantage.[68] Agnolo is also a member of a large commercial family, as are most of those mentioned in this section. This, together with the space Dante allots theft, suggests that the poet may also be concerned with a more subtle, more extensive kind of theft, the kind that is accomplished in commerce, particularly through fradulent contracts and sales (see below, chapter six).

Dante is emotionally detached from this sin to the extent that he can take pride in his virtuosity while describing it, comparing himself favorably with Lucan and Ovid. But the same is not true of the counseling of fraud.[69] To describe what he sees, Dante must "rein in his wit more than usual, so that it does not run where virtue does not guide it" (26.21–22). He is ostensibly speaking of his poetry, but he is also aware of his own temptation here—how could a political exile who had been so involved with the plight of his city not be tempted at some point to counsel deception in order to change the situation? Dante stretches so far to see into the ditch, he reports, that had he not seized a rock, he would have fallen into the flames (26.43–45). The danger is intellectual arrogance, pride and excessive confidence in one's cleverness, as Ulysses and Guido da Montefeltro amply illustrate. Dante must have had the opportunity and, so he suggests, the inclination to counsel fraud, but he rejects the Ulysses model for Aeneas, choosing the dutiful wanderer who obeys the Gods and serves the providential destiny of empire over the clever wanderer who pursues his own interests outside the bounds of civilized life.[70]

[68]*Chiose anonime,* cited by Singleton in his commentary on Hell, 437.

[69]An attempt to deny this definition of the sin of the eighth section was made by Anna Hatcher, "Dante's Ulysses and Guido da Montefeltro," *Dante Studies* 88 (1970), 109–17, but I find it over-subtle.

[70]Dante has reason to identify with Ulysses, the central figure of this canto, not only because of the temptation to counsel deception, but also because of the journey he made to an unknown world. Dante describes his own journey in sea metaphors and seems to be haunted by the fear of making the mistake Ulysses did of trusting too far in his own capacity: when he reaches the shore of Purgatory, in sight of which Ulysses drowned, he girds himself with the reed of humility, and when he reaches the top of heaven, he looks down once

Pride in his own powers and accomplishments is what dominates the figure of Ulysses in the tradition Dante drew on: his cry to the Cyclops is almost fatal to his ship (Ovid, *Metamorphoses,* 14); in his debate with Ajax he boasts of his deeds, all feats of persuasion or guile, and gloats that as Ajax is body, he is mind (*Metamorphoses,* 13). From the Trojan point of view, Ulysses is treacherous (cf. *Aeneid* 2, Sinon's story, and 3, the Trojan curse on Ulysses' land). There is a more sympathetic tradition of Ulysses, the wise man who triumphs over passion and adversity, in Apuleius, Cicero, and Horace, but that view is not reflected in the *Comedy.* The selfish desire to increase his own knowledge when it can serve no social purpose moves Ulysses to abandon all his social responsibilities, public and private, to abandon his father, his son, and his wife, to leave his land without its lord, all to experience "human vice and valor," in a "land without people" (26.99,117) at an age when men are supposed to share the fruits of their experience with others, as Dante asserts in the *Convivio.* What is the point of more experience now except to indulge his curiosity? Dante believes in the tremendous desire to know, as he reveals in the *Convivio,* but knowledge must serve a purpose, religious or social or both. Ulysses pursues knowledge that serves neither, so instead of guiding his country to virtue, he leads his boatload of old and tired followers to destruction in sight of the mountain of Purgatory. It is the highest mountain ever seen

---

more on Ulysses' "mad course" (Pr. 27.82–83). For Dante, Ulysses is an anti-Aeneas, wandering to indulge his own curiosity rather than to establish a new civilization. Neither son, nor father, nor proper love for wife could restrain Ulysses, he says, making the contrast with Aeneas who left Troy with his father on his shoulder and his son's hand in his. Guido notes that the son, father, and wife should have been sufficient to keep Ulysses from his "vagabunda inquisitione" (537), but he commends Ulysses' speech to his men (540 ff.) as Benvenuto does, though cautiously (2.294). Amilcare Iannucci, "Ulysses' 'Folle Volo': The Burden of History," *Medioevo Romanzo* 3 (1976), 410–45, offers a careful analysis of Dante's treatment of the hero as a Christian tragedy, his sin being the seeking of knowledge beyond imposed limits. For an overall view of the Ulysses problem, see J. A. Scott, "*Inferno* XXVI: Dante's Ulysses," *Lettere italiane* 23 (1971), 145–86.

(26.133–35), an achievement he still takes pride in, but it can only be reached in humility and awareness of sin. What is punished in his flame is pride of intellect that has been turned to antisocial purposes, first to the deception of others on a grand scale and then to rejection of duty to family and homeland.

Guido da Montefeltro also has enormous pride of intellect and accomplishment: " I knew all the maneuvers and secret ways and practiced them so well that the report reached the ends of the earth" (27.76–78). But he also turns his gifts to the wrong purposes. After a successful military career, he retired late in life (at the age when "one should draw in the sails" (27.81), he says, showing that he meant to avoid Ulysses' error) to repent his sins in a monastery, but he could not resist the temptation to do once more what he did so well. He is so sure of himself that he cannot imagine himself being fooled, and yet, because he is so eager to exercise his ability, he allows himself to be duped and destroyed. He blames the pope for luring him out of the cloister, saying his plan for salvation would otherwise have worked. But he knew all along what sort the pope was (27.85–99); he knew he was making war not on infidels but on Christians, and right at Rome, that he had no respect for his office or sacred orders or vows, that he suffered a "proud fever," and his words were "drunken." The rhyme words *lebbre, febbre, ebbre* ("leprosy," "fever," "drunken") emphasize the corrupt, diseased nature of his thought. Guido had ample reason to distrust the pope, having engaged in battles against the church all his life (according to the Ottimo, 1.462). The early commentators on this passage mince no words about Boniface, Pietro calling him "the prince of hypocritical clerics" (240), Guido da Pisa, "depraved by a perverted conscience and exalted by arrogant pride" (559), and Benvenuto "a great tyrant among priests" (2.298). Boniface acts here as a tyrant, and men do not have to obey tyrants, particularly in sinful acts; Pietro says the pope ought not to have ordered Guido to sin nor he to do it, noting that even the pope is subject to divine law (241). Romagna has always been plagued with tyrants and their wars, Dante says, and the commentators support him (the Ottimo, 1.461, Benvenuto, 2.305), laying much of the blame on the greed and intrigues of the popes. The Ottimo comments that canto 26 deals with the deceptions of laymen, canto 27 is concerned with the deceptions of the clergy (1.457). It is, of course, precisely what Guido advises the pope to do to his enemy—make a promise he will not keep— that the pope does to him, and, like the inventor who was burned in his own machine, it is only just that Guido should be so deceived.[71]

The lesson here is for those who give aid and counsel to tyrants, that they cannot protect themselves. But this is not a simple case of the deceiver deceived; Guido's advice enabled the pope to take the enemy stronghold, which he then destroyed. For that destruction Guido must bear some responsibility, just as Ulysses bears responsibility for the consequences of his cleverness. According to Dante's Virgil, Ulysses suffers in the flame because of the wooden horse, the betrayal of Achilles, and the theft of the Palladium (26.58–63), deeds that deceived and finally destroyed a nation, betrayed a friend, and desecrated a temple. Ironically, the horse, as Virgil points out, was the gate from which the noble seed of the Romans issued (26.59–60), who were to eclipse the Greeks, making the victory Ulysses takes pride in a temporary one and making him an instrument of his enemies' triumphant destiny. The social consequences of the kind of deception Guido and Ulysses advise cannot be calculated or controlled by the counsellor, however clever he is, but his guilt must be determined on the basis of those consequences. One modern scholar suggests a connection between the wooden horse at Troy and the secret

---

[71]Boniface seduces Guido by offering to absolve him of the sin before he commits it, using the keys with which he claims he can open and close heaven. Guido, who cannot resist another opportunity to display his cleverness, uses the excuse that it would be worse not to obey the pope, but in his very answer ("Father, since you absolve me of that sin into which I *must now fall*," 27.108– 09) he reveals the weakness of his position. He knows that he will sin as he should know that he cannot be absolved before he sins, something the devil who comes for his soul points out.

reentry of Corso Donati's forces into Florence with the collusion of Boniface and Charles of Valois; he also notes that it was the taking of the Colonna stronghold, which Guido advises, that removed the last serious enemy to Boniface's legitimacy.[72]

That Dante intends Florence to see an immediate threat to itself from deceptive political practices is evident from the beginning of the section, when the poet connects the divided flames of the souls with the funeral pyre of Eteocles and Polynices, the brothers who caused the war at Thebes by greed, deception, and betrayal. The flame of their pyre divided because even after death their hatred was intense, a fit symbol of the struggles that now divide Italian cities. Dante forecasts similar trouble for Florence from Prato, assumed by early commentators to be a reference to the neighboring city, Florence's daughter, which wants her to fall because of her iniquity or out of envy of her wealth and power (Guido, 517, the Ottimo, 1.442, Benvenuto, 2.261). Benvenuto also identifies Prato with the cardinal, Niccola da Prato, who was sent to Florence in 1303 to reconcile warring factions; he failed and laid the city under interdict, after which there were various disasters, including civil war and fire (2.262–63). Pietro mentions the destruction of cities by fire in connection with the flame of the souls, saying that a city can be destroyed by one word, or one counsel, as it can be by fire (231).

The effects of evil counsel in the ninth section of fraud are even more direct and widespread: divisions in church and state. The enormity and horror of the sin is suggested by Dante's allusions at the beginning of the canto to the suffering in wars.[73] Those who cause them, like the souls in the previous canto, take pride in their accomplishments, but they acted not

---

[72]Ricardo J. Quinones, *Dante Alighieri* (Boston: Twayne, 1979), 125–28.

[73]The continuous shifts in allegiance in those wars make one wonder what purpose they serve: Apulia is the scene first of the battle of Turnus against Aeneas, forces opposing the future Rome, then of the Punic wars in which Apulia fought with Rome, then of crusades under Robert Guiscard against Saracens and Greeks, and finally of the defeat of the new empire, the betrayal of Manfred, and the deception of Conradin.

simply out of pride, but out of calculated malice. These souls are eager to identify themselves and their actions to Dante. The poet Bertran de Born, the supreme Provençal poet of war,[74] and Mohammed, the greatest schismatic in Christendom, according to popular belief,[75] define the sin and the simple, straightforward justice of its punishment: as they severed the body of human institutions, so their bodies are now hacked apart by a devil's sword:

MOHAMMED:
seminator di scandalo e di scisma
fuor vivi, e però son fessi così

disseminators of scandal and schism
they were in life, therefore they are so rent.
(28.35–36)

BERTRAN:
Perch'io parti' così giunte persone
partito porto il mio cerebro, lasso!
dal suo principio ch'è in questo troncone.
Così s'osserva in me lo contrapasso.

Because I separated persons so joined,
I carry my brain separated, alas!
from its source, which is in this trunk.
So one can see in me the retribution.
(28.139–42)

[74]Whether Bertran had the kind of political effect he attributes to himself here is not certain, but as William Paden points out in "Bertran de Born in Italy," in *Italian Literature, Roots and Branches,* ed. G. Rimanelli and K. J. Atchity (New Haven: Yale, 1976), 39–66, Dante's audience thought he did; the same is true of the attribution to him of the lament for the young king, which Dante echoes in this canto. On Bertran's role in Dante's poem, see Teodolinda Barolini, "Bertran de Born and Sordello: The Poetry of Politics in Dante's *Comedy,*" *PMLA* 94 (1979), 395–405.

[75]The popular medieval belief was that Mohammed was a Christian, or was trained by Christians. The Ottimo reports that he was taught by a heretic monk and some say, but it is not true, that he was a cardinal who turned against the church when he failed to get the papacy (1.482).

The souls Dante meets in this section, which is concerned with serious divisions in the major institutions ordained for life on earth, represent all those most responsible for guiding men in that life, religious leaders, political figures, and poets. It includes Mohammed, who supposedly split the Moslems off from Christianity, and his son-in-law, who continues the work by creating sects within Islam; Curio, who encouraged Caesar to cross the Rubicon, splitting republican Rome and causing civil war, which Dante sees as a crime against the official government, even though it led to the empire; Mosca, who instigated the murder that began the Guelph-Ghibelline feud in Florence, about whom Dante had asked Ciacco in canto 6; and Pier da Medicina, who fomented discord among nobles from which he reaped the benefits, who now warns truthfully of betrayal and murder, too late to be of any use, but not too late to incite to revenge. The single poet is Bertran de Born, who not only encouraged nobles to fight wherever he could, for self-serving reasons, but also incited members of Henry II's family against each other and their father. He is proud of what he did, comparing himself favorably with the biblical Achitophel and boasting of his wounds. Because he so severely failed in the poet's responsibility to guide men and betrayed his gift of language, he now carries his head in his hand like a lantern, which lights the way for no one; in contrast, Statius will describe Virgil as holding a light behind to help others see (Pg. 22.68–69). Dante admired Bertran's talent, praising his poetry in the *Convivio* and *De vulgari eloquentia,* but must condemn him here because of the political consequences of his words, and because he, who could use his poetic gift to the same ends, must dissociate himself from such examples.

Throughout the circle of fraud, Dante presents souls who undermined the institutions of church and state by destroying the trust and denying the love and justice on which they must be based. In the tenth and final section of fraud, he groups those who falsify the basic elements of social and political life: alchemists, who change the natural elements of the universe; impersonators, who take on the identity of others; counterfeiters and liars, who falsify the fundamental elements of exchange and communication—coins and words. Counterfeiting is even worse than tampering with the elements, because it threatens political stability directly.[76] The last scene in the circle of fraud is, fittingly, a violent exchange of fists and words between the liar, Sinon, whose false words helped to destroy Troy, the future Rome, and the counterfeiter, Adam, whose fake florins caused severe economic and political problems for Florence, the would-be Rome.

Fraud is the most complex circle of Hell in its structure and substance, the deception and manipulation of others in a variety of ways. But the last circle of Hell, treachery, is a far worse sin because of the objects of deception, those to whom one is bound by special ties, although it is much simpler in its conception. It is one sin, divided according to the relation between the sinner and his victim, a sin of conscious commitment in a much more intense way than any of the others because here one must not only conceive the betrayal, one must decide to deny the special loyalty that binds one to the object. There are four categories of traitors: betrayers of family, of nation, of guest, and of benefactor, all special bonds on which the stability of any society must depend. The Ottimo calls benefactors "those who give being as to worldly status" (1.530), a kind of surrogate parent. For contemporary readers, benefactor seems to mean "lord," *dominus,* a political more than a personal connection (Guido, 676, Benvenuto, 2.489, and the Ottimo, 1.545, who says that both the last sections of Hell involve the breaking of the *dominicale fidanza* that a lord has in his subjects). One might expect either betrayal of family, because it is the archetypal sin against another, or betrayal of nation, because

[76]The Ottimo points out that some aspects of alchemy are all right, like the attempt to alter towards a more perfect form, or to make alloys, but faking is wrong (1.494–95), cf. Jacopo (1.453). According to Jacopo, both alchemists and counterfeiters are falsifiers of coins, of money (1.312). Both the Ottimo and Benvenuto (2.432–3) cite Aristotle on the importance of money, invented for the common use and good of men, Benvenuto going into more detail about the evolution of money from barter to metal, weight to sign.

of the number of victims, to be the worst, but instead it is the betrayal of an obligation one has willingly assumed, a breaking of an implicit contract, on one side to protect, on the other to be grateful. These relations are the quintessential social relations and cannot be denied without destroying society itself.

There are political overtones in all the regions of the ninth circle: several of the souls in the first section, Caina, murdered their relatives to take over their lands and powers; the second section, Antenora, is made up entirely of political traitors;[77] Tolomea is named for and inhabited by souls who betrayed guests for political reasons; and of the three souls in the Giudecca, two assassinated the first Roman emperor. Antenora is named for the Trojan who, like Ulysses, was involved in the theft of the Palladium and the deception of the wooden horse, but against his own country; in it, Dante encounters a traitor to Florence, involved in the shameful defeat at Montaperti, and pulls his hair out, participating not only as an offended Florentine, but also as an instrument of divine vengeance.[78] Tolomea is so named either for the son of the high priest in 1 Maccabees 16, who killed his guest, a public official traveling to keep the country in order, or for the king of Egypt, brother of Cleopatra, who had Pompey killed, or for both; this name has meaning for the histories of both chosen nations, Rome and Israel. Perhaps implicit in the ambiguity of the name is the confusion between church and state, the interference of the church in secular affairs, which so troubles Dante in his own period, and which is reflected in the presence of the archbishop Ruggieri and of Fra Alberigo in this section. The souls here are those who have killed their guests (one cannot overstress the sanctity of hospitality in the Middle Ages), but the deed is particularly offensive to Dante when the motivation is politi-

[77]Villani mentions several of them and tells their stories, noting that they appear in this canto of the *Comedy* (*Istorie Fiorentine*, 7.4 and 79).

[78]One soul asks "qual diavol ti tocca?" (32.108), meaning "what the hell is wrong with you?" but literally "what devil touches you?" Dante is, of course, the "devil" who helps punish the soul, a role he gladly assumes among the traitors, as in his refusal to open Alberigo's eyes with the words "e cortesia fu lui esser villano" (33.150: "and it was courtesy to be rude to him").

cal, as it is in every case he mentions. Indeed, Dante is moved by the souls he sees not to sympathy for them but to attacks on their cities, Pisa in 33.79 and the Genovese in 33.151, as if the whole city were tainted by the sin.

The impulse to betray is so strong that it continues even in Hell; there is always one who will name his "brothers," and Dante quickly learns to play them against each other in order to find out what he wants to know, to betray in his turn. This is, of course, the fruit of betrayal: it draws others into the sin so that, almost inevitably, the betrayer is betrayed. When the Florentine traitor refuses to give his name, another soul identifies him; the first, in fury, names not only the one who gave him away, but a host of others, as if their shame somehow lessened his. One soul gnaws on the skull of his enemy, the hatred so strong that it impels him to devour even what has no substance.[79] Dante goes out of his way to shock the audience with the last souls he sees before he reaches Satan, because he wants to impress on us the lessons he draws from them: Ugolino gnaws on Ruggieri's skull, Fra Alberigo is in Hell although his body is still alive on earth. Ugolino's story, the last extended comment by a soul in Hell, is reminiscent in many ways of the first told by Francesca in canto 5.[80] By the echoes in these two

[79]In fact, this passion to destroy the enemy affects even Dante, who tears the hair and kicks the head of Bocca in canto 32. The cannibal act is an apt symbol of the banquet at which the crime against the guest is committed, literally in the case of Alberigo, which is picked up in the fruit metaphors scattered throughout the episode. Dante does not allow us to shrink from the horror of the scene; indeed, he leaves us with a particularly disturbing doubt: Ugolino describes his sons offering themselves as food when they see him chewing on his hands from hunger; after the sons die, the father, blind from hunger, gropes for them and the last line he speaks is "then hunger did more than sorrow could" (33.75). Presumably he means that hunger killed him before sorrow, but since two lines later he is again gnawing at the skull, his teeth "strong on the bone like a dog's" (33.78), Dante forces us at least to entertain the thought that he might also have tried to eat his sons. The mere fact that one can consider it, even to reject it, is sufficiently horrible for Dante's purpose in characterizing betrayal.

[80]Both are gracious to the poet, unlike so many in Hell, because they seek his sympathy, wanting him to view them as they see themselves, as victims,

stories from the beginning and end of Hell, Dante is saying that the selfish impulse which moves all sinners, the satisfaction of the sinner's desires with no thought to the consequences for anyone else, is the same. It is destructive to the self and to others, whether it consumes them literally, as in Ugolino's case, or figuratively, as in Francesca's; it is passion which devours them and their partners, who are also their victims. Sin is finally, after all the intricate distinctions Dante has made through the cantica, selfishness, the indulgence of the self at the expense of all other obligations, and therefore, by definition, antisocial. That is why it is possible to consider, even for a moment, that Ugolino may have tried to feed on his sons. Dante's view of treachery is that a man who can commit it is no longer human. Ugolino says he could not weep when he found himself locked in the tower because he had turned to stone inside (33.49), but he was stone long before, when he committed his own acts of betrayal, a point Dante makes most forcefully through Fra Alberigo. His soul is in Hell, but his body remains on earth, inhabited by a demon, a particular "vantaggio," "privilege," of this section: as soon as an act of treachery is committed against a guest, the soul goes to Hell. In other words, the soul that commits such an act is already damned, incapable of moral judgment as it is incapable of feeling. Dante is making a startling point about this kind of treachery;[81] but he is also calling attention to the main lesson

---

and both distort their stories in order to win him over. Both are shut into small spaces and killed with those they love, with the implication that they are imprisoned and destroyed by their own vices, which also destroy those they love. Francesca tells her story partly to condemn her husband, who will end up in this last circle of Hell because he killed his brother, as Ugolino speaks in order to condemn his enemy, Ruggieri, blaming him for the death of his sons, though Ugolino, long before he was imprisoned in the tower, had sacrificed his family to political ambition and revenge. See Villani, *Istorie Fiorentine*, 7.120 and 127.

[81]It is unorthodox if we take it literally, despite certain biblical passages: in John 13:27, Jesus gives sop to one who will betray him "and after the morsel, Satan entered into him"; in Psalm 54:16, "let death come upon them [friends who betray] and let them go down alive into hell." Guido comments that just

of this cantica, that we create hell by allowing ourselves to be dominated by these impulses. Once we give in to them, our feelings are dead; the lake of the heart becomes the frozen lake of Cocytus, with pure evil—Satan—at its core.

Around the outer limits of the ninth circle stand four giants who, at a distance, appear to Dante to be towers. Dante's first view of the city of Dis, as of any medieval city, was its towers; here at its center we see the corrupt city for what it really is, not a city at all, but an anarchic mass, devoid of all human feeling, frozen in a lake of ice, guarded by naked, mostly mindless force.[82] Perhaps because they are seen as towers, the giants are meant to suggest the pride of the magnates. Benvenuto says that a high tower figures pride, that the giants are proud rulers who presume against God and subject men to their own will, mentioning in this connection that the giant at the end of Purgatory represents the king of France (2.457–58). Pietro suggests that the giants signify earthly powers, bound and reduced to impotence by God (263). The first giant Dante sees here is Nembrot, who built the tower of Babel to reach heaven, leading to the confusion of tongues, the destruction of communication among different peoples; his pride harmed not only his own, but all peoples. The rest are classical figures who were involved in rebellion against the gods, and Antaeus, who fought the Christ figure, Hercules. With the giants around the edge and Satan at the center of the circle, it is rebellion against the highest ruler, God, and betrayal of the Creator that dominates the circle, the ultimate treachery and the supreme arrogance committed by the highest classes of creature, angels and giants, those just beneath the divine in the hierarchy.

At the center of the corrupt city, Dante sees its lord literally consuming his subjects, but otherwise impotent, imprisoned in

---

as the apostle had said "I am alive, but not I, Christ lives in me," so a man obstinate in sin might say "the demon lives in me" (705).

[82]Antaeus seems to be an exception, the kind of giant nature left off creating because the combination of huge body with reason was too potent (Hell 31.49–57).

the corruption he has helped create.[83] The Satan Dante sees is a perverted reflection of the God he aspired to be, three heads, with the three traitors in his mouths. All of them betrayed their greatest benefactor, and all of them betrayed God, either in himself, as Satan did, in his human form (Christ), as Judas did, or in his vicar (the emperor), as Brutus and Cassius did. Brutus and Cassius had both fought with Pompey on the side of the Roman republic; both had been pardoned by Caesar and given high office, which they accepted, and yet they plotted and carried out his murder. Dante makes an important distinction between Cato, whom he places in Purgatory because he fought Caesar as an enemy of the Roman state but remained true to his principles, and Brutus and Cassius, who changed sides and whose allegiance should have been to the empire once it was established as well as to the emperor who had befriended them. The objects of betrayal in the final section of Hell are universal benefactors: God, who bestowed creation on all creatures, Christ, who died to redeem mankind, and the founder of the empire, which exists to restore mankind to paradise. In sinning against any of them, the implication is, we commit the worst of all sins and ultimately betray ourselves.

Dante shows, through the cantica of Hell, that we choose in our acts to inhabit the city of Hell, to turn our own city into Hell. He reminds us that Hell is a city as he enters the last circle, when he asks the muses to aid him, as they aided Amphyon to enclose Thebes (32.11), an allusion to the creation of a city by eloquence.[84] Dante has also created such a city,

[83]Benvenuto (2.552) says that the long arms of Satan figure the long power of this king who has many kings under him, his power extending east and west.

[84]Jacopo notes that according to Statius, Amphyon was so polished and graceful a speaker that everyone went to work on the walls of Thebes just to hear him (1.488). The Ottimo calls him a "most wise and ornate speaker, through whose wise and ornate speech the state and the well-being of the city of Thebes grew and was preserved" (1.549). Boccaccio, in the *Genealogie Deorum Gentilium Libri*, ed. Vincenzo Romano (Bari: Laterza, 1951), interprets

modeled on his own city, Florence, which, like Thebes, is destroying itself by its selfishness and total lack of moral order. Benvenuto goes into lengthy detail towards the end of his commentary on Hell to show the reader how the city of Hell reflects the earthly city:

> Considera ergo quod sicut imperator, rex vel dominus stat in medio civitatis, ita Lucifer stat in centro istius civitatis; et sicut apud regem stant nobiles et magnates, qui sunt sibi magis familiares et amici, ita de prope Luciferum stant isti proditores sub umbra alarum eius; et sicut circa palatium, ad portas et in platea stant custodes, ita hic in circuitu circa lacum stant gigantes magni et fortes, tamquam satellites et stipatores deputati ad custodiam tanti regis, per quorum manus omnes transeunt ad curiam eius. Et sicut postea in tota terra per diversos vicos et contratas stant cives, mercatores et artistae, ita in tota ista civitate sunt fraudulenti et violenti per diversas bulgias et circulos; quia in omni contrata inveniuntur diversae fraudes mercatorum et artistarum, et ita diversae violentiae divitum et nobilium, qui nituntur suppeditare alios quantum possunt; et sicut in suburbiis civitatis stant rustici, viles et incogniti, ita hic extra civitatem fortem et muratam stant incontinentes; et sicut communiter extra civitatem est flumen per quod transitur ad civitatem, ita hic est Acheron magnus fluvius per quem transitur ad istam civitatem maximam omnium, quae continet in se magnam partem civium omnium civitatum mundi. Et sicut longe a civitate stant strenui et bellatores in campis qui gerunt bella, et philosophi et heremitae qui speculantur in solitudine; ita hic in campo herboso et amoeno stant viri illustres, philosophi et poetae separati ab omni turba confusa aliorum gloriosi . . .

Amphyon's building the city in the same way, that he persuaded ignorant, crude, and obstinate men by his mellifluous speech, to come together, live civilly, and surround the city for public defense, 1.274.

Consider that, just as an emperor, king, or lord is at the middle of his city, so Lucifer is at the center of this city; and just as there are nobles and magnates with the king, who are his servants and friends, so near Lucifer are the traitors, beneath the shadow of his wings; and as at the gates and in the courtyard of the palace there are guards, so here around the lake are great and strong giants, like attendants assigned to care for the king, through whose hands all must pass to enter his court. And just as in the whole land, in different villages and towns, there are citizens, merchants, artisans, so in this whole city, there are the fraudulent and violent in different sections and circles; for in every town different frauds of merchants and artisans are found, just so different kinds of violence by the rich and noble, who strive to be supplied by others as much as they can; and just as in the suburbs of cities there are peasants, common and unknown, so here outside the strong walled city are the incontinent; and as there is usually a river outside the city by which one crosses into the city, so here is the great river Acheron by which one crosses to this greatest city of all which contains in itself the great part of the citizens of all the cities of the world. And just as the strong warriors who wage war in the fields, and philosophers and hermits who speculate in solitude are far from the city, so here in the lovely green field are the illustrious men, glorious philosophers and poets. . . . (2.561–62)

The political side of Dante's message was clearly not foreign to contemporary readers. But the message of Hell is not unrelievedly negative. At the end, Dante tells us that Satan's fall caused the mountain of Purgatory to rise on the other side of the earth; that is, he helped establish the place of man's restoration even before he tempted man to fall. Just as his body provides Dante and Virgil the means of beginning their climb out of Hell, so his fall provides for mankind the place to climb from the sinful state to salvation.[85] The knowledge of evil in the self and the state, which Dante has described in such detail in Hell, should provide the means to begin the move towards a new self and a new society, which Dante begins in Purgatory and completes in Paradise.

[85]The colors of his three faces are echoed in the three steps to the gate of Purgatory, because the knowledge of evil is essential to a proper confession. The colors also suggest the political factions of Dante's time, which, like Satan, work against the divine order: the black and off-white faces, the Black and White Guelphs; the off-white and red, the Guelphs and Ghibellines, whose emblems changed, but who always had red on white or white on red. See Villani, *Istorie Fiorentine*, 6.43.

FOUR

Society in Transition: Purgatory

DANTE'S PURGATORY, where individuals learn to become citizens of the ideal society, is situated on an island on the surface of this earth. It is potentially accessible to the living—Ulysses sailed within sight of it—but only in humility and acceptance of the divine order. This realm partakes more of earthly existence than Hell or Paradise, because Dante believes and wants his audience to believe that it can be established here. With the right leadership in church and state and the good will of individuals, the earthly paradise could be achieved. Dante subtly shows the relation between the individual moral struggle and the political situation in Italy, the microcosm and the macrocosm, by his use of the image of horse and rider. In the *Convivio*, 4.9.10, he had described the emperor as the horseman who rides the human will; in Purgatory, the individual souls are horses, spurred and whipped by the examples of virtue and vice on each ledge, and Italy is a riderless horse, become a wild beast because the emperor does not sit in the saddle with his hand on the bridle and correct it with his spurs (Pg. 6.88–96). At the center of Purgatory, canto 16, Dante states quite explicitly the role of the emperor in the moral struggle of the individual: Marco Lombardo, the model courtier, tells Dante that whatever corruption exists on earth is the fault of men, not of the stars, since we have the judgment to distinguish good from evil and free will to choose between them. At the same time, the individual needs guidance in making his choice, hence the need for both laws, with someone to enforce them, and guides, the empire to lead us in this world, the church to lead us to God.

Man is a social animal whose behavior is affected by his social setting and whose actions can affect his society. The extraordinary individual might be able to save himself, but most men need the help of their fellows. Dante sees almost all vice and virtue in terms of their effects on others and, therefore, cannot separate personal morality from the public context. He brings the two together in the central cantos of Purgatory, which are also the central cantos of the *Comedy*, because the main political and moral message of his poem is that in a well-functioning society, all men benefit from the virtues of others, but in a corrupt society, the bad individual disrupts the function of church and state, and corrupt institutions lead the individual astray. Reform must come from both directions. If this seems paradoxical, it is because the individuals Dante is thinking of, to whom he is addressing the poem, are those in a position by both talent and birth to affect the affairs of other men. They are those of strong intellect and will who have power in the world and can learn to control their own actions and influence those of church and state.

Dante presents Purgatory as a realm of opposing forces and tendencies, like life on earth, in which the individual must strike the proper balance. The atmosphere alternates between day and night, and the souls change their activities accordingly from action to contemplation. No one can climb at night, but no one wants to without the grace that fuels desire; similarly no one can leave his ledge before he is purged, but no one wants to leave before he is ready. This balance between freedom and law reflects the ideal harmony of Paradise. Balance and control are the essence of Purgatory, control in the laws which are freely accepted and imposed by the souls on themselves, balance in the examples of vice and remedial virtue that follow and precede each section, the good and bad rulers, good and bad within families, and Ghibellines and Guelphs. Purgatory embodies neither the absolute evil of Hell nor the absolute good of Paradise, but rather the tendency to evil controlled by the opposing desire for good.

Since the souls Dante meets here are in transition, moving towards the dominance of good rather than evil tendencies, they cannot provide examples of extraordinary vice and virtue. Instead, Dante draws these examples from the two spheres of secular and religious history. He focuses on the two chosen peoples, Rome and Israel, presenting scenes from the Old and New Testaments and from ancient history and literature.[1] At the end of Purgatory, he fuses the two histories in the procession of the books of the Bible and the pantomime of church history in relation to secular rule. Just as the historic examples have served throughout Purgatory to inspire the individual soul, so the individual in the Earthly Paradise (Dante, in this case) becomes a part of the procession of providential history that unfolds for him, and Dante's poem becomes an instrument of that history, a divinely destined successor to the books of the Bible. When any individual completes the process of purgation, when his desire to do good is stronger than his inclination to sin, he becomes a citizen of the ideal state, a *cive* of "that Rome of which Christ is a Roman" (Pg. 32.101–02), whose model is Paradise.

In Hell, the model journey was the national movement from Troy to the promised Rome under Aeneas; in Purgatory, Dante adds a second paradigm, Exodus, the journey of Israel from the slavery of Egypt to the promised land under Moses. This is the model he offers for the entire *Comedy* in his letter dedicating *Paradiso* to Can Grande, because it includes the anagogical as well as the moral and the historical; he introduces it in the second canto of Purgatory, when the souls sing *In exitu Israel de Aegypto* as they approach the island. For Dante, the goals of the two peoples, Rome and Israel, are the same; when they are achieved, the earthly paradise will be restored. In order to bring that about on this earth, mankind needs the guidance of both church and state. Dante makes a special attempt in this cantica to defend the function of the church, whose corruption

[1]Rome includes all of classical culture, since Dante's sources of Greek history and legend were all Roman.

200

he had so severely criticized in Hell and will attack again in Paradise, although he is careful even here to have the church represented by the purely spiritual angels. He presents the sacrament of confession as the essential first step in purgation and acknowledges the power of the papal indulgence and of excommunication; he uses hymns, prayers, and uplifting examples to encourage the souls and gives the history of the church its place within the procession of providential history, though not without an indictment of its current corruption. At the same time, Dante expands the political outlook of his audience from the Italian cities, which continue to command his attention, to the larger regions of Italy, Tuscany, Romagna, Lombardy, Sicily, and beyond to Provence and France and the rest of Europe and ultimately to the whole world, from the regions of the Ganges and the Tigris and Euphrates to the island of Purgatory on the other side of the planet. Purgatory, like Italy, is a kingdom, loosely tied by linguistic and cultural bonds, with no political organization and no center; it is neither city nor empire, like Hell and Paradise, but simply a passage, a roadway from one to the other.

In order to complete the passage, the individual, like the nation and the race, depends on his fellows. In sharp contrast to the anarchy and isolation, the utter selfishness, of the inhabitants of Hell, the souls in Purgatory show concern for each other, offer support and guidance. They reveal from the very beginning a sense of community, and more and more, as Dante moves through the realm, a sense of responsibility, a need to serve. In Purgatory, they help and comfort each other when they can; when they cannot, they offer sympathy. They have a community of interests in the desire to rise to heaven, which enables them to speak for each other, not, as in Hell, to betray, but rather to praise when the other is held back by humility, or to express a common need, to make an effort that serves the other as well as the self. Many are presented in friendly pairs, often from opposing political factions, such as the princes in canto 7, Currado and Nin in canto 8, Oderisi and Provenzan in canto 11, Guido and Rinier in canto 14. In this atmosphere they can welcome the stranger, Dante, with pleasure not hostility or fear, because any new object of joy enhances the potential joy of all; in Paradise, the actual joy is reflected in increasing intensity, as light is by mirrors. The souls express the harmony they are beginning to feel in the hymns they sing together, a structured unity provided by the words and music they all know but enabling them to give expression to a deeper desire for real union; in Paradise, the souls are able to create the visual symbols of their beings spontaneously, because they all reflect and are one with the divine will. The basic element of this harmony is love, the natural love that all men feel for their fellows unless they are distracted by the wrong objects. Love, we learn at the center of the cantica, is the motivating force for all action, good or bad; since wrongly directed love causes sin, rightly directed love can help make up for sin, even if it comes from another. This is the basis of prayers for the dead: the debt the sinner must pay to divine justice can be made up partly by the love of others, expressed in their prayers.[2] Dante is making not only a theological, but a psychological point: the love of one's fellows, relatives, or friends, can help one to withstand the temptations of the wrong desires and strengthen the desire for the right. That is why social community is so important, even in the individual process of salvation.

Every social unit, as outlined in *Convivio*, 4.4., and *Monarchy*, 1.5, plays a part in the process: the family, the circle of friends, the city, and the nation. Family is, of course, the basic political unit in Florence (cf. chapter one), and Dante emphasizes the family through Purgatory in various ways. Souls speak of their living relatives, to ask for prayers, to send messages of comfort and good news of their own unexpected salvation, or to lament the decline of their lines; and women are far more prominent in Purgatory than in the other two realms.[3] At the same time, Dante enlarges our sense of family

[2]See Aquinas, ST, Supp., 2.71, on the efficacy of prayers for the dead.
[3]Women figure prominently among those who can help in the struggle for good, not only as wives and daughters, but also as the incarnation of virtues.

by having the souls address each other as brothers, all sons and daughters of Adam and Eve. The presence of the first parents is felt throughout Purgatory: Dante speaks of his body as "quel d'Adamo" (9.10, as does Virgil, 11.44), and of mankind as "sons of Eve" (12.71) and "daughters of Adam" (29.86); Omberto alludes to the "common mother" of all men (11.63); the drama in the valley of negligent princes recalls the temptation of Adam and Eve when the serpent is described as "perhaps the one who gave Eve the bitter food" (8.99). And in the Earthly Paradise, we are reminded of their role in losing that home for mankind (30.52, 32.37), but we are also offered the possibility of returning to it by our communal efforts. Dante is building, through the cantica, the sense of all men as members of one family, which is basic to the concept of one universal nation. The link binding us all as fellow human beings should be as strong as the link binding us to those closest to us.

There is another "family" in Purgatory, the family of poets, joined in their artistic relations as fathers and sons, and important in two ways: on the one hand, they help to trace Dante's development from a lyric to an epic poet, from one who, like the souls in Hell, indulges in the expression of his own feelings and needs, to one who, like the prophets and the saints, carries the divine message to all mankind; on the other hand, they provide the guidance man desperately needs, while the formal guides, pope and emperor, are notoriously deficient. Human art, Dante had Virgil explain in Hell (canto 11), imitates nature, which imitates God. Thus ideally poetry and the visual arts reflect the divine order in one way, the church and state in another. Dante, who is being groomed to carry the divine message, is more self-consciously the artist in this cantica than in either of the others. He emphasizes the role art plays in life on earth, selecting other poets to guide himself and Virgil, like Sordello and Statius, discussing developments in tradition and

---

The nymphs who represent the seven virtues in the Earthly Paradise appear as women on earth and as stars in heaven, like Venus, the goddess of love and the planet whose light appears in the first canto. The Virgin Mary is an example of every virtue.

taste on the first and last ledges and letting poets dominate the last two ledges of Purgatory. Even God is presented as a sculptor and author: God created the sculpture on the ledge of pride, though we see it only because Dante describes it in his words, just as God composed the Bible, which we read because men took it down. God also created history, but we act it out and we understand it because Dante explains it to us, not only in the Earthly Paradise, but throughout the *Comedy*.

Dante relies more on the visual arts in Purgatory than in the other parts of the poem, presumably because of their didactic value for life on earth. He even seems to structure Purgatory as a dynamic heptatych, a series of corresponding panels opening out from the center:

ANTE-PURGATORY (Cato; drama of serpent and angels)
DREAM (eagle)
SINS (pride, envy, wrath, sloth)
DREAM (siren)
SINS (avarice & prodigality, gluttony, lust)
DREAM (Lia)
EARTHLY PARADISE (Matelda; procession of bible, mime of church and state)

Each of the seven ledges within Purgatory proper is structured in a similar way: angel/examples of virtues/souls/examples of vices/angel.[4] The angel at the end of one ledge is the angel for the beginning of the next, so although each ledge appears to be distinct, it is connected, moving one into another, unlike the circles of Hell. The main variation from this structure on the ledge of avarice, which is the most populous, calls attention to the three functions ordained to guide man through life:

[4]The structure for the separate ledges was observed by Enrico De'Negri, "Tema e iconografia del *Purgatorio*," *Romanic Review* 49 (1958), 81–104. I have extended the concept to the structure of the entire cantica. Note that the figures who serve as examples of virtues and vices are quite distinct from the souls who are actually in Purgatory.

ANGEL

    SOUL (pope)

        EXAMPLES (virtues)

    SOUL (king)

        EXAMPLES (vices)

    SOUL (poet)

ANGEL

Pope, king, and poet are all caught up in their own desires, but the poet completes his purgation and becomes free to move with Dante and Virgil as they pass through the circle. That is, church and state are still held back by their selfish impulses, while Dante frees poetry to serve mankind. Virtually all the souls Dante meets in Purgatory are public figures, statesmen, poets, the kinds of people who must have their own lives in order for them to lead others. They are here not just because as important people they have greater didactic value, but because they can and must embody political virtues, and the virtues and vices of each ledge are set within a social-political context.

Geographically, the whole of Purgatory looks towards the goal Dante describes in the *Monarchy,* the achievement of happiness in this life typified by the earthly paradise; the Earthly Paradise at the top of the mountain is what the souls are striving to attain for themselves and for mankind. At the bottom of the mountain, the Ante-Purgatory extends from the shore to the valley of negligent princes, which is a pale reflection of the Earthly Paradise those princes should have worked to restore. In between, there is only a road leading upwards in a spiral through the seven ledges on which the souls can prepare themselves to enter the Earthly Paradise. The road represents the common bond of the souls in Purgatory, their desire to reach the Earthly Paradise.

Instead of the many and varied guardians of Hell, Purgatory has only an angel at each ledge and two historical figures, Cato in Ante-Purgatory and Matelda in the Earthly Paradise, all of whom serve as guides rather than guards. Cato and Matelda are counterbalancing figures: Cato an old man, Matelda a young woman, Cato a Stoic pagan, Matelda a devout Christian. Both were directly involved in the major political struggles of their time and both are surprising choices for Dante: Cato is not only a pagan and a suicide, but a defender of republican Rome against the future empire; Matelda is a Christian countess who fought literally and figuratively to defend the church against the emperor and tried to leave her strategically located lands to the church when she died.[5] Instead of condemning them for their anti-imperial actions, Dante exalts them for the purity of their motives and their courage in support of their beliefs. Cato sacrificed his life in the cause of moral liberty and Matelda defended the reform pope against the corruption of political power exercised within the church. Leaving her lands to the church was a mistake, but well-intentioned, like Constantine's Donation, which was far more harmful but does not deny him heaven. Dante carefully establishes the proper political balance between the extremes these two represent through the courtier, Marco Lombardo, at the center of Purgatory; Dante asserts the importance of the two suns, church and empire, to rule the world, and condemns the church for trying to do it alone.

It is Cato who dominates the opening of Purgatory. He is the first figure Dante meets in this cantica, as Virgil was in Hell, and he is, like Virgil, an ancient Roman and an old and worthy man. As Virgil was the poet-supporter of empire, Cato is the moral statesman, enemy of empire and of political greed; Dante sees himself both as a poet of empire in the Virgilian tradition and as a political martyr like Cato. Virgil acknowledges Cato as one who gave up his life for liberty, a sentiment Dante also expresses in the *Monarchy*, 2.5: in order to fill the world with the love of freedom, Cato showed how great free-

---

[5]The early commentators I consulted all identify the Matelda in the Earthly Paradise as the countess of Tuscany, though modern commentators have made various other suggestions, as will be discussed later in this chapter.

dom is by preferring to die rather than live without it.[6] Cato opposed Caesar because he saw him as a rebel to the state, as one who brought civil war, and as a potential tyrant. The liberty he chose is essential to the moral life—one has to be free in order to choose virtue, but the knowledge that one has such a choice is basic to any sense of moral responsibility and it is this sense that distinguishes the souls in Purgatory from those in Hell, who blamed everything but themselves for their actions and situations. Cato is therefore the ideal representative of the moral life, as Matelda will be of the active life, and it is he who speaks for the laws which govern the moral universe of Hell and Purgatory; liberty without law creates the apparent anarchy of Hell.[7] Cato views Virgil as a rebel against the laws of Hell, as he had considered Julius Caesar a rebel against the laws of Rome. Virgil had himself called Cato a lawgiver in the *Aeneid* (8.670), and Cato may be perceived as a secular Moses figure in the *Comedy:* as Moses led his people across the desert and away from slavery, so Cato led his army across the desert and away from tyranny.[8] As a figure of moral rectitude, Cato is also a counter to the Veglio di Creta, the

[6]In Lucan's poem, *De bello civili,* Cato tells Brutus he would willingly be a scapegoat for the nation in order to avert civil wars and wishes his own blood might redeem nations, his own death expiate the sacrilege of war, 2.312. On medieval views of dying for the fatherland, see Ernst Kantorowicz, "Pro patria mori," in *The King's Two Bodies* (Princeton: Princeton University, 1957) 232 ff.

[7]Cf. Dante's letter to the Florentines (Ep. 6), in which he accuses them of shrinking from the "yoke of liberty" (*iugum libertatis horrentes*) in opposing the Roman emperor. Marco Lombardo (Pg. 16.80) says man is "subject freely" (*liberi soggiacete*) to greater force and better nature. The souls in Hell act as if they were not bound by any moral laws; they are, however, subject to divine justice. It is interesting in this regard that Virgil does not feel himself bound by the laws of Hell proper ("Minos me non lega," Pg. 1.77), though he must ultimately return to Hell. Although a virtuous man, he too fails to acknowledge God's law fully.

[8]See Robert Hollander, *Allegory in Dante's Commedia* (Princeton: Princeton University, 1969), 158 ff., for a detailed study of this connection. See also Carol Kaske, "Mount Sinai and Dante's Mount Purgatory," *Dante Studies* 89 (1971), 1–18.

statue in Hell which represents the continuing corruption of mankind, the only other figure of whom Dante uses the word *veglio* in the *Comedy*.[9] Cato dissociated himself completely from political and moral corruption to such an extent that Dante could ask of him in the *Convivio:* what mortal man was more worthy of representing God than Cato (4.28.15)?

Cato is, for Dante, the perfect figure of the man who in maturity gives the fruit of his life to others, who thought of himself as born not for himself, but for his fatherland and all the world (*Convivio,* 4.27.3).[10] But to live for the world rather than for himself, Cato has to divest himself of certain earthly ties, or to see them in a different light. When Virgil tries to move him with thoughts of his wife, Marzia, Cato stops him; though he loved her in the other life, he now sees her as an inhabitant of Hell, which is also how he sees Virgil. Cato is the one figure in Purgatory who shows no reverence for Virgil as a poet, but treats him simply as an intruder in the realm of the saved. This reproof should have prepared Virgil and Dante to withstand the temptation of Casella in the next canto, but it does not; when Dante sees his old friend, he cannot resist asking him to sing as he used to, and all the souls stop to listen.[11] There is nothing wrong with the shared experience, nothing wrong even with the substance of the song, but it is

[9]See Giuseppe Mazzotta, *Dante, Poet of the Desert* (Princeton: Princeton University, 1979), chapter one, on this connection and on Dante's use of Cato as a figure of redemption. To the early commentators, Cato stands for virtue and honesty (Pietro, 296), virtue and solicitude for earthly politics (Jacopo, 2.14); Benvenuto praises his honesty and virtue though he questions his suicide (3.17 and 36). It is possible to read a line of Cato's in Lucan's *De bello civili* as intuitive faith in the Judeo-Christian God: "Iuppiter est, quodcumque vides, quodcumque moveris," 9.580.

[10]The Cato in Purgatory offers a clear contrast between his own self-sacrifice for liberty and the self-indulgence of Ulysses, who ignored divinely set limits to satisfy his curiosity. The audience is reminded of Ulysses' ill-fated journey and death in sight of Purgatory at the end of the first canto (1.130–32).

[11]See Robert Hollander, "*Purgatorio* II: Cato's Rebuke and Dante's *scoglio*," *Studies in Dante* (Ravenna: Longo, 1980), 91–105, and John Freccero, "Casella's Song (*Purg.* II, 112)," *Dante Studies* 91 (1973), 73–80, on the significance of Dante's poem in this context.

wrong to be a passive audience here, particularly for Dante, who takes pride in hearing his own words sung, instead of participating as the souls had done in the singing of the hymn at the beginning of the canto and, more important, instead of using his poetry to move others to act. On the contrary, his poem has contributed to their negligence, pleasing them so that they think of nothing else (2.116–17; "parevan sì contenti,/come a nessun toccasse altro la mente"). Dante must learn to turn his poetic gifts to a higher purpose, to serve mankind and not himself, like Cato.

Negligence is the problem of all the souls in the Ante-Purgatory, as Cato underlines rather sharply: "qual negligenza, qual stare è questo?" (2.121: "what negligence, what stay is this?") They neglected their religious obligation in one way or another: they died excommunicate, cut off by the church from the sacraments (like Manfredi), or by violent death before they could receive the last rites (Jacopo, Bonconte, Pia), or they neglected religious duties throughout their lives in a private or public sense (Belacqua and the negligent princes).[12] Indeed, even Casella is there early because he benefited from a special indulgence, not because of his own actions.[13] Dante is acknowledging the role the church plays in salvation by administering the sacraments, though not altogether without qualification. The souls must wait outside Purgatory for a period of time related to their neglect of the sacraments, unless the time is shortened by the prayers of others, since man's love, like God's, can counterbalance the church's power. But they will enter at some point, because their own motivations and beliefs are, finally, what matter to God.

Even Manfredi is saved although he was long an enemy of the church, several times excommunicated, the object of a cru-

---

[12]The negligence of the princes cannot be merely of religious rituals, since the very religious Henry III is among them, but rather of the divinely ordained duty to guide the world towards unity.

[13]The Jubilee was not supposed to benefit the dead, but it seems to have here. See Amerindo Camilli, "La bolla giubilare di Bonifacio VIII e le indulgenze per i defunti e il ritardo di Casella," *Studi danteschi* 30 (1951), 207–09.

sade by Urban IV, refused holy burial and was even disinterred at the order of a bishop and perhaps of the pope, and a notorious sinner ("orribil furon li peccati miei," 3.121: "my sins were horrible").[14] If Casella's presence reveals the special grace that can be obtained through the church, Manfredi's offers a striking, if not shocking, example of the grace God grants despite the church. Manfredi was widely reputed to be an Epicurean heretic like his father (see Giovanni Villani, *Istorie Fiorentine* 6.46, Benvenuto, 3.102), and was believed to have committed terrible crimes, perhaps even the murder of relatives, but he was also the last major figure in the Hohenstaufen line who might have continued the empire in Italy; he fought courageously and died in that cause and incurred the wrath of the church because of it.[15] In Purgatory, Manfredi appears as a leader, at the head of a group of souls wandering like sheep. They are all excommunicates, cut off by the church from the assembly of Christians, sheep abandoned by their shepherd, but they instinctively form their own assembly and follow the divinely chosen leader, Manfredi.[16]

Unlike the souls in Hell who went immediately to the right circle, consciously committing themselves to their sinful lives,

[14]Louis La Favia, "Per una reinterpretazione dell'episodio di Manfredi," *Dante Studies* 91 (1973), 81–100, points out that Manfredi was the object of the strongest kind of excommunication, anathema, which was inflicted only on intransigent heretics and the most stubborn opponents of ecclesiastical authority. Villani repeats the story of the pope's involvement in the disinterment *Istorie Fiorentine,* 7.9, but says he cannot confirm it; he does, however, cite Dante as one who accepted it. The vindictive treatment of Manfredi's body by the church is subtly contrasted with the emperor's removal of Virgil's body for more honorable burial, alluded to in 3.27 and explicitly mentioned in 7.6.

[15]Brunetto Latini (*Trésor,* 1.97.1–9) accuses him of murdering his father, brother, and two nephews; Benvenuto (3.102 ff.) describes his strengths and talents, but also his vices, his greed to rule leading him to commit all kinds of crimes, and reports the part he was supposed to have played in the death of a brother.

[16]In Ante-Purgatory, the souls frequently reveal their lack of and need for a leader, in their sudden flight and dispersal without direction after Cato's reproof (3.1–3) and in their reckless speed to announce Dante's living presence (5.42), "like a troop running without a rein."

210

those in Ante-Purgatory must learn the way. When they first arrive, they are as ignorant as Dante and Virgil, but they learn from others, and as they learn they are ready to help in their turn: Manfredi's group leads the two poets to the next stage. The spirit of friendliness and cooperation, even of affection, as when Casella attempts to embrace Dante, is characteristic of the souls here.[17] The elements of the good society (the virtues of love for family, friends, and country, of faith in God, and forgiveness) are all present in the Ante-Purgatory, along with the leaders, but not yet in a properly ordered structure. Those who might have imposed the proper order on earth, the negligent princes, sit up in their valley contemplating their failures. The sense of community among these souls is in sharp contrast to what was seen in Hell, and Dante underscores that change by contrasting individual souls with infernal counterparts. He emphasizes the qualities essential to the good society by reminding us at the beginning of Purgatory of the antisocial effects of their opposites. Manfredi invites contrast with his father, Frederick, whom he was said to resemble in talent and heretical belief, but Manfredi is saved because he lacks his father's obstinacy in error and his intellectual arrogance.[18] The same point is made explicitly in the story of Bonconte da Montefeltro, son of the Guido who was condemned for fraudulent counsel in Hell 27; Bonconte was killed in the battle of Campaldino, which his actions helped to bring about, though he was guilty more of recklessness than deception, exiling Guelphs from Arezzo in 1287, which led ultimately to the bat-

[17]Even Sordello, who first appears alone and aloof, is filled with love for his fellow countryman and admiration for his fellow poet, Virgil. The one notable exception is Belacqua, who sits by himself in the shade, cut off as much from God as from his fellows.

[18]The heretical aspect is underscored by an implicit contrast with Mohammed. Manfredi reveals his wounds to Dante the way Mohammed had, inviting a comparison which is particularly apt, since the church accused Manfredi of being more Saracen than Christian. Manfredi, however, identifies himself by his relation to the good women of his family, his grandmother, whom Dante will see in Paradise, and his daughter, who is still alive, both called Costanza; he does not name his emperor father.

tle. Like his father, he is the object of a struggle for his soul, but in the son's case the angel wins, because the son died truly repentant, with the name of Mary and a tear.

The souls of the others who died violent deaths remind us of those in the lowest circles of Hell because their stories involve violence and betrayal, but they offer a sharp contrast in that they show no rancor for the crimes committed against them and make no plea for revenge. They all show restraint and a strong sense of public responsibility. Instead of contributing to the destructive violence of feuds, they help stem it with their forgiveness of others or their awareness of their own responsibility for the situation. Jacopo del Cassero, *podestà* of Bologna, was elected *podestà* of Milano, but on his way there, he was ambushed and killed in the Padovan marshes, which he calls the "bosom of the Antenorans" (5.75), those descended from the Trojan traitor for whom a section of the ninth circle of Hell was named. The treachery of the murder recalls that circle, but Jacopo's admission that he deserved some of his enemy's wrath and that he might have saved himself (5.77–81) is very different from the behavior of souls in Hell.[19] The only nonpolitical figure among the violent deaths, and the first woman Dante meets in Purgatory, is Pia, a victim of a murder which might have become a public problem if avenged. She recalls Francesca, the first woman Dante met in Hell, who was also murdered by her husband, though apparently with better cause; but unlike Francesca, who took pleasure in the thought of her husband's eternal pain, Pia does not seek revenge or betray any bitterness.

Six other victims of violent deaths are alluded to briefly at the beginning of canto 6, perhaps because they are contemporary and their stories would be well known, but perhaps also because the quick review suggests the enormous number of such victims in contemporary Italy. Three of them were

[19]Commentaries report that he went out of his way to infuriate his enemy, the tyrant Azzo d'Este, attacking his friends and insulting him, not surprising given the nature of the enemy, but certainly reckless in a public figure. See the Ottimo, 2.67, Jacopo, 2.58, Benvenuto, 3.152.

caught up in precisely the kind of feud Pia does not encourage: Conte Orso (6.19) was killed by a cousin, apparently in the course of a feud over the possession of castles between brothers—one a Guelph, the other a Ghibelline—and their descendents, which was alluded to in Hell, 32.55–58 (cf. Villani, *Istorie Fiorentine,* 6.69); an Aretine judge (6.13–15) was murdered in the hall of the tribunal by a relative of a man he had sentenced to death in the normal course of his duties, the murderer also an outlaw (6.14);[20] and the murdered son of another judge, Marzucco of Pisa (6.17–18), whose father forgave rather than avenged his death, a fact which the son, in contrast to Dante's cousin in Hell 29, does not seem to resent. Two other souls were directly involved in the Guelph-Ghibelline struggles plaguing most of northern Italy and died as a result of them, Federigo Novello (6.17) and Guccio dei Tarlati (6.15).[21] The sixth soul is Pier de la Broccia, (6.22–24), chamberlain and favorite of Philip III of France. Pier was killed as a result of the envy and intrigues of the queen and other enemies at the French court. Both the name, Peter "of the Brush," and the situation, the royal favorite envied by other courtiers, recall Pier della Vigna, the suicide of Hell 13, but that Pier, though innocent, damned himself rather than face public disgrace; this Pier, who is not necessarily innocent (see Pg. 6.20–21), accepted his fate, public execution. All the figures in this group were involved in public life, and all were the victims of the public and private problems that kept Italy and Europe divided. Now they all ask others to pray for them, looking for that love which can help pay the debt of justice and could also,

[20]See Silvio Pasquazi, "Canto VI," *Lectura Dantis Scaligera, Purgatorio* (Florence: Le Monnier, 1967), hereafter cited as LDS, 194.

[21]Marzucco's son, Gano, was killed by Ugolino's men; Ugolino's involvement in feuds was graphically demonstrated in Hell 33, and he becomes a symbol for the problem throughout Italy in Purgatory, 6.83, when Dante speaks of Italy's people inside the cities gnawing at one another. Federigo is seen with "le mani sporte" (6.16), "his hands outstreched," but very close in sound to "mani sporche," "dirty hands," a possible suggestion of guilt. Guccio is identified by Pietro, Jacopo, and the Ottimo as the one who drowned in flight from the Aretine Guelphs; according to Pietro, 327, it was an ambush.

on a larger scale, resolve the factional struggles and feuds they suffered from.

The major symbol of factionalism in Hell is the Florentine Farinata, who is also recalled in the Ante-Purgatory in two encounters. The poet Sordello appears to be, like Farinata, a solitary, proud, antisocial figure, "sola soletta ... altera e disdegnosa" (6.59 and 62), and like Farinata, he is drawn into conversation by the presence of a compatriot. In Hell, however, recollections of the shared homeland quickly led to factional disputes and verbal attack, whereas in Purgatory the thought leads to visions of Italy and then of Europe. The visions are disturbing, to be sure, but nonetheless properly motivated and moving in the right direction, from the smaller to the larger political unit, rather than from city to faction, as in Hell. The other scene that recalls Farinata is Dante's meeting with Giudice Nin Visconti and Currado Malaspina. In contrast to Farinata and his companion, Cavalcanti, who are so obsessed with their particular concerns, party and family, that they ignore the larger needs of city and land, Dante presents in Currado and Nin two men who served publicly, one within a strong family tradition of honor, the other despite the corruption in his family and in his administrators. For both men, family and public service are inextricably linked. Like the pair in Hell, Currado and Nin are of opposite factions, Nin a Guelph, Currado a Ghibelline; like them, they are concerned with family and nation, and like Farinata, Currado tells Dante about his future. But in every other way, the encounter is a contrast. Whereas Farinata and Cavalcanti never exchange a word and show no compassion for each other despite their bonds of city, married children, heretical beliefs, and eternal fate, Nin and Currado share their temporary exile in Ante-Purgatory amicably, as they share the news and the pleasure of Dante's live presence. Whereas Farinata and Dante had exchanged taunts and distressing views, Currado prophesies his family's hospitality to Dante in response to Dante's compliments to their liberality and valor. Farinata's family has been hated by Florence for generations; Currado's is honored from his grandfather, who supported the emperor Frederick II, to his grandson, who will be Dante's host. Currado, like Farinata, is concerned for his land, but his land remains a bastion of honor, known throughout Europe, despite the corruption all around, because it has had good rulers. Giudice Nin, on the other hand, who was also an important leader in his lifetime, is now concerned only with his wife and daughter, as Cavalcanti was with his son. He deplores his wife's remarriage, which seems to be a figure for shifting political alliances: she has moved from the Pisa Visconti (Guelphs) to the Milano Visconti (Ghibellines), a betrayal within the family, so to speak.[22] Thus Nin continues to be the victim of betrayal by his own people as he had been in life: his grandfather, Ugolino, who shared the *podestà* of Pisa with him (cf. Hell 33), had sided with Archbishop Ruggieri of the opposing faction in order to betray Nin and run him out of the city, but when he left Pisa, Nin became captain general of the Guelph league and was made a citizen of Genoa.[23] Despite all the obstacles, personal and public, Nin attempted to serve the common good, as he saw it, not just within one city, but in a larger political context of united cities, albeit in a league against the empire.

There is a movement outward in Ante-Purgatory from the separate cities that dominated the *Malebolge* in lower Hell toward larger regions of Italy and Europe. All but one of the victims of violence in cantos 5 and 6 come from major cities of northern Italy, Jacopo from Bologna (killed in Padovan territory en route to Milano), Bonconte from Arezzo (killed by Florentines), Pia from Siena (killed in the Maremma), the oth-

[22]They will not offer her as honorable a burial as his family would have, presumably because they will be in exile; see Giuseppe Petronio, "Canto VIII," *LDS*, 279.

[23]As we know from Hell 33, Ugolino would eventually be betrayed in turn by Ruggieri. Villani describes the event in *Istorie Fiorentine*, 7.120, noting that Ugolino's downfall was prophesied by a man of his court, Marco Lombardo, who will play an important role for Dante later in Purgatory. Nin was also betrayed in his Sardinian lands by his deputy, Fra Gomita, a barrator mentioned in Hell 22, who set his master's enemies free for bribes. Benvenuto makes the connections with Hell 22 and 33 in his commentary on Nin (3.226).

ers from Arezzo, Pisa, the Bisenza. Their stories, together with the love Sordello expresses for Mantova, lead Dante to his lament for Italy at the end of canto 6. The long speech (6.76–151) attacks all those responsible for her troubles: the emperor, the church, the various factions, and Florence. There is no emperor because his own greed and the church, in defiance of God's will, keep him out of Italy. What the emperor Albert, "uom sanza cura" (6.107: "a man without care"), fails to do, Florence is eager to, that is, shoulder the burden for the rest of Italy. That it is unable to do so is clear from its own situation, the continual change of laws, money, and customs, precisely the lack of stability which government was instituted to prevent.[24] The political divisions so stirringly described at the end of canto 6 are contrasted at the beginning of canto 7 with the unifying force of language. The Italian poet Sordello, who lived in France and wrote in Provençal, calls the Latin poet Virgil, "gloria di Latin," "glory of the Latins," as though Latin, French, Italian, and Provençal were all one.[25] In the sense that they are all Latin languages, they are of course one tradition, with their roots in Rome; politically, the lands also have their roots in Rome and the empire as their common tradition, but they refuse to accept it. The poet crosses national boundaries, reversing the effect of the tower of Babel, while

[24]Benvenuto says that what Dante attributes to Florence can be said of every land on earth at different times (3.192); he describes Italy in an extended metaphor as the most beautiful house in the world, whose summit is Rome (3.184–85), and Florence as a beautiful woman wearing all kinds of ornaments, sitting on feathers, but filled within with every kind of evil and disease (3.191–92). Pietro's comments on this passage focus on the need for government and the emperor, without whom tyrants abound, who consider private rather than public good (325 ff.).

[25]In De vulgari eloquentia, 1.15.2, Dante says that Sordello took what was best in the idiom of Mantua and its neighbors, making one speech of many, and then, being a man of great eloquence in poetry and speech, abandoned his native vulgate, with the implication that he moved on to something better, Provençal. That is, he became as eloquent as possible in his native tongue and then moved on to an established language of art. On Sordello in the Comedy, see Teodolinda Barolini, "Bertran de Born and Sordello," PMLA 94 (1979), 395–405.

princes do not, not even the emperor, whose prime function is
to unite nations: Albert sacrificed the needs of Italy and Europe
to his own wants in Germany. Villani says of Albert's father,
Rudolph, that he was magnanimous and valorous in arms,
feared by Germans and Italians, and that he might have
become lord of Italy without contest, had he chosen to come
(*Istorie Fiorentine,* 7.54), but that he failed to receive the impe-
rial blessing because he was concerned with increasing his
power in Germany and left Italy to his sons (7.145).

Sordello is the poet to make this point because he devoted
much of his poetry to reproving princes and nobles and
encouraging them to honorable action. In the famous lament
on the death of Blacatz, he calls the major princes of Europe
cowards for not protecting their realms; his list includes the
emperor Frederick II, Louis IX of France, Henry III of
England, Ferdinand III of Castile and Leon, James I of Aragon,
Thibaut of Champagne (king of Navarre), Raimon VII of Tou-
louse, and Raimon Berenger IV of Provence, and he will point
out many of their successors to Dante when they reach the val-
ley of negligent princes. In other poems, Sordello urged noble
action against evil enemies, awareness of one's duty to oneself
and others, moral behavior in a social setting, and the impor-
tance of reproving the evil.[26] When he urges war it is not for
pleasure or profit, as Bertran de Born did, but for national
honor and prestige. He stands apart from his fellows at first,
presumably because, like Dante, he is both an expatriate,

[26]See particularly the long poem, *Ensenhamens,* by Sordello in *Le poesie,* ed.
Marco Boni (Bologna: Libreria Antiquaria Palmaverde, 1954). C. M. Bowra,
"Dante and Sordello," *Comparative Literature* 5 (1953), 1–15, thinks it likely
that Dante knew the *Ensenhamens,* although there is no proof. He notes the
similarities in ideals of public service owed both to man and God and points
out the similar standards Dante and Sordello apply to kings (citing Sordello's
planh). Silvio Pasquazi, "Canto VII," *LDS,* 249, comments that both Sordello
and Dante "who objectifies himself in Sordello," are sorrowfully aware of the
civil and political disorder of Christianity and Europe. Sordello guides both
Virgil and Dante, as Statius will later in Purgatory, the pagan classical poet
slowly giving way to the Christian as Dante absorbs what Virgil can teach him
and has less need, though no less desire, for his presence.

forced by political circumstances to live among strangers, and a moralist, whose sense of corruption keeps him aloof from his fellows.[27] But the presence of Virgil releases an expression of love for their city and of admiration for Virgil's poetic mastery and impels him to action on their behalf; he guides the pilgrims to the valley at the foot of the mountain, where he points out the negligent princes of Europe. He continues to deplore their failures, as he had done in his own poem, and as he does so, he extends Dante's scope from Italy, which occupied him in canto 6, to all of Europe.

The setting recalls the *Aeneid, 6*, where Anchises showed his son the future leaders of Rome, those who would found cities, extend the dominions, impose laws, justice, and peace, and found a new Golden Age, in short, everything government was instituted for, but which the rulers in this valley failed to provide. The Golden Age Virgil speaks of is equated by Matelda in canto 28 with the Earthly Paradise, which Dante claims in the *Monarchy* the empire can restore. The princes sit in a valley which is a pale reflection of that Paradise and contemplate nightly the temptation of man by the serpent, which led to the fall and necessitated the creation of church and state to guide man in exile from Eden; that is, they are constantly reminded of their unfulfilled purpose. They sit in the proper hierarchical order with the emperor at the head and the marquis below the kings, at peace as they ought to have been in life but were not. They now represent the ideal they did *not* achieve.[28] They are

[27]Sordello eloped with Cunizza, the wife of his lord, Count Ricciardo di San Bonifazio, from the court of Verona to her brother, Ezzelino, at Treviso, c. 1223. Later, because of a secret marriage, he was again forced to flee and spent some time in southern France at the court of Raymond Berengar, and c. 1245 at the court of Countess Beatrice, wife of Charles of Anjou. He followed Charles to Italy to fight Manfred in 1265, was captured, ransomed, and eventually given castles in the Abruzzi. Thus, like Virgil (and Statius), his career moves him through much of Italy and parts of France. See Bowra, "Dante and Sordello."

[28]An interesting change in the hymn-singing occurs in the valley: one soul begins and the rest join him, suggesting that this society is functioning properly, the leaders leading and others following. All this occurs in the presence

not men who did nothing, rather, for the most part, men who were concerned with limited territorial claims and wars, with political maneuvers to advance or protect their holdings, not with the larger needs of Europe or Christendom, and often with adverse effect to their own lands, either in the heirs they left or in the expense and suffering they caused.[29]

The problems of Europe are the problems of Italy on a larger scale. The princes are, for the most part, former enemies, in some cases related by marriage, now sitting and singing in peace with each other, though too late to help their subjects, and suffering because of the defects of their sons and heirs. The emperor Rudolph is here with his defeated rival, Ottokar, who refused to recognize him as emperor; Ottokar's son was defeated and humiliated by Rudolph, but later reinstated and married to his daughter (see Villani, *Istorie Fiorentine, 7.54*). The political defects of Rudolph's son, Albert, were noted in canto 6; the moral failure of Ottokar's son is mentioned in Purgatory, 7.101–02, and in Paradise, 19.125. The king of France, Philip III, sits with his son's father-in-law, both lamenting the evils of Philip IV, of whom Dante has much to say in canto 20. But Dante reminds us that Philip III himself died in flight from a battle in which he lost most of the French fleet. The battle was against Pedro III of Aragon, who sits nearby with Charles of Anjou, uncle of Philip III; Pedro and Charles engaged in wars and intrigues over Sicily (see Villani, 7.85). Charles had earlier fought and defeated the imperial heir, Manfredi (Villani, 6.89 and 7.9); Pedro was married to Manfredi's daughter. Another of Charles's enemies, William of Monferrat, once a friend (as he had once been a Ghibelline but became a Guelph), is also here, but lower than the rest.[30] There

---

of divine grace, represented by the angels who guard the valley and drive the serpent out.

[29]In the case of France and Montferrat, they caused it themselves while the sons of Anjou and Aragon brought it on other lands, Apulia and Provence.

[30]According to Bowra, "*Dante and Sordello*," Montferrat led the league against Charles but could not control it, 13. On the relations of the various princes in the valley, see above, chapter one, fn. 20.

is a particular bitterness in the fact that Sordello, who had described so many of their predecessors over half a century before, points them out to Dante, and nothing has improved, fulfilling the implied prophecy in his poem.[31]

The meeting with Sordello and the sight of the kings of Europe, emphasizing as they do mankind's desperate needs, elicit a troubled response in Dante, a series of frightening images culminating in the dream of the rape of Ganymede by Jove in the shape of an eagle. The rape may be taken as an allegory of Dante's own plight: he too feels himself lifted out of his normal life, taken away from his companions, in order to serve a divine mission, the cause of empire; the form the god takes in the dream, the eagle, is the symbol of the empire. Dante's emotions reflect both exaltation at the importance of the mission and terror at the dangers of failure. As he is about to enter the gate of Purgatory, he is assailed again by an ambiguous image: the sound suggests the opening of the Roman treasury when Julius Caesar took it over from the republican guard. For Lucan, who was presumably Dante's source, the scene is the violation of the temple by an outlaw, against the legal government, an indication perhaps of Dante's unworthiness to enter;[32] at the same time, from the perspective of divine providence, Caesar takes the treasure that rightly belongs to the empire, the destined government of the world, and in that sense Dante has every right to enter, because he too is serving that providential order and that empire. In order to be able to serve, however, Dante must purge himself of vice, like the souls in Purgatory. The corrupt individual cannot properly serve society; so Dante must assume the burden of his own sin—the seven P's carved on his forehead—make a ritual

[31]Dante clearly has Sordello's poem in mind and covers most of the same lands, France, England, Aragon, Navarre, Provence, and the empire, though the imperial dynasty is not the same; but he does mention a grandson-in-law of Frederick II, Pedro III. The king of England is Henry III in both cases, and of the others, all but two of those in Sordello's poem are represented by sons or sons-in-law, one by a brother as well.

[32]The Ottimo (2.145–46), citing Lucan, says the doors lament because the treasure will be used to kill citizens and destroy liberty, to exile virtue and make vice public.

confession to the angel and a total commitment to the journey without looking back (9.132).[33]

Service to society is the underlying subject of the first four ledges of Purgatory. Though Dante divides the road up the mountain according to the seven capital sins, his explanation of the impulse to sin is much simpler: all actions are motivated by love or desire, instinctive or consciously willed (17.91 ff.). Love cannot err, desire may err by too much or too little force, or by the wrong object. The only wrong object we can love is the harm of another person, and that is the basis of the first three sins in Purgatory. Just as the last three sins in Hell, violence, fraud, and treachery, are social sins which involve human objects, so the first three in Purgatory are directed against others. Dante describes pride as the hope to excel by the suppression of rivals; envy is the opposite, the fear of losing power or fame because of others' success; wrath is the desire to hurt in order to avenge an injury. Inasmuch as wrath is an excessive reaction to offense, sloth—the failure to act—which is the result of too little force of love, is its opposite. On each of the four ledges that house these sins, Dante shows the failures of religious and secular leaders to use their gifts or position for the good of others (pride), to put the good of others before their own (envy), to forgive personal injury in order to avoid public harm (wrath), and to discharge assigned duties (sloth). The last three ledges, where the sins of excessive desire (greed, gluttony, and lust) are purged, present mankind's ordained guides, a pope, a king, and several poets, who failed in their roles because they indulged their own desires.

Pride, the desire to rise by another's fall, is the basic human sin, as Dante underscores by presenting the thirteen examples of pride (more than he gives for any other sin in Purgatory) so that the opening letters of each *terzina* form the acrostic UOM, "man," five times over.[34] Dante deals with three kinds

[33]Robert Davidsohn mentions that some crimes were branded on criminals' foreheads, *Storia di Firenze* (Florence: Sansoni, 1956–68), 8 vols., 5.613.
[34]In gluttony, Dante will see the letter *m* of the word *omo,* "man," in the skulls of the gluttons, who indulged themselves to the exclusion of others'

of pride in the souls and in the examples, pride of birth or being, pride of art or accomplishment, pride of power or possession, all divine gifts, intended to be put to the service of mankind, to be used with a sense of responsibility rather than of vainglory. In the carved examples drawn from the Bible and antiquity, Dante concentrates on the abuse of power and its destructive effects. He shows tyrants and their victims, rebels against the hierarchy of authority: Lucifer and the giants who attacked the gods; kings who refused to rule by God's will, like Saul and Rehoboam, who were defeated or driven out;[35] and kings destroyed in revenge for their victims, Sennacherib, Cyrus, Holofernes. Many brought disaster on their people: Nembrot's attempt to build a tower to heaven resulted in the division of his people and the confusion of tongues;[36] Sennacherib's attacks on God's people led to the annihilation of his entire army, Holofernes's to the rout of his people. Cyrus and Holofernes have their heads cut off, a symbol of the nation without a head, because in their pride they led their nations to destruction. These examples of the abuse of public responsibility for personal satisfaction and the consequent effects on whole nations are a much stronger indictment of rulers than the episode of the negligent princes, who only failed to act, and they constitute a powerful threat to current rulers. The final example of pride, the city of Troy, is meant as a threat to Florence. "Proud Ilion," as Virgil and Dante call it, is totally destroyed by its pride and can only rise again centuries later as Rome. That Dante connects Florence with Troy is suggested

---

needs. In Paradise, the *m* of *terram,* "earth," will form the eagle of empire and represent monarchy, the government that brings all men together.

[35]Saul, who ignored God's command, was abandoned by him and defeated in battle; he is shown dead on his own sword. Rehoboam, who not only refused to lighten the burden of God's people but boasted that he would increase it, is shown in flight from those he oppressed. Jacopo quotes him comparing his father's benevolent rule contemptuously with his own intended tyranny, an active rejection not only of God but also of a good heritage (2.138).

[36]As Giulio Marzot, "Canto XII," *LDS,* 419, points out, the tower represents a particularly serious loss for one who, like Dante, aspires to the unification of peoples and languages.

by his sarcastic reference to the well-governed city, "la ben guidata" (12.102), not long after the reference to Troy.

The selfish and destructive abuse of power is countered by the three examples of humility at the beginning of the ledge, all figures of the highest authority, God and two kings, who humble themselves in order to serve their subjects: although Mary is the first example, as she will be of every virtue, offering herself to do God's will, implicit in the scene of the annunciation is the humility of God's allowing himself to be born as man in order to redeem man from the consequences of his pride; God, in other words, becomes less than himself in order to serve his own creatures. Trajan is the emperor who accepts a public rebuke from the widow asking justice for her dead son, the ruler corrected by his subject and persuaded to do his duty rather than leave it to another, like the negligent princes.[37] And David, king and poet, is both more and less than king (10.66: "più e men che re"), when he dances humbly before the holy ark to praise God, an act which Dante contrasts with Uzzah's presumption at putting out his hand to steady the ark, taking on a task not assigned to him which is punished by sudden death. In Dante's letter to the cardinals, he justifies his criticism of the church, saying he is not like Uzzah steadying the ark, but simply trying to keep the oxen that draw it on the right path, while the cardinals are leading it astray (Ep. 8.5). Dante may be making an oblique reference to this letter when, in the first line of canto 12, he describes himself and Oderisi, poet and artist, walking together "come buoi che vanno a giogo," like oxen in a yoke, putting their art to the service of God and man.

[37]Trajan was a pagan who, according to legend, was brought back to life by the prayers of Pope Gregory I so that he could be baptized and saved (cited by Aquinas, ST, Supp., q.71, a.5), an illustration both of the effect of prayers and of the proper function of the pope vis-à-vis the emperor, as spiritual guide. Benvenuto, noting how hard it is for the mighty to humble themselves, cites the example of the emperor Frederick Barbarossa when he subjected himself to Pope Alexander, "a most violent enemy," and the pope "responded arrogantly: 'I will walk on the asp and the basilisk, and trample the lion and the dragon'" (3.295).

The souls on the ledge work at combating their own tendencies to pride by praying for the good of others and by humbling themselves. The individual souls, all Italians from the recent past, two political leaders and one artist, exemplify the most socially unproductive kinds of pride: pride of birth, pride of talent, and pride of power. Pride of birth involves taking credit for things one has no control over rather than contributing to the public good, which Umberto Aldobrandesco now counters with a condemnation of the family's arrogance as the source of all its troubles and of his own contempt for others, forgetting the common heritage of mankind and his obligations to it. The illuminator Oderisi has already reached a new perspective on his talent and worldly fame, accepting his place in the scheme of history, content with the contribution he could make to it while recognizing that another now does better work and receives the honor, generously implying that Dante will soon take that honor in poetry.

Provenzan Salvani, who represents pride of power and position, remains in the background and allows the illuminator to speak for him. Provenzan is a Sienese Ghibelline and descendant of political figures; his grandfather was appointed consul of Siena by Emperor Otto IV in 1212, his father helped shape the city's constitution. Provenzan's accomplishments would seem to merit some pride: he held every elected position in the commune, he worked with the *popolo* for a democratic program and taxed the rich apparently to win popular support; a strong adherent of Frederick II, he later forced his city to support Manfredi and Conradin. But his feats seem also to have helped destroy him and many of his fellow citizens: many Sienese were slaughtered in revenge for their victory at Montaperti; as the most important Ghibelline in Tuscany after Montaperti, he was himself captured and killed by the Florentines at the defeat of Siena, 1269, his head cut off and carried about on a lance, fulfilling, according to Villani (*Istorie Fiorentine*, 7.31), the prophecy that his head would be higher than all others, which in his pride he had taken to mean victory. (Compare the examples of kings whose pride led to the destruction of their people and those whose heads were cut off in retaliation for their oppressions, canto 12.) Since Provenzan was one of those who wanted to destroy Florence and is now in Purgatory, while Farinata who saved it is in Hell, one wonders if Dante is giving another hint that God intends the destruction of the city. Guglielmo Aldobrandesco was also Sienese, but a Guelph allied with the Florentine Guelphs and involved in an earlier but not lasting peace between the two cities in 1254; though Dante's emphasis in this canto is on Siena, the connections between the two cities must bring Florence to mind for Dante's audience as an example of national pride to be humbled.

Despite his fabled pride, Provenzan provides the most dramatic example of humility in the service of others among the souls: in order to raise the ransom for a captured friend, he sat and begged in a public square, an act of love that wiped out the time he would have had to spend in Ante-Purgatory.[38] Like the prayers of the living, this gesture of love helps pay the debt of justice. The giving of the self for the good of others is the essential counterbalance to pride. Similarly, to combat envy, which is the fear to lose by another's gain, one must put the good of others before the self and identify the good of the self with the good, rather than the harm, of others. As Jacopo says, envy must be countered with charity to others, not loving worldly glory and honor in themselves but as things ordered towards something else (2.145).[39] The three examples of charity presented by Dante encompass all the forms of love essential to a good society, love for mankind in general (shown by Mary at the marriage of Cana), love for friends (as shown by Pilades

[38]The material on Provenzan's background comes from Folco Tempesti, "Provenzan Salvani," *Bullettino senese di storia patria*, NS 7 (1936), 3–56. Tempesti says there is a possibility that Provenzan made this gesture to dramatize the greed and cruelty of Charles and mobilize opposition to him, 34, but Dante treats it as a simple act of charity.

[39]Gianni Grana, "Canto XIV," *LDS*, 499, notes that envy is a blind egoism that goes beyond the personal sphere of harm to the individual to the broader one of civil life, where it causes disorders and subversions.

when he offered himself to save Orestes), and love for one's enemies, which Christ preached in the sermon on the mount.[40] There are only two examples of the vice; both are a sibling's envy of divine favor, the worst form of envy because it occurs where love is most natural. This kind of envy is echoed in the rivalry between Florence and Siena, whose names recur through the cantos of pride and envy. They are neighbor cities with many common interests, who should be allies, and hurt themselves by their hostility.

The souls on this ledge are learning to give and take the support of others: temporarily blinded, they lean on one another for mutual support (13.59), they work together to supply what their eyes cannot give them (14.1 ff.). They can now admit their indebtedness to the selfless love of others, as Sapia does when she explains that she is in Purgatory ahead of her time not because of any deed of her own, but because a poor hermit and comb-seller, Pier Pettinaio, remembered her in his prayers. The souls have begun to think of themselves as part of a community, as citizens of one society: when Dante asks if there are any Italians among them, Sapia answers that "each is a citizen of one true city . . . who lived in Italy as a pilgrim" (13.94–96: "ciascuna è cittadina/d'una vera città . . . che vivesse in Italia peregrina"). This new sense of fellowship contrasts strikingly with their former factionalism: Sapia, a Sienese, had prayed God for the defeat of her enemies at great cost to her own city and arrogantly exulted over the victory that cost the life of her nephew, Provenzan Salvani, as well as of many of her fellow citizens. The battle in which Sienese Ghibellines were defeated by Florentine Guelphs represents the kind of factionalism so often criticized in Hell, which plagued Siena as it did Florence, leading the people of one city to side with a party in the other against their own compatriots and some-

---

[40]Benvenuto uses the reference to Orestes to speak of Agamemnon as the most glorious emperor of all kings, dukes, and princes, and victor at Troy, killed by his wife and her lover, a relative and a priest (3.356); the victorious king killed by an angry woman echoes Holofernes and Cyrus on the ledge of pride.

times against their own families. Factionalism is the form envy takes in the political sphere.

The self-destructiveness that results from the political envy of parties and cities is extended through the valley of the Arno and the region of Romagna by another soul on the ledge of envy, Guido del Duca, whose very names suggest that leadership which is lacking.[41] Guido goes through the cities of the Arno one by one, identifying them not by name but in terms of the beasts their inhabitants have become. The early commentators agree in identifying the cities; so there seems to be little doubt that the pigs are the Porciani from the Casentino, the curs the Aretines, the wolves Florentines, and the foxes Pisans (Jacopo, 2.158–59, the Ottimo, 2.245–46, Benvenuto, 3.380–82, and Pietro, 396, who also makes a connection with the animals in Boethius's *Consolation,* 4). All the inhabitants of the region flee virtue as if it were a serpent; that is, they have the warped perspective of Hell in which God or good is the enemy. Even the grandson of Guido's companion will "hunt wolves" along this river (14.58–60), becoming a predatory beast himself. The figure in question is a fierce *podestà* of Florence, Fulcieri da Calboli, who worked with the Blacks to condemn and destroy the Whites, 1302–03. Villani reports that he got Whites to confess to crimes whether or not they were guilty and then had them executed (*Istorie Fiorentine,* 8.59), and Dante reports that Fulcieri sold their flesh while they were still alive, like cattle, and then slaughtered them (14.61–62), a particularly vicious display of factionalism. Fulcieri's grandfather, Guido's companion in Purgatory, is Rinier da Calboli, a *podestà* of Faenza, Parma, and Ravenna in the second half of the thirteenth century, the honor of his house but without an heir to his valor (14.88–90), a fact which leads Guido into a lament for the region. He describes the Romagna in terms of poisonous plants rather than animals, "venenosi sterpi"

[41]Guido was a member of the Onesti family of Ravenna, a judge of Alberghetti and *podestà* of Rimini, and died shortly after 1229. Dante calls him "lo spirto di Romagna" (15.44: "the spirit of Romagna"), as though he should represent the region.

(14.95), reminiscent of the suicide wood in Hell, underscoring the self-destructiveness of this kind of corruption and contrasting it with the "garden of the empire" that Italy was meant to be (6.105). Guido had similarly prophesied that Fulcier would leave the "trista selva," "the sad wood," Florence, so bloody that it could not renew itself ("rin*selva*") for a thousand years (14.64–66). In contrast to the current corruption, Guido recalls other good men who have died without heirs in a kind of political *Ubi sunt,* a lament for the transitoriness of political virtue. Of the dozen or so good men and families he names, all were nobles, Guelphs and Ghibellines, all active in public life.[42] Their virtue manifested itself in their public lives. Now they are gone and corruption has taken over their cities. They were men who served the common good rather than petty factions, like the two souls here, Rinier da Calboli, a Guelph who died fighting the enemies of his *patria,* and Guido, a Ghibelline, who was remembered for his courtesy and generosity.

Another such model of virtue and service to his society, the courtier Marco Lombardo, dominates the ledge of wrath. His function in life was to guide by words, as the poet's is, so he is a fitting choice to guide the poets through the fog of wrath, but it is significant that Dante chooses a political figure rather than a poet to give the main philosophical discourse in Purgatory. Dante chooses a man who lived the theory, a most worthy figure, according to the commentators.[43] His knowledge is of the world and its ways (16.47: "del mondo seppi e quel

---

[42]Several served as *podestà* of Ravenna, Faenza, or Siena. For details about them, see T. Casini, "Dante e la Romagna," *Giornale dantesco* 1 (1894), 19–27, 112–24, 303–13, and 4 (1897), 43–57.

[43]Pietro calls him a most honorable man of the court, "probissimum hominem curialem" (409); the Ottimo (2.284) says he was valued in arms and courtesy, lived and died honorably; Benvenuto identifies him as a Venetian who called himself Lombard because he was involved with Lombard lords, arranging alliances and truces for them, a man of noble spirit and virtue, but indignant and quick to anger (3.431–32). He not only offers the central philosophical discourse, but also turns Dante's attention to his goal by asking for prayers from above instead of from those on earth, a shift that occurs almost at the middle of the *Comedy* (16.50–51).

valore amai"), what Ulysses claimed to seek. But Ulysses sought it for his own satisfaction, whereas Marco used his knowledge to serve his society as he uses it here to teach Dante. He not only guides Dante and Virgil physically, but explains moral order to them: the relation of love and free will, the need for reason to direct the individual, and the need for church and state to guide that reason. Marco explains the function of government in the context of personal morality.

Like most other souls in Purgatory, Marco is distressed by the corruption in his own region, Lombardy, which brings in the third major region of northern Italy, adding its catalogue of corruption to those of Tuscany and Romagna. Like the souls on the previous ledge, he contrasts the vicious present with a better past: there are only three good souls left between the Adige and the Po and they are old and long for death (16.115–26).[44] But Marco differs from the other souls in offering both a philosophical and a historic reason for the decline. First he denies the responsibility of the heavens for earth's corruption, granting only that they inspire our inclinations (16.73 ff.), but pointing out that we have the judgment to distinguish good from evil and the free will to choose between them; thus the corruption in the world is our fault (16.82–83: "se'l mondo presente disvia,/in voi è la cagione"). But having established this personal responsibility, he modifies it somewhat, indicating the need for external guidance to keep the simple, naive soul from pursuing the wrong inclinations. That is why there

---

[44]When Ciacco reported that there were only two just men left in Florence (Hell 6.73), he did not name them; Marco names three here, leaving no doubts in other people's minds that they might be included. The Ottimo says Currado was a man of honor, devoted to his family and the governing of cities, that Guido honored worthy men and gave generously, and Gherardo delighted in all things of worth and valor (2.292); Benvenuto calls Guido a "zelator reipublicae, protector patriae" and relates that Currado was a standard-bearer for his republic who, when his hands were cut off in battle, carried the flag with his stumps (3.448–49). On Dante's view of Gherardo, who may have been involved in the murder of Jacopo del Cassero and in the death of a bishop, but was probably a good host to Dante and a devoted lord of Treviso, see Girolamo Biscaro, "Dante e il buon Gherardo," *Studi medievali* NS 1 (1928), 74–113.

are laws and someone to enforce them, why God gave two suns to Rome—the empire to lead us in this world, the church to lead us to God. Now that the latter has put out the former, usurping a role it was not intended to play, it leads the world astray.[45] The greed of the church sets the wrong example for mankind, and that bad guidance is the cause of the world's problems (16.103–04); by confusing the two governments, the church of Rome soils both itself and its burden (16.127–29). If the image of the two suns for the balanced relations of church and empire was startling, the historic cause Marco adduces for the corruption is even more so: valor and courtesy existed in his land, he declares, before Frederick ran into trouble, but now one can pass through all of it without meeting any good men (16.116–20). Frederick II, the last important Roman emperor, whom Dante condemned to Hell as a heretic, is here praised as the protector of the virtuous life; Dante thus balances his condemnation of Frederick with a positive judgment on his rule, as he will balance his condemnation of Boniface somewhat with indignation at the attack on him (canto 20). The implication is that by fighting the empire in Frederick and his line, the church has made it impossible for virtue to flourish.[46]

[45]See chapter two for the two suns and the sun and moon in the church-state controversy. The Ottimo comments that the church does not want emperors because it wants to be emperor, as Boniface was said to have donned the crown and sword and made himself emperor (2.291); Benvenuto notes that Boniface knew laws and scripture and wrote on canon law, but did not divide spiritual from temporal power, and comments that people can more easily derive vices than virtues from the habits of the clergy (3.441–42).

[46]Although Dante's argument in this passage seems quite clear, there are some who attempt to explain it away, e.g. Rocco Montano, "Canto XVII," LDS, 613–56, who points out that Marco is not yet purged of sin, that he is a Ghibelline with no theological qualifications, that his "saints" are men of ancient nobility, not of religion; Montano suggests that Marco is pure, sterile reason not integrated with grace, the empire without Revelation. Pietro Mazzamuto, "Canto XVI," LDS, 547–612, in contrast, makes a direct connection between the political views Dante expresses through Marco and the historic situation, noting that Dante's views in Purgatory are consistent with his political letters and the Monarchy.

Dante places this discussion at the center of the *Comedy* because it is the basic message of the poem, conveying the crucial relation between the function of empire and personal salvation. He also locates it in the section of wrath, because although excessive rage and desire for revenge are harmful to individuals and to society, with the effects often felt by innocent victims, anger properly directed towards evil and corruption is the source of all reform. That is why Marco Lombardo's attack on the corruption of his region and of the church is set between examples of extraordinary forgiveness and vindictiveness, distinguished by its object—family, stranger, and enemy.[47] At the same time, Dante focuses not on the object of the attack, but on the innocent victims, actual or potential. His point in this episode is that in society the leaders must be able to control their own and others' excessive rage, to show forgiveness when punishment or revenge would do more harm than good, but also be firm in the exercise of justice when evil threatens the common good.

The opposite impulse to excessive wrath is sloth, which Dante defines as insufficient love for the right object; it is a failure to act altogether or to discharge the necessary or assigned task, and can therefore be as harmful to the commonweal as uncontrolled wrath. The examples of vice and virtue on the ledge of sloth are set entirely in a national context.

---

[47]When Mary finds her son, Christ, in the temple, instead of the anger a parent might be expected to show, she only asks why, but when Procne learns of her husband's attack on her sister, she kills her own children to avenge it. When Pisistratus's daughter is kissed in the street by a stranger, and his wife, invoking the glory of their city, demands revenge, he only asks, "What shall we do to those who wish us ill if we condemn those who love us?" But when Haman receives a small offense, he wants to punish an entire people. When Saint Stephen is stoned by an angry mob, he prays God to forgive his enemies, but when Amata's daughter is sought in marriage by Aeneas, the mother kills herself rather than see her enemy succeed, causing grief to the innocent daughter, which is described at length (17.35–39). Amata's opposition to Aeneas, who would bring the future glory of Rome to her people, is suicidal in a national as well as personal way, but like Haman's attack on the Jews, the other chosen people, it is not successful.

Sloth is shown in God's two chosen nations, who reject their destiny, the Jews who refused to cross the desert even after God parted the waters for them and never reached the Promised Land, and the Trojans who gave up along the way and did not follow Aeneas to Italy, their promised land. Since these are the two model journeys for Dante in the *Comedy,* the message for Dante's audience is to follow him in his program of action or risk losing religious as well as political salvation. The countering virtue, zeal, is shown in a religious context by Mary, who rushed to share the news of her pregnancy with Elizabeth, both women carrying God's messengers who would spread the Word as Dante continues to do, and in a political context by Caesar rushing westwards to extend the empire, as Dante hopes to. The soul Dante sees is the abbot of San Zeno, identified by his position rather than his name, presumably because he failed to do his duty properly as abbot. Now, however, he is worried about a successor, the current abbot, a bastard deformed in mind and body (18.124–25), whose father clearly abused his responsibility as a secular lord by appointing one so unfit. This situation to some extent counterbalances, though certainly does not negate, Marco's attack on the church for usurping temporal power. At the same time, the abbot's fleeting reference to the destruction of Milano for its defiance to Frederick Barbarossa (18.119–20) is a gratuitous reminder to Dante's audience of the dangers of such opposition to the divine will working through the empire.

The episode of sloth is a moment of transition between two opposing types of sinful tendency: desiring the wrong object, harm to others (pride, envy, wrath), and excessive desire for objects that are not bad in themselves (avarice, gluttony, lust). It is possible, however, to be deceived in the nature of the object desired, as Dante shows in the dream of the siren, canto 19: he sees a hideously deformed woman, but as he stares at her, his look transforms her into an object of desire. He begins to see what he desires as something worth desiring and gives himself into its power. Such self-deception can be particularly powerful in a strong mind and particularly harmful when it occurs in leaders. Dante concentrates on principal leaders of mankind in the remaining ledges of Purgatory, as one might expect after Marco's explanation of their importance not only to a good life on earth but also to salvation. In avarice, Dante sees a pope, a king, and a poet, but only the poet will function as a guide. In the remaining sections of Purgatory, Dante meets only poets; by reassessing his relation to them and their tradition, he further prepares himself for the role heaven thrusts upon him in the Earthly Paradise, when Virgil crowns him pope and emperor over himself, when he as poet becomes the surrogate guide to the world, since the other two do not function.

The ledge of avarice is distinct from all the others in a number of ways: it is so crowded that Dante and Virgil have to edge their way through it, because Dante sees it as the major source of corruption in his world; and in a break from his normal pattern, Dante includes a New Testament reference among the examples of the sin, because avarice is particularly connected with the clergy, in whom it is especially harmful to the balance of power in the world;[48] he also modifies the pattern of presentation of souls by having one appear before the examples and another after them. This variation places particular emphasis on each of the souls, because they represent the three major guiding functions, pope, king, and poet. There is no emperor, both because Dante argues in the *Monarchy* that an emperor could not experience greed since he would possess all and also because in the pope and the king of France Dante has the two

[48]Normally Dante draws examples of virtues from the New Testament and from ancient history and examples of vices from the Old Testament and ancient history; the other exception is in gluttony, which includes an Old Testament example among the virtues. The examples of avarice include two kings, who murdered for wealth, a king and a consul of insatiable greed to the point of madness, a king's treasurer, who tried to plunder God's temple, and an apostle's wife, who kept money intended for God's people. Jacopo adds political details to two of these, that Pygmalion murdered his brother-in-law for a kingdom as well as for gold (2.231), and that Crassus took a bribe to lift a seige (2.234–35). Crassus' mouth was filled with gold after he was killed because of his insatiable thirst for wealth.

worldly leaders whose greed most obstructs the empire in
Europe. It is that role which singles out the French house for
extra attention in this section, although it has already been
attacked with other national monarchies in the valley of neg-
ligent princes.

The three souls Dante speaks to on this ledge are a pope
whose greed knows no bounds until he achieves the richest
office in the world (the papacy), a king whose descendents turn
every political and private situation to profit, and a poet who
gave too freely. Dante begins with the pope because he asso-
ciates greed throughout the *Comedy* with the clergy, and
because, as Benvenuto points out, the papacy properly admin-
istered can be the highest honor and service (3.511: "Summus
honor, summum onus, summa servitus, summus labor"), but if
carried out badly it can be the gravest danger to the soul, the
summit of evil, misery and shame ("summum periculum ani-
mae, summum malum, summa miseria, summus pudor"). Ben-
venuto notes that the papacy in the primitive church was not
something to be envied since it usually involved suffering and
martyrdom, whereas now it is sought with such ambition that
fraud, gifts, and promises intervene to get it; the pope is obli-
gated to many creditors and will have to answer to God for all
who perish by his negligence (3.513–14). The Ottimo cites a
number of gospel passages that warn of the dangers of earthly
possessions or forbid them altogether (2.334). The pope Dante
chooses, Hadrian V, was in office only thirty-eight days, in
1276, but that was long enough to learn the futility of greed
for material goods.[49] It took the richest office in Christendom

[49]Dante seems to have combined elements from stories of popes Hadrian IV
and V not, I think, by mistake but because he was consciously tampering with
history in each of the three souls he presents in order to make a more striking
case. See Gioacchino Paparelli, "Canto XIX," *LDS,* 741 ff., on the confusion of
the two: if, as now seems likely, Dante knew the *Policraticus,* he made the
wrong attribution intentionally. He may also have known that Hadrian V left
his vast wealth to his family, not to the church, therefore his religious conver-
sion was not total. Paparelli suggests that Hadrian's conversion was political,
that from an anti-Hohenstaufen, pro-Angevin, he became, when pope, an
opponent of Angevin expansion and encouraged the emperor Rudolph to

to teach him that earthly wealth and power do not satisfy; ironically, he had nowhere to turn but to God. Worse even than the cynicism of this story is the fact that so few popes seem to have learned the lesson. Hadrian now seems to see the papacy in the proper light, in terms of its dignity, its universality, and the purity of its origins, suggested by the Latin words with which he introduces himself to Dante: "scias quod ego fui successor Petri" (19.99: "know that I was a successor to Peter"). But when Dante kneels to honor that position, the pope corrects him, telling him that he is only a fellow servant (19.133–35), refusing to set himself above the poet either as a man or as pope, who was supposed to be the servant of God's servants.[50] The pope's last words are a recollection of his niece, a tacit acknowledgment that the only worldly attachment of lasting value is the love of others.

The king is Hugh Capet, who died in 976 after a reign of nine years, the ancestor of the current king, Philip IV. Hugh identifies himself by the bad seed he engendered, which he longs to see punished, not out of a personal need for revenge, but because he identifies with divine justice; the corruption his greed gave rise to is part of his purgatorial suffering. What Pope Hadrian learned in a month, Hugh's family has not learned after three centuries of power in Europe, that earthly power in itself cannot satisfy. He tells Dante that he, the son of a butcher, took over the kingdom when the last king became a monk and gave the crown to his son (20.52–60); as with Celestine in Hell 3, the abdication of assigned responsibilities leaves the way open to corruption. Here again, Dante

---

Rudolph to come to Italy to be crowned. He also connects the choice of Hadrian with the attention to the French dynasty in canto 20. He notes that Dante treats avarice in Purgatory in civil and social terms (746), that he makes no real distinction between private and social ethics, between religious and political creeds, 750.

[50]Hadrian presents a striking contrast to the simoniac pope Dante encountered in Hell 19 where the poet also stood above the pope, but like a confessor quoting Scripture at him. Here Dante tries to kneel and it is the pope who cites Scripture.

seems to be playing with history, confusing the story and legend of Hugh Capet with that of his father.[51] His main point seems to be to put a criticism of the French kings into the mouth of their ancestor. Listing their increasingly sordid deeds with the sarcastic introductory phrase *per amenda*, "to make amends," he describes their seizure of lands, interference in international politics, particularly against the empire, interference in local politics, poisoning of churchmen, and even the selling of their own children. The contemporary commentators accept and embellish Dante's points: Pietro blames Charles of Anjou for the deaths of Manfredi and Conradin, the last of the Hohenstaufen line, and of Thomas Aquinas for fear he would become pope (436); the Ottimo relates that Charles brought Corso Donati and the Blacks back into Florence, causing the exile of the Whites along with wars, fires, and destruction, and repeats the rumor that Philip had Thomas Aquinas poisoned because he had reproved him, and Philip feared he would become pope (2.364–65). What worse outrage could avarice commit, Hugh asks, than selling one's child, in what appears to be a rhetorical question until he answers it: the attack on Christ through his vicar. The vicar in question is

---

[51]Villani (*Istorie Fiorentine*, 4.3) says Hugh was Duke of Orleans, but that many say his father was a rich merchant, a butcher who was made a duke for his wealth. Benvenuto, clearly aware that there are different traditions, explains that when Dante was studying in Paris (for which there is no evidence), as a "very diligent investigator of memorable things," he discovered the truth about Hugh's origin, so the other reports are fictions (3.526). Pio Rajna, "Ugo Ciappetta nella *Divina Commedia*," *Studi danteschi* 37 (1960), 5–20, reports that the confusion between father and son was not unusual and came about naturally: originally "Capeto" applied only to the father, later to the son as well, and finally exclusively to the son. He notes the conflation of various French princes in the *Memoria Saeculorum* of Goffredo da Viterbo, which Dante might have known or known of; he also relates the story of a *chanson-de-geste* about Hugh Capet, son of a gentleman, prodigal knight, grandson of a butcher by his mother, and dependent on his butcher-uncle for money. Rajna suggests that Hugh himself is a prodigal, but that Dante uses him primarily to show up the greed of his descendents. Incidentally, Rajna also points out that Louis IX does not appear in Paradise, to the distress of French critics, probably because of the acquisition of power during his reign.

Boniface VIII, one of Dante's arch villains but, as pope, Christ's spiritual representative who should be beyond the jurisdiction of the French king. Both Boniface himself and the succeeding pope, Benedict, made the analogy with Christ.[52] Every act of the French dynasty seems to be in defiance of the responsibilities of a king to his people and to God.

The third soul on the ledge, the poet Statius, first appears as a Christ figure in his role as teacher, as is fitting for a poet. The pope represents Christ as spiritual leader, the emperor Christ as king, the poet (particularly Dante), Christ as teacher. Statius's entrance is heralded by an earthquake which reminds Dante of the birth of the gods Apollo and Diana, reinforced by the souls' cry of *Gloria in Excelsis,* echoing the angels at Christ's birth. Statius appears on the road behind Dante and Virgil as the risen Christ did to his apostles on the road to Emmaus and expounds doctrine to them as Christ did, satisfying the thirst Dante said could only be satisfied by grace. That is, Dante feels his needs exceeding Virgil's capacity; for his own task as poet, he must have more than reason to guide him. He is beginning to make the transition from Virgil to Beatrice, and he does it with the help of another Roman epic poet, one strongly influenced by Virgil but, unlike Virgil, a Christian. To make Statius a Christian is once again to tamper with or at least to stretch history, despite a few indications in Statius's poetry that he intuited one God and perhaps even the Trinity; "triplicis mundi summum quem scire nefastum/illum, sed taceo" (*Thebaid,* 4.516–17: "the summit of the triple world whom it is forbidden to know, but I am silent"). Dante makes a plausible case for Statius's silence, since he lived during the early persecutions, and the silence helps to explain the long period of purgation, so that he can still be here when Dante arrives. Dante chooses Statius because he needs a poet who is both Christian and an epic poet, whose vision encompasses the history of a people, as Virgil's did and as his own does. Poets

---

[52]See Pietro Fedele, "Per la storia dell'attentato di Anagni," *Bullettino dell'Istituto Storico Italiano* 41 (1920), 195–232.

are the chosen messengers of God in the *Comedy*, Dante in order to save his world, Virgil to lead Dante to the point at which he can take on that mission. It is no coincidence that Dante and Virgil come along just as Statius is about to rise; it must be that the presence of the poet who saved him, Virgil, with the added presence of the poet he can help, Dante, touches off the final impulse to rise in Statius. He feels ready because he is and because he can serve a function at that moment.

Poetry was and is a tool of salvation for Statius, as it is meant to be for Dante's audience. His debt to Virgil is both moral and artistic. He acknowledges the artistic debt first, calling the *Aeneid* his "mamma" and nurse, and certainly his major epic, the *Thebaid,* owes a great deal to Virgil. The moral debt is more involved; he was saved from prodigality by lines in the *Aeneid* which he misread.[53] The point is not so much that Statius made a mistake, though there is irony in the fact that he is saved by the words rather than by the intended meaning, as though God were operating through the poetry without Virgil's knowledge, but that Statius could find whatever he needed in Virgil, as one might in the Bible. He goes even further, citing lines from Virgil's fourth eclogue, and claims that Virgil's poetry led him to God, like one who carries a lantern behind him in the dark, helping those who come after but not himself (22.67–69). This is the strongest indication in the poem of the justice of Virgil's damnation; since he had the material of salvation if he could save others, he could also have saved himself. Statius thus helps to wean the audience from Virgil, who will leave the poem before the end of Purgatory, and to remind us that Dante, like himself, serves God's plan. Statius provides a link between Virgil and Dante; together they represent three stages in poetry, history, and faith. Virgil lived in pagan Rome

---

[53]"Quid non mortalia pectora cogis/auri sacra fames" (*Aeneid* 3.56–57), an attack on greed, "to what do you not drive mortal breasts, o accursed hunger for gold?" By taking the *quid* to mean "why" and *sacra* to be "sacred," Statius construes the passage: "Why do you not control mortal appetites, o sacred hunger for gold?" which becomes an attack on prodigality.

under the emperor who prepared the world for Christ's birth, wrote of the fall of Troy and the origins of Rome, and is condemned to Limbo. Statius lived in a Rome slowly becoming Christian, under an emperor who avenged Christ's death (21.82–84), wrote of the civil wars of Thebes (not unlike those of fourteenth-century Italy) and is about to be a citizen of heaven. Dante lives in a Christian world without a functioning emperor, though he hopes to see one who will restore the Earthly Paradise; he writes of the corruption of church and state and the ideal society that might be, and will return to earth with a message and a promise of salvation. Virgil, like the pagan emperors Augustus and Titus, served God's purpose without knowing it; Statius served it hesitantly and therefore not very effectively; Dante serves it completely.

Having established that poets are the only fit guides available to contemporary society, and having placed himself in the epic tradition as successor to Statius and Virgil,[54] Dante must now reassess his own poetic heritage, the vernacular lyric tradition, acknowledge his debt to it, and show why he has passed beyond it. The discussions of the last two sections are primarily concerned with poetry but set within the context of the two sins of physical self-indulgence, gluttony and lust. Two strains run through both sections (cantos 23 to 26), moral corruption and poetic limitations, with one common link, self-indulgence at the cost of public good. As in Hell, Dante shows that what seems merely personal has social effects. Gluttony and lust are simply aspects of selfishness, the excessive indulgence of personal desires to the detriment of one's responsibilities. The souls named in gluttony are a pope, an archbishop, a powerful noble, a *podestà,* and two poets, Forese Donati and Bonagiunta da Lucca, the latter also a notary. They are all men of some importance in their communities, drawn from the three spheres that provide guidance to mankind; while they were indulging their appetites, the world around them was falling

[54]In canto 27, Virgil puts Dante between them, a protective gesture but perhaps also an indication that Dante is Virgil's true heir and should precede Statius.

apart. Dante speaks only to the two poets among the gluttons; with the first he discusses the corruption of Florence, as he had in the circle of gluttony in Hell, with the other he discusses self-indulgence and awareness in poetry. The attack on Florence is directed at the outrageous dress of contemporary women (canto 23) and the bestiality of contemporary politics, particularly of Forese's brother, Corso (canto 24). Style in clothes may seem to be a superficial issue, but for Dante and his society, the habits of personal life—food, sex, dress—are all signs of deeper corruption, worldliness, and selfishness. Decrees were passed in Florence limiting the extravagance of dress in the early fourteenth century because of the social disruption it could cause, and two of the early commentators take Dante's promise of heavenly revenge to apply not just to the women at fault but to the whole city: the Ottimo says that God will send war, fire, division in cities, exile, and death, for the sins of the women and their husbands who consented to them (2.442); Benvenuto thinks Dante means the internal discord, civil war, exile, and fire after 1300 (4.63).[55] The violence and anarchy unleashed on Florence by Corso Donati and his followers is simply another manifestation of the lack of control that is eating away at the city (see Villani, *Istorie Fiorentine*, 8.48 and 96). Corso's death, prophesied by his brother, Forese, in canto 24, is symbolic of the whole situation: Corso is dragged to death by the horse he was riding; the rider driven by the animal suggests that passions rather than reason are in control.[56] Perhaps the beast is the rabble he thought he was leading, which finally destroys him.

[55]Even Bonagiunta's reference to the woman who will make Dante's visit to their city pleasant is interpreted in political terms by the Ottimo (2.450): the woman is the White party, which will so attract Dante by its virtue that it will get him exiled from Florence and make him appreciate the abstinence and continence of Lucca.

[56]Villani's account of the death is somewhat different (op. cit. 8.96), so Dante's may be another instance of his shading history to make a more effective point. According to the Ottimo, Corso was drawn by the beast which draws sinners, that is, by sins (2.454); for Benvenuto the beast is a devil (4.80). Pietro says, "For the tail of the beast, read the end of his bestial will," and cites

The problems in poetry are not so dramatic, but they are related. The difference between what Dante does and what other early poets did is revealed by his description of his poetic technique: "I note what love inspires and express it as he dictates" (24.53–54). Dante presents himself as a tool of divine inspiration, a good attitude for one who is about to receive a difficult mission from heaven, but it indicates a shift from the self-centeredness of his early poetry, where he talks about his own feelings even when he is trying to praise Beatrice. There is a self-indulgence in those lyrics that is related to the rhetorical showiness of the poets who are here put down; Bonagiunta, the Notary (Jacopo da Lentini), and Guittone d'Arezzo are said to have been held back by a knot which only the "dolce stil nuovo" loosed (24.55–57). They are limited by their provincial outlooks, as well as by their style; the three poets are connected with regional schools of poetry, the Notary with the Sicilian school, Guittone with the Tuscan, and Bonagiunta with the Siculo-Tuscan. In *De vulgari eloquentia*, Dante takes two of them to represent the culture of their cities, Bonagiunta for Lucca, Guittone for Arezzo, and he attacks Guittone for never directing himself towards a courtly vulgate, never rising above the municipal to a national language. Dante sees himself as a national poet, writing in what would be the

---

Seneca's "bestial wrath delights in blood and wounds" (465). The examples of vice in these two sections suggest the same connection between personal and public lack of control: gluttony is represented by the centaurs who disrupted a wedding feast, a public celebration of love and union, and by those Jews in Gideon's army who could not control their thirst and lost the glory of victory. The examples of virtue include the Roman matrons who drank water rather than wine, symbols of the strength and self-control of Rome at its height; Daniel, who refused the wine of his captor and grew in wisdom and understanding of visions and dreams by his abstinence; and the Golden Age, when all human society was in harmony and hunger and thirst were simply but adequately satisfied. The examples of lust are, as they were in Hell, connected with rulers and set in public contexts, perverted lust (homosexual) represented by the cities of Sodom and Gomorrah, bestial lust (heterosexual) by a queen, Pasiphae; allusion is also made to the emperor Julius Caesar, who was called "queen" because of his relations with the king of Numidia.

court Italian, if there were an Italian court.[57] Because Dante believes in language as a unifying force within a nation, he rejects those who do not contribute to it and exalts those poets whose difficult style prepared the way for him to develop what in Paradise approaches a new language.[58] It is not surprising that Dante should look to poets who worked complicated ideas into their poetry or devised new poetic modes, but it is curious that he should reject two "poets of rectitude," Guiraut de Bornelh and Guittone. It would be easy to say that Dante wants to eliminate rivals in the more serious matter, but this seems unlikely when he does so much to exalt Statius as well as Virgil. What he seems to imply is that in serious content and mode of poetry he follows the Latin epic poets, who deal with morality within the context of history, while in the concern with love and vernacular style he follows Guido and Arnaut Daniel. The combination is, of course, entirely new, and he is well aware of that. What he tells us in these cantos is that he has found a language which speaks on the highest

[57]A case can be made for Guittone's attempting the same, but not so successfully. See Mazzotta, *Dante, Poet of the Desert,* chapter five, for a discussion of these cantos as a "sustained reflection on literary history and the powers of literature to engender a moral conversion." On Dante's treatment of poets, including the lyric poets and his changing attitudes towards them revealed in the *Comedy,* see Teodolinda Barolini, *Dante's Poets: Textuality and Truth in the* Comedy (Princeton: Princeton University, forthcoming).

[58]Bonagiunta had attacked Guido Guinizelli for being too learned, too subtle, too obscure in "Voi che avete mutata la mainera," and Guido had praised Guittone lavishly as his father in "O caro padre meo, de vostra laude," and received a rather patronizing answer "Figlio mio dilettoso, in faccia laude." Dante seems to reverse both judgments, another instance of his rewriting history; by having Bonagiunta praise Dante's style and Dante call Guido the father of his circle, he implies that Bonagiunta can now see what is better in Guido. He is far more direct in having Guido himself scorn those who used to praise Guittone as paying more attention to report than to truth (26.121–26). Instead, Guido now looks to Arnaut Daniel, a Provençal poet as a "better craftsman of the mother tongue" (26.117), suggesting that the vernacular traditions are one, but also that the "dolce stil nuovo" is the real heir of the highest Provençal poets.

level to his audience, to all Italians, and is worthy to convey his message. It is important for him to make this point before he enters the Earthly Paradise, before he becomes surrogate emperor and pope, before he takes his place in the procession of the Bible and providential history and assumes his divine mission. He may be shaken as a man by Beatrice's personal accusations, but he must be confident in himself as a poet, and we must have confidence in him in order to accept the implications of that episode.

Virgil testifies to Dante's capacity as a moral being and a poet when he takes leave of him, telling him he is ready to stand on his own and assume the role of guide to men:

> libero, dritto e sano è tuo arbitrio
> e fallo fora non fare a suo senno:
> per ch'io te sovra te corono e mitrio.

> your will is free, straight, and healthy,
> and it would be wrong not to follow it
> therefore I [poet] crown you [poet] king
> and bishop [emperor and pope] over yourself.[59]
> (27.140–42)

Among the early commentators, there is a difference of opinion: the Ottimo (2.498) interprets the gesture to mean "I make you ruler and pastor over yourself" (*rettore* and *pastore*); Jacopo (2.330) takes it to apply only to poetry, with Virgil admitting Dante's superiority, "quasi a dire: che tu se' sovra me; e però soggiunge ed io ti corono della corona e mitria poetica sovra mia scienzia poetria, ed arte" ("as if to say that you are above me, and therefore he adds and I crown you with the poetic crown and miter over my poetic knowledge and art").

---

[59]Singleton notes that the crown and miter were used for the emperor and concludes that Dante does not mean to include the church, (see his commentary on Purgatory, 665), but since both were also used for the pope (Ernst Kantorowicz, *The King's Two Bodies* [Princeton: Princeton University, 1957], 491), the argument does not hold.

Benvenuto sees it as rule, "regem et dominum" (4.158). It seems more consistent with Dante's stand throughtout the poem and in the *Monarchy* to assume that when he as a poet takes on a function for all mankind in place of the divinely instituted leaders, it must be for both emperor and pope, not for only one, and that is why he uses both *corono* and *mitrio*. The empire was, according to the *Monarchy*, instituted to restore mankind to the earthly paradise, the church to guide him to the heavenly; the poet can, indeed must, help in both.

Dante has also come to represent mankind purged and ready to return to its home, the Earthly Paradise. He has become, as Kantorowicz puts it, not only a member of the mystical body of Christ, which is the church, but of the mystical body of Adam, which is humanity (*The King's Two Bodies*, 492). The earthly paradise was intended for all men, not only Christians (28.77–78: "questo luogo eletto/a l'umana natura per suo nido," "this place chosen for human nature as its nest"), a point that will be made more clearly in Paradise. It is also, as its single inhabitant suggests to Dante, the place the ancient poets dreamt of when they spoke of the Golden Age (28.139–41), a period of peace and justice, without need of law, punishment, or war, and that is what man strives to restore. Benvenuto comments that the Golden Age according to ancient poets was a time of virtue, of great peace, justice, and liberty, and that it existed under Saturn in Crete and also under the emperor Augustus in Italy (4.180). The earthly paradise can be achieved on this earth by the concerted effort of all men pursuing the virtues of the active life, as the early commentators point out: Pietro, interpreting the moral sense of the scene, says that man, purged from the principal vices and sins, enters completely a certain state of life sweet as paradise; he cites Isidore on the active life, which makes us use earthly things well, and suggests that Lia, in Dante's dream, represents the active life of the primitive church and the Old Testament, and Matelda represents the active life of the new church and New Testament (492, 495). Pietro contrasts the active life described in Purgatory with the contemplative life of Paradise, but I think Benvenuto is closer to Dante when he comments that we only see Rachel, who represents the contemplative life, at the end of Paradise (4.154); that is, Paradise is also concerned with the active life. Jacopo divides human life into active and contemplative, the first serving as a road and gate to the second, but notes that the body and its passions must be at peace, for which civil life was ordained (2.319); he interprets the seeds which come from the Earthly Paradise as the virtues which take root in human hearts, if men are disposed to them (2.334), making a direct connection between this life and that. The rivers of Dante's Earthly Paradise are Lethe, which destroys the memory of sins committed, and Eunoe, which restores the memory of good deeds, both important in creating the kind of confidence that makes an active life of virtue possible.

Because Dante's interest is in the active life, he focuses on the figure of Lia (Leah) rather than on Rachel in his dream; he sees Lia gathering flowers and singing, and she describes not only her own activity but that of her sister, Rachel, who gazes into her own eyes in a mirror all day. The dream occurs at the hour when Venus first shines on the mountain with the fire of love (27.95–96), the light that has hovered over Purgatory from the first canto, representing properly directed love which inspires the soul to good and useful action and binds men together in a harmonious society. The imagery of love dominates both Dante's dream and the appearance of Matelda, which brings the dream to life. Matelda signifies the ideal object of a man's desires in contrast to the siren dream in canto 19;[60] she offers herself to Dante intellectually, ready to answer

[60]The dream is recalled by the rhyme words *smaga, vaga, appaga* (27.104–08, cf. 19.20–24, *dismago, vago, appago*). When Beatrice appears, she too will recall and replace the siren's "io son, io son dolce sirena" (19.19) with her "ben son, ben son Beatrice" (30.73). For Dante, the first step towards God is the love of a woman; Eve drove mankind from Eden, Beatrice or her equivalents will bring him back. Hugh of St. Victor connected the love between man and woman, Adam and Eve, with human fellowship, saying that woman was made from man so that she might look to him as to her beginning, just as all men, coming from one, should be one and love one another as if they were one (*Sacraments*, 1.6.34).

any question. She transforms the object of his desires from physical to intellectual, preparing him to meet Beatrice. Matelda awakens love and desire in him in a state of innocence, leading him to love of God through his creation, reminding him of the hymn which praises God's creation, "Quia delectasti me, domine, in factura tua." Beatrice, through the same kind of love, will lead Dante to the direct vision of God, but she will also give him the mission for which he has been chosen by heaven. Love, for her, for God, and for mankind, will enable him to carry it out.

We know, of course, who Lia and Rachel are, and who Beatrice is for Dante, but Matelda has been something of a puzzle. Early commentators had no doubts. For them the name could only evoke the countess of Tuscany: Pietro calls her a most magnificent lady, a most excellent woman, who built, by gift, a vast number of churches, waged war on the emperor, and, when she neared death, offered all her patrimony at the altar of Saint Peter in Rome, which even today is called the patrimony of the church (497); Jacopo says she is an allegory for the active life, that she was a wise and powerful woman, polished in virtuous habits, the qualities that suit the perfection of the active life (2.331–32). Benvenuto (4.151–55) describes her at length as the most splendid, illustrious countess, surpassing all others in her brilliance, the feminine sex in her virtues and virile habits; he says she was well-versed in matters of war and even more so in religious observance, gave generously to the poor, and was powerful in her realm, which included Mantua, Parma, Reggio, and Ferrara; that she was educated, had a large collection of books, and knew Italian, German, and French well. It is fitting, Benvenuto feels, that she should lead Dante through the paradise of delights and show him the church militant, in whose service and honor she had fought so magnificently during her life and which she made her heir after her death. Benvenuto also connects her with Cato, who was placed at the entrance of Purgatory to prepare souls to climb the mountain, as Matelda, for the excellence of her virtue, is put here to teach and show the purged souls how to cross over the waters, through the church.

It is obvious from the early commentators that Matelda was still a well-known figure in the fourteenth century and that the name would suggest the countess to Dante's readers. Villani also gives her a good deal of attention, making it quite clear that hers was a popular story still in northern Italy; he mentions her role in the war between Gregory and Henry, her war on Robert Guiscard, her family history and wide building, along with the intimate details of her marriage, her defeat of Henry III in Lombardy and of Henry IV, who returned what he had taken from the church, and finally her death (*Istorie Fiorentine*, 4.18, 20, 22, 27, and 29).[61] The contemporary life of Matelda by Donizo, which records her public activities and her relations with emperors and popes, describes Matelda as another Martha for her actions (a New Testament equivalent of Leah, both figures for the active life) and also as a Mary for her concern with the faith (Mary, like Rachel, is a figure for the contemplative life).[62] She is a fit representative of the active life and the church militant because she actively fought for the church in its struggles against the empire. She supported a reform pope, Gregory VII, against Henry IV; that is, although she opposed the empire, she supported the battle against corruption in the church, against worldly concerns and imperial interference in church matters, and she put all she had to the service of what she believed. If, as a devout woman, the count-

[61]The historical facts are somewhat different: Matelda willed her lands to the papacy but was forced to change the disposition and make Henry V her heir in 1109; her intention was clear enough, however, so that the lands continued to be disputed for over a hundred years until Frederick II finally surrendered them in 1220.

[62]Donizo, *Vita Mathildis*, ed. Luigi Simeoni (Bologna: Zanichelli, 1930–4), 2.170–72. It is an intriguing coincidence that a form of Dante's name occurs in a line of Matelda's life near her own name: " . . . iam dicta tibi supra dante Mathilda" (2.509), just as it does in Virgil's *Aeneid* near Cato's name: " . . . his dantem iura Catonem" (8.670). If Dante knew the life of Matelda, as he certainly knew the *Aeneid*, he might have been struck by this curious link between the two he selected as the human guardians of Purgatory.

ess mistakenly bestowed political power and possession on the church, her intentions were honorable; she is presumably to be included among those who followed Constantine in shedding imperial plumage on the church (32.138) with good intentions.[63]

The other Mateldas who have been suggested, the thirteenth-century German mystics, are interesting because of their otherworldly visions, but they are not as suitable symbols of the active life as the countess; of course, since Dante does not name her until the last canto, he leaves us free to associate the woman he sees in the Earthly Paradise with various figures, a restored Eve, Proserpine, Astraea (connected with the Golden Age), or even the *donna gentile* who temporarily took Beatrice's place in Dante's mind. But the Countess Matelda, who was directly involved in the struggle of papacy and empire, and still a powerful legend in Dante's time, seems a far more suitable person to alert Dante to the procession of the Bible, which includes the chariot of the church and culminates in the drama of church-state history. As a political figure who stood for morality and adherence to spiritual values against worldly powers, she is a fitting balance to Cato; as a woman whose actions influenced the power struggles of her time, she is a fitting symbol of the active life, who washes Dante in the river of Lethe to erase the memory of his sins and leads him to drink of the river of Eunoe, which restores his memory of the good already done so that he may be fortified and encouraged to act. Because Matelda's role is to emphasize the importance of action in the world, it is she who shows Dante the procession of providential history, which works like Dante's poem, dramatizing history and drawing its audience (Dante in the one case, us in the other) into it.

[63]Cf. Dante's description of the Donation as a good intention that bore bad fruit, "buona intenzione che fè mal frutto," in Paradise, 20.56. When Beatrice tells Matelda to answer Dante's question in canto 33, Matelda feels obliged to justify herself "as one who looses herself from guilt" (33.120), indicating a sense that she can be at fault.

Beatrice, Dante's individual source of salvation, appears in the procession representing all the forms God takes in order to save mankind, as the universal church (the spouse of God), as Christ (the savior in history), and as the emperor (his regent on earth).[64] Later, when she sharply reproves Dante, he sees her as an admiral on the poop, which connects her briefly with the pope (the pilot of the ship of the church). Beatrice must remind Dante of his failures, because, if he is to correct others, he cannot stand outside as an observer of the moral scene; he must first accept the truth and reform himself. His confession takes place in the Earthly Paradise where man fell and to which he is destined to return, and it occurs amidst the procession of the Bible and the symbols of church and state, the instruments God established after the fall to help man return. Those institutions exist for the individual, and Dante's mission is to restore them so that they can resume their proper function in leading mankind back, but before he can begin, he must accept responsibility for what he is. Even now, like the sinners in Hell, Dante still tends to blame others, as evidenced by the frequent complaints about Eve's losing paradise (29.24–30, 32.31–32). The procession, however, utters the name of Adam, to remind Dante and his audience that anyone who consents to sin is guilty, and the greater the responsibility, the greater the guilt, not only of Adam in relation to Eve, but of churchmen and secular rulers in relation to the individual Christian. What Beatrice accuses Dante of could be said of any figure of importance in the world, that despite the special gifts he had received, he allowed himself to be corrupted and followed false images of good; his only hope for salvation was the sight of the souls in Hell (30.136–38). This is precisely the point of Dante's poem for his audience. Just as Christ descended to Hell to rescue the Jews of the Old Testament and gave new meaning to the pagan culture that preceded him, so Beatrice descended to Hell to summon Virgil to lead Dante back to her, religion

[64]Her connection with the three figures is established by the phrases which herald her arrival, see fn. 15, chapter 1.

acknowledging the need for reason and pagan learning in order to prepare the soul for the lessons of theology and grace, Christianity acknowledging the role of Roman history and the empire in its destiny. By admitting to the sins Beatrice names, Dante associates himself with the souls in Purgatory and dissociates himself from the souls in Hell; he accepts the transitoriness of worldly goods and the need to face and accept his responsibilities before he takes on responsibility for others. Once he does this, he is able to contemplate the image of Christ in the griffin in his two natures, human and divine, which is essential to understanding man's two goals, the earthly and the heavenly. Dante is now ready to join the procession, to assume his proper role in the providential plan.

At the tree of the knowledge of good and evil at which Adam and Eve sinned, which is the tree of divine justice in which the eagle of empire lives, Dante witnesses the drama of the church's role in the world.[65] Beatrice tells Dante he will only remain in the Earthly Paradise a short while and then will become eternally a citizen of that Rome of which Christ is a Roman, that is, the heavenly city, but because he must carry the message of what he has seen to the world, he must watch the drama under the tree. The drama is staged more for Dante's audience than for him; he is simply the divinely chosen intermediary. It occurs here in the midst of his own purgation because the correction of relations between church and state, the restoration of their proper functions, is essential to the salvation of individual souls. Dante's mission is to help restore the institutions, theirs is to guide souls to salvation. Canto 32, which describes the drama, is the longest in the *Comedy*

[65]Cf. Pg. 32.48, the griffin's only words, "so is preserved the seed of all that is just," and 33.71, God's justice seen morally in the interdict on the tree. Early commentators connect the tree with obedience (Pietro, 524, Jacopo, 2.379) as well as with the knowledge of good and evil (Benvenuto, 4.247 and the Ottimo, 2.560, who also mentions the tree of life, citing Peter Lombard and Bede). Robert Kaske connects the meanings of knowledge and justice in "Sì si conserva il seme d'ogni giusto," *Dante Studies* 89 (1971), 49–54. The drama itself was discussed earlier, in chapter two.

because it carries the central lesson for Dante's audience, the need to restore those institutions to the function God intended. The following canto, the last in Purgatory, assures us of that restoration. After warnings of God's wrath, a hymn describing the destruction of the temple by heathens, and the prayers of the righteous for revenge, Beatrice announces in the words of Christ to his apostles that she will disappear but shortly return, meaning that Christ will come back in one of his roles. Since she goes on to say that the eagle which left its feathers on the chariot—the empire—will not long be without an heir, it seems most likely that she is prophesying an emperor, as the early commentators assumed. Pietro says the imperial eagle (*aquila imperialis*) will not be without an heir (532), cf. the Ottimo (2.584).[66] Benvenuto identifies the eagle with the Roman empire and connects this prophecy with Virgil's in canto 1 of Hell (4.272–73). He suggests that just as one emperor gave riches that led to the insatiable greed of prelates and destruction of the world, so another Roman emperor will take them back and free the church by killing the whore, that is, the pastors of the church who are married to the wolf of avarice (cf. chapter two). Although the prophecy is veiled, as Beatrice herself comments, the message Dante is to carry back is the lesson of the drama and the coming of the emperor.

Dante ends his journey through Purgatory renewed and restored like a new plant with new leaves (33.143–44: "rifatto sì come piante novelle/rinovellate di novella fronda"), recalling both the reed of humility at the shore of Purgatory and the tree of justice that was renewed by the chariot of the church. Dante, as the humble tool of the divine, will now help keep that tree green. His audience, if it has been persuaded by his lesson, should be ready to do the same. If they have not only recognized their wrongs in the examples Dante has set before them, but have also acknowledged the effects of those wrongs

[66]Jacopo identifies the eagle with the emperor Constantine (2.396), and speaks of a leader who will persecute the evil pastors of the church; God's vengeance, he says, will take enormous ruling power (*signoria*) and great force (2.394).

on their society, if they can accept their responsibility for the corruption in the church and the government and forego their own selfish desires and ambitions and consider the common good, then the Earthly Paradise may be achieved in their world. What such a society could be, with men of different talents and functions working together in joyful cooperation and in harmony with the divine will to the benefit of all, is demonstrated in Paradise.

FIVE

The Ideal Society:
Paradise

PURGATORY prepares the individual to assume a fitting and use-
ful role in the ideal society; Paradise provides the model for
that society. At each level as he rises through the planets,
Dante sees a harmonious group of souls, beginning with those
who were motivated more by their own needs than by a con-
cern for others, but who nonetheless served God and mankind;
they appear as they acted in life, as individuals within the
group. As Dante moves up, however, he sees souls who have
submerged their individuality in a symbolic figure (wheels, a
cross, an eagle, a ladder), which represents the way they lived,
putting the common good above their own. Their greatest per-
sonal desire was to serve others. The souls work together
impelled more by the common will, which is ultimately God's
will in which all others find peace, than by their often conflict-
ing personalities. Towards the end, Dante sees all the souls
together as flowers in one garden and, in the final vision, as
petals of one rose. But even within this all-encompassing single
figure, the souls are revealed in their distinct individuality, in
the human features that had not always been visible to Dante
before. What he shows symbolically in the rose is what he said
directly in the *Monarchy,* that in the ideal society, which
should include all mankind, men can achieve their highest
individual potential.

The rose is the heavenly city (30.130), the joyful kingdom
(31.25), the just and pious empire (32.117) whose emperor is
God; it is the model for the political and moral life on earth.
God's love is the motivating force of the physical universe and
of the human soul, which should move in harmony with each

other as Dante's soul does at the end of the poem. The souls in Purgatory were inspired by love temporarily misdirected; the souls in heaven are moved in varying degrees of intensity by love rightly directed, and express their love for God through service to man. Since they are motivated by the same impulse, they can work in harmony for the same ends despite different means: those who sought truth through knowledge (in the Sun), though they may have been intellectual enemies, can form the perfect figures of the circles; those who served justice through the state, whether pagan, Jew, or Christian, form the eagle in the planet of Jupiter. All those who seek truth on earth not for themselves but to serve God and man, however they may go astray in the pursuit of it, are figuratively forming that circle; all who serve justice through its highest secular expression are a part of the eagle.

Paradise is in every way the antithesis of Hell. In contrast to the souls in Hell who were driven by selfish impulses which had antisocial effects, the souls in Paradise are inspired by love to act for the good of all. The structure of Paradise is informed by God, who is both center and circumference, at once filling and containing the heavens, whereas Hell is formed by the absence of God and the negative presence of his antithesis, Satan. Heaven is filled with light and motion, like a magnet drawing all upwards and to the center, where God is seen as three circles of light from which flows the river of grace. Hell is a vast emptiness, surrounded by futile activity, darkness, cacophony, like a funnel that draws downwards to the three-headed figure of Satan, frozen in the ice into which have flowed all the wastes of human corruption and misery from the rivers of Hell. In Hell, the circles are separate and distinct, and within them the selfishness of the souls cuts them off from each other, except for expressions of hatred or revenge. In Purgatory, the souls begin to help one another and move freely from one section to the next when they have purged themselves of each selfish impulse, climbing the road that unites the different sections and leads to the Earthly Paradise. In Paradise, though the souls are seen at first in separate spheres, they are actually parts of one universal human society, a society which by its very unity of will enables them to realize their highest individual potential, manifest in the increased powers of the resurrected body. To achieve this desired unity, Dante does not deny the great variety in man or in the universe, he affirms it. Harmony through diversity is a theme of the cantica, reflecting the Neoplatonic concept of perfection through the realization of all possibilities. This is the basic principle of human society as Dante sees it: individuals have different talents, different capacities, which they must pool for their own and others's good. He makes this point in a different way in each of the first four heavens: the differing natural capacities are discussed in the Moon, different ranks according to merit in Mercury, the variety of tendencies and talents in Venus, and various modes of seeking truth in the Sun. Dante shows how the differences in men are related to the workings of the physical universe, all part of the total harmony.[1]

On earth, the model of the ideal society can be realized within the secular sphere only in the empire and within the religious only in monastic orders. It is not to be found in the church hierarchy headed by the pope, because that confuses secular and spiritual functions. This distinction is clear from the arrangement of the souls in the planets: the kings and emperors who appear in the eagle, the sign of the Roman empire, as the exponents of justice on earth are placed in the second highest planet, Jupiter; above them, in Saturn, Dante places the church, not in the person of good popes, which might have implied a supremacy of papal authority over imperial, but in the figures of monastic leaders, men who chose to leave the world in order to serve God and who, even when they were forced to deal with the world, refused any political power

---

[1]The universe Dante presents in the first canto is a reflection of human life in that it is composed of diverse elements all moved by the same source, all natures having different fates, being moved to their source more or less intensely by instinct (1.109–14); the motion of the heavens in its most perfect conjunction is a harmony of opposites, four circles forming three crosses (1.39).

in it. Their position acknowledges the precedence of spiritual values over temporal, of the contemplative over the active life, but carefully removes the church from direct participation in the secular political sphere. It is true that above Saturn, in the heaven of the fixed Stars, Dante sees the whole population of heaven, the church triumphant, as a garden and meets Peter, the first pope. But Mary, not Peter, is the center of the garden, and Peter was in any case the leader of a church that was little more than a community of the faithful, living, as Dante describes them, an ascetic life and preaching the word of God, much like the ideal religious who are featured in Paradise. Peter also condemns the corruption of his successors in the papacy in no uncertain terms.

Paradise is filled with religious figures, particularly in the Sun and Saturn and the fixed Stars, but they are either members of orders or disciples of Christ. The one pope Dante sees, apart from Peter, is John XXI, and he is presented as a scholar rather than as pope; we know that Gregory I is also in Paradise only indirectly by reference to an error in his teaching, but he himself is not seen. The absence of popes as popes is one of the most striking features of Dante's Paradise. The religious figures Dante concentrates on (Bernard, Benedict, Peter Damian, Francis, Dominic, Bonaventure, Thomas Aquinas) were leaders, most of them administrators, often of large communities, but always separate from the secular state. They did not attempt to usurp secular political power; indeed, if they discussed the relation between church and state, as many of them did, they spoke as political moderates, recognizing the rights of the state and warning the church not to interfere. Within the church, they fought for reform and against wordliness and corruption; far from seeking a position of power within the ecclesiastical hierarchy, they attempted to avoid it. They have a clear sense of their function, which is to imitate Christ in the simple life and to lead others to do the same by teaching and example, precisely the role Dante wishes the church to play. The role of protecting order and meting out justice in the world, on the other hand, belongs to the secular state, whose leaders dominate the heavens of Mercury, Mars, and Jupiter, and also appear in Venus and even in the Sun.

Paradise does not offer, any more than Hell or Purgatory, a clear political structure or program. But it does give the basic elements of the perfect society through the souls who embody them. The souls are first presented grouped in the three lower spheres according to their motivations, in the higher spheres according to their functions. The first group, in the Moon, are those who wanted to devote themselves to a religious life, but were forced to break their vows and return to the world in order to serve the worldly needs of others. Their contribution to society may not be as tangible as that of the other groups of souls, but in their willingness to accept their own limitations and lesser positions without envy or hostility, they contribute in a passive way to the peace and well-being of the whole. The next group, in Mercury, were active in the world in order to win fame and glory; they served mankind, and thereby God, though for personal reasons, and prepared the world for the nobler actions of others. The souls in Venus were moved by love for other men, love that could lead them into sin (Cunizza's affairs, Folco's early passion), but also inspire them to good (Rahab's aid to Joshua, Folco's life as monk and bishop). In the fourth heaven of the sun, Dante sees souls whose lives were more ordered to the common good, which is subtly underscored by the fact that they are the first group to appear in a symbolic figure; they are the wise, the teachers and moralists, who guide others to knowledge and correct their actions. Beyond the Sun, in Mars, are those whose love for God and man inspired them to sacrifice themselves in the cause of defending and spreading the faith, the crusaders and martyrs; and after them, in Jupiter, the rulers who imposed order and justice on the world and, in Saturn, the contemplatives and monastic leaders who mediate between God and man and who gave structure to the religious life on earth. These are the seven spheres that together constitute the ideal society. In the last three heavens, Dante returns to the sources of human existence, first in the Stars, where the founder of the church, Peter, along with James and John, examines Dante on the theological virtues essential to a properly directed life, and the founder of the human race, Adam, discourses on language, the essential tool of social life; then, in the Primo Mobile, where the angels translate God's will to action in the universe, and finally, in the Empyrean, where the source and unifying force of all is God's love.

At the beginning of Paradise Dante claims two of the three guiding functions for mankind, the moral, which belongs to the emperor, and the didactic, which is the poet's. If he can describe his final vision of God—and the whole cantica is an attempt to reconstruct that experience—he will prove himself worthy of the crown of laurel which signals the triumph of emperor or poet (1.29). He compares his own quest to describe the vision to a sea journey on untraveled waters, not, like Ulysses, abandoning his responsibilities to seek an unknown destination, but accepting the mission imposed on him by heaven and knowing his goal before he sets out. The classical model for Dante's journey in Paradise is Jason, who is mentioned near the beginning of the cantica (2.16–18) and again near the end (33.94–96). Jason's is the first great human quest in classical myth. Benvenuto da Imola says Jason was the first to sail the great sea, as Dante is the first poet to treat of Paradise; as Jason acquired great treasure, Dante achieved the *summum bonum,* Dante's great ship being his work; as Jason drew armed soldiers from base matter, so Dante drew strong meanings from vulgar (Italian) words; as Jason took great heroes and poets with him, like Hercules and Orpheus, Dante took Virgil and Statius and others; as Jason triumphed over the dragon, the oxen, and the giants waging civil war, so Dante over earthborn vices with their discord and battles (4.340–41).[2] Jason set out to win back his usurped kingdom by performing tasks in

[2]Paolo Pecoraro, "Canto II," *Lectura Dantis Scaligera, Paradiso* (Florence: Le Monnier, 1968), hereafter cited as *LDS,* 50, notes that Dante represents himself in Jason. In the *Ovide moralisé,* roughly contemporary with the *Comedy,* Jason is interpreted as Christ who comes to save mankind disinherited by mad excesses from the noble heritage of heaven and cast into the "city of shadows," 7.709 ff. The golden fleece is the flesh Christ assumes.

which he tamed a series of antisocial forces: in yoking the fire-breathing oxen, he controls the destructive element (Dante tried to guide the "stubborn oxen who lead the ark of the church astray" in his letter to the cardinals, 8.5); and in setting the warriors born of the dragon's teeth against each other, he exorcises the destructive element. It is this aspect of his quest that Dante alludes to in canto 2, probably in reference to what he has attempted to do in Hell and Purgatory. But Jason's quest was completed by the attainment of the golden fleece; whatever else Jason did (and his betrayal of Medea and Hypsipyle put him in Hell), he did bring back the golden fleece.[3] When Dante alludes to Jason's quest in canto 33, he is presumably thinking of himself in the same way: whatever may become of him as an individual, he has given his golden fleece, the poem describing his vision, to mankind. Dante thus moves beyond his other classical model, Aeneas, although he will still use him in the Cacciaguida episode; Aeneas's quest was to found the civilization that would be Rome, Dante's is to carry the divine message to the heirs of that civilization so they can found the earthly paradise. In Paradise, Dante rises temporarily above the human condition, as Glaucus did, and is able to see something of the divine plan.[4] To make his journey, which is the writing of the poem, Dante offers himself as a "vessel" (1.14), a tool of the divine like Paul, the "chosen vessel," "vas d'elezion" (Hell 2.28).

Although Dante conceives of Paradise as one harmonious society, he presents it in separate parts, broken down by the motivating qualities of the souls or by the roles they play. The first group he sees in the Moon, the planet of reflected light, is the only one in which the virtue is passive, not active. These souls had good intentions, but their courage did not suffice to

---

[3]The good act is not contaminated by the subsequent fate of the actor, nor can it, of itself, save him. Compare Julius Caesar, who is in Limbo, although his actions in spreading the empire according to God's plan are praised by Justinian in Paradise and the souls on the ledge of sloth in Purgatory.

[4]The Glaucus episode is referred to briefly during the Jason story by Ovid, *Metamorphoses* 7; Jacopo interprets Dante's allusion to it to mean that the virtuous man can by his actions become blessed like the angels (3.27).

carry them through.[5] They are in Paradise because their desires never wavered and they never succumbed to evil impulses in their own actions, but they partake least of God's light because they have the smallest capacity for it and they did the least to oppose evil in others. They are represented by two nuns who were forced out of the cloister against their will and made to marry and live in the world, bowing to external pressures and allowing themselves to be used by selfish men for self-serving purposes, a telling contrast to the contemplatives in Saturn who also renounced the world and were forced back into it, but by spiritual men for God's purposes, bowing to the greater need of others. The souls in the Moon seem to recognize and accept their limitations. They are as satisfied as any souls in heaven with the joy they have and as ready to share it with Dante, because they now know that they could not absorb any more. Instead of resenting or envying others for having more, as Dante seems to expect them to (3.65: "Do you desire a higher place?" he asks), they are happy with their lot because they are in harmony with the divine will, which is the essence of existence in Paradise; the joy of this perfect realm is such that anyone who partakes of it is satisfied. The contrast with the imperfect earthly society, where men continually strive to get more than they deserve or need, and destroy others out of envy or greed, is obvious.

There is no reason to assume that failed nuns, or religious of either sex, are the only souls who belong symbolically in this sphere. They are not only women, since Piccarda speaks of them as "questi altri beati" (3.50), which must include men, and they are all here because they did not fulfill their vows (3.55–57). The emphasis in the Moon is not on the nature of the vow, the examples adduced in the various discussions being as much political as religious, but on the sanctity of it. Dante seems to be concerned not only with vows, which are promises made directly to God, but also with oaths, promises made to

---

[5]Dante makes it clear that the souls in the Moon gave in to force in order to escape danger, out of fear; in other words, that they lacked courage (4.73 ff., 4.101, 4.110–11). Their defective wills are symbolized by their reflected light.

men with God as witness, which are the basis of political stability (and commercial as well, inasmuch as business contracts also depend on such oaths).[6] The early commentators seem to have extended Dante's meaning beyond purely religious vows: Pietro Alighieri cites civil law on free contracting (574); Jacopo likens the vow to a written contract in which the affirmation and will of the parties is one and speaks of the promise or "stipulation" made in such a contract (1.56).

Because one cannot retract a promise that is freely given, one must be sure that it is wisely given in the first place; that is, recognize one's capacity and swear to no more than can be accomplished. The lesson of the sphere is not a simple need for commitment and action, but the more specific one of rational commitment within the limits of one's capacity to act.[7] Although Dante meets only one soul, Piccarda, and sees one

[6]Livy, from whom Dante took the Mucius story, one of his examples of commitment made, mentions no vow, but relates a statement made publicly in the Senate, *Histories,* 2.12. "Vow" does not seem to have the technical meaning for all writers in the Middle Ages that it has for us, e.g., the *veu* Alis makes in *Cligés* is a purely political promise (2,650, 2,652). The modern commentator Sebastiano Aglianò speaks of the "dramatic character of the pact" (*patto*) in his article on vows in the *Enciclopedia Dantesca,* 5.1151, and Susan Noakes in "Dino Compagni and the Vow in San Giovanni: *Inferno* XIX, 16–21," *Dante Studies* 86 (1968), 41–63, comments on Dino's use of religious language to describe the political commitment and shows how the two spheres necessarily intersect.

[7]Dante's play on the words "vow," *voto,* and "empty," *voto,* and their plural *voti,* in 3.28, 30, and 57, stresses the importance of the theme for him. Dante underscores the lesson not just with human examples or even philosophic discourse, but with cosmic analogy as well. The same laws operate for men and for the heavens: the individual's capacity to act is related to his capacity to absorb God's light, just as the moon's light depends on its capacity to absorb and reflect the physical light of the sun. Moon spots are ascribed not so much to rarity and density as to differing capacity, different powers that result from different formal principles. The word for "power" in the planets is the same as the word for "virtue" in the soul, *virtù.* God's light, which is love and grace, works through the heavens as physical light does with mirrors, reflecting from soul to soul. This is also how good operates in society, increasing in effect by the number of objects and participants. (On Beatrice's explanation of rarity and density, see Bruno Nardi, "La dottrina delle macchie lunari," in his *Saggi di filosofia dantesca* [1930; 2d rev. ed., Florence: La Nuova Italia, 1967], 3–39).

other, Costanza, he presents his audience with three sets of examples, different aspects of vows and commitment: Piccarda and Costanza represent those who broke their religious vows because they lacked the courage to hold to them; Mucius and Saint Lawrence are cited as examples of total commitment despite great physical suffering, one to a political, the other to a religious cause; and Agamemnon and Jephthah as examples of reckless vows made for political reasons which are kept at great cost to others. In every case, the action or lack of it affects others: the first pair allow themselves to be passive accomplices to wrong, the second are active for good and move others to good by their examples, the third sacrifice innocent victims to their needs. Political motives are involved in every case: marriage for political purposes in the case of the women, Lawrence tortured by the Roman government because he would not turn over church treasures to the emperor, Mucius caught in a plot to assassinate an enemy of Rome, Agamemnon and Jephthah victors in national wars.[8]

Dante's audience knew Piccarda as the sister of Corso Donati, a major political figure in contemporary Florence, noted for his violence. The commentators identify her without hesitation, and Jacopo notes that Corso had to make a certain connection in Florence and, having no one else to use, took her out of the cloister (3.47–48). From what we know of Corso's activities, and even Piccarda speaks of "men used more to evil than to good" (3.106), her acquiescence in his plot must carry some guilt.[9] Costanza, who was also forced out of the cloister, eventually gave birth to the "third wind and last

[8] As Dante tells the story of Mucius in the *Monarchy*, 2.5 (cf. *Convivio*, 4.5.13), citing Livy as his source, the enemy was Porsena, whom Mucius had determined to kill; when he failed and was captured, he burned his own hand to punish it and show his continued devotion to the cause. The Ottimo goes into some detail on political intrigues in the Jephthah story (3.100–01).

[9] Her subsequent life seems to have been a kind of penance: "Iddio si sa qual poi mia vita fusi" (3.108: "God knows what my life was then"). Like Francesca in Hell and Pia in Purgatory, Piccarda is the first woman Dante meets in the *cantica* and like them, she is the victim of violence. Francesca, however, had brought the violence on herself by her affair with her brother-in-law, for

power of Swabia" (3.119–20), assumed by most commentators to be the emperor, Frederick II, the last powerful emperor in Italy; Dante calls him the last emperor of the Romans, "l'ultimo imperadore de li Romani," in *Convivio*, 4.3.6.[10] That Costanza had been a nun has no historical basis and was probably the result of popular identification of Frederick with Anti-Christ, who was expected to be born of a nun. Dante exonerates Costanza by making her "beata," even though he accepts the story that she had been a nun. It seems likely that, for Dante, whatever else Frederick may have been, as Roman emperor he served the divine plan, and that Costanza served God's purpose better in giving birth to him than she would have as a nun; Dante had Frederick's son, Manfredi, whom he

which she seems to feel no guilt but rather desires revenge on her husband; Pia was apparently an innocent victim but shows no resentment, indeed great restraint, in alluding to the act; Piccarda suffered the effects of her brother's violence through her life, but seems to accept her fate as just and does not seek revenge or even identify the men responsible. Corso's activities were criticized in Purgatory 24 by his brother Forese. Ernesto Sestan, in his article on Corso in the *Enciclopedia Dantesca*, 2.559, reports that Corso not only took Piccarda out of the cloister to make a useful marriage for his own purposes, but also forced a widowed sister out of the convent in order to take control of her wealth and her children's inheritance.

[10]Most scholars agree on Frederick. Among the early commentators, Jacopo (3.50–51) and the Ottimo (3.61) offer another identification, Curradino, son of Constance of Bavaria, the last claimant to the throne in that family. They implicate Frederick instead in the events leading to the marriage, but even the Ottimo mentions the possibility of Frederick as the "third wind." Both Pietro (563), and Benvenuto (4.377–78) assume it is Frederick and go into some detail about the events, involving the pope and the bishop of Palermo in opposition to Tancred, Constance's nephew and heir to her father Roger. Benvenuto adds the detail that Constance was already fifty, which was why she produced a "monster," and because of her age many women came to see her when she gave birth, not believing the report, cf. Giovanni Villani, *Istorie Fiorentine* (Milan: Società Tipografica dei classici Italiani, 1802), 5.16. That she was older than her husband, though not by such a margin, Benvenuto and Villani both claim, she being over thirty while Henry was twenty-one. Benvenuto remarks that Costanza had less excuse for allowing herself to be so used than Piccarda since she was older and was persuaded not by a relative, but only by a priest (4.378–79).

admires, identify himself as her grandson in Purgatory, 3.112–13.

Dante leaves the moral judgment of both women's stories somewhat ambiguous, as their actions were.[11] He does, however, contrast the incompleteness of their will with the total commitment of Lawrence and Mucius (4.82–87), noting that such whole and firm will, *voler intero* and *salda voglia*, is all too rare. It is not coincidental that both men suffered by fire, the external flame testifying to the ardor within. By using the two as models of perfect devotion, Dante implicitly equates devotion to the empire with devotion to God; indeed, in the *Monarchy*, 2.5, he uses Mucius as an example of the miracles committed by Romans that prove the divine destiny of their empire, Dante praises the total devotion of Lawrence and Mucius because they act in the service of a good cause and sacrifice themselves for it. He condemns Jephthah and Agamemnon, on the other hand, because they sacrifice others to their needs, specifically their own children for military success, when they should have admitted that their vows were a mistake rather than compound the mistake by carrying them out: "più si convenia dicer 'mal feci,'/che, servando, far peggio" (5.67–68). Dante clearly sees them not as tragic figures who serve their countries at great personal cost, but as ambitious and selfish men.

Because freedom of the will is the greatest gift God gave man, surrender of that freedom in the making of a vow is the greatest gift man can make to God. Once he has made it, he cannot retract it, he can only substitute an even greater sacrifice (5.55–60), with the dispensation of the church, whose role

---

[11]Dante's confusion about the relative responsibilities of Piccarda and Costanza is one of the two questions Beatrice has to ask for him as Daniel did for Nebuchadnezzar (4.13–14), a reference that recalls the latter's dream of the statue described in Hell 14, which represented the corruption of mankind and the succession of kingdoms through history, a connection Dante presumably wants us to have in mind here in reference both to political implications of this section and to the history of empire in the next. Jacopo (3.58–59), and the Ottimo (3.71–72) both connect this passage with the statue in Hell 14.

is to mediate between man and God. A vow, whether personal or public, can only be changed with the formal consent of God's spiritual representative. The political nature of the promises described in this sphere, or the actions that led to the breaking of them, has been noted. The frequency of recklessly destructive or of broken oaths in contemporary Italian history and the chaos that resulted from them is a recurrent theme of the *Comedy*. There is no question of Dante's sense of the importance of a vow properly made and adhered to for political stability and security. The most important political message of these cantos is that one must exercise great prudence and wisdom in making any vow, but once it is made, one must be faithful to it or be prepared to pay heavily for the privilege of getting out of it, no matter how good one's intentions or how heavy the external pressure.

In sharp contrast to those who bowed to pressure and failed to do what they had sworn, the souls in Mercury were active in order to win honor and fame (6.113–14). They participate less fully in God's light than souls seen in higher spheres because they put their own honor and fame first, but they rejoice in the fact that their reward is commensurate with their merit and that they contribute to the total harmony of heaven: "diverse voci fanno dolci note;/così diversi scanni in nostra vita/rendon dolce armonia tra queste rote" (6.124–26: "different voices make sweet notes, so different positions [seats] in our life render sweet harmony among these wheels"). They accept not only the justice of their situation, the limited justice of reward suited to the deed, but also the need for diversity, the fact that different ranks, like different notes, create the harmony of an ideal society. If even the society of heaven is based on diversity, how much more so must society on earth be. Recognizing the need for different functions and being willing to assume the most fitting one is related to the recognition of one's limitations, which was considered in the Moon. In Mercury, each accepts his assigned role: Justinian reformed the laws; Belisar led the army; Romeo formed national alliances by arranging marriages.

Romeo de Villeneuve is mentioned very briefly as an exemplary public servant who discharged his duties with extraordinary success but little earthly reward. He served as chamberlain to Count Raymond Berengar IV of Toulouse and arranged the marriages of all four of his daughters to kings, to Louis IX of France, and his brother, Charles of Anjou, king of Naples and Sicily, to Henry III of England, and his brother, Richard of Cornwall, king of the Romans.[12] These marriages, like the conquests of the empire, though on a different scale, were a way of unifying Europe and thus served a higher purpose than the one intended by Romeo, of strengthening and enriching the house of Raymond. Despite his achievements, or more likely because of them, Romeo was undone by the envy of others at the court and departed without honor or riches to beg his bread (6.139–42), as Dante puts it somewhat melodramatically, presumably seeing a connection with his own undeserved exile. He is another example of a devoted courtier destroyed by envy, like Pier della Vigna in Hell and Pier della Broccia in Purgatory, though unlike them he departed of his own free will. His fate illustrates the vanity of desires for earthly reward, which motivated the souls in Mercury.

Though the souls in this sphere were inspired by earthly glory, their actions served a greater cause. Both Romeo, a count's chamberlain, and the emperor Justinian served the cause of unified government, one by arranging state marriages, and the other by reforming the laws by which the Roman empire, the main subject of discussion in their sphere, governed the world. In Mercury, the empire is the instrument of divine justice and revenge; in Jupiter, the empire will be the embodiment of divine justice. The souls in Jupiter serve that justice by preserving order and right, those in Mercury serve it by punishing or avenging wrong. That the divine will and the Roman will are one is suggested by lines 6.55–57: "Poi,

[12]Villani, in his history, names these four (6.91); the Ottimo identifies them but without naming the kings of England and France (3.174). Benvenuto gives the same countries but misidentifies the king of England as Edward (4.457); Pietro (594), and Jacopo (3.106) include the king of Aragon along with those of England, France, and southern Italy (Puglia).

presso al tempo che tutto 'l *ciel volle*/redur lo mondo a suo modo sereno,/Cesare per *voler di Roma* il tolle" ("then, near the time that all *heaven willed* to lead the world back to its serene way, Caesar, by the *will of Rome*, took it"). The only soul to speak in this sphere is Justinian, and he is the only soul in the *Comedy* whose words fill an entire canto uninterrupted, as befits the highest ranking spokesman for the empire. He relates the history of the Roman empire, a fitting role for the emperor who, by reforming its legal code, gave it the form that was to endure through the various changes of dynasty. He begins his description with a reference to Constantine, who turned the eagle against the course of heaven (6.1–2), who moved the empire counter to its divine destiny, a reference to the Donation, which supposedly left Rome in control of the papacy when the secular government moved to Constantinople. Justinian's references to Pharsalia, Pompey, and Cleopatra (6.65 ff.) suggest that eastward movement of empire is generally bad, echoing the message of the statue in Crete, the symbol of human history which turns its back on the east (Hell 14). Constantine reversed the normal relation of pope and emperor by bestowing secular power on the spiritual organ; Justinian exemplifies the proper relation, the emperor guided by the pope in matters of faith, when he is led out of heresy by another pope, Agapetus. Justinian had believed that Christ had only one nature, divine, and had to learn that he was also human, an aspect of the divinity important not only for the redemption of man, discussed in canto 7, but also for the significance of worldly institutions in history.

Justinian concentrates on the early history and prehistory of the empire, the series of dedicated Romans, beginning with the self-sacrifice of Pallas fighting for Aeneas, who gave their lives or service to the state when it was a kingdom and a republic and finally when it became an empire under the Caesars.[13] Under the empire, Rome served the divine purpose directly by

---

[13]There is a certain emphasis in his speech on the numbers 3 and 7, the battle of 3 against 3 after more than 300 years, the 7 kingdoms, the 3 empires, all of which reinforce the sense of divine destiny at work; cf. *Monarchy*, 2, on the miracles of Roman history, which make the same point.

preparing the world for the redemption; first when heaven wanted the world to be at peace, Julius Caesar spread its dominion east and west; then Augustus defeated the enemies who had killed Julius and established the peace in which Christ was born; under Tiberius the empire was granted by God, "the living justice" (6.88), the "glory of avenging his wrath," that is, of crucifying Christ in order to pay man's debt for original sin. Necessary and just as this act was in terms of the punishment of human nature and the divine nature of Christ, it was eminently unjust and therefore it too had to be avenged. Once again Rome, under Titus, was the instrument of vengeance. Thus the Roman empire plays an essential role in the redemption of mankind. In the *Monarchy*, 2.12, Dante used the crucifixion as yet another proof of the validity of the Roman empire, claiming that Christ's expiation would not have served its purpose had his death not been legal, that is, carried out by a legal government. By choosing to die under Roman jurisdiction, God sanctioned Rome's authority in the world. Under Charlemagne, the empire protected the church, but now the empire itself is being attacked by Christians, by those who oppose it under the standard of the lilies and by those who appropriate its own standard, the eagle, for partisan purposes; France, the Guelphs, but also Florence with its florin are suggested by the lilies. This is the only time in the poem that Guelphs and Ghibellines are named, and they are both condemned, even the Ghibellines, who purported to be supporters of empire, because they have allowed their partisan and self-serving ambitions to obstruct the divine course of the empire. The eagle should represent world government, not a party, and the lilies should nestle within the eagle's wings, as they do in the symbolic figure in Jupiter (18.112–14). God, Justinian warns the "new" Charles (Charles II of Naples), will not give up his standard for the lilies (16.106–11); those who usurp the power God gave the empire oppose not only a secular force but the divine will.

The early commentators seized on this passage, sensing its importance for Dante; canto 6 inspires by far the longest commentaries of any canto in the four commentators I consulted. Pietro cites a series of Roman writers, historians and poets, as does Jacopo, along with Aquinas's *De regimine principum,* to show that reason in man operates like God in the world, that man is a social animal, living in a multitude, who resembles God not only in that he is ruled by reason, but in that the multitude of men is ruled by the reason of one man (Pietro, 588–9). The Ottimo cites Aristotle's *Politics* on the need for rule by one and reminds us that in the *Monarchy,* Dante said the ruler should be the emperor of Rome (3.177). Jacopo points out that anyone who opposes the Roman empire opposes justice and the divine will (3.87). He condemns the church for wanting the empire to be vacant, for encouraging its enemies, even blessing traitors to the crown, to the extent that almost all Italians are drawn into the sin of dividing the congregation of the faithful, obstructing the empire that was sanctioned by the great miracles God performed under its holy standard (3.105). He condemns the Ghibellines even more than the Guelphs for involving the empire, which should be moved only by justice and reason, in partisan hatred (3.105); he denounces the French through history first as opponents of empire, going back as far as Julius Caesar (3.94), and then as derelict emperors, failing to protect the church with the result that the empire was transferred to Germany (3.104); he fills out the history of empire under the Germans up to the contemporary Henry of Luxembourg, making it quite clear that the empire of the Romans described by Justinian is still alive in the German claimants.

The empire binds men formally in a political society under one government; love binds them emotionally and inspires them to act, providing the force which makes that government work. It is the diversity in men that makes society necessary and love that makes it strong. The souls of Venus, the realm of human love, illustrate the generosity of love on which a good society depends: they are so full of love (8.38: "sì pien d'amor"), that they can find as much joy in pleasing Dante as in their heavenly activities. At the same time, they offer the fullest expression in Paradise of the diversity within society and the purpose it serves. When Dante is asked the fundamental question, "Would it be worse for man on earth if he were not a citizen?" (8.115–16: "sarebbe il peggio/per l'omo in terra, se non fosse cive?"), he unhesitatingly replies "Sì." This is because men are born to exercise *diversi offici*, different functions; one is born a lawgiver, another a soldier, a third a priest, and a fourth an intellectual/artisan (8.118–26). God assigns the functions, or at least the tendencies, and men should not interfere with them by trying to make priests of soldiers and kings of priests. Natural inclinations should be fostered for the common good, not for selfish needs, but men insist on imposing their will over nature's (and God's) and that is the cause of their trouble (8.139–48).

The diversity that operates in human nature is amply illustrated by the souls themselves and by their concerns. They represent different functions in society as well as different aspects of love in human relations: Charles Martel, the soul who discourses on the need for organized society, is a king, who also shows friendship for Dante; Cunizza, a noblewoman and the lover of the poet Sordello represents both sexual passion and charity; Folco (Folquet of Marseilles), a love poet who became a monk and later a bishop, illustrates sexual love that is redirected towards God; and Rahab (who is pointed out but does not speak), a biblical prostitute and a type of the Christian church in exegesis, represents human love at its lowest, involving greed and lust, and at its highest, devotion to God.[14] The group of souls is carefully balanced to include two men and two women, two who are connected with the political sphere, one of them a king, and two with the religious, one a bishop. And it is no coincidence that all three of the modern figures are also connected with poetry, and thereby testify to the role it plays in society. The king, as befits one who should both support poetry and look to it for support, recognizes Dante as

---

[14]For Rahab in exegesis, see Jean Daniélou, *Les Figures du Christ dans l'Ancien Testament* (Paris: Beauchesne, 1950), 217–32.

a poet of love, citing a line which connects Dante with this heaven and the inspiration of Venus; the bishop had begun as a love poet, progressing like Dante from the limited concerns of selfish love to the greater needs of mankind;[15] and the noblewoman had been the lover of the poet Sordello, who was himself concerned in his own poetry and in Dante's *Comedy* (Pg. 7) with the responsibilities and failures of political leaders. Since the impulse to love others is good, if properly directed, it is the source of great good to the community, as in Dante's service to the empire, Folco's to the church, Rahab's to God, and Cunizza's charity to those in need. The early commentators who knew of Cunizza's affairs and marriages emphasize the positive side of her love: Jacopo says that she thought it *villania* to deny her love to any who asked courteously for it and comments that as she was generous and courtly (*curiale*) with earthly love, so, allegorically, these are with divine love (3.148). Benvenuto describes her as pious and compassionate to the wretched people her tyrant brother afflicted, her excess turned to the benefit of her fellows, his to their harm (5.2).

Both love and justice, the two social qualities that permeate Paradise, are directed outward, towards others, and should continually increase in scope. The souls reveal that broadening of scope geographically as well as socially: Charles Martel is the son of Charles II of Naples and Mary of Hungary, the grandson of Charles of Anjou and the son-in-law of the emperor Rudolph; he was the king of Hungary and heir to Provence, as he reminds Dante, and should have been heir to Naples and Sicily; he might have been a force for unity in

---

[15]Folco had been a lyric love poet, like Dante, but gave up his life in the world to become a monk and ultimately a bishop. He was involved in the persecution of the Albigensian heretics, which Dante would presumably approve as he approves Dominic's battle against heresy (canto 12), if he knew of it, but he does not mention it, nor do Folco's *vidas* or *razos*. Folco also wrote crusade poems, which Dante probably did know, an interest he would certainly applaud as he shares Folco's anger at the modern popes who no longer pursue that cause.

Europe had he lived.[16] Folco goes beyond Europe to include the Holy Land as part of his world; he identifies his origins by reference to the Mediterranean, which connects Europe with the Near East, and to rivers in Spain and Italy and a town in North Africa, bringing all those disparate regions together. He had written crusade poems, encouraging action in that region, and he berates popes who have forgotten that cause.

The primary concern of these souls now, as it is Dante's, is the corruption that exists in their spheres on earth: Charles Martel and Cunizza are troubled by their own relatives as well as by the larger political scene. Both have brothers who rule their lands badly, one a tyrant, the other a miser, both examples of the negative side of diversity in human nature. Cunizza's brother is the notorious tyrant Ezzelino da Romano, who was named among the violent in Hell 12; Charles's brother is plagued by avarice, his own or others' (8.82–84), which threatens the entire "ship" of state (8.80–81).[17] But neither Charles nor Cunizza is limited by family concerns; both see the larger needs. Charles is troubled by the misrule that led to the Sicilian rebellion, taking those lands from the imperial inheritance (8.71–75); Cunizza by resistance to imperial authority (Padua's assertion of independence that will cause her defeat by Can Grande in 1314, 9.46–48) and by treachery to the imperial party (the bishop of Feltre's betrayal of Ghibellines who took refuge with him, 9.52 ff.). Their concerns are reflected indi-

---

[16]Dante apparently met the young king. Villani describes Charles's passing through Florence where he stayed twenty days on his way to meet his father in 1295 (*Istorie Fiorentine*, 8.13); his retinue of two hundred French and Provençal knights, dressed in scarlet and dark green, their saddles silver and gold, adorned with the Hungarian arms, gold lilies and red and silver circles was, Villani says, the most beautiful company a young king ever had, and apparently it made an impression on Dante as well.

[17]Benvenuto reports that there were several brothers, among them, Charles, who died young, Louis, who was simple and useless to the world and therefore became a friar, and Robert, who was learned and moral, loved books, wrote good sermons, and should have been a friar (4.484, 503); Villani also mentions Robert's interest in theology (*Istorie Fiorentine*, 12.10). He is apparently an example of one forced into the wrong profession.

rectly in the objects of Folco's attack. When he praises Rahab for helping Joshua achieve his victory in the Holy Land, for which she "seals this order in the highest degree" (9.116–17), Folco presents Joshua's victory as the model for the crusades which current popes have forgotten (9.126). It is ironic, of course, that a prostitute should be the highest representative of love, while the church she "figures" is prostituting itself on earth; but like Rahab, the church leads a double life, one part devoted to the faith, another selling itself for worldly profit. This connection is implicit as Folco turns back from Rahab to the issue of ecclesiastical corruption, the church's neglect of the Gospels and the doctors for the decretals and the pursuit of the florin, the coin with which Florence, in the devil's service, corrupts clergy and laity alike (9.127–32). Folco brings the focus back to the great enemies of empire, the church, and Florence, Dante's favorite sources of the political ills of his world.

Attacks on corruption in high places increase as Dante rises through the heavens, because the higher spheres are peopled by leaders of mankind on earth, those responsible in various ways for the common good, first teachers (in the Sun), then warriors who defend it (in Mars), rulers (in Jupiter), and finally spiritual guides (in Saturn). In the early heavens the emphasis is on diversity, in the higher ones on unity. In the Sun, which is a turning point in the journey, Dante reaches the climax of diversity, the greatest number of individual souls to be seen or named in any sphere of Paradise, and at the same time the beginning of a special unity, the appearance of all the souls in one symbolic figure, in this case concentric circles.[18] The souls in the Sun represent the great variety in fields of human knowl-

---

[18]Kenelm Foster, "The Celebration of Order, *Paradiso* x," *Dante Studies* 90 (1972), 121, says that Dante's twenty-four wise men "represent a harmony . . . of diverse aspects and functions reflecting the various ways in which mankind may participate in one divine wisdom." The physical sun, the fourth and therefore middle point of the journey through the seven planets, is also a mediator between earth and the intelligible sun, God, as the souls are between men and truth.

edge, all essential to the civilized life on earth: the liberal arts, particularly grammar and logic, philosophy, theology, exegesis, law, history, natural science, and morality. The variety is underscored by the geographic range of the figures named: many of them of course from Italy, but also from France, Germany, the Low Countries, Britain, Spain, Greece, North Africa, and the Near East. If there is a geographic center to this circle, it is Paris, where many of the souls studied or taught or both.[19] Benvenuto notes both the geographic distribution ("like stars in the different parts of heaven, so these doctors come from different shores and provinces"), and also the interconnection of their work ("and as stars illumine themselves and others with their rays, so these doctors by the rays of their writings sent from one to another and commenting one on the other," 5.94–95).

Indeed these scholars used or abused each other's works to a striking degree: Albert wrote commentaries on Peter Lombard and on Pseudo-Dionysius and attacked the ideas of Siger; Thomas Aquinas wrote on Peter Lombard, Boethius, and Pseudo-Dionysius and attacked the ideas of Anselm, Siger, and Joachim; Bonaventure commented on Peter Lombard, drew on Anselm, Hugh, Richard, and Pseudo-Dionysius and attacked Joachim, who had attacked Peter Lombard. The point Dante is making is the interdependence of their work, the thought of one stimulating or provoking the thought of the next, with human knowledge and understanding enriched at each stage. The conflict of ideas is an important element of their work, reflected in the circles they form, which Dante compares to millstones, suggesting the whole process of grinding grain by contrary motion, as these souls work by contrasting opposing ideas to move closer to the truth. The dialectical method, which many of them practice, depends on the opposition of

---

[19]From the first circle, Albert, Thomas, Peter Lombard, Richard, and Siger all taught or studied in Paris, and Pseudo-Dionysius was the patron saint of France. From the second circle, Bonaventure, Hugh, Peter Comestor, and Peter of Spain were all in Paris.

different ideas, whether right or wrong, in order to progress to better understanding; for this process, the more minds at work, the more can be learned.[20] But the circles suggest harmony as well as opposition, matching "motion to motion and song to song" (12.6), reminding Dante of parallel rainbows, of echoes, and finally of a pair of eyes that must move together for the most effective vision; he compares the movement of the single circle, and of the double circles, to a dance, a form which imposes harmony on disparate elements (10.79–81). Marriage, an act which imposes unity on disparate elements, is also an important figure all through this sphere, carrying on the theme of love from the previous planet but containing it within an acceptable structure, however figurative.[21]

Of the two circles, the one introduced by Thomas Aquinas is made up primarily of scholars and philosophers, systematizers of thought and compilers of learning, those who pursue God's truth;[22] the other, presented by Bonaventure, is mainly mystics, exegetes, reformers, men concerned with God's love as expressed in vision, in revelation, or in imitation of his life. The one characteristic shared by all the figures in both circles

[20]Those who used the dialectical method in their work were Aquinas, Albertus Magnus, Peter Lombard, Richard of St. Victor and Siger in theology, Gratian in canon law (he called the *Decretum* the *Concordia discordantium canonum*); Anselm wrote an introduction to dialectic, *De grammatica*, Pseudo-Dionysius provided opposing approaches to the knowledge of God, positive through names, negative through exclusion of the imperfections of creatures, Orosius reconciled opposing views of history, and Solomon weighed opposing sides in making judgments.

[21]Beginning with the image of the church as the bride of God rising to greet her bridegroom (10.140–41), which balances the actual adultery of the church condemned at the end of the previous canto (9.142, cf. Hell 19) with the ideal model, Dante carries the theme over into the lives of Francis, who loves and marries Poverty, and Dominic, who loves and marries Faith; both saints were sent by God to rescue his bride, whom he had married with his blood (11.32).

[22]Fiorenzo Forti, "Canto x," *LDS*, 369, distinguishes rationalists in Thomas's circle from mystics in Bonaventure's. Benvenuto comments that it is suitable that Thomas introduce the figures in his circle since he knew their writings intimately (5.38); Jacopo, after listing his major works, says Thomas defined much in theology that Augustine had left undefined (3.168).

is that they are teachers, whether of theology, philosophy, the arts, or morals. Together, they provide the basic reading list for Dante's educated citizen. Thomas is a key figure for Dante because of his vast works covering all the important areas of thought, because of the systems he imposes on the material, and because of his balanced view of spiritual and secular needs (see introduction). Bonaventure is the other major "doctor" in this sphere because of his mystic writings, the influence of his *Itinerarium Mentis ad Deum,* the "journey of the mind to God," which might also be a description of Dante's poem, his acceptance of the role of secular learning in the service of theology (in the *Breviloquium*) and of secular society in human life, but also perhaps because of the coincidence of parallels between his life and Thomas's.[23] They were contemporaries, who were appointed to chairs of theology in the same year, 1256, and died in the same year, 1274, Bonaventure at the Council of Lyon, Thomas en route to it; both studied and taught at Paris, both wrote commentaries on Peter Lombard, and both refused bishoprics, although Bonaventure was made a cardinal-bishop shortly before he died.

Bonaventure's circle, with a few exceptions, does not boast the same profusion of stellar intellects as Thomas's; it includes several not known at all for their writings, others who wrote only basic texts, still others whose primary concern was in seeking the mystical prophetic significance of God's word, rather than in working out the logical inconsistencies in nature or theology. It does include the one medieval pope Dante sees in heaven, John XXI, though he is identified as

[23]See Matthew M. de Benedictis, *The Social Thought of St. Bonaventure* (1946; reprint, Westport: Greenwood, 1972), for views culled from various works, particularly the *Collations on the Hexaemeron* and the *Commentary* on Peter Lombard's *Sentences,* which show that Bonaventure, like Dante, sees man as a social animal who needs the contributions of others in order to live properly and who owes his service to others, to succor, teach, and correct when necessary. Bonaventure also believes the government should have one head concerned with the common good so man can turn his earthly exile into an outpost of the heavenly kingdom, a thought reminiscent of the end of the *Monarchy.*

Peter of Spain, author of a manual of logic, not as pope,[24] and Joachim of Fiore, whose book of figures probably influenced Dante's symbols in Paradise, as his prophecy of a third age of moral and spiritual regeneration may well have done.[25] Dante allots to this circle roughly a third the space he gives the other (fifteen as compared to forty-two lines), but he does give it equal symbolic value, because this circle provides the basic tools of grammar, logic, morality, and knowledge of God's word on which the others build.

Thomas's circle includes major thinkers, like Thomas himself, his teacher Albertus Magnus, Boethius, Pseudo-Dionysius, and Siger of Brabant,[26] as well as men who made important

[24]Benvenuto calls his *Summae logicales* a useful introduction (5.89). Peter also taught and wrote on medicine and he was the pope under whom the condemnation of 1277 was issued, but whether he was in sympathy with it has been questioned. See J. M. DaCruz Pontes, "Un nouveau manuscrit des 'Quaestiones libri de anima' de Petrus Hispanus Portugalensis," *Recherches de Théologie ancienne et médiévale* 43 (1976), 167–201, for various questions about Peter's life and views. During his brief pontificate, Peter worked to reconcile the elected emperor Rudolph with Charles of Anjou, which Dante would have approved.

[25]An exegete who emphasized the harmony of the Old and the New Testaments, Joachim was also a reformer who attacked the corruption of the contemporary clergy. The Spiritual Franciscans identified themselves with the age of the Holy Spirit, and Joachim's ideas were attacked by Bonaventure and Thomas, who said there would be no age of perfection on earth. His book of figures probably influenced Dante's poetic concepts, see Marjorie Reeves and Beatrice Hirsch-Reich, *The Figurae of Joachim of Fiore* (Oxford: Clarendon, 1972). Joachim also attacked Peter Lombard's doctrine of the Trinity, and that view was condemned at the Fourth Lateran Council, the work not the man, as the Ottimo points out correctly (3.307); cf. Reeves, *The Influence of Prophecy in the Later Middle Ages* (Oxford: Clarendon, 1969), 32.

[26]Thomas and Siger were public adversaries in Paris and Thomas refuted several of Siger's views, but their ideas were condemned together in 1270 and 1277. Siger expressed the conflict between reason and faith in the double truth, the concept that the truth known by reason and the truth known by faith cannot necessarily be reconciled. He also denied creation *ex nihilo* and the immortality of the soul; for a shift in his views on the individual intellect, see Edward P. Mahoney, "Saint Thomas and Siger of Brabant Revisited," *The Review of Metaphysics* 27 (1974), 531–53. Whether or not Dante knew of the shift, he clearly feels that even if Siger's reasoning led him to the wrong con-

contributions to knowledge in particular areas, like Gratian in canon law and Orosius in history, who influenced Dante on the concept of Rome as the chosen nation of God. [27] Boethius is not named, but he is identified by his place of burial. He is yet another of those public servants who is undone by envious rivals, like Pier della Vigna, Pier de la Broccia, and Romeo, and he is the one with whom Dante can most closely identify himself.[28] In the *Convivio* Dante cites Boethius as a model for one whose misfortune justified his writing about himself, and

---

clusions, it was in the pursuit of truth; the remark, "silogizzò invidiosi veri" (10.138) is interpreted by Benvenuto to mean that Siger "disputed happy truths, abandoning logical fallacies" (5.47), probably a more positive view than Dante intended. Pietro calls Siger a great philosopher and theologian, "magnus philosophus et theologus" (623). See Etienne Gilson, *Dante and Philosophy*, trans. David Moore (1949; reprint, New York: Harper, 1963), 257 ff. for a modern discussion of Siger in the *Comedy*.

[27] There is some question about this identification; Orosius is called "quello avvocato dei tempi Cristiani/del cui latino Augustin si provide" (10.119–20: "that advocate of Christian times whose Latin (writings) Augustine used") and has been identified with both Ambrose (whom some early commentators prefer) and Orosius (the choice of most modern scholars). Pietro (623), and Jacopo (3.176) give Ambrose, citing his conversion of Augustine; the Ottimo, (3.255) gives both Ambrose and Orosius, noting that Orosius was *really* an advocate and defender of Christian times in the book he wrote at Augustine's behest; Benvenuto (5.44–45) mentions both, but prefers Ambrose as more worthy of this circle, *even if Dante meant Orosius,* which he thinks probable since Dante shows in his writing that he was very familiar with him. Forti, on the other hand, points out that a *piccioletta luce,* "a little light," would not be suitable for Ambrose, "Canto X," 374; he also cites an early commentator, Buti, who identifies the soul as Orosius. On Orosius and Dante, see Charles Davis, *Dante and the Idea of Rome,* (Oxford: Clarendon, 1957), 55 ff. Orosius, who attempted to reconcile Augustine's views of Rome and its place in the providential plan with the Eusebian view of history, is the more likely candidate, I believe.

[28] Boethius wrote about subjects of major concern to Dante, the conflict between free will and predestination, fortune and philosophy as forces in men's lives, and he also helped to pass on much of ancient thought, Aristotelian as well as Neoplatonic, to the Middle Ages, though he did not complete his project of translating Aristotle and Plato into Latin; he wrote widely on the liberal arts, logic, mathematics, music, philosophy, and theology. The Ottimo (3.256) mentions Boethius's translations from Greek to Latin and his learning in all the liberal arts as well as natural science and morals.

in Paradise as one who moved from martyrdom and exile to peace in heaven (10.124–29), a connection Dante's ancestor, Cacciaguida, reinforces by echoing the description (15.145–48).

Probably the most surprising figure in either group is King Solomon, the fifth in Thomas's circle.[29] He was, of course, known to medieval Christians as the author of the Song of Songs, the Old Testament book of love, and of the Book of Wisdom, as well as of Proverbs and Ecclesiastes, and therefore has a place among scholars, but Thomas praises him for such profound wisdom that he had no second (10.112–14). Dante allows that praise to stand unchallenged for almost three cantos until Thomas explains what he had meant (13.95 ff.): that Solomon asked only for enough wisdom to be a good king, not for knowledge in other realms, so that it is among kings that he has no equal. But through the sphere of the wise, while he presented all the other teachers, Dante has tricked us into thinking of Solomon as the wisest of all. In a sense, of course, he is, not just among kings but among men, because he accepts his role and chooses only to do it well, and he puts his wisdom to the immediate service of society in his judgments as king. From Dante's point of view, there can be no greater wisdom. It is not a coincidence that, although Dante focuses on the scholarly achievements of most of the figures in this sphere, he has chosen in the main men who also had responsible administrative positions in the world.[30] It is also significant that

[29]Early commentators are somewhat disturbed by Solomon's presence here, noting that there is some dispute among theologians over whether he was saved or damned, See Pietro (623), and Benvenuto (5.42). Jacopo notes only that there are varying opinions about Solomon (3.175).

[30]Albert was the provincial of an order and a bishop, Peter Lombard a bishop, though only for two years, Boethius a consul, the real Dionysius (not the author) a bishop, Isidore an archbishop, Richard a prior, Bonaventure the general of his order, Illuminato and Augustin officials of the Franciscans, Hugh a prior, Peter Comnestor chancellor of the University of Paris, Peter of Spain pope, Chrysostom metropolitan of Constantinople, Anselm archbishop of Canterbury, Rabanus archbishop of Mainz, and Joachim an abbot. All of them led active lives in addition to their teaching, but are here because it was through their teaching that they had the greatest effect on others.

among all the churchmen, it falls to Solomon's lot to describe the important Christian doctrine of the resurrection of the body, the promise of full perfection of all human powers. Resurrection is an affirmation of the human state, whose glory is achieved not by denying the earthly part, but by perfecting it, and it is fitting that it should be described by a king, the role best suited to help man approach such a state in life. It is interesting that Benvenuto sees the sphere of the Sun as central to Dante's Paradise, just as a king is to his kingdom, implying that these souls, by the disciplines they teach, impose order on the world as the sun does in structuring the day and the year: the sun is like the king, who has Saturn as a counsellor because counsel is an old man, Mars as his leader of war, Jupiter as his judge, Venus as the provider since she gives all delights to the kingdom, Mercury, the god of eloquence, for his ambassador, and the Moon for his herald or watchman, *praecone* (5.30).

The souls in the Sun appear in concentric circles; in Mars, they appear in a cross within a circle, as if they somehow came out of the previous sphere.[31] In fact, what the others teach, these do. Benvenuto says that the doctors in the Sun illuminated the faith with doctrine and writing, the soldiers in Mars fought for the faith of Christ with the shedding of their own blood; the doctors fought with tongue or pen, but are not as worthy as these who fought with hand and sword and exposed their lives (5.120). Dante underscores that contrast by having Cacciaguida echo in Mars the words which described Boethius in the Sun. Thomas had said of Boethius: "the holy soul who reveals the fallacious world . . . came from martyrdom and exile to this peace" (10.125–29). Cacciaguida says of himself:

---

[31]The white cross on the red background (the planet Mars is red) recalls the arms of crusaders, which are no longer taken up in the right cause. It was thought that the vapors of Mars also signified the death of kings and transfer of kingdoms, a subject Dante treats in this sphere, particularly in relation to Florence. Dino Compagni (Cronica, 2.19) relates that when Charles of Valois came to Florence and sided with the Blacks, a red cross was seen over the prior's palace, which was taken as a sign of God's anger at Florence (the cross was formed by vapors following the planet Mars).

"disencumbered from the fallacious world ... I came from martyrdom to this peace" (15.146–48). Both saw this world as deceitful, both came from that martyrdom to this peace, but for Dante, it is better to fight against the iniquities of the world, as Cacciaguida did, than to learn to rise above them in the mind.

The souls in Mars all fought in God's cause; those Dante sees fought wars for Israel or Christendom against the infidel, but this is not the only way to serve the cause. Dante himself is given his mission here and his crusade is to fight evil with his words and guide others to the establishment of an earthly paradise, the restoration of the holy land throughout the world. He instinctively offers that sacrifice before he knows where he is (14.85–90), clearly moved by the spirit of the planet, which is his proper sphere of action; he endures his martyrdom in life by suffering exile and isolation and hostility. But he is somewhat hesitant, identifying with Phaethon, who destroyed himself and harmed the earth by taking on a task he was not fit for; Dante wants to reform but not to destroy. He is also torn between the fear of losing the few friends he has, if he speaks the truth, and the fear of losing lasting fame if he does not (17.109–20). What Dante has to relate will indeed give a bitter taste to many as he fears, but it is essential food and vital nourishment; if it strikes the mighty, that will be cause for honor to him, Cacciaguida reassures him, presumably in that he had the courage to take on such opponents. They are the most important audience for his poem, those in the best position to put into effect, in Italy at least, what Dante is preaching. He was shown the examples of famous men because they will have the greatest impact on his audience. This didactic justification for Dante's method comes in the central cantos of Paradise, right after the praise of the foremost contemporary defender of the empire in Italy, Can Grande (17.76 ff.), and the criticism of the church for betraying the last emperor (17.82). The juxtaposition makes it clear that Dante's poem is intended to serve the cause of the empire.

The central figure in the planet is Cacciaguida, Dante's

ancestor, who lived in Florence when it was small and vir-
tuous, not yet greedy or a major opponent of empire, and who
himself followed an emperor, Conrad III, on the second cru-
sade and fought and died for the faith. Cacciaguida's account
of his own life is very brief, but it suffices to establish Dante's
credentials as one born to a class that serves society at the top
levels. [32] His very name suggests one who "hunts a leader," as
Dante and all his world are now doing. His meeting with
Dante recalls Anchises and Aeneas but his message is quite dif-
ferent. [33] His Florence attempts to be a new Rome, usurping a
destiny that does not belong to it and from which it must fall.
The distinction between the destinies of Rome and Florence is
implicit in the contrast between the prophecies Anchises and
Cacciaguida make: Anchises shows Aeneas the heirs of his line,
the future glory of Rome. Cacciaguida speaks of the past his-
tory of Florence when it was small and modest and of its pres-
ent corruption; the only future glory he mentions is that of
Can Grande, an imperial vicar but not a Florentine. The future
that Dante is to establish in the world is not that of Florence,
except within the much larger context of Rome as the empire
which embraces the world.[34]

The Florence of Cacciaguida's time was the model of a small
city, contained within its walls, its boundaries marked by the
statue of Mars and the Baptistery, symbols of its two patrons,

[32]There is some question whether the Conrad III of the second crusade cre-
ated any knights in Florence, as Conrad II had, see Singleton's commentary on
Paradise, 266. What matters to Dante is that his audience see him as the de-
scendent of an old, modestly noble Florentine family that had once served God
and the emperor.

[33]Dante thinks of Anchises when he first sees Cacciaguida, who speaks Latin
words reminiscent of the Aeneid. Dante thus identifies himself with Aeneas
here, and Cacciaguida identifies him with Paul by the question "to whom as
to you were the gates of heaven twice opened?" (15.29–30), to which the only
answer is Paul.

[34]Early commentators contrast the corruption of contemporary Florentine
figures with virtuous ancient Romans in some detail, e.g., Benvenuto (5.151–
52). On the corruption of a city by the invasion of foreign elements, which
Cacciaguida goes into at length, Pietro cites Aquinas, Aristotle, and Seneca
(658).

past and present. Dante said in Hell (13.143 ff.) that because Florence had given up its patron Mars for John the Baptist, it would always suffer from the art of Mars, war. In this sphere of heaven, Dante shows that the two spirits of fighting and of self-sacrifice for a cause can work together. John the Baptist is a martyr, one who sacrificed his life for God as the souls in Mars do; Florence now rejects his example and follows that of the pagan god, but only in the negative sense of civil war, not in the positive of crusade for good. Civil war is the inevitable result of the reckless growth of the city: when it was one fifth its current size, every citizen, even the humblest, was of pure blood (16.46–51); now that it has taken in foreign elements, it has created its own corruption. A city is like the human body: if it has too much food, its functions are disrupted, and if it overindulges too regularly, it may destroy itself, a point Dante has made before in the circles of gluttony in both Hell and Purgatory. Benvenuto picks up this analogy in his comments on Cacciaguida's words: just as a superfluity of goods gives rise to disease, so the confusion of men is the cause of frequent sedition (5.167).

Cities rise and fall, their great families grow old and decline, new ones emerge, but there is a moral as well as a natural reason, as the historic works of Eusebius, Orosius, and Bede had taught Dante. In this case, the main source of trouble is the church; if she, "the most degenerate people in the world" (16.58), had not been a stepmother to the emperor, Florence might have been spared the infusion of destructive elements. Jacopo (3.256) explains this passage as meaning that if the empire had remained at peace with the church, all worldly monarchy would have continued properly ordered, cities would not have attacked each other, they would have remained in their own territories; there would have been vicars to keep the evil elements out of the cities and preserve their virtue. If the great families of Florence had controlled their pride, Dante implies, they might not have fallen, leaving the way open for the mob to rise; if Buondelmonte, who would never have been there if the city had not expanded into the countryside, had not reneged on his betrothal, the feud that split the city open might have been averted. The murder of Buondelmonte, which set off the feud, tood place at the foot of Mars' statue, as if the city had offered him in sacrifice to the god (16.146–47), acting like pagans. In a kind of litany, Cacciaguida names the great families of the past whose glory is gone, or who are altogether extinct, but he also alludes to those who engaged in the most destructive feuds, the Buondelmonti and Amidei, the Cerchi and Donati. When the people of Florence were "glorious and just" (16.151–52), their emblem was never turned upside down in defeat nor reversed in color to distinguish factions. Villani mentions that Florence's standard of the white lily on the red field appeared when the Christians took the city of Damiatta in 1221 (*Istorie Fiorentine*, 5.40), but in 1251 when Florence threw out the Ghibellines after it had defeated Pistoia without their help, it changed the standard to a red lily on a white field in order to distinguish itself as Guelph (6.43). The Ottimo (3.383) notes that the lily is naturally white, but it became red because of the divisions in the city; that is, by changing its standard, the city declared its commitment to bloodshed, to the negative aspect of Mars.

The enormous amount of attention given to this one city at the center of Paradise is dictated by Florence's position, in Dante's eyes, as the center of secular opposition to the empire in Italy and the epitome of secular corruption. Dante himself will be a victim of the perfidy of his native city, Cacciaguida tells him, which will act as a stepmother to him (17.47), as the church does to the empire; in his exile, Dante will suffer the bitterness of living on the charity of others and of enduring the company of fools and evil men who will turn on him.[35] But he will also know the hospitality of the great Lombard (Bartolomeo della Scala), whose standard bears the "holy bird," the eagle, on a ladder (17.72), a more fitting home for Dante than the lilies of Florence. It is no coincidence that the souls in the

---

[35]Dante met with other exiled White Guelphs in 1302 in an attempt to reconquer Florence, but he did not join them in later attempts. See Nereo Vianello, "Canto XVII," *LDS*, 602–03.

two highest planets in Paradise, Jupiter and Saturn, appear in the same figures, an eagle and a ladder, since Dante associates this family with the highest level of service to God and man. Cacciaguida alludes to the deeds of one member of the family, Can Grande, who in the time of the *Comedy* is only nine, but who, before this part was written, became the imperial vicar of Henry VII, a distinguished warrior and effective ruler. He will be the foremost servant of the empire in Italy, helping to do the work of the *veltro,* a connection suggested by his name "great dog"; his deeds will be "incredible to those who will witness them" (17.92–93). Can Grande would, in fact, win many victories in north Italy and serve as imperial vicar of Verona and Vicenza and eventually as captain general of the Ghibelline league in 1318; he refused to relinquish his imperial title or function after the death of Henry when the pope, John XXII, refused to recognize either of the imperial candidates, Ludwig or Frederick. A letter from Can Grande to Henry states that he saw in the empire the only possibility for an ordered civil life and for the peace necessary to the serene development of all human activity to obtain the greatest good of peoples, concepts very similar to Dante's in the *Monarchy,* indicating that Can Grande's loyalty to the empire was as much a matter of principle as of party.[36] Dante dedicated the Paradiso to him, suggesting that he thought of Can Grande as the most receptive audience for his poem and probably the one in the best position to put into effect, at least in Italy, what Dante was preaching. Although his name implies a connection with the *veltro* of Virgil's prophecy, it is unlikely that Dante intended an absolute identification of the two; more likely, he saw Can Grande as the one figure in Italy who might help consolidate imperial power there. Can Grande might be the "heir to the eagle" in the sense that he remains to care for the imperial cause, but he is not himself a candidate for the crown and

[36]The letter is cited by Raoul Manselli, "Can Grande ed il mondo Ghibellino nell' Italia settentrionale alla venuta di Arrigo VII," in *Dante e la cultura veneta,* ed. Vittore Branca and Giorgio Padoan (Florence: Olschki, 1966), 47–48.

therefore not powerful enough to carry out the full task of driving greed back to hell and reforming church and state in Europe. Dante has carefully brought together at the center of Paradise the most important issues of his poem, the corruption of Florence, the church's treacherous opposition to the empire, the imperial vicar who fights stubbornly for the cause, and the role of his own poem in serving that cause. At the center of Purgatory, the courtier, Marco Lombardo, discussed the problem of church and empire in general terms; here Cacciaguida, a fighter, presents the issue to Dante as one on which he must act, through his poem.

Before he leaves this sphere, Dante sees something in Beatrice's eyes that even his memory cannot retain, a fleeting ·vision of the divine, but she directs his eyes back to the souls in the cross saying "non pur nei miei occhi è paradiso" (18.21: "Paradise is not only in my eyes"). Paradise is not just the vision of God, but the reflections of his virtues in others. Just as Dante sees God's light in Beatrice, he must continue to see self-sacrifice, as he has in Mars, and justice, as he will in Jupiter, in those who embody them. Pointing out the notable figures on the cross, Cacciaguida describes Paradise as the "tree that lives from its top" (18.29), that has its roots in God. That is the model for the tree Dante saw in the Earthly Paradise, the tree of justice, which housed the eagle whose ideal form appears in the next sphere. Paradise is also a tree that shelters the eagle of empire, which the souls of these two spheres serve, those in Mars by fighting to establish or protect God's government so those in Jupiter can carry out his justice; on earth both activities are functions of the empire. Cacciaguida points to eight other figures, all secular leaders who fought for God's people, Israel or Christendom, against the infidel, to establish the state in which justice might operate, the only justifiable war. Among them are Joshua, who destroyed Jericho, a city of sin, and led the Jews to the Holy Land in what might be called the first crusade (cf. 9.124–26), and Judas Maccabeus, who freed the Jews from Syrian tyranny and restored the temple at Jerusalem, the ideal city in biblical tradition, the equivalent of

Rome in the secular sphere; Charlemagne, whom Justinian named among the Roman emperors and who defended Europe from the Saracens in Spain and southern France; Godfrey, who led the first Christian crusade and became the king of Jerusalem; and Robert Guiscard, duke of Apulia, who led the Norman struggle to free southern Italy from the Saracens. Cacciaguida, who fought and died on the second crusade, returns to take his place in the cross as the ninth figure.[37] He is the one ancestor Dante chooses to acknowledge in the *Comedy,* the crusader who, like Dante, must leave his beloved Florence in order to fight God's battle.

The object of the struggle waged by the souls in Mars and by Dante in his poem is the establishment of the universal Christian empire on earth, through which divine justice can operate for all men. That empire and its relation to divine justice is seen symbolically in the souls of Jupiter and the eagle they form. In this sphere, the individual subordinates himself completely to the harmony of the whole; it is the only heaven in which no individual soul speaks. Together the souls first spell out a biblical message, then form the figure of the eagle, and finally the eagle speaks with one voice. The essence of the eagle is its unity; it is the symbol of justice on earth in God's ordained instrument, the empire, and through it we learn the workings of justice, the basis of divine justice, which is mercy (canto 20), and the greatest obstacles to justice, the corrupt church (canto 18) and bad kings (canto 19). The message of this sphere is that justice must be adminstered in love: "Diligite justitiam . . . qui judicatis terram" (18.91 and 93: "love justice, you who judge the earth"), the words of Solomon from the Book of Wisdom. (Dante's emphasis on the first three letters *DIL,* and their possible relation to the DXV prophecy was discussed

[37]The number nine among warriors suggests the nine worthies, some of whom are here: Joshua, Judas Maccabeus, Charlemagne, and Godfrey; the classical trio is not, nor is Arthur from the medieval group; David, the missing Old Testament figure is in the next planet. Benvenuto (5.214) notes that some mistakenly identify the "artista" of 18.51 as David, which suggests they may also have had the worthies in mind.

in chapter two.) It does not seem far-fetched to assume that Dante intends us to make such a connection, that the savior Beatrice foretold in Purgatory will be a soul of this sphere, a just king. It is, of course, God who designs both the words and the eagle that emerges from them (18.109–11), as he used human language to reveal his message in the Bible and the empire to carry out his plan for the redemption. An analogy is to be made with human history: we can read God's message in the movements of men, as Dante does in his poem.

From the last letter, the *M,* the souls form an eagle, the "sign that made the Romans revered in the world" (19.101–02); the eagle declares that it is exalted for being just and pious, "giusto e pio" (19.13), words that evoke Aeneas, showing that the tradition of justice and piety was present in the very seeds of the empire. The *M* suggests *Monarchy,* the rule of one who, as Dante explains in his work of that name, stands above all other earthly rulers, beyond greed and ambition and therefore able to serve pure justice. In Purgatory, *M* was the human skull, the bare outlines stripped of the self-indulgent flesh, the essence of man; here it is the essence of the highest order of mankind on earth, brought together in one figure. Jacopo calls the eagle made by the souls the principal sign of earthly monarchy, in which one elected to such office is sole lord over the others, and all temporal positions depend on him; just as man is one essence in which soul dominates, so in the world there should be one temporal signory, which should be the rule for all human acts that come under temporal jurisdiction (3.281). Benvenuto (5.223–24), suggests that the souls of just kings and rulers who constitute the one body of the eagle show figurally that all kingdoms of the world depend *de jure* on the Roman, in which justice is most vigorous, as can be proved in various ways, and all kings are subject to the Roman prince as different members of the human body are to the head; the natural order is like the universe, in which an animal with many heads is a monster (perhaps a reference to the church-state controversy, see chapter two). Around the eagle in Jupiter other souls form lilies; since the lily is the symbol of France, of Florence, and of the Guelphs, all enemies of the empire, the suggestion is that ideally all political factions and powers should come together under the monarch, the Roman emperor.[38]

Having established that the empire is the organ of divine justice, Dante focuses on the source of the smoke that vitiates the light of justice on earth (18.118 ff.), the papacy and the papal curia. He makes it clear that in opposing the empire, the church runs directly counter to God's justice. Now there is buying and selling in the temple, which Christ condemned by his own act, in the very temple built by miracles and martyrdom, the church (18.121–23). The sacrifices made for the faith are undone by the guardians of the faith. War is now waged with excommunications instead of swords, that is, against other Christians. The sacraments, "the bread which the pious father denies to none" (18.129), are being used as a weapon, the "pious father" is not the pope, but God, and he offers his bread to all, but the pope withholds it for political purposes. Dante reminds the pope that Peter and Paul, who died for the vineyard he is laying waste, are still alive, as we will soon see, threatening retribution, but the pope says he does not know "the fisherman" or "the pole" (perhaps a pun on Paul's name), because he is so devoted to the one who was "drawn to his death by leaps," a rather casual reference to Salome's dance. The pope is devoted to John the Baptist, not out of self-sacrifice, but because the saint's face appears on the florin.[39]

[38]The lily is also associated with Mary in the Annunciation, and the eagle can also symbolize Christ; thus Dante may be suggesting Christ in the eagle as the supreme judge, represented on earth by these kings. The suggestion of Christ does not, however, deny or supercede the reference to the Roman empire, as Joseph Chierici suggests in *L'Aquila d'oro nel cielo di Giove* (Rome: Tiberino, 1962). Kenelm Foster, "Paradiso XIX" *Dante Studies* 94 (1976), 71–90, sees grace as the unifying principle of the eagle, which goes beyond the secular monarchy of the symbol. Aurelia A. Bobbio, "Canto XVIII," *LDS*, comments in response to Chierici that the eagle could hardly be Christ himself, since it denies knowledge of the elect, 651.

[39]Umberto Bosco, "San Francesco," *Cultura e Scuola* 13 (1965), 612, connects this picture of the greedy pope with John XXII's persecution of the spiritual Franciscans. Villani (*Istorie Fiorentine*, 9.169) mentions that John had his

In contrast to the pope's selfish greed, the *molti amori* of the eagle have no separate desires; they can speak as one, in the first person singular, for each other and for mankind, because their wills are in perfect harmony. The eagle reveals the scope of the empire's jurisdiction over all mankind, in answer to a question that has plagued Dante throughout the *Comedy:* how can a man who has never heard or read of Christ, but whose thoughts and acts are good, be justly condemned? The answer is that he can be saved if he believes in Christ, even without knowing him, and an example is given in canto 20 in the pagan Ripheus. Many who cry "Christ, Christ," as if they believed, will be much further from him than one who never knew him (19.106–08), and Christians will be condemned at the Last Judgment by the saved Ethiopian, representing those born where Christ is not known.[40] The eagle also lists the Christian kings whose bad deeds will be read in the Book of Justice. They are contemporary kings from all over Europe and the Middle East, all motivated by private ambitions rather than the common good, by lust for power or wealth or pleasure. Many

---

own coin minted, of the same alloy and stamp as the gold florin, with his name beside the lily, for which he was severely criticized. He dates that minting in 1322, which would be too late for Dante to know of it unless it was spoken of earlier; in any case, it is an interesting verification of Dante's judgment.

[40]The repetition of "Christ" in 19.106 weakens rather than strengthens the appearance of faith. The repetition rhymes with Christ in lines 104 and 108, with a negative reference to those who did not believe or did not know Christ, the four occurrences of the word forming a kind of cross:
                                                    Cristo
                                            Cristo Cristo
                                                    Cristo
which is partially interspersed with the rhyme words *segno* (the eagle, symbol of empire), *regno* (the heavenly kingdom), and *legno* (the cross of Christ), lines 101, 103, 105. Dante is emphasizing the contrast between the true faith that can be found in those who did not know Christ directly and the hypocrisy of those who mouth his name. The salvation of the "Ethiopian" seems to have troubled Jacopo, who assumes that these lines mean that many Christians will be closer to the depths of hell than some Gentiles and will suffer greater penalty, but they will all be in hell (3.298–99); Benvenuto, however, understands and accepts Dante's meaning, saying the Ethiopian will damn false Christians when the souls are divided into the saved and the damned (5.246).

of them are familiar figures to the readers of the *Comedy,* since
they were mentioned in Purgatory 7 as the source of distress
to their virtuous fathers: Albert of Austria (son of Rudolph),
Philip IV of France (son of Philip III), Edward I and II of
England (son and grandson of Henry III), Wenceslas of Bohe-
mia (son of Ottokar), Charles II of Jerusalem (son of Charles
of Anjou), and Frederick II of Sicily (son of Pedro III of Ara-
gon).[41] Their bad deeds, which are outlined here, in contrast to
their fathers' decent though negligent lives, strongly suggest
the increasing corruption of the contemporary world; they are
guilty of every kind of sin, treachery, violence, fraud, counter-
feiting, greed, pride, lust, and sloth. It may well be that the
fathers' failure to act aggressively for good leaves the way open
to such evil. The eagle, to give greater force to his list, employs
the rhetorical device of anaphora, and the first letters of the
repeated phrases spell the acrostic *LUE,* pestilence, because evil
kings are the disease of the Christian world. The Ottimo com-
ments that Christian princes should guide their subjects to
honorable life, should lead by example so that others may be
secure in their civil and political lives, but these used their time
in vice and sin to the harm and death of souls and bodies and
of the substance of their kingdoms (3.448).

  Although the figures in the eagle never speak separately, the
major ones are named, so we have a sense of the role of the

[41]It is not clear whether one or both Edwards are meant, because in Purga-
tory 7, Edward I was singled out as a good offspring. On the other hand, he
was responsible for the failure of a major Lucca banking house, the Ricciardi,
who had served him for many years, and Dante did spend time in Lucca during
his exile, where he could certainly have heard the story from their point of
view, see below, chapter six. On Philip IV, Benvenuto notes that his crimes are
described in Purgatory 20, but here Dante names only his very greedy baseness,
"avarissima viltate" (5.247). Dante does, however, specifically mention Philip's
falsifying of coins and the ensuing trouble for his country; he also alludes to
Philip's death, caused by a boar-hunting accident. Villani describes Philip as
handsome and clever, but self-indulgent and open to bad counsel, which was
harmful to his country, and reports that his three daughters-in-law were all
caught in adultery, a result, it was said, of the sins of the family in incestuous
marriages and the father's attack on Boniface, *Istorie Fiorentine,* 9.65.

individual within the operation of the empire, a relation most effectively expressed by an analogy: as the eagle lapses into individual songs, which Dante cannot comprehend, the poet compares the sensation to the sky when the sun sets and the individul stars become visible. Similarly, in the eagle and in the proper operation of world government the individual may be invisible within the whole, because the more powerful light overwhelms it, but it is always there. The souls named also illustrate the scope of the empire in Dante's view, extending from Israel and Troy to modern Italy. The pupil is David, who sang of the Holy Spirit, "il canto dello Spirito Santo," a poet as well as a king, one who praised God in his words as well as his actions; he now knows the real value of his song, not just as the expression of his own feeling for God, but perhaps as a means of moving others to love God. In the brow are five leaders, the Roman emperors Trajan, who put justice before pride in accepting the widow's rebuke,[42] and Constantine, who moved the empire and made it Greek, in opposition to its divinely ordained destiny, in order to "yield to the shepherd"; he now knows that his error, committed with good intent, does not harm him, although it may destroy the world. Benvenuto (5.260) calls Constantine a just prince, but his Donation "damnable" because it caused the corruption of the prelates of the church. The others are a second Old Testament king Hezekiah, the medieval king William II of Naples and Sicily, renowned for his devotion to justice and his support of the church, though not to the detriment of his own authority. William is contrasted to the current kings of Naples and Sicily (20.62–63) mentioned in canto 19. The last soul named is the Trojan, Ripheus, whom Virgil praises for his justice ("Ripheus, justissimus ... et servantissimus aequi," *Aeneid* 2.426-27: "Ripheus, the very just ... and devoted servant of justice"); he presents the strongest example in the *Comedy* of the operation

---

[42]Cf. Purgatory 10, where Trajan and David were both cited as examples of humility, a connection Dante apparently intends us to make because he alludes to the Purgatory scene in connection with both kings. Similarly, the acrostic *LUE* recalls the other, *UOM*, composed from the examples of pride in Purgatory 12.

of grace.[43] God showed him by grace the future redemption and he believed in it; that is, his devotion to good, expressed through his actions as a just king, opened the way to his salvation. This is the closest Dante comes to affirming the power of good works alone; he does insist that the theological virtues were present in Ripheus's soul (20.127–29), but it was his good deeds that attracted the grace: "tutto suo amor là giù pose a drittura:/*per che,* di grazia in grazia, Dio aperse . . ." (20.121–22: "down there he gave his love to right, *for which* God opened to him, from grace to grace . . ."). This affirmation of the value of service to the public good in a leader is a tremendous encouragement to Dante's audience to follow the example. There is, of course, bitter irony in the fact that pagan kings have served divine justice, while the church now opposes it and Christian kings abuse it.

In Jupiter Dante presents the symbol of the highest secular order, the empire; in the last of the seven planets, Saturn, he presents the highest form of religious life, but his model is the monastic community, not the church hierarchy under the pope. The souls Dante sees are contemplatives, men who tried to remove themselves from the world and to renounce worldly power and wealth in order to devote themselves entirely to prayer and meditation.[44] Having shown the height of the active

[43]On Dante's treatment of Ripheus as a leader, although there is no suggestion of high rank in the *Aeneid,* see chapter one, fn. 16. The eagle is described as the sign of the world and of its leaders, "il segno del mondo e dei suoi duci" (20.8, cf. 19.101–02); the sphere is responsible for justice on earth (18.116 and 93), and those who may be expected to rise to it, or fail to do so, are kings (19.112 ff.). Ettore Paratore, "Canto xx," *LDS,* 724, points out that Ripheus was among the top level of Trojans, but was not a king. Benvenuto notes that Ripheus was a Trojan warrior, but he also describes the souls in the eagle as kings, rulers, princes 5.223, 257, and 262).

[44]The Ottimo comments that the previous two cantos dealt with those who acted within political regimes pleasing to God, the present canto with men who virtuously followed the influence of Saturn in the contemplative life remote from the turbulence of the world (3.466); Benvenuto (5.272), describes the souls in the previous sphere as illustrious spirits of the active life, civil and political, whereas these serve God through the contemplative. Bonaventure places contemplatives above the clerical hierarchy, which is in turn above the secular (*Collationes in Hexaemeron* 22).

life with the crusaders in Mars and the just rulers in Jupiter, Dante seems to be reaching a climax with the contemplatives, but in fact, the two figures he sees are men who tried again and again to remove themselves from the world in order to live the contemplative life, but who were followed by the world and forced to deal with it, even to some extent to work within it. They are contemplative by choice, active by necessity. The symbol Dante chooses for this planet, the ladder, is a traditional symbol for contemplation, but it works particularly well for Dante in that the contemplative not only tries to ascend to God, but must also descend from time to time to deal with men, as the souls do here to speak to Dante. Dante does not deny the supremacy of contemplation as the highest human activity, but he does seem to reject it as an exclusive lifestyle. In the *Convivio* (4.27–28), where Dante gives the suitable occupations for different ages in life, he suggests that a man should retire to a monastery and give himself solely to God only when he is old and has given his prime and the maturity of his experience to the service of society.

The monastic life, as conceived by Benedict in his rule, is the model of a perfect, autonomous society, incorporating a Roman sense of order, discipline and authority; it is an empire in miniature, in which the abbot is elected by his monks and serves for life, heeding the advice of senior monks but appointing all officials. The rule was meant to establish a peaceful life in the monastery by discipline and self-control, to assure salvation for the souls of all its members, the same goal Dante envisioned for his world government.[45] The monastery was to be a microcosm of the world, with young and old, rich and poor, noble and plebeian, erudite and uneducated, exclusive only by sex and vocation. In a sense, the ideal monastery is an

[45]A noble by birth, Benedict had fled the corruption of life in Rome and become a hermit, but found the eremitic life unsuitable for all monks and even dangerous for some and founded a cenobitic monastery and eventually Monte Cassino, with a rule which was austere but not extreme. The rule divided the monk's day among communal religious services, manual labor, private study of Scripture or meditation, and eating and sleeping.

attempt to return to the Golden Age, which in classical myth was ruled by Saturn, as Dante notes (21.25–27), when men could live without possessions, without need, in peace and harmony and justice; Matelda's description of the Golden Age, which equated it with the Earthly Paradise in Purgatory, 28.139 and following, is similar. The monastic community at its best is a religious model for the secular ideal Dante wants to see restored on earth for all mankind through the empire. But religious communities do not retain their purity for long in the fallen world. The only figures named in this circle are founders of religious orders or houses, who acted to combat the corruption they saw around them. The aspect of the contemplative life Dante focuses on is the establishment of a society to practice it; the ones who give order to that society are chosen to represent the contemplative life in the *Comedy*.

The choice of Benedict is self-evident: he adapted monasticism to the West and gave it the basic rule which was the model from the sixth century on. Peter Damian, on the other hand, is a more idiosyncratic choice. Dante may be acknowledging that fact when he asks Peter why he should have been chosen to come to Dante; Peter's answer, that the ways of God are so mysterious that even the highest angels in heaven do not know why (21.91 ff.), may well be an answer to those in Dante's audience who would ask why *he* was chosen for his mission.[46] What presumably appealed to Dante in Peter is the

[46]Dante may have been familiar with Peter's life and works and may indeed have stayed in monasteries founded by him or which carried on his tradition. J. P. Whitney, *Hildebrandine Essays* (Cambridge: Cambridge University, 1932), 97, says that Dante spent time at Fonte Avellana, according to an inscription in the monastery, and also at Gubbio and Ravenna, where he would have heard about Peter. Alfredo Zini, "San Pier Damiano in Dante," in *San Pier Damiano nel IX Centenario della Morte* (Cesena: Centro Studi e Ricerche sulla antica Provincia Ecclesiastica Ravennate, 1972), 2 vols., 1.254, assumes that Dante had a deep knowledge of Peter Damian's life and works. Paolo Amaducci, *Nel Cielo dei Contemplanti* (Rome: Alfieri e Lacroix, 1922) puts forth the thesis that the *Comedy* was influenced by Peter Damian's work on Exodus, a view that has not gained much support, but Amaducci also offers arguments for Dante's knowledge of Peter's works. Paolo Brezzi, "Il canto XXI

combination of his role as a reformer of religious and secular mores, his position on the relation of empire and church, and his enforced public activity. Though he became a hermit, and Dante has him speak nostalgically of his hermitage (21.106ff.), he was frequently drawn away from his refuge to carry out tasks for the church. Perhaps the role that most involved him in all aspects of public life was that of papal legate: he was sent to Milan in 1059 to reconcile practices of penance with church law, to France in 1063 to arbitrate between Hugh of Cluny and the bishop of Macon, to Germany to reconcile Henry IV with his estranged wife Berta di Savoia in 1069, and to Ravenna when it rebelled against the pope in 1072. His travels gave him the opportunity to spread his message of reform throughout Europe and he took advantage of it. He criticized nobles, plebeians, and religious alike for their bad habits and their abuse of public position, as Dante does, but he was particularly concerned with the clerical abuses of simony, clerical marriage, the free use of excommunication, and papal wars against Christians.

For a man who wanted to be a hermit, Peter Damian shares a remarkable number of Dante's concerns. In a letter to the cardinals, which has similarities with Dante's epistle 8, Peter compares himself to a watchman crying out the dangers he sees, the world going from bad to worse; in Paradise, 21.126, Dante has him say that the cardinal's hat is going from bad to

---

del Paradiso," in IX Centenario, 1.247, suggests that Dante may have chosen Peter because of his political views, although Dante does not mention them. Walter Ferretti, "Il pastore dei laici nella chiesa secondo San Pier Damiani," in IX Centenario, 2.235 and 236, discusses the letters to the emperor and to the cardinals. Vincenzo Poletti, Pier Damiani e il secolo decimo primo (Faenza: Fratelli Lega, 1972) and Whitney give details of Peter's life. He became a prior in 1043 and attracted so many followers that new houses had to be founded; he was made a cardinal in 1059, a position he tried to refuse until the pope threatened excommunication for disobedience. He was not happy with the see, although it gave him an important position in the college of cardinals, because it was not populous and offered little in the way of pastoral work, and he succeeded in being relieved of it in 1070 to return to his monks, a responsibility he felt he had neglected.

worse, perhaps an echo of that letter. Peter complains that education is neglected, laws scorned, attention given only to worldly gain, robbery, theft, perjury and sacrilege; he reminds the cardinals that the episcopate does not consist of soldiers, servants, and good mounts, but of honorable customs and holy virtues, of setting a good example (Zini, "San Pier Damiano," 257). Peter's remarks about the rich life and the horses are also echoed in the words Dante has him speak in 21.130–35 about the pastors so weighed down by wealth and indulgence they have to be lifted on their palfreys, their cloaks so large they cover both beasts under one skin. Equally attractive to Dante would be Peter's position on the relation of church and state. In his *Disceptatio Synodalis,* a work many have proposed as a source for the *Monarchy,* Peter takes the traditional Gelasian position of the distinction between the task of church and state and the harmony of their function and defends the emperor's right to interfere in a papal election in order to safeguard the rights of the church; by the same token, he grants the pope rights over the empire when it is vacant.[47] In a letter to the emperor, Henry II, Peter praises him for having expelled an unworthy bishop from his see in Ravenna; in a letter to Henry's son, the king of the Romans, he says that the church needs both priest and king, that Christ was both, but after him the functions were divided between pope and emperor (Ferretti, "Il pastore," 235–36). Peter is thus the ideal churchman for Dante, by choice a hermit with no personal ambitions of power or wealth, of necessity a public figure with a moderate view of church and state relations, and a driving will to fight corruption.

The contemplatives can scorn the world because they have

---

[47]On the *Disceptatio* as a source, see Arrigo Solmi, *Il Pensiero politico di Dante* (Florence: La Voce, 1922), Karl Vossler, *Mediaeval Culture,* trans. W. C. Lawton (1929; reprint, New York: Ungar, 1966), 2 vols., 1.272, and most recently Paolo Brezzi, "Il canto XXI," 1.247. Gustavo Vinay, who edited the *Monarchia,* expressed doubts, see 289, fn. 24. For a bibliography on Dante's knowledge of Peter Damian, see Zini, "San Pier Damiano," 253–54. On papal rights, see Ep. 1.5 and Whitney, *Hildebrandine Essays,* 126.

their eyes fixed on heaven, but it is precisely this perspective that enables one to serve the world best: one must see it for what it is, be fully aware of the futility of earthly power and wealth, if one is to guide the world and not be corrupted by it. After his meeting with the contemplatives, Dante is able to look down on the earth and see its "vile semblance" (22.135); what makes us so fierce seems nothing more than a threshing-floor (22.151: "l'aiuola che ci fa tanto feroci," cf. 27.86), reducing the world to the receptacle of heaven's wheat and chaff. The point is that Beatrice continues to focus Dante's attention on the earth because that is the reason for his journey, not the vision of God, which is its goal, but the effect that vision will have on earth. Once Dante has completed his journey through the planets, which revealed the different functions of man in the world culminating in the microcosm of the ideal society in Saturn, he is able to see the symbol of the macrocosm, the garden of the church triumphant.

In the sphere of the Stars, which are responsible for individual human traits and tendencies, for the variety in the human race, Dante sees human society together in all its diversity. The garden presumably includes all those Dante saw in the other spheres within one symbol;[48] that garden is a gathering of individual flowers, a foreshadowing of the final vision of the single rose, in which each soul is a petal of the same flower but each retains its individuality, the perfect manifestation of human society as one harmonious whole composed of distinct individuals. Dante returns here to the garden imagery of the Earthly Paradise because mankind in its redeemed state is the highest fulfillment of Eden; the goal of mankind as a whole (cf. *Monarchy*, 3.16) is to restore the Earthly Paradise in this life. This garden, the model for the Earthly Paradise, is where all the rest of Paradise has been leading, "all the fruit gathered from the turning of these spheres" (23.20–21). Benvenuto

---

[48]There has been some argument over whether the souls in the Stars are to be thought of as yet another separate group or as all the heavenly souls together; Cesare F. Goffis, "Canto XXIII," *LDS*, 823 ff., shows that it must be all.

interprets these lines to mean that here, "in that Rome of which there is one prince, who rejoices in the great number of citizens," we have the armies of virgins Dante saw in the Moon, the active from Mercury, the amorous from Venus, doctors from the Sun, warriors from Mars, kings and princes from Jupiter, contemplatives from Saturn, all seven "armies" chosen and sent to different battles by their leader, now recalled and gathered before the highest leader and emperor to receive their deserved reward and triumph in order to inspire others to fight well (5.316). In the presence of the whole community in its nearly perfect form, Dante becomes more than himself for the divinely ordained task; Dante can now sustain Beatrice's smile because of what he has seen (23.47–48). The individual rises to his full potential within the perfected community.

Dante conceives of the garden as representing both the fellowship of man in society, the "sodalizio eletto" (24.1), and a family. The microcosm of the smallest social unit, the family, is here identical with the macrocosm of the empire, and Dante's language through these cantos emphasizes both.[49] Everyone is born into the family of man, but not everyone becomes a member of this society. To be part of the perfect society, one must have the proper guidance, and one must be inspired by the motivations presented in the lower spheres and by the theological virtues. These are the basic virtues without

[49]Language of the family: Mary, as mother, 23.121 ff.; Peter to Beatrice as sister, 24.28; Dante to Peter of Paul as brother, 24.62; Dante to Peter as father, 24.124; Dante to James of John as brother, 25.94; Dante to Adam as father, 26.92–93, and Adam to Dante as son, 26.115; Peter to Dante as son, 27.64. Language of empire and secular state: *regno, civi,* 24.43: Mary as *regina coeli,* 23.128; Peter as *primopilo,* a Roman military officer, 24.59; Peter as *baron,* 24.115; James as *barone,* 25.17; Christ's *vicari,* 25.15; *nostra basilica,* 25.30 ("royal hall," glossed by Jacopo, 3.371, as "domus regia"); *nostro imperadore* of God, 25.41; *aula, conti,* 25.42; *stuolo* (troops), 25.54; *sommo duce* of God, 25.72; *corte,* 24.112, 25.43, 26.16. Giacinto Margiotta, "Canto XXV," *LDS,* 901, comments that Dante's use of feudal language reveals an orientation towards justice, a virtue which is human and social rather than theological, citing Donadoni.

which the others cannot fully operate. In this sphere of great-
est variety, Dante returns to what holds human life together:
to the origins of the church (with Peter, James, and John), and
the beginning of the family of man (with Adam), to the basic
elements of Christian life (faith, hope, and charity) and of
social life (language). In his treatment of the theological vir-
tues, Dante emphasizes not abstract definitions but visible
manifestations, the social effects in deeds or in writings, as if
the virtues could be known only from their operations among
men, just as God could really be known when he became man.
Faith is authenticated by works and proven by the conversion
of the world to Christianity; hope is based on merit, works as
well as grace, and love is proven not only by Scripture and
philosophy, but also by the creation and redemption (26.58–
63). Man's existence is the result of love and depends on love
for its perfection.

Dante emphasizes the human factor rather than abstract the-
ory in the operation of language as well. Rejecting the view he
espoused in De vulgari eloquentia, 1.6.4–7, that one strain of
Hebrew was created by God and remained pure until the time
of Christ, Dante has Adam explain that speech is natural and
therefore, as a product of human reason, liable to change: the
language Adam spoke was extinct before Nembrot built his
tower, because no product of human reason can endure with-
out change.[50] All men speak, but how they speak is a matter of
individual choice (26.130–32). This fact both diminishes lan-
guage, in that as a product of man and nature it is corruptible,
and exalts man's gift of expression. Just as all men are influ-
enced by the stars but respond differently, and just as all men
are petals in the eternal rose but each with a different face, so

[50]Dante expressed the same view about mutability in language in De vulgari
eloquentia, 1.9.6, but dated it from the confusion of tongues as the result of
Nembrot's tower, and attributed the creation of language to God. Here he
makes language a purely human product, which must evolve from its incep-
tion. See Aristide Marigo, in his edition of the D.v.e. (Florence: Le Monnier,
1957), fn., p. 60, on the originality of Dante's view, and Nardi, "Il linguaggio,"
Dante e la cultura medievale (Bari: Laterza, 1949), 217–47.

all men speak, but each in his own way. Variety is the essence of human existence and speech is the basis of civilized life on earth, the essential means of communication, however imperfect.

Dante's own testimony to the power of language is his poem, to which he gives a striking affirmation in the midst of the examination on the virtues, calling it the "sacred poem to which heaven and earth have put their hands" (25.1–2: "il poema sacro/al qual ha posto mano e cielo e terra"). Pietro's comment on this passage is that Dante, who has been approved in faith, is now approved in poetry (699). Since this passage precedes his reference to David as the *sommo cantor*, the implication is that Dante sees himself and his poem as contributing to the same purpose as the Bible, as he hinted when he joined the procession of the books of the Bible in the Earthly Paradise, a view that seems to be confirmed by the encouragement of the saints. The desire he expresses to be crowned with the poet's garland in Florence follows his symbolic crowning by Peter, who circles him (24.151–53) as the angel had Mary (23.94–96), and who later enjoins Dante to tell the world what he has heard (27.65–66). Dante contrasts the heavenly crowning by Peter with Florence's refusal to recognize him (25.8–12), just as, one might add, Florence refuses to recognize God's will in accepting the emperor. Dante will continue to fight because he has hope, not just of the future life, but also of some improvement on earth, and James tells him that he has seen God's court in order to strengthen his own and others' hope (25.43–45). Like Paul, Dante has been granted a vision of heaven during his mortal life; like Paul, he had been a sinner before his conversion and is temporarily blinded by a divine light, and his sight will be restored by Beatrice as Paul's was by Ananias, a connection made by John (26.12). All of these analogies reinforce our sense of Dante's mission and of the poem as a message from God. As the apostles carry Christ's word to man in the New Testament, so Dante is to carry the saints' words to man in his poem.

The basic message of the poem is the threat to all men from

sin and corruption, particularly in high places, and the desperate need to find the proper guide to correct that. Adam defines original sin as going beyond the limits set, "il trapassar del segno" (26.117), a definition which fits any and all sin, but particularly the political activities of the papacy, which Peter goes into in some detail in the following canto. Peter, who represents the beginning of the church, which was instituted to combat sin, accuses the contemporary church of being the worst source of sin and of preventing the empire from fulfilling its function to impede sin. Peter complains that his place, "il luogo mio," is usurped and therefore in God's view empty like the empire, but the papacy is vacant because it is improperly filled.[51] Rome has become a sewer of blood and stink, doing the devil's work instead of God's (27.25–27). The church actually works against salvation, for which it is condemned by its founder, while the individual Christian, Dante, who has proven himself to be in possession of the essential tools of salvation, the theological virtues, is ready to carry Peter's message of reform. Peter, like Benedict and Peter Damian in the previous sphere, contrasts the sacrifices of the early leaders of the church with the current greed and presumption, but he focuses on his own followers, the popes, who usurp not only Peter's place but Christ's in presuming to select which Christians will be favored and which condemned (27.46–48). Jacopo notes that the church divides Christians by putting the Ghibellines on the left as enemies of the church (3.408); Benvenuto comments that every place has been infected by the church out of insatiable greed, and particularly that most Guelph city, Florence ("guelphissima civitas," 5.391–92). Providence, Peter assures Dante, which ordained Scipio to defend Rome's glory, will soon give aid. Once again, as in Jupiter, Dante makes it clear that it is pagan Rome that did God's will, while Christian Rome, con-

---

[51]The Ottimo (3.583) says the seat is vacant because Boniface was elected by deceit and simony and therefore is not properly the pope; Benvenuto (5.403) comments that there is no one to govern because Boniface usurps both powers. Jacopo (3.404), remarks that cupidity is the result of the defects of bad pastors who do not guide their subjects.

trolled by the church, obstructs it, at least until a new leader comes. In his comments on this passage, Benvenuto connects the "future Roman prince" with the *veltro* who will exterminate cupidity in the world (5.393 and 404). Since Dante has repeatedly shown that the church cannot avoid corruption when it concerns itself with secular affairs, it is clear that it can only be restored to its original purity and function when it is deprived of secular power, and that is presumably what the Roman prince, the *veltro,* must do.

As he moves closer to the final vision, Dante seems more, not less, obsessed with the role the church plays in the world's distress. Even in the Primo Mobile, the heaven of angelic intelligences that move the universe, where we might expect to pass beyond human responsibility, Beatrice echoes Peter's attack and prophecy. Because the world is not now governed, men born innocent turn corrupt; that is, without the proper guidance everyone reenacts Adam's fall. Greed motivates all action, but before long these circles will change the course of events, the poops will turn where the prows now are (27.146), a line that recalls the end of Ulysses' journey (Hell 26.140–41).[52] The church reenacts Ulysses' mad flight and will therefore meet the same fate. Its leaders must be destroyed so that the fleet can be turned around. Beatrice also attacks those who teach errors out of vanity or greed, or who abuse scripture for their own purposes (29.82–126) and neglect the truths Christ gave men in the Gospels; the message is not simply one of neglect through pursuit of worldly goods, but outright perversion of the church's purpose on earth. Selfishness is always at odds with the common good and with God's purpose, as Dante showed in Hell. The devil, Beatrice reminds us, is constrained by all the weights of the world (29.57). Evil, greed, selfishness is not power but slavery.

In his description of the angels, Dante again emphasizes their relation to human life. He insists that they were created

---

[52]Beatrice actually says before January is no longer winter, that is, 9000 years, but this is understood to be sarcastic; cf. Benvenuto (5.405), the large number means small, that it will not be long.

with the substances they move, not long before, as Jerome said, because they would be imperfect if as movers they existed without the objects of their moving (29.37–45). Dante claims that angelic powers were increased after the fall; those who chose God were strengthened with grace and merit, raised in their powers once they committed themselves to the right side. We are told that receiving grace is worthy of merit because it depends on the receiver's desire (29.65–66), another encouraging lesson for Dante's audience. The angels are of incalculable number, arranged in nine orders, each angel different from all the others, just as all men are different, but they are ranked according to capacity or function; the nine orders are grouped in triads, in relation to the Trinity. Dante's nine heavens, moved by the angels, can be similarly grouped in triads: the movements of the first three, Moon, Mercury, Venus, cause souls to act primarily out of concern for themselves, though their actions serve others; the middle three, Sun, Mars, Jupiter, cause them to act for others directly by teaching, defending, governing; the last three affect human lives by mediating between God and man, either by prayer and contemplation (Saturn), by distributing tendencies (Stars), or by moving the heavenly bodies (Primo Mobile).[53] Since angels represent the church in Purgatory, it does not seem untoward to suggest that Dante thinks of them in Paradise as models of the spiritual, unworldly church on earth. The celestial hierarchy described by Pseudo-Dionysius is Dante's model for the earthly, with separate orders of being each with a different function, all serving one ruler. Bonaventure (*Collationes in Hexaemeron*, 22) relates all nine orders to nine orders of human life: the first three monastic, the middle three clerical (pontifical, sacerdotal, and ministerial), the last three laymen (princes, officials, and the people); the first three are contemplatives, the last actives, the middle group partakes of both. Dante's connections are

---

[53]Gregory gave different orders for the angels in the *Moralia* and in Homily 34, and Dante followed the latter in the *Convivio* (see 1.136, fn., in Busnelli-Vandelli edition [Florence: Le Monnier, 1954]).

similar to Bonaventure's if we relate the angels to the motivations of souls in the spheres, but with two significant differences: where Bonaventure has popes, Dante has kings and emperors, and where Bonaventure has priests, Dante has crusaders. Jacopo, noting that the angels are divided according to the diversity of their acts and offices, gives the functions of the angelic orders and their influence, direct or indirect, on human life (3.420ff. cf. Ottimo, 3.605). The Ottimo comments that men cannot be ordered like the angels in terms of their natural powers, but according to habit, tendency and will: The highest are given to speculation and knowledge, the lowest to indulgence of the flesh, but those in between, if they can direct their habits to actions, are upright men suited to the political life (3.629–30), that is, good citizens.

The angels in Paradise are contained within the divine mind and moved by its love. Love is the great binding force between the angels and God, the universe and God, men and God, and men and men. Dante reaches the final vision because of his love for Beatrice and hers for him, and he will see it because of Bernard's love for Mary and hers for him and for all mankind. The love of human beings for each other, which holds society together, also prepares the soul to love God. Mary is the final stage in Dante's journey because she initiated it; she sent Beatrice apparently to rescue Dante but actually to enlist him, as we now know, in her son's cause, the salvation of mankind. Even the sending for Dante involved the cooperative effort of many souls: Mary sent Lucy for Beatrice, who got Virgil to bring Dante through Hell and Purgatory to her, and then she brought him through heaven to Bernard, who presents him to Mary. Bernard is the guide for the final stage of the journey because he combines all the significant qualifications. He is a mystic, devoted to Mary, a major interpreter of the biblical book of love (the Song of Songs), a clerical reformer who fought corruption in Rome, a political activist who preached and gathered the second crusade, a political moderate who warned the papacy against becoming involved in secular affairs and asserted the pope's responsibility to serve rather than to rule, and even something of a poet. He appears to Dante as an old man, reminiscent of and complementary to the figure of Virgil: Dante's first guide was a poet who sang the origin and the future glory of the Roman empire, his last guide is a saint who preached love to mankind and spiritual care to the papacy.

Dante's last view of human society in the *Comedy* is the single rose in which each individual is a separate and distinct petal. Like the garden in the Stars, the rose is described in terms of the family of man and of the city/empire, the microcosm within the macrocosm.[54] The composition of the rose reflects the makeup of the human race on earth, with Jews and Christians in equal number (32.38–39), men and women, adults and children;[55] in this sense it is a more satisfactory model than the limited monastic community of Saturn. There is some question why Dante chose to emphasize the children, who are there on the merits of others, not their own, and are childish in appearance and voice (32.46–48), despite the traditional teaching on the resurrection that everyone appears in a state of physical perfection, of maturity.[56] The Ottimo (3.707) says

[54]Language of family: the rose as bride of Christ, 31.3; Bernard as "tender father" to Dante, 31.63, "holy father," 32.100; Ruth as great-grandmother to David, 32.11; Adam as father, 32.122, 32.136; Peter as father of the church, 32.124; Anna, mother of Mary, 32.133–34; Mary, mother and daughter of Christ, 33.1, and the face that most resembles his, 32.85–86. Language of the secular state: *città*, 30.130; *regno*, 31.25 and 31.117; *oriafiamma* (standard of victory), 31.127; *reame*, 32.52; *corte*, 32.98; *patrici, imperio*, 32.116–7; Mary as *regina*, 31.100, 31.116, 32.104, 33.34, and as "Agusta," 32.119; she presides as empress, surrounded by her "patricians," 32.115–20.

[55]The Jews are "those who believed in Christ to come," 32.24; whether Dante would include Ripheus, the Trojan, and other saved pagans among them, is not made clear, but it seems likely.

[56]See Aquinas, ST, Supp., q.81, a.1; childhood and age are defects, but the resurrection is without defect of human nature, therefore men and women will rise at the age of bodily perfection, young adulthood. Pietro specifies age thirty (733), citing Augustine's *City of God*, 22.

the "pueri" must be different from the other blessed souls in appearance and sound, but does not think of them as small children; Singleton suggests that Dante wanted the contrast of youth and age, noting that Bernard is presented as an old man, which is also unusual (commentary on Paradise, 540). It seems more likely to me that Dante is calling the audience's attention once again to the fact that he is describing the ideal society as it might be on earth, where it must include young and old.

The rose also includes a place for the man who should have ruled such a society on earth, and specifically excludes those who obstruct it. There is an empty seat with a crown above it reserved for the emperor Henry VII, who "will come to set Italy straight before she is ready" (30.137–38). Because the crown is especially noted, it must be more than a saint's halo; it is the imperial crown, which confers a special dignity even in Paradise. At the same time, Beatrice reminds Dante that the pope who opposed Henry, "secretly and openly" (30.143), will be thrust into Hell, pushing "the one from Alagna" down even further into his hole. This reminder that Boniface, who was captured at Alagna, got his comeuppance in the first life is a warning to the current pope. Paradise thus awaits the coming of an emperor, Hell the coming of two popes, Dante's way of bringing the church-state conflict into the highest sphere of heaven. The chronicles of Dino Compagni and Giovanni Villani reflect the same attitude towards the participants: Dino explains the election of Henry as the result of the church's need for a defender, particularly given the attacks of the king of France, who had caused the death of Boniface and was taking advantage of the church in every possible way. The church wanted someone just, wise, powerful, a son of the church and lover of the faith, and they found Henry, Dino declares (3.23). God wanted Henry to come to Italy to defeat and castigate the tyrants of Lombardy and Tuscany, and the emperor came, bringing peace like an angel of God (3.24), but the devil, "the enemy who never sleeps," began to sow discord (3.28), in which the Florentines played a major role. They oppressed their own citizens for money to support treachery and rebellion against the emperor, and to bribe the pope (3.31–32).[57]

The ideal city of Paradise is Rome, in its essence, the only city which is both *urbs* and *orbis*, "city" and "world," once the center and the circumference of the state. Benvenuto comments that Mary, the empress of this eternal Rome, is called *Agusta*, like Livia, as Christ is somewhat improperly compared to Octavius, the "highest and most excellent emperor," "summus et praeclarissimus imperator" under whose rule Christ became man (5.500–01). Beatrice had told Dante in Purgatory (32.101–02) that in Paradise he would become a "citizen of that Rome of which Christ is a Roman," and when he sees the rose, Dante compares his amazement to that of a barbarian at his first sight of the earthly city (31.31–34). This is the center of civilization, the hope of all who suffer from anarchy and violence, the end of the journey to the "just and sane people," which Dante began, he reminds us, in Florence, the archenemy of the civilizing forces of empire, the barbarian of Italy, so to speak. The sight of mankind in the rose, the model for the earthly paradise Dante seeks in the *Monarchy*, prepares Dante for the final vision of God, because the perfected society of man is a reflection of God. The God he sees is, like that society, diversity within perfect unity, Dante comes away from the vision in complete harmony with the divine will and the universe it moves, anxious to serve it: "ma già volgeva il mio disio e'l velle,/... l'amor che move il sole e l'altre stelle" (33.143–45: "but already the love that moves the sun and the other stars was turning my desire and will").

When Dante first saw the rose, he felt like a pilgrim who had reached the temple of his vow (31.43–44), a reference to

[57]Villani describes Henry as "good, wise, just, gracious, brave, strong in arms, honest, catholic, of a magnanimous heart, greatly feared and respected" (9.1), the perfect prince, while Clement was "greedy for money, a simoniac who sold all the benefices at his court for money," a man of lust who kept a mistress and who had a master of necromancy summon the soul of his dead nephew, which produced a vision of both of them condemned to hell for simony (9.58).

the sacrifice he offered in Mars, where he accepted the mission Beatrice had described to him in the Earthly Paradise. The completed poem is the discharge of that mission. What Dante offers in the *Comedy* is a model in broad outlines for the ideal society on earth, first all the traits that must be excluded from it (in Hell), then the remedies to counter them (in Purgatory), and finally its essential elements and functions (in Paradise). A political society should be unified under one rule, with every individual contributing to the common good according to his or her abilities, motivated by love and justice so that all can realize most fully the potential in each. The community must have certain officers: secular rulers and officials (judges and lawgivers), fighters to defend it, teachers and intellectuals to order and enhance all aspects of earthly life, and religious guides to ensure by prayer and example that it remain in harmony with the divine will. But the religious guides must be solely concerned with the spiritual life, completely renounce worldly power and wealth, never interfere in any way with the secular workings of the government; in short, they are to be the monastic leaders of Saturn, closer to God than any of the other separate groups of souls, but leaving the operation of society in the hands of the rulers (of Jupiter) and the warriors (of Mars), with the help of the teachers (in the Sun). There is no place in Dante's ideal society for the bureaucracy of the church. This is not to say that Dante wishes to dispense altogether with priests and bishops, or even with the pope; they are necessary to minister to the spiritual needs of men, as evidenced by Folco in Venus and by the many bishops in the Sun, but they must be kept free of any involvement with the workings of the state. Those members of society who fulfill none of the particular roles can contribute in other ways, motivated either by love (like the noblewoman, the priest, and the young king in Venus), by the desire for glory (like the souls in Mercury), or by the peaceful acceptance of their own limitations and destinies, filling whatever slot others design for them (like the souls in the Moon).

Such is the political society Dante envisages. For the individual within that society, there is a lesson at each stage: the need to make a commitment based on a reasonable assessment of oneself and the situation (Moon), to act firmly on that commitment (Mercury), fortified by love for one's fellows (Venus) and by all that human learning can offer (Sun); to sacrifice oneself, if necessary, for the common good (Mars), to serve justice rather than self-interest (Jupiter), and to dedicate one's actions to God's will (Saturn). A society made up of such individuals will be the restored earthly paradise (the garden of the Stars), a reflection of the celestial hierarchy (Primo Mobile), and of God himself and the eternal city of the Empyrean.

SIX

Exchange and Communication, Commerce and Language in the *Comedy*

ATHOUGH Dante seems to be primarily concerned in his poem with the leaders of the church and the major secular governments in Italy and Europe, men who can move their institutions towards the ideal universal government, his audience would have included many from the commercial world, some of whom were also in a strong position to influence international politics. It is therefore not surprising that Dante should speak to them in the technical language of finance and trade and that he should be concerned with financial activities throughout his poem. He accepts commerce as an essential part of life in a complex society, as a basic form of exchange, like language, though vulnerable to the same kinds of abuses and in need of the same kinds of control. It seems fitting to conclude this study of Dante's political vision with a survey of his views on commerce and language as they appear in the *Comedy.*

Dante's connection with the commercial world was personal. He was the son of a banker or money-changer, the brother-in-law of a moneylender; he himself engaged in some business and was a member of a guild, the "Arte dei medici e degli speziali," primarily involved with drugs and spices, though he probably joined the guild to further his political career.[1] Commerce and literature were not mutually exclusive

---

[1] Forese Donati, in the exchange of insulting sonnets with Dante, implies that Dante's father was a moneylender (72a) and states that he was a money-changer (74a), see *Dante's Lyric Poetry,* ed. Kenelm Foster and Patrick Boyde, (Oxford: Clarendon, 1967) 2 vols.; given the tone of the insults, it is possible that the first is an exaggeration, but the second is likely. Giuseppe Garrani, *Il*

in Florence; the best known contemporary chroniclers, Dino Compagni and Giovanni Villani, the men who mediate most directly between their society and later generations, were merchants, not to mention the Venetian merchant and travel-writer Marco Polo. Letters by merchants in the Datini archives, dating from the later fourteenth century, reveal not only an interest in books, but a particular interest in the *Divine Comedy*. Datini himself, who had many books and was in frequent contact with booksellers, cites Livy, Valerio, Seneca, and Boethius, and argues in his letters about philosophy and divine justice, as well as the law.[2] A notary writing to Datini cites Dante twelve times in his letters, obviously expecting his correspondent to recognize the source; other merchants request copies of parts of the *Comedy* or cite Dante, in one case the very apt passage from Hell 27 about taking in the sails at an age when one should give up the life of trade.

We know that Dante reached this audience, and we can assume that he was speaking, at least in part, to them. That their response to his poem might have been expected to play a part in giving reality to his vision is suggested by the role merchants and bankers played in the contemporary world. Italian merchants were involved in international trade from an early date; they not only bought and sold goods, they also bought raw materials, like wool and silk, manufactured or refined them, and sold the products. In 1159 there were enough Italian merchants at the Champagne fairs to organize themselves and their money-exchanges under a captain; official exchanges were established in port cities by 1200 to facilitate maritime commerce. The wide variety of currencies (virtually every city

pensiero di Dante in tema di economia monetaria e creditizia (Palermo: Cassa di Risparmio, 1965), 12, thinks he probably was a banker. Jeremy Catto, "Florence, Tuscany, and the World of Dante," in *The World of Dante*, ed. Cecil Grayson (Oxford: Clarendon, 1980), notes that Dante's sister married a moneylender and that Dante himself first appears in Florentine records in 1283 or 1284 as the owner of a debt, 8.

[2]See Enrico Bensa, *Francesco di Marco da Prato* (Milan: Treves, 1928), 63. Giovanni Livi, *Dall'archivio di Francesco Datini* (Florence: Lumachi, 1910) cites the letters mentioned here, see particularly 24.

or lord, not only in Italy but even in France and Germany, had its own coins) made monetary exchange difficult, but the practice of paper transactions, keeping accounts of purchases and sales to be settled at a later date in a specified currency, enabled merchants to extend credit, to receive deposits to be drawn on or transferred, and to use those deposits for investments.[3] In the case of the larger merchant-banking houses, the amount of money held was often substantial and was drawn on not only by other merchants for commercial ventures, but also by kings and popes and cities to finance governments and armies. Banking companies served as agents to collect papal taxes, which brought money into Italy, allowing Italian banks to balance their foreign currency payments and facilitating Italian trade.

The most striking feature of Italian banking and trade in this period is its scope; companies employed large numbers of people and established agents in different cities throughout Europe. The Bardi of Florence had warehouses, offices, and staff in ten Italian cities from Genoa and Venice to Palermo and Bari, as well as in Avignon, Barcelona, Bruges, Cyprus, Constantinople, Jerusalem, London, Majorca, Marseilles, Paris, Rhodes, Seville, and Tunis.[4] Commercial ships traveled the Mediterranean from one end to the other, not to speak of the Danube, the Black Sea, the Atlantic, and the North Sea. A company from Lucca sent agents as far as Greenland to collect papal tithes; in 1292 five of the top six taxpayers in Paris were Italian merchants. Italians were involved in some way in the affairs of virtually all the countries and major cities of Europe. In England, Italian companies financed English troops against France and Scotland, obtained royal concessions to silver

[3]See Raymond deRoover, *Business, Banking and Economic Thought in Late Medieval and Early Modern Europe*. ed. Julius Kirschner (Chicago: University of Chicago, 1974), 120 ff., on the development of accounting. Cf. Armando Sapori, *The Italian Merchant in the Middle Ages,* trans. Patricia Kennen (New York: Norton, 1970), 30.

[4]See Sapori, *Italian Merchant,* 51; the information in this paragraph is drawn from Sapori (also his *Studi di storia economica medievale* [Florence: Sansoni, 1946], 587 ff.), and Roberto Lopez, *The Commercial Revolution of the Middle Ages, 950–1350* (Cambridge: Cambridge University, 1976).

mines, served as royal collectors in local counties, and ran public exchanges and customs in major ports. The Ricc[i]ardi were a part of the English government, paying out fees for service to the crown, collecting taxes, controlling customs and money exchange and recoinage; the list of their debtors included many government officials, earls, archbishops, bishops, abbots, revealing the extent of their involvement in the entire country.[5]

For Italy's merchant-bankers, the whole civilized world was a potential or actual market, an imperfect foreshadowing of the united world Dante would like to see for all men. Like religion, commerce linked northern Italy with the rest of Europe and made the Italian cities sensitive to all the vagaries of international politics. It gave their wealthy citizens considerable influence in the world, but it also left them vulnerable to events they could not control. Princes often refused to pay their debts or called in huge sums on short notice, and many large companies failed as a result. The Ricciardi of Lucca, for example, were caught between two belligerents, Philip IV of France and Edward I of England, financing both sides of the war in Gascony. When Edward and the pope, Boniface VIII, both recalled large deposits, the Ricciardi were unable to raise either sum; Edward seized their assets in England, Philip arrested their representatives in France, and Boniface refused to help them retrieve their money until it was too late to save them. As one house failed, another took over, but the number of major failures of Tuscan companies while Dante was writing the *Comedy* cannot have failed to impress him.[6]

[5]Richard W. Kaeuper, *Bankers to the Crown, The Riccardi of Lucca and Edward I* (Princeton: Princeton University, 1973), 83, 151; the list of debtors is given on 60 ff. The name is spelt with an *i* in Italian studies.

[6]See Sapori, *Studi,* 579, on the four major Italian companies succeeding each other as royal bankers in England, the Ricciardi, the Frescobaldi, then the Bardi and the Peruzzi, the latter three all from Florence. On the failure of the Ricciardi, see Kaeuper, *Bankers to the Crown,* 209 ff, Garrani, *Il pensiero di Dante,* 34–36. Kaeuper lists among the failures the Ricciardi in 1301, the Franzesi in 1304, the Macci, 1312, Frescobaldi, 1315, and Cerchi Bianchi in 1320, 10.

In the major cities of northern Italy, the world in which Dante lived, commerce dominated. Guilds loomed large in local politics, merchant-bankers ran communes. In Florence, political power in the late thirteenth and early fourteenth centuries was almost exclusively in the hands of great banking, commercial, and industrial families; the three major guilds, of wool (Arte della Lana), cloth (Calimala), and banking (Cambio), made up 71 percent of the priorate.[7] Distinctions between the rich bourgeoisie and the nobility were not sharply made in the commercial cities; indeed, nobles often joined with rich merchants to form new urban patriciates, and members of large families were as likely to look to business to make their fortunes as they might elsewhere to the church or the military.[8] Partnerships originally formed for individual enterprises were

[7]On Florence, see Marvin Becker, *Florence in Transition*, vol. 1, *The Decline of the Commune* (Baltimore: Johns Hopkins, 1967), 17. Cf. Lopez, *Commercial Revolution*, 70: "Italian communes were essentially governments of, by, and for merchants." See M. V. Clarke, *The Medieval City-State* (1926; reprint, Cambridge: Speculum Historiale, 1966), 120, on the development of political offices from guilds, and Daniel Waley, *The Italian City-Republics* (New York: McGraw-Hill, 1969), 63, on elections by guilds. On Florentine bankers in local politics, see Gino Masi, "I Banchieri Fiorentini nella Vita Politica della città sulla fine del Dugento," *Archivio giuridico 'Filippo Serafini'* 105 (1931), 57–89, and "La Struttura sociale delle fazioni politiche fiorentine ai tempi di Dante," *Giornale dantesco* 31 (1928), 3–28.

[8]See Sapori, *Studi*, 708; Roberto Lopez and Irving Raymond, *Medieval Trade in the Mediterranean World* (1955; reprint, New York: Columbia, 1961), 92, and Lopez, *Commercial Revolution*, 67. DeRoover, *Business, Banking*, 342, notes the unusual social mobility in north Italy because of trade. He cites examples of partnership formulae which begin "a nome di Dio, e guadangnio," ("in the name of God and gain," dated 1308), 71, and an entry in an account book, "Al nome di Dio, amen, di guadangno, e di buone venture ke Dio ci dea" ("In the name of God, amen, of gain, and of good fortune which God may give us," 1253), 345. The move into commerce was widespread in north Italy and from an early date. I. Capecchi and M. P. Puccinelli, "L'economia pistoiese ai tempi di Dante," *Bullettino storico pistoiese* NS7 (1965), 171–83, point out that Pistoia developed artisans and trade rather than agriculture from the twelfth century, when it was small, because of its numerous ponds and canals, that the wealthier families went into banking, and that moneychangers held posts in the city government.

replaced by standing companies, usually made up of brothers or other members of the same family, sometimes of families connected by marriage, which pooled capital to increase their trade and profits and to minimize their risks and losses. Families were political as well as economic forces in cities like Florence. Dante felt the negative effects of the interrelation of politics and economics when he was accused of barratry, the misuse of public funds, a common charge made by a victorious faction against its defeated rivals, which often resulted, as in Dante's case, in the confiscation of property. The sentence against Dante was renewed in 1315, condemning him and his sons to death and destruction of their goods and giving any who met him license to offend him in person or goods.[9]

Dante's attitude towards commerce is essentially a moderate one, accepting it as a fact of life, a potential benefit to society, as long as it serves the common good and does not harm the community in order to advance individuals. He presents the distribution of wealth as the result of divine providence in the passage on fortune (Hell 7) and justifies craft and manufacture hence, implicitly, trade in his description of art as the daughter of nature and granddaughter of God (Hell 11).[10] The importance he accords both to personal property and to a stable currency is manifest in his teatment of their abuses; he discusses in some detail a variety of economic and monetary sins, not

[9]Francesco Mazzoni, "Teoresi e prassi in Dante politico," in Dante Alighieri, *Monarchia, Epistole politiche* (Turin: ERI, 1966), lix, cites the sentence against Dante. There seems to be no evidence that Dante was actually guilty of barratry, see Garrani, *Il pensiero di Dante*, 89, fn. 139.

[10]*Arte* can refer to the work of an artist or artisan, of anyone who practices a profession or craft; *arte* is the official name used by guilds to signify the occupation, and Dante uses it in *Convivio*, 4.6.6, to mean whatever men do in their work, for example, "operazione od arte," "l'arte di cavalleria." In the *Convivio*, Dante lists three licit ways of acquiring wealth, of making money by craft or trade or service, "per arte o per mercatantia o per servigio meritante" (4.11.7), as opposed to theft and robbery. The focus in the *Convivio*, however, is on the negative aspects of wealth, the dangers of desiring and possessing it; even its distribution is attributed to random causes, whereas in the *Comedy*, Dante treats wealth as an important element in the workings of providence.

just greed, but plunder, squandering, usury, fraudulent buying and selling of different kinds of goods, theft, and counterfeiting. Each one appears in a separate section of Hell, and several are attacked in Purgatory and Paradise as well. He employs the technical language of commerce literally, in connection with the abuses, and metaphorically, applying it to spiritual treasures and moral debts.[11] The technical language and commercial details would have been a particularly effective means of reaching the members of the audience attuned to them and would presumably have added a whole other sphere of application to Dante's message, as this chapter will show. The metaphorical use of the same language seems to be Dante's way of countering "corporal usury," which is forbidden, with "spiritual usury," which multiplies the benefits of God's gifts, a distinction made by canonists and theologians.[12]

Dependent as Europe was on the activities of merchant bankers and international commerce, it was by no means consistently in favor of them. The ancient prejudice against merchants, which assumed that the search for profit always involved greed and fraud, was still alive, but there were moves towards accommodating commerce in medieval theology and law, both canon and civil.[13] I will very briefly survey those areas most relevant to Dante's concerns in the *Comedy,* giving the dominant views on the major issues reflected in Dante's attitudes. The concept of trade for profit was still being argued, whether it was fully moral to make a profit on a sale, and, if so, how much, and whether one could legitimately recover any more than the original sum on a loan, and, if so, under what circumstances. The key to the first question was the "just

[11]Dante goes far beyond the simple metaphorical use of treasure, such as the Egyptian gold in Exodus that was interpreted as pagan learning to be put to Christian use in biblical exegesis. See Augustine, *De Doctrina Christiana,* 2.40 (60), and *Glossa Ordinaria,* for Ex. 3:22 and 12:35–36.

[12]John W. Baldwin, *Masters, Princes and Merchants* (Princeton: Princeton University, 1970), 2 vols., 1.271, hereafter cited as MPM.

[13]Baldwin, MPM, 1.262, notes that in ancient times when one wanted to insult a wanderer, like Ulysses, one called him a merchant, as Nausicaa's father did.

price" and what components could be calculated in establishing it; the key to the second was the charge of usury, at what point it could be applied. Medieval thinking, in theology as well as in law, went well beyond Aristotle's views in these matters. Aristotle had acknowledged the importance of private property and the need for money in the functioning of the state, but he condemned retail trading as unnatural and usury as worst of all. The same mistrust of merchants and their work is found in Peter Lombard's *Sentences,* where he says that soldiers or merchants unwilling to give up their professions should not be received as penitents because they could not exercise those professions without sin (4, d.16, q.4, a.2). But the major thirteenth-century commentators on the *Sentences,* Albert, Aquinas, and Bonaventure, modify his position considerably. They recognize that countries are not necessarily more self-sufficient than individuals and must rely on the services of those who can procure supplies for them, that in a complex society one cannot always buy directly from the producer.[14]

In the *Summa Theologiae* Aquinas takes a moderate stand on commercial activity: he defends the concept of private property as conducive to efficiency, order, and peace in the state (2.2ae, q.66) and includes among sins of commutative justice attacks on others' possessions and persons (2.2ae, 2.64). He discusses both sales and loans as voluntary commutations (q.77 and q.78), condemning the sale of something for more than its just price as fraud (q.77, a.l); money was instituted to measure

---

[14]See deRoover, *Business, Banking,* 337, and John W. Baldwin, "The Medieval Theories of the Just Price," *Transactions of the American Philosophical Society* NS 49 (1959), 63–66 hereafter cited as JP. Bonaventure recognizes the necessity of an army to defend the faith, of trade so that lands can live (Commentary on *Sentences* of Peter Lombard, *Commentum in quattuor libros Sententiarum Magistri Petri Lombardi,* 4, d. 16, dub.15), and admits that a merchant can act without sin if he does not practice deception; Aquinas says that those things without which the republic cannot be maintained are not vices, but ordered to virtue, provided the merchant acts without fraud and according to a licit contract (Commentary on *Sentences* of Peter Lombard 4, d.16, q.4, a.2). Giles of Rome *De regimine principum* 2.3.12, mentions five ways to acquire money, which include trade and transporting goods.

value, and the price must be the equivalent of the value, even if the law punishes only an excessive discrepancy.[15] But Thomas does not demand full disclosure by the seller as long as he does not actively deceive the buyer; that is, the seller does not have to state an obvious fault in the object for sale, nor does he have to inform the buyer of other sellers who can offer a lower price. In opposition to Aristotle, Thomas even allows a moderate profit (moderatum lucrum), not as an end, but as payment for labor or to accommodate changed circumstances. In a letter to James of Viterbo, Thomas acknowledges not only that price can change with different places or times and can be affected by risk, by labor, and expense, but also that a sale on credit is not necessarily usurious, that it can be useful for the common good of merchants as long as it does not involve fraud.[16] The line between credit sales and usury is a thin one. In the discussion on usury (q.78), Thomas states the main arguments against profit on loans: that money is meant to be consumed in use, so one cannot sell both it and its use; since ownership is not transferred in a loan, the borrower assumes the risk, so the seller has no claim to compensation.[17] In the De Malo, Thomas notes that positive law permits some usury for the common good of the multitude rather than incur greater harm (q.13, a.4, r.6); he makes an interesting distinction

[15]See Francis A. Richey, *Character Control of Wealth according to St. Thomas Aquinas* (Washington: Catholic University, 1940), E. VanRoey, "La monnaie d'après St. Thomas d'Aquin," *Revue Neo-Scholastique* 12 (1905), 27–54, 207–38, for Aquinas on wealth and money; on monopoly and just price, see Sapori, *Studi*, "Il 'Giusto Prezzo' nella dottrina di San Tommaso e nella practica del suo tempo," 189–227, Raymond deRoover, "La Doctrine scolastique en matière de monopole et son application à la politique économique des communes italiennes," in *Studi in onore di Amintore Fanfani* (Milan: Giuffrè, 1962), 6 vols., 1.151–79.

[16]See Ovidio Capitani, "La *venditio ad terminum* nella valutazione morale di S. Tommaso d'Aquino e di Remigio dei Girolami," *Bulletino dell'Istituto Storico Italiano per il Medio Evo* 70 (1958), 229–363; cf. Alfred O'Rahilly, "Notes on St. Thomas," *Irish Ecclesiastical Record* 31 (1928), 159–68.

[17]Ownership does not change legitimately in usury any more than in fraud, theft, robbery, or simony, so all gain must be restored to the rightful owner, according to canon law, Baldwin, MPM, 1.303.

between the usurer who lends what is *his* and may hope for amicable recompense, and the simoniac who gives what is Christ's for a reward, whereas he should hope only for the honor of Christ and the utility of the church. There are other passages in the *Summa* which are not directly concerned with usury but imply a positive view of investment and profit, for instance, criticism of the servant's pusillanimity for burying money rather than trading with it (2.2ae, q.133), and praise of large expenditure for great works as part of the virtue of magnificence q.134.[18]

Aquinas's views on usury and just price seem fairly moderate for a theologian, since theologians tend to have more rigid views than canon or civil lawyers, but Remigio dei Girolami, Dante's contemporary and fellow Florentine, is even more accommodating. Remigio recognizes the need to stimulate sales and avoid losses, real or possible, and accepts the desire for profit and the competitive nature of trade. He also justifies a limited usury if necessary to develop business, by increasing the price of sale for late payment to the one who lent the money, provided he is a business rival, as simply a way of getting back what was unjustly taken. Remigio recognizes the importance of credit sales for commerce and the importance of commerce for the city or kingdom. Although he condemns usury and the evil effects of greed, Remigio counts among the seven special gifts God gave Florence the abundance of money, noble coinage, the wool industry, skill in manufacture of arms, and vigorous building.[19] It seems safe to say that commerce was so important a part of public life in the thirteenth and fourteenth centuries that even theologians accepted it and contented themselves with limiting its excesses. Innocent IV did, however, point out the danger that if usury were permitted, the

---

[18]See Jacob Viner, *Religious Thought and Economic Society* (Durham: Duke, 1978), 63–64, who cites Richey, *Character Control.*

[19]See Charles Davis, "An Early Florentine Political Theorist: *Fra Remigio dei Girolami"* Proceedings of the American Philosophical Society 104 (1960), 667, and Capitani, "la *venditio ad terminum,"* 340 ff., for text and commentary of *Determinatio utrum sit licitum vendere mercationes ad terminum.*

rich would put their money into usurious loans rather than into agriculture.[20]

In law the attitudes were even more tolerant. Having a tradition of free bargaining to establish price in Roman law, which outlawed only excesses of more than 50 percent either way, medieval civil law accepted an agreed price as just except in the case of enormous discrepancy between it and true value; a judge could determine the just price, but monopolies were not permitted to fix prices (Baldwin, JP, 17–29). Canon law accepted resale at a profit if it was caused by necessity, if the goods were improved, or if labor or expense were involved. The canonist and theologian Huguccio permits even a cleric to resell at a higher price, as long as it is the just price, and to profit from his craft in order to maintain himself. Twelfth-century decretals accepted the sale of goods on credit at a higher price than what was in effect at the time of the contract if there was any doubt as to the value of goods at the time; by the thirteenth century, risk was accepted as part of the cost in a sale, though not in a loan. Loans present a special problem. They were supposed to benefit from another's need; the word for loan, *mutuum,* was interpreted as meaning a transfer of ownership, what is mine (*meum*) becomes yours (*tuum*).[21] If the lender expects not only a return of the goods (object or money) but something more, he is selling time, since money is consumed by its use and cannot bear fruit; the borrower has assumed all the risk, since he must replace the loan even if he loses it. As Noonan points out (*Scholastic Analysis of Usury,* 81), a strict application of these theories would have involved the better part of Siena and Florence in the practice of usury. In fact, the Fourth Lateran Council, 1215, condemned Jews

[20]See John T. Noonan, *The Scholastic Analysis of Usury* (Cambridge, Mass.: Harvard University, 1957), 49.

[21]On credit sales, see Baldwin, JP, 39–52, and Viner, *Religious Thought,* 81–85. On loans, see Noonan, *Scholastic Analysis of Usury,* 39 and 48, citing Gratian and Bonaventure, and T. P. McLaughlin, "The Teaching of the Canonists on Usury in the 12th, 13th and 14th centuries," *Medieval Studies* 1 (1939), 81–147, and 2 (1940), 1–22, particularly 1.100; cf. Viner on usury, 85–99.

who extorted "heavy and immoderate usuries," "graves et immoderatas usuras," or Christians who associated with Jews who failed to make restitution for such, giving rise to the question whether moderate usury was acceptable.²² Cino da Pistoia, Dante's friend and fellow poet, who was also a lawyer, says in his commentary on the Codex that canon law permits usury as interest (*interesse*) either because of delay in payment or of the utility the purchaser enjoyed from retaining the object, but forbids usury from a loan contract unless loss is sustained.²³

The fact that civil law seemed to permit usury (by virtue of regulations to control the extent of it) further complicated the issue. Garrani lists more than a dozen Italian communes whose statutes controlled the rates of interest in the thirteenth century: Pisa, Milano, Verona, Bologna, Viterbo, Parma, Vicenza, Como, Torino, Casale, Ivrea, Moncalieri, Val Trompia (*Il pensiero di Dante*, 84). The Council of Vienna (1311–12) attacked the problem by declaring that civic officials offend God when they permit usury in their statutes and should be excommunicated (McLaughlin, "Canonists on Usury," 1.84, 2.10). Of course, the cities themselves raised money by forced loans on which they might pay annual dividends, but this was not considered usury because the loan was forced and the lender could not demand a refund, and because the town made a gain from the capital it was refunding in dividends. There were any number of ways devised to avoid the charge of usury. McLaughlin, citing Hostiensis, *Summa de usuris,* gives thirteen of them; they include various modes of temporary transfer of property, with the fruits of the property serving as the interest, compensation for damages of various kinds, selling at a higher price than the current worth in anticipation of higher value at a later date (*vendens sub dubio*), gifts freely offered by the debtor (*gratia dans*), labor, which may be compensated, and direct

²²See McLaughlin, "Canonists on Usury," 1.99, and Benjamin N. Nelson, *The Idea of Usury* (Princeton: Princeton University, 1949), 16.
²³McLaughlin, "Canonists on Usury," 1.88–89; interest is technically distinct from usury as compensation for damages incurred from a loan, see Noonan, *Scholastic Analysis of Usury,* 106, and Baldwin, MPM, 1.282–86.

usury from heretics and infidels, which some justify as a way of bringing them into the fold.[24] It is significant that *cambium,* "money-changing," is not listed among the evasive devices, nor is it mentioned by the canons which condemn sales on credit, although most commentators assume it should be (Noonan, *Scholastic Analysis of Usury,* 180). Ptolemy of Lucca seems to defend profit in money-changing, noting that money is not necessarily a fixed measure; that is, that money used for exchange is different "in species" from money used as a measure, but he does not develop the argument (Noonan, 182). Money-changers were distinguished from moneylenders by their public functions; official exchanges existed at fairs, ports, and in major commercial centers. Raymond deRoover suggests that exchange was the origin of banking, noting that by 1200 exchanges were being made in Genoa by paper rather than by hand.[25] But the changers charged interest, which they covered

[24]McLaughlin, "Canonists on Usury," 1.125 ff. Those in which the fruits of the property serve as interest are: *feuda,* the return of a fief to the church as security, in which the fruits may be enjoyed without being deducted from the debt as long as the vassal is freed from service during the same period; *pro dote,* property given to the bridegroom as security for a dowry that could not be paid, in which the fruits need not be deducted because a dowry is not always sufficient to support the burdens of matrimony and a dowry must be kept intact for the public good; *stipendia cleri,* clerics may take revenue of pledges placed with them for loans if they are ecclesiastical benefices they are recovering from laymen; *venditio fructus,* essentially a rent charge, the revenues of land sold for a limited period of time, allowed because of the uncertainty involved; *lex commissoria* by which the seller is allowed to regain possession for the same price, while the revenue goes to the purchaser. Compensation for damages includes: *fidejussor,* compensation to those who put up security for clerics in debt to merchants and were forced to pay damages; *pretium post tempora solvens,* late payment to cover possible damages; *poena nec in fraudem,* penalty for nonexecution of contract, as long as it is a penalty and not indemnification of the lender. Usury for heretics and infidels, *cui velle jure nocere,* is based on Ambrose, "ubi jus belli, ibi jus usurae," where it is right to make war it is also right to make usury, but Hostiensis does not accept this because harm to another cannot be justified.

[25]See deRoover, "L'Evolution de la lettre de change, XIVe–XVIIIe s.," *Affaires et gens d'affaires,* 4 (Paris: Colin 1953), 23–24, and Kirschner, "Raymond deRoover on Scholastic Economic Thought," in *de Roover, Business, Banking,* 32.

in the rates of exchange. Money would be lent in one place and currency to come due in others, though it would in fact be repaid in the first, treated as a double exchange; in some contracts the middle step was omitted, making it clear that the transaction was a ruse. The exchange, despite the profit, was not technically usury because it involved not a loan but a commutation of moneys, although Hostiensis saw the danger of the concealed loan (deRoover, *Business, Banking,* 203). Money-changers also received moneys on deposit, which they would transfer by request from one account to another, allow to be overdrawn, or invest for a return.

A related development, which also served to procure profit without incurring the charge of usury, was the partnership (*societas*), in which two or more people pooled money and labor, and the risk, like the profits, was shared. Interest might be as high as 50 percent, but it was covered by payment in other currencies, or by the risk incurred, and is rarely mentioned by theological commentators. According to Lopez, interest on sea-loans was acceptable at first because of the risk involved, but was condemned as usury in the thirteenth century (*Medieval Trade,* 168). There is argument among scholars about the relative importance of the avoidance of usury and the pursuit of profit in the formation of commercial partnerships or companies, but there is no question that this is one of a wide variety of practices instituted in order to avoid the charge of usury, practices that seem clearly usurious by any strict interpretation. The fact is that commercial growth was in conflict with strict theological theory and the result, despite the attempts by moderate theologians to accommodate to some extent the needs of business, was widespread and ingenious subterfuge.

That Dante was aware of such practices is beyond doubt. He attacked the worst excesses in various subtle and direct ways in the *Comedy.* At the same time, he takes a moderate position on the question of commerce and accepts it as a necessary part of civilized life, while he deplores certain abuses as harmful to the common good.[26] The best indication of Dante's attitude towards trade is his treatment of money. He is concerned with money as a basic instrument of exchange, an essential tool of society, very much in the way language is. Indeed, Dante often connects the abuse of language with the abuse of money: the first example of gibberish in Hell occurs in the section of the first economic sinners, the miser and prodigals, who attack each other with words as they did the providential order with riches; blasphemers, who defy God with words, are in the same division of the seventh circle as usurers; liars and counterfeiters are together in the last section of the eighth circle as the worst practitioners of fraud. The liar Sinon tells the counterfeiter Adam: "S'io dissi falso, e tu falsasti il conio" (30.115: "If I spoke false, you falsified the coin").[27]

Money was invented to measure the value of objects in order to facilitate exchange: it gives numerical expression to the basic factor of human need, the universal measure of all exchange.[28] Currency expresses the natural standard of value. Coins based on numbers represent the value of objects, so that goods and services may be exchanged; words, based on letters, represent the essence of objects, so that knowledge and ideas may be exchanged. Both are essential tools of civilized life, and the higher the level of civilization, the more essential these tools become. As a social animal, man has to rely on his fellows to provide the necessities and the luxuries of life, but to procure them he has to be able to express his needs and to pay for them. Trade, like language, can be a force for unity: just as the Italian language, despite regional dialects, unites a country

[26]Both Sapori, *Studi*, 536, and Garrani, *Il pensiero di Dante*, 68 ff., particularly 78, comment on Dante's acceptance of commerce.

[27]In Purgatory, 12.105, Dante couples corruption by words in official records (*il quaderno*) with corruption by money in customs and weights (*la doga*).

[28]Baldwin, *JP*, 74. See Alfred Sohn-Rethel, *Intellectual and Manual Labor* (London: Macmillan, 1978), for a discussion of the relation between commerce, particularly coinage, and abstract thinking; see also R. A. Shoaf, *Dante, Chaucer, and the Currency of the Word* (Norman: Pilgrim Books, (1983).

hopelessly divided politically, and Latin brings together the various countries of Europe, so a strong currency, like the florin and the trade that depends on it can bring together the most distant parts of the inhabited world; Benvenuto da Imola notes that the florin is the common coin, universally accepted, "valde communis moneta et universaliter expenditur per totum" (2.431). As cities and countries have different dialects and languages, they also have different currencies, but just as they can fix on a common language to facilitate communication, so they come to one or two reasonably stable currencies to facilitate trade. Indeed, cities in Italy as well as in Germany banded together in order to have one currency (Garrani, *Il pensiero di Dante*, 115 ff.). Apart from the church, the only organizations with regular representatives throughout Italy and even Europe and the Middle East were the large commercial companies, who brought the various regions together by transporting news as well as goods. And the merchants who traveled throughout the world, unlike their fellows in the various separate states of Italy, were "Italians" united by both a community of interests and the hostility of their hosts.[29]

[29]All commercial Italians seem to have been called "Lombards" at first (Sapori, *Italian Merchant*, 14) and were persecuted as a group in France (ibid. 17–18); they banded together officially under a captain of Lombard and Tuscan merchants "Capitaneus mercatorum lombardorum et tuscanorum" in 1278, and he negotiated for them with the French king; later they formed a society of Italian merchants, "Universitas mercatorum italicorum," 1288 (ibid. 19). Garrani, *Il pensiero di Dante*, 13, notes that these organizations were self-disciplinary; he also mentions that commercial families joined togehter in caravans in order to be safer in their travels. Italian companies that were fierce rivals at obtaining wool in England apparently shared ships to transport it (Kaeuper, *Bankers to the Crown*, 42). F. P. Luiso, "Su le tracce d'un usuraio fiorentino del s.XIII," *Archivio storico italiano* NS 42 (1908), 3–44, cites a document of the Curia in 1294 in which Giovanni Gianfigliazzi promised in his own name and that of the merchants from Florence and Lombardy residing in Provence at the time to pay a sum in order to abolish or modify a royal decree on usury, 24. When the king of England needed large sums, he could count on the Ricciardi to raise them from among the Italian banking community (Kaeuper, 301). In the Datini archives, letters about merchants in Spain mention the "detti Italiani" apropos of royal permissions and restrictions (Livi, Dall'archivio, 52).

Money, like language, can be used for a variety of useful purposes, to buy and sell, to build, to finance government, support art and education, and help the indigent, but it can also be used to bribe and blackmail, to buy power and impede justice. Similarly, language can be used to explain and to teach, to control or correct, to encourage towards good, to amuse and comfort, but it can also be used to seduce and deceive, to lead astray and destroy. Both are susceptible to corruption and must be controlled, language by the rules of grammar, money by officially imposed standards of weight, material, and value.[30] The social and political damage that can be done by false documents or counterfeited coins is self-evident. Hell offers ample evidence of the evils of abuses of language and of money and of the connection between them: Hell itself is both a vast mouth ("l'ampia gola d'inferno," Pg. 21.31–32) and the city of wealth, Dis; the feet of simoniacs, who sold the sacraments for gold and silver, are seen as grotesque tongues projecting from the "mouths" of baptismal fonts; the ditch of thieves is a "fierce throat," and the principal thief defies God with his words.[31] When Dante goes through the gate of Purgatory, it reminds him of the Roman treasury despoiled by Caesar (9.133 ff.), but the treasures of Purgatory are the language of prayers, a currency by which the living can help "pay the debt" of the souls, and the language of poetry, the treasures shared by poets and offered by them to their audiences. In Paradise, where communication moves beyond language in new words and paradoxical concepts, symbols and music, the souls themselves

---

[30]Garrani, *Il pensiero di Dante,* 139, mentions a particularly intriguing way of regularizing monetary circulation, by the use of imaginary money, which existed only as a standard against which real monies could be measured, the "Fiorino a Fiorino" in Florence, and the Sicilian "oncia."

[31]Counsellors of fraud, who teach others to gain power and wealth by deception, are also tongues, spurting from the "throat" of their *bolgia,* and the three worst traitors, those who sell out their benefactors, hang from the three mouths of Lucifer. This is the essence of Hell, turning the mouth, the instrument of communication through which reason speaks, into an organ of pure consumption.

are the treasures, the jewels, and financial imagery is used to express the highest kind of spiritual wealth.

Dante himself is both a poet and a merchant in the *Comedy*, using the beauty and force of his language to guide his audience. As poet, he serves as a messenger, an intermediary between God and man, besieged by his countrymen in the otherworld to take their messages home, like a merchant in foreign parts, and charged by heaven with an important message for his countrymen on earth. As merchant, he travels through the universe on the "ship of his wit" to acquire the most valuable goods available to man and bring them back to sell to his countrymen for their own good. He serves an important function for society, but he is also making a profit in the reputation he clearly expects to gain from the poem. His primary purpose is not self-enrichment, but if he is offered the poet's crown by his native city, he will accept it. The same heavenly source disposes men to trade and to eloquence. The Ottimo, in his commentary on Fortune (Hell 7), makes the connection between eloquence and trade through the god Mercury, who was, he says, called "Iddio d'eloquenza, perch'è Iddio dei mercatanti," the god of eloquence because he is the god of merchants, who know how to buy and sell softly (1.120–21). It is tantalizing to project this onto the heaven of Mercury in Paradise and suggest that that is where good merchants must be, among those active for honor and fame in the world. Well-known commentaries on classical mythology connect Mercury with business as well as with eloquence. Fulgentius interprets Mercury as *Mercium curum*, "concern with wares," noting that every merchant might be called Mercury. He has winged feet because the feet of merchants move everywhere, as if winged; he has a staff with serpents because trade sometimes gives a kingdom, sometimes a wound; his head is covered with a helmet because business is always hidden. He is called Hermes, because *ermeneuse* is explanation, and explanation in words is necessary in business. He is a thief because there is no difference between the robbery and perjury of businessmen and of thieves.[32] In the commentary on the *Aeneid* attributed to Bernard Silvester, Mercury is both a star and eloquence; he is patron of robbery because he deceives the souls of listeners and controls merchants, since those selling goods further themselves with eloquence. He is the guardian of merchants (*mercatorum cura*) and activity of minds (*mentium currus*) because he reveals carefully contrived matters.

From the beginning of the poem, Dante uses financial imagery to describe his own journey and experience as well as the spiritual debts and treasures of the souls he sees, slowly replacing "corporal" with "spiritual" usury. When he is stopped by the wolf of avarice in the first canto, he feels like one "who would willingly acquire" (1.55: "che volontieri acquista"), but "when the time comes that makes him lose," he weeps and is depressed, as if he had sought worldly gain too eagerly and lost. On the other hand, Beatrice, moved by the unselfish desire to save Dante, rushes eagerly to Virgil and describes her desire in similarly financial language: "al mondo non fur mai persone ratte/a far lor *pro* o a fuggir lor *danno*" (2.109–10; "no one on earth was so swift to make a profit or to avoid a loss"). Dante asks Virgil later to find some "compensation" for the time they must rest so it will not be lost (11.13–15), treating knowledge as treasure to be stored up, an approach that becomes much more obvious in Purgatory and Paradise. For the most part, however, financial language in Hell is applied to sin and evil: as they approach the ninth sec-

---

[32]Fulgentius, *Mitologiarum Liber I*, ed Rudolfus Helm (1898; reprint, Stuttgart: Teubner, 1970), chapter 18, and *The Commentary on the First Six Books of the Aeneid*, ed. J. W. and E. F. Jones (Lincoln: University of Nebraska, 1977), 4.222 ff.; the commentary was translated by E. G. Schreiber and T. E. Maresca (Lincoln: University of Nebraska, 1979). Mercury as eloquence was, of course, well established by Martianus Capella's *De nuptiis Philologiae et Mercurii*. Thomas Aquinas connects trade with lying words, ST, 2.2ae, q.77, a.4: "difficiliter exuitur negotiator a peccatis labiorum." There is an interesting analogue to Dante as poet and merchant in some versions of the Tristan story, in which the hero disguises himself in his wanderings both as a merchant and as a minstrel.

tion of fraud, Dante describes it as the "ditch in which those who acquire their load by dividing pay their fee" (27.135–36: "'l fosso in che si paga il fio/a quei che scommettendo acquistan carco"). Hell is a great sack which holds the treasure of evil (7.17–18: "la dolente ripa/che 'l mal de l'universo tutto *insacca*"); a simoniac comments that on earth he put wealth, here he puts himself, in a purse (19.72: "sù l'avere e qui me misi in borsa"); the weights born by the hypocrites "make their scales creak" (23.101–102: "li pesi fan ... cigolar le lor bilancie"). Hell itself is the "city of wealth" (8.68: "la città c'ha nome Dite"), who resides at its center (11.64–65: "'l punto/de l'universo in su che Dite siede"), and sinners are its treasure, the booty Christ took away from it (12.38–39: "colui che la gran preda/levò a Dite").

In Purgatory, the treasures are intellectual and spiritual, but sin is still treated as a debt that must be paid.[33] The debt can be repaid in different species: in time—the negligent spend an equivalent amount of time and the excommunicates thirty times as long waiting to get into Purgatory as they spent excluded from the sacraments; in prayers of the living, which the souls in the first half of Purgatory beg Dante to request for them; and in their penance, their suffering: "come Dio vuol che 'l debito si paghi" (10.108: "as God wants the debt to be paid"); "qui convien ch'io questo peso porti ... tanto che a Dio sodisfaccia" (11.70-71: "I have to carry this weight until God is satisfied"); "di tal superbia qui si paga il fio" (11.88: "here you pay the fee for such pride"); "cotal moneta rende/a sodisfar chi è di là troppo oso" (11.125–26: "such coin does one pay in satisfaction who is too daring here"); "e ancor non sarebbe/lo

---

[33]Aquinas speaks of the expiation of sins in Purgatory in terms of debts, profit, and compensation, ST, Supp. 2.71, particularly a.4. Jacques Le Goff, *La naissance du Purgatoire* (Paris: Gallimard, 1981), notes the financial language in that passage, although he points out that the text was put together by Thomas's disciples from his work. See also Jacques Le Goff, "The Usurer and Purgatory," *The Dawn of Modern Banking*, Center for Medieval and Renaissance Studies, UCLA (New Haven: Yale University, 1979), 25–52, for connections between the concept of Purgatory (the salvation of sinners) and the development of capitalism.

mio dover per penitenza scemo se ... non fosse ... Pier Petti-
naio in sue sante orazioni" (13.125–28: "and my debt would
not yet be reduced by penitence if not for Pier's holy prayers").
Dante recognizes and feels the weight of his own debt: "già lo
incarco di là giù mi pesa" (13.138). Before he leaves Purgatory,
he is accused by Beatrice of following false images of good,
which "render no promise in full," for which he has to pay
with tears of repentance (30.132, 144–45: "che nulla promes-
sion rendono intera/... alcuno scotto/di pentimento che
lagrime spanda"). The debt of penance is carefully reckoned
and must be paid in full by the individual's account, although
he may transfer funds from other sources, such as prayers.
That is because on earth he set his heart where sharing is for-
bidden (14.87), because earthly goods are lessened by partner-
ship (15.50: "per compagnia parte si scema", whereas heaven's
goods are increased by the number of possessors (15.55–56:
"per quanti si dice più lì 'nostro,'/tanto possiede più di ben
ciascuno" "the more [souls] there say 'our,' so much more
good does each one possess"). Dante, who still has an earthly
perspective, does not understand these words and asks, putting
the question clearly in terms of material wealth, how a good
distributed among many possessors can make them richer than
if it is possessed by one (15.61–63: "com'esser puote ch'un ben,
distributo/in più posseditor, faccia più ricchi/di sè che se da
pochi è posseduto?"), but Virgil explains that love reflects
between God and souls as among so many mirrors, constantly
increasing in power, like light, a superb example of "spiritual
usury."

Dante does know enough in Purgatory to seek "profit" in
Virgil's words (15.41–42: "io pensai ... prode acquistar ne le
parole sue", a sign that his values are sound, and Beatrice will
later show him things for the "profit" of the world that still
lives badly (32.103: "in pro del mondo che mal vive"). Dante
speaks of his own poetry as money he spends: "più non
spargo/rime, lettor; ch'altra spesa mi strigne,/tanto ch'a
questa non posso esser largo" (29.97–99: "I lay out no more
rhymes, reader, because another expense presses me so that I

cannot be generous with this one"); and of Guido Guinizelli's poems as something that makes even their ink precious (26.112–14: "li dolci detti vostri/ . . . faranno *cari* ancora i loro incostri"). Statius credits the *Aeneid* with giving his poetry all its value, "without it I would not have weighed a dram" (21.99: "sanz' essa non fermai peso di dramma"), and claims that to have been alive when Virgil was, he would give a year more than he owed in exile, that is, he would increase his debt of penance, prodigal now of his love.[34] Dante counts what other poets teach him as intellectual pay: "tu m'appaghe, " he wants to say to Virgil (15.82), and to Bonagiunta he does say "te e me col tuo parlare appaga" (24.42). Guido speaks of what Dante learns on his journey as cargo he is loading on his ship (26.73–75: "de le nostre marche. . . esperienza imbarche"). Dante is consciously storing up this treasure from the beginning of Paradise (1.10–11: "quant'io del regno santo/ne la mia mente potei far tesoro"), but it is a heavy load under which he may tremble (23.64–66). Nonetheless, Dante is confident his boat is big enough to handle it (23.67–69). Dante has in fact come for the cargo with good money of his own: "assai bene è trascorsa/d'esta moneta già la lega e'l peso" (24.83–84: "the alloy and weight of the coin have been well examined") Peter says of Dante's answers on faith, and then asks him if he has it in his purse (24.85). "I do, so shining and round that there is no doubt of its minting," Dante answers (24.86–87: "Sì ho, sì lucida e sì tonda,/che nel suo conio nulla mi s'inforsa"). (Cf. Hell 11.54, "quel che fidanza non imborsa.") But even Dante does not have wealth enough in his words to describe the beauty of the Virgin (Pr.31.136–37: "e s'io avessi in dir tanta divizia/quanta ad imaginar").

Dante is surrounded by spiritual treasures in Paradise, where God as supreme ruler establishes their value: "Qui veggion l'alte creature l'orma/de l'etterno valore, il qual è fine/al quale è fatta la toccata norma" (1.106–08: "here the high creatures

---

[34]Cf. Matelda, who gives Dante more than she had promised, sure that it will be no less valued for that (28.137–38), i.e., one can be prodigal of learning as well as of love.

see the stamp of the eternal value which is the end to which the mentioned rule was made"). His is the true light that pays all souls in full (3.32). Free will, the gift God "prizes" most, is the treasure sacrificed in a holy vow (5.19–29). Peter Lombard offered the church his *Sentences* as his "treasure" (10.108); Francis offered his followers unknown wealth, "ignota ricchezza" (11.82), a good cargo for whoever follows him (11.122–23: "per che qual segue lui ... discerner puoi che buone merce carca"). Dominic and Faith gave each other a dowry of mutual salvation (12.63, "mutüa salute," perhaps a play on *mutuum*, "loan," this being a true exchange). Dante speaks of Cacciaguida as "my treasure," "il mio tesoro" (17.121); the heavens are very rich coffers filled with wealth (23:130–31: "quanta è l'ubertà che si soffolce/in quelle arche ricchissime", which Dante tries to assess (24.17–18: "de la sua ricchezza/mi faciendo stimar"), wealth that is secure and without longing "oh sanza brama sicura ricchezza" (27.9). The souls in Paradise are jewels, 9.37, 10.71; topazes, 15.85, 30.76; rubies, 19.4.

The sense of inexhaustible wealth that pervades Paradise does not bring with it fiscal irresponsibility. Even here, there is an awareness of the enormous debt that has to be paid in order to make this wealth possible: original sin was a debt so great that man, although he had contracted it, could not pay by himself (7.97–98: "non potea l'uomo ne' termini suoi/mai sodisfar"). Only God, who had created all, not for his own profit (29.13), but to share with others, could, in the person of Christ, satisfy it with his army, which "cost so much to rearm" (12.37–38: "l'essercito di Cristo, che sì caro/costò a rïarmar"). Eve's palate cost the whole world (13.39: "a tutto 'l mondo costa"), but Christ's suffering "satisfied" the debt and "turned the scales" (13.41–42). Still the world forgets "how much blood it cost" to disseminate God's word (29.91–92). Trajan, however, now knows "how much it costs" not to follow Christ (20.46–47), because he has been in Hell. In the midst of this perfect society, where all treasures are shared, there is a deep distress for the abuses on earth, distress that reminds us of the worst abuses of Hell. Some are political abuses, described in financial imagery, some are actual economic abuses. Charles Martel warns his brother, Robert, not to be driven by greed and stinginess to "overload his already laden boat," but to look to fighters who are not concerned with filling their own coffers (Pr. 8.76–84). The eagle of justice condemns both the king of Rascia, Stephen Urosh II, for counterfeiting Venetian coins (19.140–41), and the king of France, Philip IV, for filling his coffers by falsifying the coin (19.119: "falseggiando la moneta" and debasing his own coinage. Cunizza decries the impious pastor who trades in human lives: "the vat to receive their blood must be too large, and he who weighed it ounce by ounce very tired" (9.55–58). Cacciaguida laments the effects of commerce on his native city with a nostalgic recollection of the old Florence before the excessive display of wealth (15.100–02) and the reckless increase in the size of dowries (15.103–05), before husbands deserted their wives to trade in France, (15.119–20)[35] and outsiders came in to the city to engage in money-changing and trade (16.61), before there was fraud in the salt customs (16.105) and appropriation of revenues for vacant sees (16.113–14), or before the "weight of felonies became so heavy some would have to be jettisoned from the ship" (16.94–96: "carca/di nova fellonia di tanto peso/che tosto fia ïattura de la barca"), a reference to the troubles of a large banking family, the Cerchi.

Cacciaguida describes the corruption brought about by secular commercialism in his city, the heavenly kings point to earthly monarchs misusing their power over the currency to the harm of nations, but most of the figures in Paradise are concerned with economic corruption in the church. Indeed, even Cacciaguida describes Rome as the place where Christ is "traded" every day (17.51: "là dove Cristo tutto dì si merca"); for Dante, the temple built by miracles and martyrdom has become a marketplace (18.122–23: "del comperare e vender

---

[35]Saint Francis was so named because his father, a merchant, was in France on business at the time of his birth.

dentro al templo/che si murò di segni e di martìri"), and the pope so cynically intent on the Baptist (the gold florin) that he has no thought for Peter or Paul (18.133–36). Peter rages that the church which arose from his blood is used to acquire gold (27.40–42), that his figure seals false privileges which are being sold (27.52–53), that rapacious wolves masquerade as shepherds (27.55), and Cahorsines are preparing to drink the martyrs' blood (27.58–59), to suck as much wealth as they can from it. Though this is a reference to Pope John XXII, Cahors is also synonymous with usury (cf. Hell 11.50). Beatrice says that unscrupulous clerics pay out money with no stamp, no official coinage (29.126: "pagando di moneta sanza conio"), in other words, that their pardons are counterfeit. But perhaps most damning of all, Benedict says that *grave usura* ("immoderate usury," such as was condemned by the Fourth Lateran Council) is not so offensive to God as the church's misuse of its funds (by monks in this case), which it has in keeping for God's people (22.79–84). The church engages in the worst kind of fiscal corruption by appropriating and misusing funds it does not properly even possess, but only administers.

Dante uses the financial imagery to such an extent, both metaphorically and literally, not only because it is familiar to his audience, whom he wishes to entice away from their concern with material wealth towards spiritual treasures, but also because the world of commerce is essentially positive, for all its abuses. Like politics and religion, trade is essential to the well-being of man in society, as long as it is practiced with a sense of public responsibility and not exclusively for personal gain. In Hell, of course, all acquisition is selfish and to a greater or lesser extent antisocial. The cantica is dominated by greed, beginning in the first canto with the wolf, the most effective obstacle to man's desire to climb the mountain of Purgatory. The monster who guards the first financial sin (avarice), a *maladetto lupo,* "cursed wolf," is Pluto, identified by early commentators as the god of earthly wealth, *Dispater* (father of wealth, Dis, see the Ottimo 1.107–08, Guido, 136, Benvenuto, 1.243–44), or as the equivalent of Dis (Pietro, 97); Pluto is

named for earth and called Dis because (*divitiae,* "riches," are born from the earth.
Hell is the "città di Dite," the city of wealth. Indeed, two thirds of the cantica, from canto eleven to the end, is devoted to sins which are "daughters of greed." According to Aquinas, drawing on Gregory and with references to Isidore and Aristotle, covetousness can be excessive in retaining or in receiving; when it involves action to acquire people's goods by force, it is violence, when by deceit, it is fraud; if it uses simple words, it is falsehood, if it adds the confirmation of an oath, it is treachery, as seen in Judas, who betrayed Christ out of avarice.[36] The last three sections of Hell, described in cantos 12 to 34, are violence, fraud, and treachery. Violence is subdivided into three sections, depending on the object (neighbor, self, or God), but within each section, the sins against persons and possessions are punished together; they are of equal importance by virtue of their location. Thus tyrants and murderers are punished with despoilers, plunderers, and extortioners; suicides and wastrels are together in the second section, and in the third blasphemers, sodomites and usurers (those who attack God directly or in his "things"). Fraud is divided into ten separate categories, each of which involves illicit gains by fraudulent practice (see below); it is committed against one who trusts or one who "has no faith in his purse" (11.54: "quel che fidanza non im*borsa*"). Treachery, the last circle of Hell, is betrayal for wealth or worldly power; whoever betrays is "consumed at the center of the universe on which Wealth sits" (11.65–66).

This pattern is carefully laid out distinct from the rest of Hell in canto 11; the three sins are connected by their moti-

[36]ST, 2.2ae, q.118, a.8: "avaritia est superfluus amor habendi divitias, in duobus excedit . . . in retinendo . . . in accipiendo. . . . Et sic in acquirendo aliena utitur quandoque quidem vi, quod pertinet ad violentias; quodoque autem dolor. Qui quidem si fiat in verbo, erit fallacia, quantum ad simplex verbum; periurium autem si addatur confirmatio iuramenti. Si autem dolus committatur in opere, sic, quantum ad res, erit fraus; quantum ad personas, proditio, ut patet de Iuda, qui ex avaritia prodidit Christum.

vation, which is malice, and by their end, which is injury (injustice), and is accomplished either with force or fraud (11.22–24). Malice "acquires hatred in heaven," an ironic contrast to the material goods acquired by its actions. The importance of possessions is revealed by Virgil in his definition of violence:

A Dio, a sé, al prossimo si pòne
far forza, dico in loro e in *lor cose,*

. . . .
nel prossimo . . . e nel *suo avere*

. . . .
Puote omo avere in sé man violenta
e nei *suoi beni;*

who uses violence against God, himself, or his neighbor,
in themselves and *in their things*

. . . .
against his neighbors and *his possessions*

. . . .
against himself and *his own goods.*

(11.31–41)

Speaking of the suicide and the wastrel, Virgil makes it clear that cutting oneself off from material substance is the equivalent of depriving oneself of life: "he repents without profit, who deprives himself of your world, gambles or wastes his substance" (11.42–44: "sanza pro si penta/qualunque priva sé del vostro mondo,/biscazza e fonde la sua facultade"). But even more significant, after he has defined the three sins and given Dante a sense of what is found in the remaining circles of Hell, Virgil returns to usury and ends the whole discussion with fifteen lines on that particular sin (11.97–111), as if it were the key to all, and, in the sense that usury means making an illicit profit, it is. In Dante's world, any financial activity might be called "usury" to discredit it.

At this point, in the light of Dante's interest in financial terminology, it is appropriate to look at specific passages in

which the economic aspect may shed light on the meaning of
the episode, not by denying other meanings, but by adding
another dimension to them. The canto of the misers and prod-
igals, the first economic sinners, opens with Pluto's "Pape
Satàn," words that have been variously explained or defended
as gibberish. But the fact that *Pape* is the form in which the
pope's title appeared on papal coins minted by Boniface VIII—
DOMINI BO PAPE or DN BON PAPE—lends weight to the "Pope
Satan" reading.[37] By hoarding or recklessly spending, these
souls, like the papacy on a larger scale, impeded the work of
fortune, assigned by providence to oversee not only the distri-
bution but also the transfer of worldly goods and power to
individuals and nations. The concept of change is emphasized
in the passage on fortune: "sì spesso vien chi *vicenda*
consegue" (7.90); "*volve* sua spera" (7.96); "*permutasse* a
tempo li ben vani" (7.79); "le sue *permutazion* non hanno trie-
gue" (7.88). The technical term for barter in a contract is *per-
mutacio* (Baldwin, MPM, 1.267). The movement of the first
economic sinners, the misers and prodigals, in opposing semi-
circles symbolizes their opposition to fortune by turning the
wheel back on itself, but it also suggests their disruption of
circulation in the market, an idea emphasized by the repetition
of "circle": "così tornavan per lo *cerchio* tetro" (7.31), "si vol-
gea ciascun . . . per lo suo mezzo *cerchio*" (7.34–35), "quando
vengono ai due punti del *cerchio*/dove colpa contraria li dis-
paia" (7.44); perhaps in the clerical tonsures mentioned twice
in the midst of these lines (7.39 and 7.46–47); and as Dante and
Virgil leave the circle, "noi ricidemmo il *cerchio*" (7.100),
"così *girammo* de la lorda pozza/grand'arco, tra la ripa secca
e'l mézzo" (7.127–28: "so we went around a great arc of that
filthy swamp between the dry bank and the slime"). *Mezzo* is

[37]The coins of the other popes in the late thirteenth and early fourteenth
centuries use PP, PAPA, sometimes PA, or PAP. Boniface's are the only ones I
could find with PAPE in this period (see Francesco Muntoni, *Le monete dei
Papi e degli Stati pontefici* [Rome: P & P Santamaria, 1972] 1.24 ff.), though
Leo VIII had one in the tenth century.

perhaps a pun meaning both "slime" and the "mean," which they ignore. If Dante is thinking of circulation, as seems likely, the inflated lips of Pluto ("quella infiata labbia") may suggest inflation.[38]

The Ottimo, in his commentary on canto 7, goes into some detail on the workings of greed in virtually every class of society: prelates commit simony, lesser priests sell unmentionables ("cose che il tacer è bello") to laymen, lay princes oppress their subjects with taxes and ransoms, occupiers of foreign cities and provinces rob and loot, as do knights in wars, judges give false sentences and false counsels for money, and merchants and artisans sell for more than things are worth or steal with defective weights, numbers, or measures; they sell on credit, a kind of usury, lend at interest, which is also usury, or buy early (1.110–11). Benvenuto also focuses on businessmen, interpreting the weights rolled by the sinners as the labors and cares of misers, whose bodies rarely rest, who rush around by land and sea, expose themselves to all kinds of dangers and discomforts, and whose souls are anxious even when the body rests (1.250).[39]

In chapter three, the political overtones of factionalism in the canto of the heretics were discussed, but there are economic overtones as well: first of all, the heretics singled out in canto 10 are Epicureans, who ignored the afterlife for the goods and pleasures of this world; second, heresy was often coupled with usury in law and criminal investigation. The Council of Vienna determined that secular officials who wrote, supported, or enforced statutes abetting usury should be excommunicated, and those who stubbornly affirmed that usury was not a sin be punished as heretics; investigation of heresy and usury was often in the hands of the same ecclesi-

---

[38]Cf. Garrani on the counterfeiter's swollen stomach, *Il pensiero di Dante*, 160 ff.; Garrani suggests that by condemning avarice, which takes money out of circulation, whereas loans put it in, Dante is distinguishing bankers from usurers who lend at excessive rates, 86.

[39]The restless movement of merchants in pursuit of gain is a classical *topos* adopted by the church fathers, Baldwin, MPM, 1.262.

astical officials, the Inquisition and the Frati Gaudenti.[40] Conversely, part of the punishment for heresy was the confiscation of property, which occurred in the posthumous condemnation of Farinata degli Uberti and his wife as heretics, nineteen years after their deaths, and resulted in the loss of all property to their sons and grandsons. The sentence of condemnation says nothing specific about their heresy, but goes into some detail on the goods to be confiscated and to be inventoried publicly within eight days and divided and sold so that the heirs could not recover the succession.[41] The Templars were also condemned for heresy at the instigation of Philip IV as a way of getting control of their vast wealth, which Dante alludes to rather critically (Pg. 20.91–93), but the Templars had engaged in moneylending, while there is no indication that Farinata was so involved. Cavalcanti, on the other hand, who lies beside Farinata among the heretics, comes from a family quite actively engaged in banking and commerce.[42] Dante may well be showing the obsessive pursuit of wealth and the anticivic loyalty to family (which in business also means the company) through Cavalcanti, who asks only about his son, as a counter and complement to Farinata's obsession with political power

[40]McLaughlin, "Canonists on Usury," 2.10–11, and Marvin Becker, "Florentine Politics and the Diffusion of Heresy in the Trecento: A Socio-Economic Inquiry," *Speculum* 34 (1959), 61, and Emilio Morpurgo, "I Prestatori di Danaro al tempo di Dante," *Dante e Padova* (Padua: Prosperini, 1865), 193–233. According to Morpurgo, the mission of the Frati Gaudenti was to safeguard peace, wipe out heresies, defend ecclesiastical privileges and the claims of widows and orphans, and particularly to oversee the repression of usury. 216.

[41]See Niccolò Ottokar, "La condanna postuma di Farinata degli Uberti," *Archivio storico italiano* 77 (1919), 159 ff., for the text of the sentence; he notes that a year and a half after the posthumous trial of Farinata, Bruno degli Uberti was similarly condemned for heresy, posthumously, and his sons lost their inheritance, dispersing another substantial part of the Uberti family fortunes.

[42]According to Robert Davidsohn, *Storia di Firenze, I primordi della civiltà fiorentina: Industria, arti, commercio e finanze* (Italian trans. Giovanni Miccoli), 6.256, no one took part as frequently in the consulate of the Calimala guild as the Cavalcanti and indeed the wool industry also had a seat in their houses; on the importance of the Cavalcanti in commerce and banking, see Masi "Banchieri," 61–62.

and his anticivic loyalty to party. The selfish pursuits of wealth and power are equally destructive to the public good.[43]

Violence, as noted above, is a sin committed against possessions as well as persons. It involves misappropriation or misuse of property: the acquisition of others' goods by force in the first section, the reckless squandering of one's own substance in the second, and the abuse of God's goods in the third, in that usury disrupts the providential distribution of wealth. Dante seems to imply that one economic crime leads to another: one of the barrators in Hell is the son of a wastrel (22.50–51); one of the wastrels, Jacopo da Sant'Andrea, inherited his wealth from his mother's family, probably involved in usury, and after he squandered it, he tried to get some back by force and then by fraud.[44] Innocent IV made an obvious connection between squandering and usury when he expressed fear that Christians were squandering their possessions in order to pay usurers (McLaughlin, "Canonists on Usury," 1.110). Two of the early commentators interpret the dogs that run after the wastrels as creditors (Pietro, 161, Benvenuto, 1.452), Benvenuto adding that creditors and their messengers persecute fleeing debtors and take parts of them (their possessions) when they catch them; it is perhaps not a coincidence that Dante's usurers brush away the burning rain like dogs bitten by insects (17.50–51). The statue of the Veglio di Creta, representing the progressive corruption of man and the transfer of power and goods from one nation to another, appears in the last section of violence, among those who defy God

---

[43]There are various suggestive details in the canto which have financial overtones: the souls appear from the waist or chin up, as busts or heads, seen against the backdrop of their tomb covers, rather like the figures on coins, and Farinata does not move except for one slight raising of the eyebrow, like an engraved figure; Cavalcanti's face is seen to the chin, *mento,* which rhymes with *talento,* "talent", and *spento,* "spent." (*Talento* means "desire" rather than the coin here, but that is not clear until the following line. 10.55–56.) Dante "reads Cavalcanti's name" in his words and penalty (10.64–65) as one identifies the figure on a coin.

[44]See Enrico Salvagnini, "Jacopo da Sant'Andrea e i Feudatarj del Padovano," *Dante e Padova* (Padua; Prosperini, 1865), 37–40 and 55.

directly: the blasphemers, who make an unnatural use of speech, the sodomites, an unnatural use of sex, and the usurers, an unnatural use of money. The statue of human and national corruption can also be read as an allegory of debased currency, the only whole part being the gold head, the crack beginning in the silver and getting worse in the copper and iron, just as the only currency that was likely to remain stable was gold, while silver, alloys with baser metals, and copper, were constantly debased (Lopez, *Medieval Trade*, 13–14, 145 ff.). The effect of such devaluation is felt by the whole nation.

Although sodomy would seem to have little to do with finance, Dante hints at a rather superficial and materialist attitude among the souls, primarily by the use of commercial language. In the encounter with Brunetto Latini, the dignity of the old poet and civil servant is diminished somewhat by the imagery from the garment industry: Brunetto squints at Dante like an old tailor threading his needle (15.21); he takes Dante by the hem (15.24) and says he will follow at his skirts (15.40); the three sodomites in the following canto recognize Dante by his clothes (16.8).[45] Brunetto says his group is lamenting their eternal losses, "etterni danni," much as a small businessman might speak of his continual losses, and tells Dante to follow his star to a "glorious port," meaning worldly (literary) success (15.55–56). Fortune is mentioned frequently in their conversation, meaning providence to Dante, but chance or personal success to Brunetto. Brunetto's book is his "Treasure," *Tesoro*, in which he hopes to achieve immortality of a limited kind, the only kind he can now aspire to, but it is clear that he thinks of literary fame as a worldly acquisition, not as a means of serving society and God. He speaks of the Florentines as a "gente avara, invidiosa e superba" (15.68), putting greed first, in contrast to Ciacco's order (6.74), perhaps revealing Brunetto's concerns as much as the city's. Brunetto appears with and

---

[45]Saint Bernard compares himself to a tailor at the end of Paradise (32.140), but there it is a humility topos, revealing a willingness to work within the limits and material given by God. The sexual implications of the sodomites' clothes imagery were discussed in chapter three.

must rejoin a group of clerics and men of letters; the three sodomites in canto 16 are with statesmen, political figures, but they mention another, Guglielmo Borsiere, a pursemaker, who is with yet another group, presumably of tradesmen or businessmen. His disturbing report of the changes in Florence prompts them to ask Dante about the city and he responds with an attack on the pride and "dismisura" brought about by the "gente nuova e i sùbiti guadagni" (16.73: "new people and sudden earnings"), as if commerce were directly involved with the unnatural turn civic life was taking, a view that sets the scene for the last sin in the same section of violence.

The early commentators give a good deal of attention to usury and four of the five consulted point out that civil law permits it: Pietro notes that civil and canon law hold that a loan should be given without hope of gain, but that civil law inhibits usury in four counsels, in other words, by restricting it, permits it; Pietro also distinguishes between the *mercator,* the merchant or trader who sells what he has bought, and the *foenerator,* the lender or usurer who sells something given by God and expects to get it back (141–42). The Ottimo gives the "emperors'" (Roman law) restrictions on usury by class, the highest percentage allowed to nobles, next to merchants, but he adds that canon law now prohibits usury (1.310). Guido da Pisa cites Aquinas (ST, 2.2ae, q.77) on the fact that civil law by allowing usury does not oblige men to sin (315 ff.), but he also points out that gratuitous gifts are permitted, as well as recompense for loss (319), and he includes selling dear and buying cheap under usury (320–21). Benvenuto, commenting on usury in canto 11, notes that civil law permits it, but that civil law is concerned only with men living peacefully together (1.379); in connection with the usurers themselves in canto 17, Benvenuto says there can be virtuous usurers, although it is rare to find any of great virtue, and reminds us that Dante puts the worst examples of any sin in Hell (1.571), from which one infers that there may be usurers in Purgatory or Paradise. He also cites the public service performed by the knights mentioned in this canto, who had great banks in large cities to subsidize the poor for the public good (1.574–75), and complains that usury has become more hidden than open, involving not only changers, merchants, and artisans, but also prelates, priests, and friars (1.575).

By placing usury in the circle of violence rather than in fraud, Dante seems to distinguish lending at a profit from fraudulent lending practices; he does not condemn all such profit under fraud ("in fraudem usurarum") as the church did.[46] He does, of course, present the usurers after he has seen Gerione, the figure of fraud, which is reasonably taken to mean that he implies the fraudulent aspects of usury. But by having Gerione invade the section of the usurers, Dante may also be suggesting the usurious aspects of fraud, inviting us to consider the illicit profit making by the various types of fraudulent practice he describes. Benvenuto interprets Gerione as the three aspects of fraud, in word (the just face of a man, because speech is proper to human beings), in the thing (the body of diverse colors, as in all crafts and transactions), in the act (the venomous tail which stings, pierces, and infects); the beast crosses mountains because daily, by letters, a fraud invented in some transaction swiftly crosses seas and mountains and spreads to other, even distant, regions (1.559–60). Pietro says fraud is continually committed at a distance by letters and embassies (181). Garrani identifies Gerione with usurious contracts, which appear to be legal (the face), but contain a hidden, illicit profit (the tail) (*Il pensiero di Dante*, 67).

Each section of fraud involves illicit profits, the first five by direct sales of what should not be sold, the last five by more subtle manipulations. The first *bolgia* contains seducers and pimps, those who sell their own or someone else's body. Pimps "coin" women (as the devil comments, 18.66: "qui non son

---

[46] In civil law, fraud, *dolus,* is any cunning, deceit, or contrivance used to defraud, deceive, or cheat another; two kinds are specified, "dolus ex proposito," intentional fraud, which nullifies a contract, and "dolus re ipsa," which is by mistake and has no remedy in law (Baldwin, MPM, 1.264). The ten categories of fraud described in Dante's eighth circle are all of the first kind.

femmine da conio," "here there are no women to coin"), turning them into marketable items.[47] Dante asks the soul he meets here, Venedico, what has brought him to such "pungent sauces," "pungenti salse" (18.51); Benvenuto explains that in Bologna, where Venedico comes from, Salse is a place outside the city in which the bodies of desperate criminals, usurers, and other infamous people were thrown (2.11), and Venedico himself notes the greed of the Bolognese (18.63). The souls of the next section, the flatterers, sell the service of their tongue; Aquinas (ST, 2.2ae, q.78, a.2) holds that recompense can be by service or word as well as money, because these can also be given monetary value. Conner ("Inferno XVIII," 98–99), points out that John of Salisbury, in the *Policraticus*, 3, offers as the main type of flatterer one who is willing to sell his wife or a woman of his household to please someone else, for whom gain, not deceit, is the main object: "filia namque decentior, aut si quid alius in familia placeat *ditiori,* publica *merx* est, exposita quidem si *emptorem* inveniat," "an attractive girl or, if something else in the family pleases the *rich man,* it becomes a public *commodity,* if he can find a *buyer*" (italics mine). Dante seems to make a similar connection, since he concludes the section of flatterers with the words of a prostitute.

The imagery of prostitution recurs frequently in the third *bolgia,* among the simoniacs who sell God's wife, the church, and God's gifts, the sacraments, which were freely given and meant to be freely given. Here the money imagery is rampant: "voi rapaci/per oro e per argento" (19.3–4: "you who are greedy for gold and silver"); "fatto v'avete dio d'oro e d'argento" (19.112: "you made yourselves a god of gold and silver"); Nicholas says that on earth he put wealth, here he puts

---

[47]See Wayne Conner, "Inferno XVIII, 66 ("femmine da conio") and 51 ("pungenti salse")," *Italica* 32 (1955), 95–103, for an analysis of various meanings of *conio,* the most obvious being "coin," but with the other possibilities including the die or stamp used in making coins (with a possible obscene reading of women easily stamped), a measure for liquids (not applicable here), and deception (possible as a double-entendre).

himself, in a purse (19.71), as if *he* were money, and Dante reminds him of the "ill-gotten money" ("mal tolta moneta") he received to oppose Charles of Anjou (19.98–99). There might even be a suggestion of coins in the physical description of the *bolgia*, a series of holes, all the same size and round, like the ones in San Giovanni; Dante is referring to the cathedral, but the saint's name also evokes the florin in the *Comedy*. The souls have become a perversion of the coins they put in their purses, their feet instead of their heads giving the seal to their authenticity (their identity), because they had subverted God's work for money.

The souls of the next two sections tamper with the providential plan in secular life. The false prophets sell another of God's gifts, the ability to foresee the future, offering their services at a price to those who would use the knowledge to counter the course of providence. Among them are also the sorcerers, who make a pretence of controlling events by the practice of magic arts, leaving their proper work, their crafts of shoemaking or spinning, to tell fortunes and cast spells; like usurers they do not labor for their gains. Barrators sell the services of government, trading in the public trust. Their section begins with the description of boat repairs in the Venice Arzanà, the city's shipyards, the core of its vast maritime trade. The activity of these souls, however, was for a different kind of profit: Lucca is full of those who turn "no" into "yes" for money (21.42), taking bribes to subvert justice and order; when a new one turns up in Hell, literally upended in the pitch, a devil tells the souls there is no place for the Santo Volto here (21.48). The Santo Volto is the image of Christ on a wooden crucifix worshipped in the city, so this is usually taken as a blasphemous reference to the soul's rear end, but since the Santo Volto also appeared in Lucca's coins, the devil might well be saying "you can't bribe your way out of this," or "you can't buy favors here."[48] This is a sin that pervades Italy: the

[48]See *Corpus nummorum italicorum*, vol. 11, *Toscana* (*Zecche minori*) (Rome: Cecchini; Milan: Hoetli, 1929); vol. 12, *Toscana* (*Firenze*), cited below, was published in 1930.

bolgia holds Sardinians, Tuscans, and Lombards, along with a Navarrese, whose prank illustrates the nature of barratry. He offers to "make seven come for his one" (22.103: "per un ch'io son, ne farò venir sette"), which sounds very much like a con-man's offer of stupendous profits; instead, he disappears, absconds with the goods, so to speak, and leaves his victims fighting among themselves.

The first five sections of this circle involve fraud in that the sinners had no right to sell what they sold; they traded in non-commercial items. The last five sections involve a more subtle kind of fraud, the concealing or abetting of illicit profits or acquisitions. The first of these is hypocrisy, using the pretense of piety, the position afforded by a religious role, for profit. The Frati Gaudenti Dante meets in this section were sent to Florence to keep peace, but actually worked for one faction; it was also their function to stamp out heresy and repress usury. It was, in fact, common practice for religious orders to offer absolution for usury in return for gifts. Davidsohn gives a series of examples of usurers giving large sums as a token of their repentance, so they could be absolved in order to avoid posthumous accusations that would deprive their heirs of the inheritance.[49] In one case the same sum obtained remission for the sins of the man's father and other relatives as well, in another the excuse for giving money to the monks was that the individual usury victims could no longer be identified, and the usurer got away with twenty pounds per year for twenty years to make up for illicit profits of five hundred pounds. Disputes among the Friars Minor led to accusations of giving absolution and promising burial in holy ground in order to get money, without proper evidence of repentance. Although Dante does not mention such actions specifically, he does have the hypocrites dressed in heavy monastic robes, like those worn by the Cluniacs, who were famous for the richness of

[49]*Storia di Firenze*, 6.448–50. Davidsohn also notes that statutes of guilds, which were well-meaning attempts to control usury, served instead to cover it "hypocritically with a veil of piety," 6.269. Cf. Morpurgo, "Prestatori di danaro," 216.

their garments; the hypocrites' robes, however, are gold outside and lead beneath, suggesting the false value they got and gave, and Dante refers to them as the very scales that weigh that value (23.102).

Theft is in some ways the most perplexing aspect of fraud, as Dante presents it. He devotes two full cantos to it, more than he gives to what would seem more important sins, like simony, hypocrisy, the dissemination of scandal and schism; he outdoes himself in the artistic treatment of it, rivaling Lucan and Ovid; and he is moved by his experience of it to violent attacks on Pistoia (25.10–12) and Florence (26.1–3).[50] All of this seems out of proportion to the crime of theft in its simplest form, even the theft of sacred objects. However, theft can also apply to more complicated acts than the surreptitious physical seizure of another's goods. Usury is described as a form of theft by theological writers.[51] The Ottimo, in a long note on avarice as practiced by merchants and artisans, includes theft in sales by defective weights, numbers, and measure (1.111) and says that Mercury represents both businessmen and thieves. In other words, theft can also be the fraudulent appropriation of others' goods by various means, including fraudulent contracts. The punishment Dante gives for theft is metamorphosis, the change of form, emphasized by his repetition of such words as *muti, trasmutò, cambiar*. When one soul watches the transformation of another, he says, "omè, Agnel, come ti muti" (25.68: "Oh, Agnel, how you change"), perhaps a pun on *mutuum*, the loan, which lies behind all these transformations but is never acknowledged. Commercial transactions were *commutationes*, and one important part of commerce was money-changing, *cambio*; indeed, one of the three major Florentine guilds was the Arte del Cambio. Since Dante considered

---

[50]On the economic life of Pistoia, see Capecchi and Puccinelli, "L'economia pistoiese"; on the metamorphoses of cities, see above, chapter 3.

[51]Noonan, *Scholastic Analysis of Usury*, 17, cites Anselm of Canterbury, Hugh of St. Victor, Peter Comnestor, and Peter Lombard; see also Nelson, *Idea of Usury*, 9; see McLaughlin, "Canonists on Usury," 1.82, for similar treatment in commentaries on the *Corpus juris canonici*.

a man's property a part of himself, as he makes clear by his division of sins in the seventh circle, the exchange of property is a kind of metamorphosis, and the illicit exchange is suitably punished by an imposed metamorphosis of man and serpent. But since the serpents are also souls, there is, as in business, a continual shifting of the roles of victim and perpetrator. In line with Garrani's suggestion that Gerione, the figure of fraud with the serpent body and human face, represents usurious contracts, I would like to suggest that it is in this *bolgia*, where serpents appear and are interchangeable with the souls, that Dante is dealing at one level with usurious contracts. Indeed, the thieves come the closest to embodying fraud, as figured by the monster with the face of a just man and the body of a serpent; thieves alternate, as fradulent businessmen must, between the appearance of a known human being and the reality of the dangerous beast. And just as businessmen prey on one another—sometimes the deceiver, sometimes the victim—so the souls alternate between the state of human victim and serpent attacker.

Fraudulent contracts are those made in order to avoid the prohibitions against usury. Beginning with the nature simile at the opening of canto 24, in which the simple peasant "sees" snow and later discovers it was hoarfrost, Dante sets the scene for deception. What one "sees" (reads) in a contract is not necessarily what one gets. The one centaur who is not with his fellows among the violent, Cacus, is here for the theft he fraudulently committed (25.29: "furto che frodolente fece"), in which he literally covered tracks so the crime would not be discovered; what fraudulent contracts do is cover the tracks figuratively. Since deception in contracts is practiced by the clever manipulation of written words, Dante emphasizes the abuse of words in speech and writing: the souls have difficulty speaking, with voices unfit to form words (24.65–66), Vanni Fucci defies God with his words in a manner more shocking than the blasphemer's in canto 14 (25.3, 25.13–15); one soul burns faster than "o" or "i" is written (24.100–01), another mixes with the serpent as black with white on burning paper

349

(25.64–66). Like well-written contracts, the serpents both bind the souls, preventing any attempt to free themselves, and also bite them, taking parts away, which Garrani interprets as an attack on their patrimony. Dante describes three kinds of metamorphosis, which might be read as three of the most popular kinds of contract made to avoid the charge of usury.[52] The first, in which the soul dissolves to dust and then returns to his former shape, suggests the false sales in which title to property is transferred for money, but only temporarily, with the lender receiving the fruits of the property as interest on his loan and eventually returning the property for the original sum. The second metamorphosis, the fusion of two beings, the serpent and the man, into a strange creature neither two nor one (25.69), suggests fake partnerships set up for one undertaking in order to mask a loan.[53] And the third, in which the serpent and the man exchange their shapes altogether but not permanently, suggests the exchange of money, the loan being set up in one currency to be paid in another, but actually paid in the first, with the interest buried in the double rate of exchange. Dante emphasizes the exchange, contrasting what he describes with what Ovid did using a series of suggestive words: "Ovidio ... *converte* ... non *trasmutò* ... le forme/a *cambiar* lor matera" (25.97–102); "ciascun *cambiava* muso" (25.123); "si rispuosero a tai norme" (25.103: "they responded to such standards"); and they change the appearance of "excess matter" (*troppa matera*, 25.124–26). "Così vid'io la settima zavorra/ *mutare* e *trasmutare*" (25.142–43), Dante concludes, "so I saw the seventh ballast change and exchange," using the word

[52]The early commentators make distinctions among three kinds of theft in these cantos, assuming that each metamorphosis must represent a different one, but they do not specify contracts; Jacopo, however, defines thieves as those who fraudulently and secretly extort others' goods through the subtlety of their wit (1.312). The connection between Dante's theft and fraudulent business practices should be considered, whether or not one accepts the specific kinds of contract suggested here.

[53]Note the emphasis on numbers in this passage: "'non se' né *due* né *uno*.'/ Già eran li *due* capi *un* divenuti,/quando n'apparver *due* figure miste/in *una* faccia, ov'eran *due* perduti./Fersi le braccia *due* di *quattro* liste" (25.69–73).

zavorra, "ballast," drawn from shipping and meaning material of little value used primarily for weight, to describe the souls in the section.

Among the five Florentine thieves who undergo the changes, Dante sees four from the merchant-banking families of the Cavalcanti, Brunelleschi, and Donati.[54] The early commentators name the souls, but give no details about them, which suggests that they were not notorious thieves in the normal sense of the word, and since they did come from banking families, it seems reasonable to assume that their "theft" was of a more commercial nature. Even Vanni Fucci, who was a thief in the obvious sense, was the bastard son of a family involved in usurping others' property and inheritance.[55] He himself was the head of a group of thieves and robbers who ambushed and killed, and so might be seen as a figure for the heads of commercial companies that committed their crimes more subtly. The canto which follows the thieves begins with a ringing attack on Florence, masked as praise for its worldwide prestige: "Godi, Fiorenza, poi che se' sì grande/che per mare e per terra batti l'ali,/e per lo inferno tuo nome si spande" (26.1–3: "Rejoice Florence that you are so great that you beat your wings over sea and land and your name resounds through Hell"). It is commerce that gave Florence its importance on land and sea and, apparently, in Hell as well.

It has been suggested that the voyage Ulysses describes, which has no obvious classical source, was inspired by the disappearance of two Genoese brothers, merchants who sailed through the straits of Gibraltar in 1291 with two ships and merchandise, seeking a new route to India, and disappeared.[56] Marco Polo and his uncles, also merchants, returned from their long sojourn in China in 1295, a journey similarly undertaken to find new sources and new markets, with vast treasures

[54] See Masi, "Struttura sociale," 24–25.

[55] Giovanni Rosadi, "Il canto XXIV dell'Inferno," *Lectura Dantis* (Florence: Sansoni, 1917), 21–22.

[56] See Bruno Nardi, *Dante e la cultura medievale* (Bari: Laterza, 1949), 153–54.

which must have inspired many other such projects of long-distance travel. Dante may have been influenced by both events, the disappearance of the one and the return of the other with tales of strange lands and customs. In his time, only merchants in search of new markets or new sources of supply ventured as far into the unknown as Ulysses did. It does not seem far-fetched to assume that Ulysses, whose stated purpose of learning more of human vice and virtue is belied by the direction of his journey, represents in part the acquisitive man who continues even in old age to pursue wealth, new sources, new markets, no matter what the risk. This might well be the "folle volo,/sempre *acquistando* dal lato mancino" (26.125–26: "the mad flight, always gaining (acquiring) on the left," the wrong side). In that case, the fraudulent counsel Ulysses gives is not simply the theft of the Palladium or the wooden horse, but the encouragement to his companions, old and tired men, to continue the quest for wealth. It is an interesting coincidence that one of the merchants in Dante's audience cites the lines by which Guido evokes Ulysses' journey (27.80–81) to describe his own retirement from business, indicating that he, at least, made such an identification (Livi, *Dall'archivio*, 24).

What Guido da Montefeltro did was to advise the pope to take illicit advantage of his enemy, to seize his property by fraud. It is not irrelevant that the pope's anger had been roused by the Colonna's theft of papal treasure. Guido, an old operator, who was attempting to live a life of repentance for his sins, was drawn back into them by the pope's promise of anticipatory absolution. This is rather reminiscent of the practice by suspected or accused usurers, abetted by greedy churchmen, of making periodic amends in order to continue to sin. There is, of course, no question of Guido's being taken for a merchant himself—he is far too well-known a political figure. But he is a classic example of the conman conned, and his story of failed, because insincere, repentance might well have been intended to strike that segment of the audience most likely to engage in it. Are not businessmen the most likely objects of the devil's simple lesson: you can't be absolved unless you repent, and you can't will and repent at the same time (27.118–19)? One wonders if that is why Guido addresses Virgil with the curious remark: "tu . . . che parlavi mo lombardo" (27.19–20: "you who were just speaking Lombard"), and why Virgil seems to be speaking a Lombard dialect instead of his Latin or Dante's Italian. Lombard was the term foreigners used for commercial Italians (Sapori, *Italian Merchant,* 14). Dante may be implying that Virgil is being taken for a traveling merchant, in order to introduce the commercial note where it would not be expected. That might explain Virgil's abrupt "Parla tu;/ questi è latino" (27.33: "You talk to this one, he's Italian").

The commercial note is retained in the next (ninth) section where, Dante says, "those who acquire their load by dividing pay their fee" (27.135–36: "si paga il fio/a quei che scommettendo acquistan carco") for the sin that "costs so much" (29.21: "la colpa che . . . cotanto *costa*"). The eighth *bolgia* contains those who gave fraudulent counsel, enabling others to sin if they so chose; the ninth holds those who actively draw others into public sin (*scandalo*) and schism (*scisma*). Schism covers the act of sundering from one's community, whether religious or political, scandal covers the act of drawing another into a serious sin (Aquinas, ST, 2.2ae, q.43). The word is regularly used in connection with usury, in discussing whether the borrower is to be held responsible for giving the lender the opportunity to sin (ST, 2.2ae, q.78, a.4). Aquinas argues that there is no active scandal on the part of the borrower, and that the usurer's scandal is passive, that he takes the occasion to sin from the malice of his heart: "ipse autem usurarius sumit occasionem peccandi ex malitia cordis sui. Unde scandalum passivum est ex parte sua: non autem activum ex parte petentis mutuum." Though "scandal" is not limited to this meaning, the word might well have such overtones for Dante's audience. Guido da Pisa, commenting on usury in Dante, says the borrower gives the opportunity of lending, not of sinning, and cites Aquinas without naming him on active and passive scandal (323). The punishment for the sin of this section is defined by Bertran de Born as the *contrapasso*. Aquinas uses *contrapassum* in his discussion of retaliation and restitution, making it clear that *contrapassum* can only apply to commutative justice. He notes that money was invented to serve the same purpose, in order to provide proportionate commensuration to equate the passion to the action in exchanges (ST, 2.2ae, q.61, a.4): "et ideo oportet secundum quandam proportionatam commensurationem adaequare passionem actioni in commutationibus; ad quod inventa sunt numismata. Et sic contrapassum est commutativum iustum" Sapori equates Thomas's use of *contrapassum* with "scambio," the exchange in a commercial transaction after equivalent values have been established (*Studi,* 200). It is probable that Dante connects financial sinners on a large scale—important businessmen, as well as religious and political leaders—with this sin. Certainly their actions can be equally influential and destructive.

In the final section of fraud, Dante places those who falsify the most basic elements of human intercourse or exchange: identity, words, metals, and coins. The early commentators connect falsifiers of metals (alchemists) with counterfeiting. Pietro distinguishes three kinds of *falsitas,* two of them involving money: (1) in the thing itself, as in knowingly spending false money, or using some other false thing, or feigning something false in one's person; (2) in a deed, as in fabricating false money or corrupting it with alchemy; or (3) in words, as in perjury (251). The Ottimo (1.495) defines alchemy as tampering with the material of money, the metals, as does Jacopo (1.453); Jacopo also says that Dante treats falsifiers of money in both canto 29 (the alchemists) and canto 30 (the counterfeiters), 1.452. The alchemists who disfigure themselves as they once disfigured metals talk about the wild spending of the Sienese (29.125 ff.); and the counterfeiters lie side by side with the perjurers, attacking each other with their fists and their words. The exchange between the counterfeiter Adam and the liar Sinon, reveals better than any other the connection between coins and words:

ADAM:

... "Tu di' *ver* di questo
ma tu non fosti sì *ver* testimonio
là 've del *ver* fosti a Troia richesto"

SINON:

"S'io dissi *falso,* e tu *falsasti* il conio
... e son qui per un fallo
e tu per più ch'alcun altro demonio"
(30.112–17).

"You speak the truth in this, but you weren't such a true
witness when you were asked for the truth at Troy."
"If I spoke false, you falsified the coin ... I am here for
one crime, you for more than any other demon."

Both lied, one in words, the other in the manufacture of coins;
both did enormous harm to the nations involved, Sinon's lie
about the wooden horse leading to the destruction of Troy,
Adam's counterfeiting of the florin to severe economic and
political problems for Florence.[57] If each counterfeit coin is to
be taken as a separate fault, Adam is indeed the worst sinner
so far encountered. Garrani suggests that Adam's swollen
stomach represents monetary inflation swelling the market
with false money, a problem known in the Middle Ages as
morbus numericus or *nummericus,* a numerical or monetary
disease, in which the increase of bad money without an
increase of goods pushes prices higher and higher (*Il pensiero
di Dante,* 160, 165). Jacopo (1.469) interprets the soul's
hydropsy, resulting from undigested humors, as an allegory for
the counterfeit coin, in which the absent carats that would
make it genuine are sick and undigested. Counterfeiting is a

[57]Garrani, *Il pensiero di Dante,* 163 ff. On Adam and other abuses of coinage
mentioned in the *Comedy,* see Flavio Valeriani, "La numismatica nella *Divina
Comedia,*" *Rivista Italiana di Numismatica* 28 (1915), 197–220; he uses the
continuing existence of certain coins as evidence for the extent of counterfeit-
ing and circulation of bad coins. I am indebted to Alan Stahl of the American
Numismatic Society for this reference.

serious attack on the economic and social order, the worst of economic sins, because it harms all strata of the population indiscriminately; it is an offense against the entire community. Benvenuto notes that falsifying money does serious harm to the common good of the republic (2.431: "cum omnis falsans pecuniam graviter delinquat contra commune commodum reipublicae").

What Adam counterfeited was the florin, the most important coin in European currency, whose value was authenticated by the stamped figure of John the Baptist, the "lega suggellata del Batista" (30.74). The importance of such a stamp in a world of myriad coins and separate currencies cannot be overestimated. The job of stamping coins was an important one and carried prestige; the names of masters of the mint ("maestri di zecca") are preserved from the early fourteenth century in Florence, and Giovanni Villani is listed among them in 1316 (*Corpus nummorum italicorum*, vol. 12). Benvenuto goes into some detail about money, citing Aristotle on the invention of coins because barter was not efficient; coins were conceived as the measure of all things: they were made of gold and silver as the most perfect metals, light, and therefore portable, and round, because that is the perfect form (2.432–33). The counterfeiter has the last word among the sinners in the section because his deed is, in fact, the most antisocial, the most generally destructive to the public good, the hardest to undo. It is one of those stunning coincidences that his name should be Adam, so that his appearance here, towards the end of Hell, serves as a kind of parallel to the mention of Adam, the source of original sin, at the top of Purgatory and the appearance of Adam late in Paradise, where he discourses on the corruption of human speech, the other basic means of exchange between men on earth.[58]

[58]The last major sin of Hell, the betrayal of those to whom one is tied by specific bonds is less overtly social a sin in its victim than fraud, though it still has politico-social overtones. One would not expect to find the same suggestions of commerce in this circle, and one does not; nonetheless, money and possessions are a factor, at least as important a motivation in this circle as

In Purgatory, there is a shift from money as the standard of material value to spiritual goods, in which words serve at least partially as a substitute coin, in prayers through the first half of the cantica and poetry or the speech of poets through the second half. The realm itself is organized in terms of a commercial transaction, according to the requirements of commutative justice: sins are debts to justice that must be paid for in exact equivalents, measured in time, penance, or prayer.[59] The payment in time and penance is made directly by the sinner, the payment in prayer by others, whose love is acceptable currency towards the total, the first sign of a spiritual good replacing a more material value. The highest part of the mountain, the Earthly Paradise, is described as the *arra,* the pledge or guarantee which God, the highest good who made man good and for good, gave man of eternal peace and man lost by "default," exchanging laughter and play for tears and suffering:

> Lo sommo Ben . . .
> fé l'uom buono e a bene, e questo loco
> diede per *arra* a lui d'etterna pace.
> Per sua *difalta* qui dimorò poco;
> per sua *difalta* in pianto e in affanno
> *cambiò* onesto riso e dolce gioco
> (28.91–96).

---

power. There are commercial elements, although Dante does not allude to them, behind the betrayal of Ugolino, which is connected with Pisa's struggle against Florence and Lucca. His audience probably knew that one of the major problems between Pisa and Lucca was Pisa's periodic counterfeiting of Luccan currency (Garrani, 118). Many of the betrayals alluded to in the ninth circle occur either to gain possessions or as the result of a bribe. Even in Satan's mouth, the central figure, Judas, is one who committed the betrayal of Christ for money.

[59]Even in the calculation of the sin's weight, however, unexpected values are applied: Bonconte, we learn in canto 5, was saved despite his sins because of one little tear, "per una lagrimetta" (5.107), to the distinct annoyance of the devil.

In the second half of the cantica, after Dante has learned the lessons of spiritual wealth, which can be shared without loss (canto 15), of love and free will as the sources of human action (cantos 16–18), and of greed as the great obstacle (cantos 19 and 20), the poet is more and more driven by the thirst for knowledge to amass the treasure of words from other poets. The shift in his perspective begins with the discussion of forbidden sharing or partnership, *divieto consorte,* in which Virgil explains how spiritual treasures increase with sharing and continues with the lessons on desire and free will, with the help of Marco Lombardo.

Marco introduces himself by saying "Lombardo fui," "I was a Lombard" (16.46), and he speaks later of an honorable man, Guido del Castello, who is best called "il semplice Lombardo," "the honest Lombard" (16.126). We are presumably intended to see both of them as counters to the Lombard who is usurer to the world. Marco offers Dante knowledge, not money. He was a courtier, not a merchant, a guide to right action in others, what Dante is and what he would like to see his audience—merchants as well as rulers and churchmen—become. Heaven, Marco explains, initiates human movements, but man by his own choice determines his actions. The cause of corruption is in us, not in the planets. We are all driven by desire, by love, which can be directed at good or bad objects, the other side of the greed for wealth or power that drove the souls in Hell, but that love must be guided by reason in order to choose the right object. To help him make that choice, man needs the guidance of the church and the empire. After Marco has established the need for church and state as man's two guides, Dante shows us the appointed guides, a pope and a royal house, distracted by greed; the royal house is not the empire, but the French monarchy, an effective obstacle to imperial power. The pope offers a simple example of greed corrected by accession to the richest office; the king, on the other hand, describes the terrible crimes to which greed drove his descendants (20.64 ff.): rapine by force and deceit, seizure of lands, murder of a prince and a holy man, betrayal of a city, selling of a daughter, the capture of a pope (Christ in his vicar), and the attack on a religious order (the Templars) to seize its vast wealth, "carrying their greedy sails into the temple" like a pirate ship (20.93: "portar nel Tempio le cupide vele").

The French monarchy offers the most striking example of the excesses of greed, committed as they are on a national scale, but there are also references in Purgatory to the public greed of cities: Siena is ridiculed for its expensive and futile attempts to find a sea passage, either by dredging a canal to a port, or by discovering an underground river, all to increase its commercial scope; Florence takes on the burden of justice for all, as it would gladly take on any other cargo. The sense is of public responsibility, but the language suggests a sarcastic reference to its commercial enterprises: "many refuse the common load, but your people answer ... 'I'll take it on [my ship]'" (6.133–35: "molti rifiutan lo commune *incarco;*/ma il popol tuo solicito risponde ... 'Io mi *sobbarco!*'"). And she continually changes her laws, money, offices, and customs to seize the advantage of the moment; again the language is suggestive, "quante volte ... hai tu *mutato, e rinovate* membre" (6.145–47), recalling the transformations and renewal of limbs of the thieves in Hell.

Dante focuses on greed in a public context in Purgatory, since the only individual examples he presents are the French king, who speaks for his posterity, and the pope, who represents an ongoing problem of the papacy. At the same time, Dante suggests that greed is the most significant sin in Purgatory, as it was in Hell in its various manifestations, by giving it several cantos and a structure which differs from the other ledges (see chapter four). He sees all three of mankind's guides on this ledge, the pope in canto 19, the king in canto 20, and a poet in 21 and 22. The poet's sin is not greed, but prodigality, purged on the same ledge because it too involves excessive concern with and misuse of material wealth, but Dante does not seem to consider it equally harmful. Virgil asks Statius how avarice could find a place in a breast with so much wisdom (22.22–23), meaning, how could a disciple of mine ... ? Statius is quick to explain that his sin was prodigality. Aquinas considers prodigality less serious than avarice, in part because the prodigal's giving is of use to the many to whom he gives, while hoarding is of use to none (ST, 2,2ae, q.119, a.3). Statius wasted not only wealth, but also the far more valuable treasure of faith, which he kept hidden for some time after he acquired it. Nonetheless, he values the poetic word of Virgil ("without the *Aeneid* I would not have weighed a dram," 21.99), and is therefore a suitable guide to Dante and his audience.

After the meeting with Statius, Dante meets only poets on the remaining ledges of Purgatory and treats his words and theirs as precious goods. He is ready to move to the most valuable riches of all, the joy and love and knowledge of Paradise and, most important, to bring them back to share with and, figuratively, sell to his audience. Paradise is a realm of treasure, there to be taken, the quantity limited only by the taker's capacity. At the same time, it is pervaded by a sense of responsibility and right, a desire to keep the books of justice balanced. The good and bad deeds of men are recorded by number in God's books like account books, "quel volume aperto/nel qual si scrivon tutti suoi dispregi . . . segnata con un i la sua bontate,/quando 'l contrario segnerà un emme" (19.113 ff.: "that open volume in which are written all their misdeeds . . . the good marked with an I (1), the opposite with an M (1,000)"). In the early cantos, the heavens of the Moon and Mercury, the concern is for keeping one's word, paying and receiving what is due; in the other spheres, the focus shifts to concern for others, particularly corruption on earth where it has most effect, in the church, in the French monarchy, and in Florence, in religion, politics, and commerce.

The subject of discussion in the first heaven, the Moon, is the vow, the promise made directly to God and freely given. Dante uses the word *voto*, "vow," for its play on "empty," promises which lack the perfect commitment of the will and cannot be fulfilled. But, as suggested in chapter five, the examples Dante gives of political commitments indicate he is thinking in broader terms than the religious commitment; he seems also to have in mind promises made to man with God as witness, oaths. Moreover, the financial language used in discussing the promises and the satisfaction for them suggests that Dante intended his audience to extend the application of what he says not only to political, but also to commercial commitments. He describes the vow as a free sacrifice of free will, a gift from God only to intelligent creatures, a treasure which once given cannot be reclaimed (5.19–30). The value of the vow is that God and man both participate; it is a contract of mutual consent (5.26–27). "What then," Beatrice asks, "could be given in compensation?" (5.31: "Dunque che *render* puossi per *ristoro?*"); "if you try to use what you have offered, you want to make a good job of ill-gotten gains" (5.32–33: "se credi bene *usar* quel c'hai offerto/di maltolletto vuo' far buon lavoro"), an improper use of money, since what is consumed cannot be re*used*. A vow cannot be cancelled except by being paid, though the offering can be exchanged, bartered (5.50–51: "alcuna offerta/si *permutasse*"); that is, the species of payment may be substituted, not the amount, and not unless the value is greater than the original promised, not unless "the thing laid aside is contained in the thing taken on as four in six" (5.59–60). Dante's query whether there is not some other way to make up the payment, "to satisfy with other goods, which will not weigh too lightly on the scales" (4.136–38), is rephrased by Beatrice in equally commercial language: "you want to know if you can pay enough with another service to secure yourself from suit for a failed vow" (5.13–15). What outweighs everything else in the scale cannot be made up by any other kind of payment (5.61–63: "quanlunque cosa tanto pesa/per suo valor che tragga ogne bilancia,/sodisfar non si può con altra spesa"). That is why vows must be very carefully made, under the guidance of Scripture and the pastor of the church and without the pressure of "mala cupidigia"; worldly gain should not be allowed to influence the decision.

The sanctity of the given word, the promise made either directly to God or calling on God as a witness, is the major issue here. Even in commercial contracts, the solemn oath was often the basis of the agreement, and as such was to be honored, whether or not the contract was later found to be usurious; pressure might be put on the creditor to release the debtor, but if that failed, the obligation stood, a principle recognized by ecclesiastical as well as civil authority: a decretal of Pope Alexander III pronounced the paying of usury preferable to the breaking of an oath.[60] Beatrice stresses the importance of making a promise that one will be able to keep. Dante had asked in the previous canto how people could be held responsible for breaking their vows when external pressure was applied, how another's violence could decrease the measure of my merit (4.21: "di meritar mi *scema* la *misura*"). Beatrice answers that the absolute will (*voglia assoluta*) does not consent to the loss (*danno*), except insofar as it is afraid of worse (4.109–10). But she has already explained that the will (*volontà*) does not allow itself to be forced, no matter what violence is used, if it does not in some way consent, and then it is no longer absolute (4.76–77). The legal points in establishing usury also depend on will, intention, and hope, *voluntas, intentio,* and *spes;* will and intention are important aspects of the financial as well as the theological question.

If the financial language throughout this section permits the reader to extend the issue of vows to oaths in commercial contracts, then Dante is arguing for truth and prudence in business as well as in religion and politics, for a careful consideration of one's needs and resources weighed against the external situation before one commits oneself to any contract with God or man. Most of Dante's audience would be more likely to make financial contracts than any other kind. The aspiring nuns in the Moon did not calculate their own weakness in the face of family pressure; political agreements are similarly made without sufficient consideration of extenuating circumstances and pressures, as commercial contracts may be made in

[60]See McLaughlin, "Canonists on Usury," 1.108 and 2.15–16, and Baldwin, MPM, 1.273. Not all contracts call God to witness, though partnerships usually do (see Lopez, *Medieval Trade,* for documents); but all call some public official, usually a notary, to witness, and all involve giving one's word.

moments of need or expectation, based more on wishful think-
ing than on realistic appraisals. In every case, the person who
gives his/her word, is obligated to see it through, no matter
what the cost. Dante puts the burden of responsibility for any
kind of religious or social commitment, as he does for any
kind of sin, on the one who undertakes it. This attitude seemed
to underlie his treatment of usury in Hell, which he placed
outside the circle of fraud, making the point that if the bor-
rower freely agrees to the contract, he is not being deceived by
the lender, even if he is overcharged. The message is to avoid
taking on a commitment of any kind that one is unable prop-
erly to fulfill, but the commercial overtones give it particular
force for much of Dante's audience.

The souls in Mercury are also concerned with the discharge
of responsibility and just deserts. Justinian, the emperor who
speaks for the heaven, tells Dante that the happiness of its souls
lies in the exact measure of their rewards with their merits, no
more, no less: "Ma nel *commensurar* d'i nostri *gaggi*/col
merto è parte di nostra letizia,/perché non li vedem minor né
maggi" (6.118–20). The soul he points out to Dante at the end
of the canto, Romeo, had in fact given his lord a higher return,
seven and five for ten, but when the lord demanded a reckon-
ing, others made him appear to be wanting: "il mosser le
parole biece/a dimandar ragione a questo giusto,/che li
assegnò sette e cinque per diece" (6.136–38). On earth he was
badly paid (*mal gradita*, 6.129), but in heaven he has finally
received what he deserves. Justinian took care in his own
labors, the reform of the legal code, to be exact, to eliminate
from the laws all excess or vanity (6.12), under the guidance of
God. What remains, then, is presumably God's will; that is, if
Roman law differs from canon law, Dante apparently accepts
the civil law as divinely ordained. If this is so, then usury, con-
demned in theology but permitted to some extent in civil law,
is, as Garrani suggests (*Il pensiero di Dante*, 86), within God's
order, according to Dante. Justinian speaks of divine justice in
the same precise and balanced terms: original sin had to be
avenged, and that revenge was put into the hands of the high-

est secular authority, the Roman empire, but the revenge, too, had to be avenged; every act has its consequences, every deed must be repaid in kind or equivalent.

Viva giustizia, "living justice," is the dominant note of Mercury, peopled by those who were active in the pursuit of honor and fame. That they include rulers and courtiers we know from the presence of Justinian and Romeo, but that they may include a variety of others is suggested by the lines that introduce Romeo: "different positions in our life render sweet harmony among these wheels" (6.125–26). The early commentators agree that the souls here were active in wordly pursuits, even if it made them less fervent in divine love (Pietro, 594), but the pursuits were useful to the community (Ottimo, 3.172, cf. Jacopo, 3.106). The Ottimo discusses prudence as the relevant virtue that governs what is useful to ourselves and not harmful to our neighbors, guarding against vice in terms of flesh, wealth, or honor (3.110 ff.). In his discussion of fortune and the workings of the heavens in Hell 7, the Ottimo, following an old tradition, connects Mercury with eloquence and business, in that merchants use soft talk to sell and buy (1.120–21). Mercury disposes to eloquence and wealth, though men must exert themselves to develop those gifts; one will never be a good speaker if he does not use his reason and intellect to converse with the wise and eloquent, nor will he be rich if he abstains from procuring wealth and merchandise (1.123). It seems reasonable to assume that the Ottimo includes merchants and businessmen among those active in the worldly life in Mercury. Dante names business, "civil negozio," among the worldly pursuits in which men can lose themselves (Pr. 11.7), but since he also includes those who follow law and the priesthood and rulers who use force and cleverness, we must assume that he only condemns those who pursue the professions for the wrong reasons, not the occupations themselves. At the end of canto 8 in Paradise, when Charles Martel has shown that man must be a citizen, and that civil life requires different offices, he mentions Solon (the lawgiver), Xerxes (the soldier), Melchisedech (the priest), and "the one who, flying through the air, lost his son," Daedalus, who exercised his ingenuity to achieve amazing feats but to the harm of his son. Daedalus seems to represent the intellectual, the artisan, perhaps also the merchant. He completes the picture of civic leadership, the lowest function in Dante's civic order but nonetheless essential to its survival.

After the heavens of the Moon and Mercury, joy and love rather than justice dominate, but love often manifests itself in concern for life on earth. Each sphere, no matter how high, offers some attack on the corruption that results from greed. In Venus, Charles Martel speaks of the stinginess and greed of his brother, Robert, Cunizza of the priest's betrayal of political refugees. In contrast, it is also in Venus that the fusion of beings through love is suggested in the verbs created from pronouns, for example, "s'io m'*intu*assi come tu t'*inm*ii" (9.81), in which it is tantalizing to see a possible echo of the definition of *mutuum,* "loan," what is "mine" becoming not just "yours," but "you." In Hell, where there was also a possible pun on *mutuum* (25.68), the fusion of beings was violent and forced, whereas in heaven it is willed out of love and accomplished by language. In the Sun, where the treasured are Peter Lombard's *Sentences,* Francis's Poverty, and Dominic's Faith, the object of attack is the worldliness of the papacy and the Franciscan and Dominican orders, in contrast to Dominic, who did not ask to dispense two or three for six, nor for the fortune of the first vacancy, nor for the tithes that belong to God's poor (12.91–93). In Mars, Cacciaguida attacks the results of commercialism in Florence. In Jupiter, the rulers of the eagle condemn the currency abuses by contemporary kings. The figure of the eagle, which denounces those abuses, rises out of the M of earth (*terram*) in a rather stylized way, suggesting among other possibilities the eagle on the imperial coins of Frederick II and later of Manfred.[61] The M on Manfred's coins, which resembled the eagle, often had globes

[61]See Rodolfo Spahr, *Le Monete Siciliane dai Bizantini a Carlo I d'Angiò* (Zurich: Association Internationale des Numismates Professionels, 1976). Frederick II had coined a small quantity of a gold coin which recalled the ancient empire in its metal and minting, as well as its name, the Augustale (Valeriani, "La numismatica," 202).

above and around the stems, like the lilies Dante describes nestling in his eagle. We know from Forese Donati's reference to the *aguglin* in his sonnet 74a (line 4), that imperial coins were not uncommon in Dante's Florence. Perhaps Dante is implying that even in its coins, the empire symbolized the ideal relation of political entities. In the highest heavens, we are told by Saint Benedict in Saturn, the realm of the contemplatives, that the abuses of church funds are worse offenses to God than *grave usura,* and in the Stars, where Dante displays the wealth of his faith, Peter delivers a stirring attack on the greed of the clergy who use the church to acquire gold (27.42) and to sell mendacious privileges (27.53). Beatrice extends the attack to general greed as they rise into the Primo Mobile, and before they leave it, she condemns the clergy's failure to guide man, turning Scripture to their own purposes and selling pardons that have no value ("pagando di moneta sanza conio," 29.126), paying their congregations in counterfeit coin.

Heaven's view is that secular and religious rulers use their positions to increase their own possessions, and pay their subjects with false coins and worthless paper. Only Dante seems to have real treasure to offer, the faith he carries "in his purse" (24.85) which was tested by Peter and found to be genuine currency (*moneta*) in its substance, its alloy (*lega*), and weight (*peso*), and the knowledge he has been offered on his journey which is the "payment" or "profit" he has gained from Virgil and Beatrice and others. He became more aware of the value of words in Purgatory as he learned the power of prayers and of poetry, and he returns from the journey to offer this treasure, the words of his poem, to his audience. If the church and the state fail in their divinely appointed function to guide mankind because of their greed and selfishness, it is left to the poet to use his tools, words, to teach and to attract men to the right way.

As money is essential to the exchange of goods and services, so language is essential to the exchange of ideas and information. As a social animal, man depends on both. But since both are products of man's ingenuity, both are susceptible to corruption, and must be controlled. Rulers impose standards of value on their currency; men of letters set the standards for their language, grammarians the basic rules, poets the elegant style. In *De vulgari eloquentia,* writing in Latin, Dante defended the vulgate as more noble than Latin because it is natural to man, a divine gift, rather than artificial and man-made; whereas in the *Convivio,* writing in Italian, he called Latin more noble because it is controlled by rules, making it incorruptible. When Adam describes speech as a human creation (Pr. 26), reversing the view of *De vulgari eloquentia,* we think not only of its limitations, but also of its achievements, like the *Comedy.* Dante is aware that in a country like Italy, with no political unity, the Italian language in the hands of educated writers can speak to all Italians. He presumably chooses to write his poem in Italian both because it can reach a wider audience in his native land and because he has greater freedom in his use of it. He helps to set its standards as he writes.

That heaven sees poets as ideal guides is clear from Beatrice's choice of Virgil to lead Dante through Hell and Purgatory, because of his adorned and honorable words (*parola ornata* and *parlar onesto,* Hell 2.67, 113), and from heaven's choice of Dante to carry its message (Pg. 33.52 ff., Pr. 17.124 ff.), "the sacred poem to which heaven and earth put their hands" (Pr. 25.1–2). Poets are the merchants of the true treasures, faith and knowledge. We are shown the power of poetry to move men to faith and morality in the influence of Virgil's words on Statius, which opened his mind to Christianity and cured it of prodigality (Pg. 22.79–87 and 22.40–41). It is, of course, ironic that Statius derived messages from Virgil's words which Virgil himself did not intend or recognize, but the point is that poets, pagan or Christian, can be God's tools, as Dante offers himself to be God's vessel (Pr. 1.14). Like any other public figures, poets can abuse their trust and gifts: Pier della Vigna, Brunetto Latini, Bertran de Born, used their words to mask the truth, to win worldly honor, to encourage to wrong. Poets can be limited in their perceptions, like the classical poets in Limbo who lacked faith, or the lyric poets in Purgatory who lack Dante's religious and political mission; or they can, like Dante, offer their gifts to God's service, as Folco, and David, and Bernard do in Paradise. It is not a coincidence that for his final vision, Dante turns to a man who was not only a theologian and a mystic, but also something of a poet.

Man needs speech because it is the only way he can effectively communicate with his fellows; animals, who operate on instinct, and angels, who have direct perception, do not need it. Only man has thoughts that his fellows cannot perceive except through his words. The positive function of speech as a civilizing, educational, and unifying force among men has a strong Roman and medieval tradition, but there is a powerful negative tradition as well; the Bible points up the dangers of speech, as do church fathers like Gregory and Augustine, for whom the highest form of speech is the "rhetoric of silence."[62] Dante draws on both traditions in the *Comedy*, the negative in Hell, the positive in Purgatory and Paradise. In Hell, he reveals the dangers: the misuse of speech in order to deceive others, the lack of control over speech that leads men to betray themselves, and the total breakdown in communication because the source of language, reason, has cut itself off from God, the good of the intellect, "ben dell'intelletto," and cannot therefore function properly. Speech in Hell is deceptive and divisive, an antisocial force. In Purgatory, on the other hand, it serves as a means of communication among men and between man and God, as a unifying force, drawing disparate elements together; it enables the souls to guide and comfort each other, to give information to Dante, and to send messages to their families. It is in every way a constructive force. The

[62]On Augustine, see Joseph A. Mazzeo, "St. Augustine's Rhetoric of Silence," *Journal of the History of Ideas* 23 (1962), 175–96. On the two traditions, see James J. Murphy, *Rhetoric in the Middle Ages* (Berkeley: University of California, 1974). Cf. my "The Relation of Speech to Sin in the *Inferno*," *Dante Studies* 87 (1969), 33–46.

souls in Paradise do not need language to communicate; like the angels, they can perceive God's and their fellows' thoughts directly, but they speak in order to communicate with Dante and sometimes out of the sheer need to give voice to their feelings. In order to convey the sense of this realm, which transcends human expression in a perfect harmony of wills, Dante moves towards a new language, creating new words, combining contradictory images, treating separate languages as one, playing with sounds and repetition of words to suggest meanings not contained in the syntactical structure. But instead of creating confusion, he brings about a deeper understanding. The souls of Paradise are one in their love for God and their fellows and in their concern for man's existence on earth; they are beyond the negative powers of speech, but the souls of Hell are prey to all of them. They are harassed by noises, laments, cries, howling, barking, all expressing pain or hostility, however incoherently. Some of the souls are impeded in their speech by their shapes (the tree-suicides and serpent-thieves), some are submerged in rivers and gurgle their words. Many of the guardians of Hell do not speak; instead they twist their tails or blow horns, bark or shout gibberish, all apparently in parody of the angelic ability to communicate directly without words. When the souls speak, they curse God, their families, anything they can blame for their situation, or they defy God. They attack each other verbally (the misers and prodigals, the wrathful, usurers, falsifiers, and traitors) and Dante as well (in the prophecies of Farinata and Vanni Fucci).

Only rarely do the souls in Hell refuse to talk; more often than not, they attempt to manipulate words in order to benefit themselves or deceive others, but in fact they betray themselves and reveal the hidden dangers of a skillful use of language. Just as Semiramis had made her "libido licit in her law" in order to eliminate a major taboo with one letter, Francesca attempts to turn her self-indulgent affair into a tragic romance by playing with the clichés of courtly love, but she reveals the self-deception implicit in the lyric love tradition by her manipulation of the details of her story.[63] Pier della Vigna's distorted syntax is an attempt to mask his perverted thinking, but instead reveals it, at the same time suggesting the emptiness in the rich, formal rhetoric of his own writing. Pier was a poet and rhetorician as well as a public official, famous for his style in Latin and Italian, poetry and prose, but here his style works against him. "You would have been more gentle if we were souls of serpents," he chides Dante (13.38–39), but serpents do not have souls that outlive their bodies, so Pier is reversing the error he made in his own life when he killed himself as if his soul would not live after the body. His speech abounds in word and sound plays: "infiammò contra me ... e li infiammati infiammar sì Augusto/che i lieti onor tornaro in tristi lutti" (13.67–69: "enflamed against me ... the enflamed so enflamed Augustus, that the happy honors became sad griefs"), culminating in "l'animo mio, per disdegnoso gusto,/credendo col morir fuggir disdegno,/ingiusto fece me contra me giusto" (13.70–72: "my soul, in contempt, believing it could flee contempt with death, made me unjust against my just self"). Both statements are attempts to justify himself, but reveal the truth he failed to see, that he abused the trust of his emperor by trying to control his heart, as he deserved the envy and anger of those he closed out, and that by committing his last act against the highest justice, he had made himself, though innocent of the crime he was accused of, ultimately guilty. By

[63]She tells the story of her affair as though it were a brief encounter rather than a long duration, presenting herself and Paolo as young lovers, though they were middle-aged when they died; she also reverses the roles of the lover in the Lancelot-Guinevere kiss in order to suggest that Paolo is the active force in their affair, but his silent weeping belies her. Though she uses the lyric clichés, the real desires keep asserting themselves: "Amor, ch'al cor gentil ratto s'apprende," a line which might have been written by Guido Guinizelli, is followed by "prese costui de la bella persona" (Hell 5.100–01: "love that swiftly takes hold of a noble heart took him for my beautiful body"), revealing the physical aspect of the love. Similarly, "Amor, ch'a nullo amato amar perdona," is quickly undercut by "mi prese del costui piacer sì forte" (5.103–04: "Love that exempts no loved one from love, seized me for the strong pleasure [I took] in him").

fleeing unjustified contempt, he incurred justified damnation. Ulysses, similarly, gives a heroic tone to his last voyage, but his words betray his failures as a husband, son, and father, and reveal the dangers to his people of persuasive rhetoric in an irresponsible leader. Ulysses speaks of the "*owed* love which *should* have made Penelope happy" (26.95–96): "il *debito* amore/lo qual *dovea* Penelopè far lieta"), revealing in his choice of words an awareness of the duty he neglected, as he reveals the empty pretense of his desire to experience human vice and valor by the goal of his voyage, the "world without people." Guido da Montefeltro speaks of his life in penance, but describes his sins with pride (27.74–78). He blames the pope for leading him back into sin, but his words reveal his awareness of the pope's perfidy, the neglect of his office, the "proud fever," and the "drunken words" (27.91–99).

Virgil, through all the abuses of language in Hell, remains as the standard for the proper use of speech: he corrects Dante when he is wrong, scolds him when he becomes too involved, encourages him when he is afraid. He controls the monsters by invoking the divine will that inspired the journey, though he is unable to control the devils in the same way, as if the classical poet had power over the creatures of classical myth, the creations of human imagination, but not over the fallen angels, whose sin is the worst extreme of his own, rebellion to God's law (Hell 1.125). But there are times when even a receptive audience cannot be moved by the poet's words, as Virgil explains to the suicide: if Dante could have believed what he saw in my verse, he would not have stretched out his hand to tear the branch (Hell 13.46 ff.). Here Virgil acknowledges the need for direct experience, but if Dante cannot believe his description, why should the audience believe Dante's? I think Dante expected us *not* to believe the literal description, but wished to call attention to a significant difference between his scene and Virgil's. Like the metamorphoses of the thieves (cantos 24 and 25), which derive from Ovid and Lucan, the voice from the bleeding tree has a different moral setting in Dante's poem. His subjects suffer transformations they bring on themselves; the classical figures are more or less innocent victims of fate, inspiring sympathy and pathos rather than the horror and moral repulsion Dante intends. But Dante shares with his classical sources a power unique to poets among men—to give existence to the impossible. They can make the dead live and move and speak, they can turn men into trees and serpents, fly through the heavens, and pass beyond time and space. Their powers approach God's, which is why they are so severely punished when they abuse them, like Pier della Vigna imprisoned in a tree, able to speak only when he is maimed, and Bertran de Born, who carries his severed head in his hand. Just as rulers alone are empowered to coin money, to establish a currency for their people, so poets have the power and the responsiblity to mold the language and to preserve its integrity.

Poets speak for their cultures, carrying messages across time as well as space: Virgil's words opened Statius's mind to the message of his Christian contemporaries; Virgil, Statius, Lucan, and Ovid all speak to Dante through their poetry. Poets converse in the *Comedy* in a way no other group can, beginning with the exchange between the classical figures and Dante in Limbo, and carrying on through the encounters of Purgatory, first with Sordello, then with Statius, and finally with Forese, Bonagiunta, Guido Guinizelli, and Arnaut Daniel. Though Dante describes the encounters as conversations, he implies that the real communication is through the poetry: "parlando cose che'l tacere è bello,/sì com'era 'l parlar colà dov'era" (Hell 4.104–05: "speaking of things it is sweet to be silent about as it was to speak of them there"); "ascoltava i lor sermoni,/ch'a poetar mi davano intelletto" (Pg. 22.128–29: "I listened to their [Virgil and Statius] words which gave me understanding of poetry"). Only with his near-contemporaries does Dante record the conversation, in which he describes his own manner of writing, providing through Bonagiunta the name of the tradition in which he worked (the "Dolce stil nuovo") and establishing through Guido the direct line of influence, from Arnaut to Guido to himself, rejecting Guiraut and Guittone. By his encounters with poets in the three realms,

Dante traces his own poetic development and informs us of the tradition he expects to be placed in. By accepting the epic poets, Virgil and Statius, as guides, who accompany him part of the way, while the lyric poets, however respected, are met and passed beyond because they are fixed in their positions, Dante tells us that he has gone beyond the lyric tradition and become an epic poet. At the same time, by leaving the epic poets behind him in Purgatory (Statius must also rise to heaven but we do not see him there) and meeting in Paradise only those poets who devoted themselves to God, Folco (who began as a secular poet but became a monk and then a bishop, and was incidentally the son of a merchant), David, the supreme poet of the Old Testament, "the supreme singer of the supreme leader" (25.72: "sommo cantor del sommo duce"), and Bernard (to whom more poems were attributed then than now, but who is given the final prayer-poem to the Virgin at the beginning of canto 33), Dante labels himself a religious poet.

The words of poets speak to men across time and even across the boundaries of language. Dante moves towards one language in Purgatory, as he is moving towards a unified people under the empire, and he does it through poets: Sordello, the Italian poet who lived in France and wrote in Provençal, addresses the Latin poet, Virgil, as "gloria di Latin . . . per cui mostrò ciò che potea la lingua nostra" (Pg. 7.16–17: "glory of the Latins . . . through whom our language showed what it could do"), where "our" must include all romance languages as one with Latin; on the last ledge of Purgatory, the Italian poet Guido Guinizelli describes the Provençal Arnaut Daniel as "miglior fabbro del parlar materno" (Pg. 26.117: "a better craftsman of the maternal speech"), which means either that Provençal is the mother tongue for lyric poets, or that Provençal and Italian are one, perhaps both. Dante then allows Arnaut to speak several lines in Provençal, fitting the words into the Italian meter and rhyme scheme, as he had done with lines from Latin hymns earlier in Purgatory, showing through his poetry how the languages can work together to convey one message. In Paradise he will use Latin words and phrases as

though they were Italian and even fit a Latin and Hebrew pas-
sage into his rhyme scheme, suggesting the single unified tra-
dition of Judeo-Christian culture.

The unifying force of language is emphasized in many ways
in Purgatory: Dante, not as a poet, but simply as a traveler
going back and forth between the realms of the dead and the
living, or between Purgatory and Paradise, is sought out as a
messenger to carry news and requests back to earth or up to
God; from Beatrice and later Cacciaguida, we learn that Dante
is also destined to carry God's message to men. Like the mer-
chant who moves between foreign lands and his own, carrying
news and messages as well as orders and goods, Dante's words
are the only connection these souls can have with the living.
Marco Lombardo, an honorable Lombard, seeking others'
good, not his own profit, a counter to the selfish merchant,
guides Dante with his words when the fog robs them of any
other kind of communication: "l'udir ci terrà giunti," he tells
Dante (16.36: "the sound [hearing] will keep us together") and
Dante answers "tue parole fier le nostre scorte" (16.45: "your
words will be our guides"). These lines occur in the middle of
Purgatory (hence of the *Comedy*) and express the essence of
the poet's use of language throughout the poem.

Words also unite souls in a common expression of love and
praise and desire, through hymns and prayers. The souls who
approach the shore of Purgatory sing "In exitu Israel de
Aegypto," all together with one voice or one melody (2.47);
even the negligent princes, who had failed to work for har-
mony on earth, sing "Salve Regina" together, harmonizing
with each other in the song (7.112–13, 125). The souls of the
proud recite the Lord's Prayer together (11.1 ff.), acknowledg-
ing their sins, forgiving others, and praying for the living, as
one. Prayers are effective in moving divine justice, not because
of their rhetorical effect or their beauty, but because they
express and affirm a commitment of love or repentance. They
represent the strength of the feeling, and it is the feeling that
moves God, but the fact of the expression is also significant.
Man must make the effort and acknowledge, even to himself,

what he feels in order to achieve what he desires; that is why
Dante must admit his sins in the Earthly Paradise, despite his
earlier ritual confession to the angel at the gate of Purgatory,
and why he must affirm his faith, hope, and charity in a public
declaration in Paradise. In both cases, his audience (Beatrice
and the apostles) knows what he feels, but his expression of
the feeling is an affirmation and commitment as well as a will-
ing communication of that feeling to others. Cacciaguida tells
Dante that he knows his will and desire, but that Dante must
give voice to them in order to better fulfill the holy love:

> perché il sacro amore . . .
> . . . .
> . . . s'adempia meglio,
> la voce tua sicura, balda e lieta
> suoni la volontà, suoni il disio,
> a che la mia risposta è già decreta

> so that sacred love . . .
> . . . .
> . . . may better be fulfilled,
> let your voice, secure, bold, and happy,
> sound your will, sound your desire,
> to which my answer is already decreed.
> (15.64–69)

Speech is the human creature's means of expressing his exis-
tence and his joy in it. God, Dante tells us, created not for self-
ish needs, not to acquire goods for himself (Pr. 29.13: "non per
aver a sè di bene acquisto"), but so that his "splendor might be
able, shining, to *say* 'I exist'" (Pr. 29.14–15; "perchè suo splen-
dore/potesse, risplendendo, *dir* 'Subsisto'"). The expression of
existence is the fullest experience of existence. Even though
the souls in heaven do not need to speak to each other because
they perceive each others' thoughts directly, they do feel the
need simply to express certain emotions. Cacciaguida's affec-
tion for God, inspired by the presence of Dante, is beyond the
comprehension of mortals, but it is "spoken" nonetheless:

"cose,/ch'io non lo intesi, si parlò profondo;/ ... ché il suo concetto/al segno d'i mortal si soprapuose" (Pr. 15.38–42: "things I did not understand, he spoke so profoundly ... for his conception surpassed the sign of mortals"). The eagle in Jupiter praises divine grace in songs that can only be known by those who rejoice in heaven, "con canti quai si sa chi là sù gaude" (19.39); the souls in Saturn announce divine vengeance in a cry "of such high sound that it cannot be imitated here" (21.140–41: "di sì alto suono,/che non potrebbe qui assomigliarsi"), which Beatrice has to interpret for Dante.

In Paradise, a realm in which thought is mirrored in the divine mind *before* it is thought (15.61–63), human language must be as inadequate as it is superfluous. From the very beginning of the cantica to the very end, Dante emphasizes the inadequacy of human speech and memory to describe the divine vision: "vidi cose che ridire/né sa né può chi di là sù discende" (Pr. 1.5–6: "I saw things that one who descends from there has not the knowledge nor the ability to retell"); "da quinci innanzi il mio veder fu maggio/che il parlar mostra" (33.55–56: "from then on, my sight was greater than speech shows").[64] One reason language fails is that human speech, as Adam explains to Dante in canto 26, is the product of human reason, susceptible to the same limitations and the same kinds of corruption, with the same development and potential for corruption as another product of human reason, currency, unlimited expansion proportionally decreasing the value of both. Speech began pure and simple; the first word for God was the single vowel "I," but soon it changed to "El" (26.133–36), and now there are myriad names in different tongues. Change in lan-

---

[64]Cf. letter to Can Grande, sec. 29, in which Dante says he lacks the knowledge because he has forgotten and lacks the power because even if he remembers speech fails him: "for we perceive many things by the intellect for which language has no terms, as Plato indicates by his employment of metaphors; he perceived many things by the light of the intellect which his everyday language was inadequate to express." Dante, too, finds ways to transcend the limitations of normal language.

guage is continuous; Adam points out that his own language was completely gone even before the tower of Babel, and Cacciaguida speaks in a dialect that differs from the one spoken five generations later in Dante's Florence. This kind of change is natural and without moral overtones, but there are other abuses which hinder the ability of language to communicate, as Beatrice points out (29.82 ff.), faulty interpretations of others' words, the willful distortion even of Scripture by learned commentators, the lies and fables of preachers who feed their flocks on wind for their own advantage, all contrasted to the simplicity and purity of Christ's word and the teaching of the early apostles who relied on the Gospels. Forgetting what blood it "cost" to disseminate God's words through the world (29.91–92), modern preachers hand out clever words and jokes, and false pardons, paying their audiences with counterfeit currency (29.126).

Dante also distorts language in Paradise, but in order to offer true value. He transcends the limitations of human language in order to convey an ideal beyond human experience. He goes further than metaphor, turning to other forms of language, to visual symbols, music, and to new poetic expression. From the sphere of the Sun on, Dante presents the souls within symbolic figures of circles, a cross, an eagle, a ladder, a garden, and finally the rose. The symbols convey their meaning without words, leaving us to work out their full significance.[65] That they rise beyond mere words is best illustrated by the eagle, the symbol of the Roman empire, God's chosen instrument to administer justice on earth, which is formed from the last letter of the biblical phrase by the souls who, in their new form, are

[65]Dante progresses from the symbols in the Earthly Paradise, which are real objects with symbolic meaning, to metaphors in the early part of Paradise, and finally to symbolic figures; for instance, the garden in the Earthly Paradise is a real garden which represents the created universe in its prelapsarian state, souls in the first part of paradise are metaphorically "plants," but in the sphere of the stars, Dante sees all the souls as flowers in the garden of the church triumphant and, in the Empyrean, as petals of a single rose.

able to speak as one, with the voice of divine justice. That single voice, coming from all the great exponents of justice, shows the difference between divine justice, which is single and perfect, and human perceptions, which are incomplete and faulty.

Music in Paradise is usually beyond human comprehension, though the sweetness makes itself felt and draws Dante to it. The motions of the heavens create music (1.76–78), a harmony that evokes Dante's desire; the souls echo that harmony in their song (Venus, 8.29–30, Sun, 10.66, 145–48), which attracts Dante although he cannot grasp the words (Mars, 14.122–23, and Jupiter, 19.97–99, where he is told that eternal judgment is as incomprehensible to mortals as the eagle's notes are to him). The sweetness and richness of sound increase as Dante rises: in the Stars, the music of an angel is such that the sweetest melody here would seem like a cloud breaking in thunder (23.97–99) and the song of a soul so divine that not even Dante's imagination can recapture it (24.23–24).

But whether he is using symbols or music to suggest the deeper meaning and harmony of Paradise, it is only through Dante's words that we can be aware of their existence. It is, finally, poetic language which conveys some sense of the ineffable. Dante is in control of his medium to such an extent that he can stretch it beyond its own limits in a variety of ways, by using Latin words, not as foreign phrases but within the Italian (the last rhyme of the poem is the Latin *velle* and the Italian *stelle*), by creating new words in Italian to suggest concepts that cannot otherwise be expressed (e.g., *inciela,* "inheavens," becoming one with heaven, *s'inluia,* "inhims," fusing two beings in one), by using repetition to suggest difference rather than similarity ("come in voce voce si discerne," 8.17, where one voice is distinguished from the other) or identity where difference is expected (as with homonym rhymes in which the meaning is apparently different but actually the same, e.g., *porti,* "harbors" and "carries," 1.112,114, where the force which "carries" is the "harbor" to which all must return), and by using paradoxical analogies (the moon is a cloud, a diamond, a pearl, and water).[66] In every case, the reader is forced to work beyond the surface words in order to arrive at the meaning, which is not so much concealed as imprisoned within the bonds of human language.

Through his poetic language, Dante provides his audience with abundant "spiritual usury" to counter the "corporal usury" of their world. He transcends the limitations of material values and goods as he moves through the *Comedy* by giving financial terms a metaphorical meaning, by turning the commercial perspective from profit and loss in money to gains in love and knowledge. Language provides the means to transform commercial thought, not by changing the words, but by changing the context and therefore the meaning. The treasure Dante offers the reader of the *Comedy* is not the face value of the individual words, which in themselves are true currency and amount to a substantial sum reckoned simply as poetry, but the meaning that lies beyond them, the moral, political, religious message of the ideal universal government whose stamp gives them authenticity and to whose enduring stability their value attests.

[66]For a more detailed study of the unusual technical devices in Paradise, see my "Words and Images in the *Paradiso:* Reflections of the Divine," in *Dante, Petrarch, Boccaccio, Studies in the Italian Trecento In Honor of Charles S. Singleton,* ed. Aldo S. Bernardo and Anthony L. Pellegrini (Binghamton: SUNY, 1983), 115–32.

Index

Sumner, B. H., 8n
sun and moon, political analogy, 26,
30n, 101–103; two suns, 76, 102,
206, 230
swords, two, political analogy, 19,
23–24, 25, 90, 96, 100–101
Sylvester, pope, 29, 85n, 91, 97–98

Tempesti, F., 225n
Templars, 83, 85, 340, 359
Thebes, 58, 135, 160, 186, 194–95,
239
theft, 71, 133–34, 168, 169, 180–82,
348–51
Thomas Aquinas, 10–13, 29, 133–34,
176, 236, 274, 276, 318–20; in DC,
94–95, 103, 123, 275–79;
Commentary on Ethics, 10n, 12,
152, 166; Commentary on
Politics, 11n, 166n; Commentary
on Sentences, 13n, 318; De malo,
319–20; De regimine principum,
16, 269; De regno, 10n, 11, 12, 13;
Summa contra Gentiles, 10n, 11;
Summa Theologiae, 10n, 11, 12,
108n, 133n, 134, 146n, 148n,
175n, 180n, 202n, 223n, 318–19,
320, 329n, 330n, 336n, 343, 345,
353–54, 360
Tierney, B., 14n, 19n–20, 21n, 22n,
23n, 25n, 26n, 27n, 34n, 94n, 106n
Tillman, H., 25n
Toffanin, G., 47n
Toynbee, P., 175n
Trajan, 54, 55, 91, 124, 125, 223,
292
translatio imperii, see empire:
transfer of
treachery, betrayal, 134, 148, 168,
189–94, 212, 336, 356n–57n
Triolo, A., 152n
Troy, 135, 171, 185, 189, 200, 222–
23, 239, 292; Trojans, 232

tyranny, tyrants, 12, 57, 154n, 155–
56, 166, 184, 185, 216n, 222, 271,
272, 336

Ugolino, 136, 191–92, 213n, 215
Ullmann, W., 14n, 19n–20, 22n,
25n, 29n, 87n, 106n, 124n
Ulysses, 89, 110, 171, 182–84, 185–
86, 208n, 229, 258, 303, 351–352,
371
usury, 71, 165–66, 319–24, 337, 341,
343–44, 348–50, 353, 362;
absolution for, 347; corporal and
spiritual, 317, 379; grave usura,
335, 366; and heresy, 339–40

Valeriani, F., 355n
Vallone, A., 130n
Vanroey, E., 319n
Veglio di Creta, 89, 160, 207–208,
341–42
veltro, 112, 115–19, 128, 285, 303;
veltri, 158
Vernani, Guido, 6n, 38, 127; De
reprobatione Monarchie, 127n, 130
Vianello, N., 284n
Villani, G., Istorie Fiorentine, 50,
62, 66n, 70n–71n, 72n, 88n, 109n,
116n, 151n, 155, 156, 159, 163–64,
176, 179n, 180, 190n, 192n, 197n,
210, 213, 217, 219, 224, 227, 236n,
240, 247, 263n, 266n, 272n, 284,
289n–90n, 291n, 307–308, 312, 356
Vinay, G., 297n
Viner, J., 320n, 321n
Virgil, 43, 45, 46, 47n, 52, 58, 75, 77,
86, 91, 111, 113, 115, 122, 137–40,
206–208, 237–39, 242, 258, 305–
306, 329, 331–32, 259–60, 367,
371–73, and chapters 3 and 4;
Aeneid, 53n, 54n, 73, 116–17,
147n, 175, 183, 207, 218, 238,
247n, 292, 293n, 332, 337, 353,

LIBRARY OF CONGRESS CATALOGING IN PUBLICATION DATA

Ferrante, Joan M., 1936–
The political vision of the Divine comedy.

Includes index.
1. Dante Alighieri, 1265–1321. Divina commedia.
2. Dante Alighieri, 1265–1321—Political and social views.
I. Title.
PQ4422.F48   1984   851'.1   83-26906
ISBN 0-691-06603-5 (alk. paper)